Praise for *The Medici Conspiracy*

"Written like a classic crime story, this true-life tale kicks off with a botched robbery and police chase. Authorities raid the villa of a Munich-based antiquarian to discover a collection of [fourth] century B.C. vases soaking off encrustations—and traces of theft—in a . . . swimming pool full of water and caustic chemicals. As the plot thickens, a cast of crooked art dealers, shady collectors, and formidable art institutions are implicated in an investigation that steers Italy's Art Squad to a Geneva warehouse filled with looted national treasures. The warehouse's owner? Giacomo Medici, Italy's most nefarious art dealer. With one of the book's main players, Marion True, the J. Paul Getty Museum's former antiquities curator, on trial for conspiring to purchase stolen antiquities . . . even the timing of this book is a work of art."

—*TIME* (Europe), named one of the ten best books of 2006

"This is a devastating charge, and anyone with an interest in ancient art and archaeology will want to examine it carefully . . . [the] book provides the most comprehensive account yet of the investigation that led to True's trial, and contains much that will be of interest to anyone trying to understand the underground antiquities market and what should be done about it. . . . Watson and Todeschini are at their best in describing the detective work that led Italy's special art police unit to Medici's warehouses and then to Robert Hecht and other dealers."

—*The New York Review of Books*

"Gripping. . . . As a portrait of venality, *The Medici Conspiracy* is both shocking and compelling." —*The Observer* (UK)

"*The Medici Conspiracy* is not, as its title might suggest, an allusion to historical Florentine intrigue—though the tale is worthy of such a connection. . . . Written like a detective story . . . the book is a thoroughly researched . . . and accessible read."

—*The Guardian* (UK)

"*The Medici Conspiracy* documents convincingly—indeed takes the lid off—the extraordinary way that some of the world's most famous museums, aided by some of the most prominent collectors, have paid corrupt dealers millions of dollars to obtain notable antiquities looted from ancient sites in Italy and beyond and then illegally exported. . . . Watson and Todeschini have written a fascinating account of conspiracy and corruption in high places. It will rock the world of the complacent collectors who ask no questions. It shows how several museums have undermined their own reputations. And it is a rattling good read."

—*The Evening Standard*

"[A] gripping crime story of epic proportions."   —BookReporter.com

"Writing with the zest and seduction of the finest crime novelists, Watson and Todeschini . . . offer an invaluable primer in antiquities . . . [and] a dramatic, fascinating, and rightfully indignant report on outrageous avarice and crimes against civilization."

—*Booklist* STARRED* review

"In light of the Metropolitan Museum of Art's recent decision to return a rare—and by the Italian government's contention, stolen—vase painted by the Greek master Euphronios, Watson and Todeschini's colorful account of Giacomo Medici, an antiquities dealer found guilty of looting last year, and his illegal business dealings, is wonderfully prescient . . . they are at their best when chronicling the international adventures of various investigators, such as the Carabinieri Art Squad's raids on various Italian criminals to recover lost loot."   —*Publishers Weekly*

"Giacomo Medici's international criminal network stretched from Italian tombaroli looting antiquities under cover of darkness to fraudulent dealers and high-profile institutions such as Sotheby's and the Museum of Modern Art in New York. Watson and Todeschini combine methodical research with the tension of a thriller and genuine passion for their subject. They explain the tricks resorted to by smugglers and write movingly of the loss of our archaeological heritage caused by the careless dismantling of ancient sites. The Taliban's destruction of the Bamiyan Buddhas caused international outrage, but Watson and Todeschini suggest that comparable damage is being done across the world every day."   —*Scotland on Sunday*

"This is not about *the* Medici but Giacomo Medici, the spider in the middle of a web of illegal art smuggling. The looting of tombs and archaeological sites is big business in Italy and, as Watson and Todeschini's book shows, some very important institutions have been caught buying the looted goods. They are particularly good at showing just what is lost when an archaeological site is compromised—beautiful objects without provenance [are] another clue to history lost. Reading almost like a thriller at times, this is an exciting exposé of a huge criminal trade."   —*Publishing News*

"This title, which combines art history with the pace of a crime thriller, exposes the illegal trade in ancient artifacts and provides a useful background to trials currently taking place. Together, the authors reveal how looted objects have appeared in some of the most prestigious museums in the world."   —*The Bookseller*

"Like a good crime novel, the pace is fast. The evolving plot is intriguingly complex. The villains are highly organized and unrepentant. The evidence is convincing, some beyond reasonable doubt. The goods are high-quality treasures and the handlers' profits enormous. The *modi operandi* include guns, chainsaws, ceramic bashing, charm, and threats. . . . The crimes against heritage involve reckless, intentional, and permanently depriving behaviour . . . the authors spare no punches—the antiquities market [is] stripped bare."
                                —*British Journal of Criminology*

"A 'true-life thriller' rich in documentation and proof."
                            —*Corriere della Sera* (Milan, Italy)

"Virtue prevails, as it must: and that is the story of this book. It is argued with a force comparable to the wrath of Cicero arraigning Verres, the rascal among connoisseurs in Late Republican times. . . . We join Peter Watson and Cecilia Todeschini in condemning the scrabblers and raiders who have supplied the demand . . . "
                                —*Times Literary Supplement*

"[A] landmark exposé..."   —*American Journal of Archaeology*

THE
MEDICI
CONSPIRACY

THE ILLICIT JOURNEY
OF LOOTED ANTIQUITIES,
FROM ITALY'S TOMB RAIDERS
TO THE WORLD'S
GREATEST MUSEUMS

PETER WATSON
AND
CECILIA TODESCHINI

PublicAffairs
New York

BOOK DESIGN AND COMPOSITION BY JENNY DOSSIN.
TEXT SET IN TRUMP MEDIAEVAL.

Library of Congress Cataloging-in-Publication Data
Watson, Peter, 1943–
The Medici conspiracy : the illicit journey of looted antiquities,
from Italy's tomb raiders to the world's greatest museums /
Peter Watson with Cecilia Todeschini.—1st ed.
p.   cm.
Includes index.
ISBN–13: 978-1-58648-402-6 (hc)
ISBN–10: 1-58648-402-8 (hc)
1. Archaeological thefts. 2. Art thefts. I. Todeschini, Cecilia. II. Title.
CC135.W39 2006
363.2'5962—dc22
2006041695

ISBN–13: 978-1-58648-438-5 (pbk)
ISBN–10: 1-58648-438-9 (pbk)

CONTENTS

Authors' Note

THIS IS A BOOK about art, about the great passions it arouses and the crimes those passions can lead to. In particular it is about very beautiful ancient sculptures and exquisitely painted Greek and Etruscan vases, art works that tell us so much about the great civilizations of the classical world, which are the foundation of the West. It is also about an ugly conspiracy to rip these grand and important objects from the ground and smuggle them abroad. It proves beyond doubt for the first time that a good number of the antiquities in many of our most prestigious museums, and held in the best-known collections, have been illegally excavated and passed through the hands of corrupt dealers, curators, and auction houses, shaming us all. The conspiracy has been the subject of painstaking investigations by the Italian authorities that have led to a series of groundbreaking trials that have shaken the world of archaeology and antiquities-trading to its core.

For this paperback edition, one or two errors have been corrected, and the text has been updated to take account of events since hardback publication in Spring 2006. This includes an entirely new chapter (Chapter 21) on important revelations in Greece.

Prologue on Fifth Avenue

On Sunday, November 12, 1972, the Metropolitan Museum of Art in New York City announced—via an article in the *New York Times Magazine*—a sensational new acquisition. It was an exceptionally rare Greek vase, a *calyx krater* in the terminology of the classical world, meaning that it was a two-handled bowl, used for mixing water and the strong, heavy wine the ancient Greeks produced (they did not drink their wine "neat"). This krater was very large, designed to hold seven gallons of liquid, and very old, having been produced in the sixth century BC. It had been "thrown" by the potter Euxitheos and decorated by the painter Euphronios, who is acknowledged to be one of the two or three greatest masters of Greek vase painting. His works are so rare that the last important piece before this one had been unearthed as long ago as 1840. About eighteen inches high, the vase showed ten massive, beautifully fashioned ochre figures on a black background. The main figure was the dying, naked Sarpedon, son of Zeus—the greatest of all Greek gods—oozing blood from three wounds and being lifted up by the twin gods of Sleep and Death. The great warrior had delicate locks of reddish hair, and his teeth were clenched in a paroxysm of death. In other figures, young men were preparing for a battle that could kill them, the delicate lines of their armor beautifully rendered—in browns, red, and shades of pink. Not the least remarkable thing about "the Euphronios vase," as it became known, was the price paid for it by the Metropolitan Museum—$1 million. This was the first time $1 million had ever been paid for an antiquity.

No sooner was the news about the acquisition made public than controversy erupted. Many—including several prominent archaeologists and museum curators—thought that the Met had been duped. Cornelius Vermeule, then acting director of the Museum of Fine Arts in Boston, pointed out that a number of comparable vases were on the market, some for as little as $25,000, and that the most anyone had ever paid for a krater of similar size and age was $125,000. John Cooney of the Cleveland Museum of Art appraised the vase at between $150,000 and $250,000, whereas Professor Ross Holloway of Brown University said $200,000 was the limit. On this reckoning, the Met had paid four to eight times what the krater was worth.

Still more controversial was the way the Met had actually acquired the vase.[1] In February 1972, some months before the public announcement, according to the account given at the time, Dietrich von Bothmer, the curator of the Greek and Roman Department, had received a letter from a certain Robert E. Hecht Jr., an American dealer in antiquities then living in Rome. Educated at Haverford College, Hecht was the heir to a Baltimore department store fortune but had been living in Europe since the 1950s. In his letter to von Bothmer, Hecht had described the vase he had on offer as the equivalent—in beauty, importance, and price—to an impressionist painting. (The Met had itself opened the age of million-dollar impressionists with its then recent acquisition of Monet's *Terrasse à Sainte-Adresse*, for which it had paid $1,411,200.) Hecht gave it as his opinion that the vase on offer was the equal of the famous calyx krater in the Louvre, generally regarded as one of the three greatest pieces of pottery known.

In June that year, 1972, Thomas Hoving, the director of the Met, along with von Bothmer and the Met's deputy director and chief curator, traveled to Zurich to view the krater. Von Bothmer later said, "When I saw the vase I knew I had found what I had been searching for all my life." Hoving was more grandiloquent.

> To call [the vase] an artifact is like referring to the Sistine Ceiling as a painting. The Euphronios krater is everything I revere in a work of art. It is flawless in technique, is a grand work of architecture, has several levels of heroic subject matter, and keeps on revealing something new at every glance. To love it, you only have to look once. To adore it, you must read Homer and know that the drawing is perhaps the summit of fine art . . . I found the drawing the finest I had virtually ever observed. One long, unhesitating line that sped from the wing of Sleep through his arm in a pure stroke was genius. . . . I tried to think of something comparable, from any time or any master. I could only think of the so-called

Alexander sarcophagus in Istanbul, the precious drawings in the illuminated Book of Hours created for the Duke of Berry by the Limbourg brothers around 1410, and the watercolor of the bird's wing by Albrecht Dürer in the Albertina in Vienna. They were all unique masterworks, yet none had the same sense of soul.

There was no haggling over price, so it was said, and Hecht hand-carried the vase to New York at the end of August. Before it went on display, the cracks that covered the surface were painted over, at museum expense, and von Bothmer began to prepare a scholarly article on the vase to supplement the piece in the *New York Times*, which had been placed via Punch Sulzberger, a Met trustee and a member of the family that owned the paper.

To begin with, both Hoving and von Bothmer were coy as to exactly how they had acquired the krater, and about the cost, though the director, who appeared with it one morning on the *Today* show on ABC TV, admitted that the vase would be insured for $2 million. Hoving had told the reporter who compiled the initial *New York Times* story that the vase had been in a private collection in England at the time of World War I. Hoving said that he didn't wish to be more specific about the owners "because they have other things that we might want to buy in the future."

The veiled explanation didn't stand much scrutiny. Many archaeologists were skeptical about Hoving's account from the very beginning because the Etruscans* had always had a predilection for Euphronios, and it was generally assumed in the profession that the krater had been discovered on an illegal dig, somewhere north of Rome. In the trade, too, it was realized that a vase by Euphronios—who, after all, was very famous, the equivalent in the ancient world of Michelangelo or Picasso—could not have lain for half a century unknown in a private collection.

Then there was Hecht, the dealer. At that time he was persona non grata in Turkey following a scandal in which, on an internal flight from Izmir to Istanbul, he had taken out some ancient gold coins to examine them. An air stewardess noticed the coins and informed the captain, who radioed ahead to the airport. On arrival, police were waiting for Hecht,

*From Etruria in Italy, the modern area stretching north of Rome to Grosseto, Siena, and Florence and into Umbria as far as Perugia.

arrested him, and seized the coins, which they discovered had been illegally excavated. The coins were therefore confiscated and Hecht expelled. He had also been arrested in Italy in the early 1960s, implicated in an antiquities-smuggling scandal, but acquitted.

The editors at the *Times* began to sense that the story they had run about the acquisition of the vase had been part of a carefully orchestrated presentation. No one likes being a patsy, and so the paper assigned a team of reporters to verify the real story. One of them, Nicholas Gage, began by delving into the customs records at New York's Kennedy Airport for August 31, 1972, the day when it was said that the vase arrived. After several hours, he found records for a vase valued at $1 million that had arrived that day aboard TWA flight 831 in the company of one Robert E. Hecht Jr. Flight 831 came from Zurich, so that's where Gage went next. In Zurich, he interviewed three dealers, each of whom said he had heard that the vase had been dug up in late 1971 in a necropolis north of Rome and was sold to Hecht by a well-known middleman for a little under $100,000. In Rome, others gave Gage the same story.

Meanwhile, back in New York, von Bothmer had been a little more forthcoming. He first of all confided that the vase could have come from England—or it could have come from Italy. "But it doesn't make any difference whether it was the 3,198th vase or the 3,199th vase found there." All that mattered, he said, was whether it was genuine or fake, and how beautiful it was. "Why can't people look at it simply as archaeologists do, as an art object?" This statement severely damaged von Bothmer's credit among archaeologists. In a letter to the editor of the *New York Times*, Margaret Thompson of the American Numismatic Society spoke for many when she wrote: "I am outraged. . . . [A]ny archaeologist worthy of the name knows that the place and circumstances of discovery are of great significance for the archaeological record." She was supported by the newsletter of the Association for Field Archaeology, which argued in an editorial that publication of the fantastic price of the krater had "at one stroke" enormously inflated the market for all antiquities. "The purchase cannot fail to encourage speculators whose objectives in acquiring ancient art . . . lie in the tax benefits to be saved by donating the objects to museums or educational institutions at their new market value. . . . As long as acquisition at any price is to be the credo of our major collections, they will fail to serve the cause of knowledge and serve only to incite resentment and encourage crime." And in fact that year, at the annual meeting of the Archaeological Institute of America (AIA), traditionally held between Christmas and New Year's Day, and called in 1972 in Philadelphia, the scholars delivered a humiliating rebuke to von Bothmer. He was a distinguished man. A German by birth, he had studied at Berlin University and at Oxford with J. D. Beazley, the great historian and connoisseur of Greek vases. Von Bothmer was wounded in World War II, in the Pacific, and awarded the Bronze Star for heroic achievement—all this before joining the Met. That year, 1972, he was one of those slated for the six-strong board of trustees of the AIA—a nomination that is normally tantamount to election. But just before the vote, a seventh nomination was made from the floor. Von Bothmer came bottom of the vote—and out.

In speaking about the vase, its English provenance was not all that von Bothmer revealed. He also confirmed that he had first seen it in the garden of Fritz Bürki, a restorer who was listed in the Zurich directory as a *sitzmoberschreiner*, or chair mender. The vase had been broken, von Bothmer said, but had been reassembled and was complete, save for a few slivers. Von Bothmer further volunteered that, at the Met, if they were offered an object without a pedigree, or provenance, their normal policy was to submit a photograph of the object to the authorities in those countries "that might consider the object part of their cultural or artistic patrimony." That procedure hadn't been followed with the Euphronios vase, however, because—it now turned out—Hecht *had* provided a pedigree. He said that the krater had belonged to an Armenian dealer named Dikran A. Sarrafian, who lived in Beirut, Lebanon. Hecht had provided two letters from Sarrafian, one dated July 10, 1971—that is, a few months before the alleged clandestine dig in Etruria. The first letter said, in part, "In view of the worsening situation in the M.E. [Middle East], I have decided to settle in Australia, probably in N.S.W. [New South Wales]. I have been selling off what I have and have decided to sell also my red figured crater which I have had so long and which you have seen with my friends in Switzerland." It mentioned a price of "one million dollars and over if possible" and a commission of 10 percent for Hecht. The second letter, dated September 1972, confirmed that Sarrafian's father had acquired the vase in 1920 in London, in exchange for some Greek and Roman gold and silver coins.

On learning all this, the enterprising Gage dashed to Beirut, traced Sarrafian, who—over several whiskies at the St. George Hotel—told him that Hecht had just been and gone. Sarrafian, according to Gage, was a small-time dealer in coins, who also organized archaeological tourism. He would not at first say what, exactly, Hecht had paid him for the vase, or why the American had flown to see him in such a hurry. He admitted to Gage that he did not collect—either vases or statues—but had inherited "a hatbox full of pieces." This is the man that the director of the Met, Thomas Hoving, would not identify to begin with because he owned other "major objects" that the museum might want.

This whole set of events—so improbable, so inconsistent and mysterious—had created a furor in Italy, as had the fact that so far as the fractures in the vase were concerned, none of them crossed any of the ten faces on the figures. This was miraculous good fortune. Unless, perhaps, the vase had been deliberately and carefully broken in order to smuggle it more easily out of the country where it had been found.

Gage didn't give up. Back in Rome, and acting on a tip, he drove to Cerveteri, the ancient site of an Etrurian city northwest of Rome, and went from door to door asking for a man known as *il Ciccione* (a modern American equivalent would be "Fatso"). According to the story he wrote later, Gage was eventually led to a two-room stone house where he found "a short, husky, unshaven man in bare feet." This was Armando Cenere, a farm laborer and mason, who confessed to also being a *tombarolo*, or tomb robber. Later in the evening, sitting by his stove, Cenere further confessed that he had been one of a team of six men who had been digging nearby at Sant'Angelo in mid-November 1971, when they had turned up the base and handle of a Greek vase. He was detailed as "lookout" while the others cleared the entire tomb, a process that took a week. They found many pieces, including a winged sphinx, which they left in a field and then tipped off the police about it. This was to divert suspicion from themselves and what else they had found.

Cenere recalled to Gage one piece of pottery that, he said, showed a man bleeding from three wounds. Shown a photograph of the Met's Euphronios vase, he identified the portrait of the dying Sarpedon. He said he had been paid 5.5 million lire (about $8,800) as his (equal) share of the payoff.

Cenere's testimony, though vivid, was not conclusive. He could have been mistaken, he could have been inventing the details, in the hope of payment, or the limelight. If he and his friends did find the vase, and it was in pieces, it was unlikely that none of the breaks would cut across at least one of the figures' faces. Certainly, Thomas Hoving didn't accept the tombarolo's version; he even said the Met was being "framed" by the *Times*.

Eventually, the case came to court in Italy. In the witness box, Cenere went back on everything he had told the *New York Times*. He and Hecht were acquitted, though the latter was also declared persona non grata in Italy, to add to his similar status in Turkey. He moved to Paris.

At the end of 1972, when von Bothmer gave his talk to the annual meeting of the Archaeological Institute of America (after which he was not voted on to the board of trustees), his subject was the myth of Sarpedon, illustrated with slides of its portrayal by the artist Euphronios. During the course of his presentation, von Bothmer showed not only scenes from the Met's krater but also an earlier treatment of the same subject on a smaller cup, or kylix. In other words, this cup was a *second* unknown work by Euphronios. Wasn't this an extraordinary coincidence—that the krater should show up after fifty years in Sarrafian's collection, and then another piece should surface at the same time? Furthermore, what von Bothmer didn't know just then was that the police investigations of the krater in Italy (following publication of the *New York Times* article) had, quite independently, uncovered rumors about the existence of a second Euphronios work—a kylix—also with a dying warrior scene. Tackled later by journalists, von Bothmer admitted that he had a photograph of the kylix but had never seen the cup itself. He wouldn't show anyone the photograph, he said, since "the owner might have a prior claim on it" (although he had used the photo readily enough in his AIA lecture). Moreover, he didn't know where the actual object was—"It's supposed to be in Norway."

Discussing the kylix, Hoving and von Bothmer got themselves into a real muddle over who had seen what, and when. In the first place, Hoving changed his story. In an interview with David Shirey of the *New York Times*, he said at first that he had never seen the kylix, or even a photograph of it. Later, he telephoned back and said, "I want to be perfectly clear that I never saw the cup. I did see a photograph." One reason for this change may have been that, late in the day, he recalled an interview he had given to a reporter from the London Sunday newspaper, the *Observer*, which was also interested in the Met's controversial acquisition, because it might have been smuggled out of Britain. To an *Observer* reporter, Hoving admitted being offered—in fact, on that very day of the interview—a kylix by Euphronios, a cup that he said was signed, was in fragments, had pieces missing, but showed Sarpedon being carried off by Sleep and Death. Hoving told the reporter the cup had been made about twenty years before the krater.

Later, still before Gage published the first of his articles, von Bothmer said it was Hecht who had the kylix and had had it since *before* he'd had the krater. On this occasion, von Bothmer also said that he had seen the kylix in Zurich, in July 1971, thus giving a different version to what he had said before, when he had claimed not to have seen the kylix and didn't know where it was. He told the *Observer* reporter that he didn't want to say too much more about the cup, because he wanted to buy it. There followed this exchange:

> OBSERVER: Isn't it a good fortune for Robert Hecht . . . that he manages to have first the vase and then the cup?
>
> VON BOTHMER: The other way round—the cup has been owned for a couple of years, I was shown this cup in July 1971. [Pause.] I stopped in Zurich and I saw the cup and I have my notes and my dates. I would put it differently—the cup at the price then being quoted me was not nearly so exciting to me until after this object [the vase] appeared. Therefore, when you have two of a kind, it takes on greater significance.

In other words, von Bothmer implied that the Euphronios krater had surfaced some time *after* July 1971, when he saw the cup in Zurich. Was he not then aware of Sarrafian's letter to Hecht, dated July 10, 1971, affirming that the krater had been in the Sarrafian family for more than fifty years and that Hecht had already—by July 1971—seen it in Zurich?

That was not the end of the confusion. A later affidavit by Sarrafian said that when he had made the vase available to Hecht, in 1971, it was in pieces and "Hecht was warned that I am not responsible for any missing pieces." This was confusing and inconsistent on three grounds. First, he also said he had authorized its restoration "three years ago"—that is, in 1969. How could that be, if it hadn't surfaced until July 1971? Second, Fritz Bürki had reported that when he received the vase in the summer of 1971, it had already been restored but "so badly I had to take it to pieces and restore it all over again." Third, von Bothmer had said earlier that when he had first seen the vase it was not yet completely restored, so he had authorized Bürki to fill in the cracks and paint them over, for a fee of $800. No one account seemed to match another.

Then there was the inconsistency about the nature of the fragmentation. In his affidavit, as mentioned above, Sarrafian had said that Hecht had been "warned that I was not responsible for any missing pieces." How could Sarrafian *know* there were missing pieces, if the vase comprised between sixty and 100 fragments, as Hoving said? And in any case why should he worry when, again according to Hoving, the enormous price that the vase commanded lay partly in the fact that it was in perfect condition or, as one later document put it, 99⁴⁹⁄₁₀₀ percent complete, with just a few slivers missing?

The price also seemed too neat: In his July 1971 letter, Sarrafian had instructed Hecht to sell the vase for "one million dollars and over if possible." How did he choose such a high target price since, until then, the highest price a vase had sold for was $125,000?

The improbabilities did not end there. Sarrafian told Gage that Hecht had taken the bulk of the money, in contrast to what he had said in the July 1971 letter, which specified a 10 percent commission to Hecht. "Bob was clever, I was stupid," said Sarrafian. "I wouldn't have given him an invoice—one dealer doesn't usually give an invoice to another—but he specifically asked for one. He said he wanted it for tax purposes . . . I gave him an invoice saying he's paid a fantastic price for the vase. I didn't even get one quarter of a million dollars for it. The bulk of the money went to Hecht."

The final contradiction, in his letter dated July 10, 1971, is Sarrafian's remark that in view of the deteriorating situation in the Middle East, he had decided to settle in Australia, "probably in N.S.W. [New South Wales]," and this was one reason he was selling. He never went. Sarrafian and his wife were killed in a car crash in Beirut, in 1977.

In other words, the confusion about the Euphronios vase—where it came from, when it was assembled, who was paid what, what its relation was to the kylix—was fairly comprehensive. No wonder Dietrich von Bothmer's fellow archaeologists, most of the trade, and journalists on both sides of the Atlantic were so skeptical about the official version. Hecht had by then acquired a controversial reputation, though Hoving, von Bothmer, and the trustees of the museum appeared not to care very much.

But there was one man who did. Oscar White Muscarella was an assistant curator at the Metropolitan Museum in the Department of Ancient Near Eastern Art. Born in 1931, he had a master's degree and a Ph.D. in classical archaeology from the University of Pennsylvania, then the foremost archaeological school in the United States and one of the top three in the world. He had been a Fulbright scholar at the American School of Classical Studies at Athens and had excavated at Mesa Verde in Colorado, at Swan Creek in South Dakota, at Gordion in Turkey, and at five sites in Iran, in one of which he was director and in three others co-director. In 1974, he had just turned forty and was the author of one well-received academic book and at least twenty-six articles. His career also boasted another unusual distinction: Although he was still at the Met, he had been fired three times.

It was a murky story that turned on—or appeared to turn on—Muscarella's inability to cooperate with his colleagues, either in the field or in the museum itself. In fact, the objections to Muscarella had more to do with his involvement in museum politics than with his work. He had been active in championing the rights of women, who were paid less at the museum than men for identical positions, he had objected to the museum's architects cutting down some large ("magnificent") magnolia and elm trees to create space for a new wing, and perhaps most important, he had been one of several junior curators who had set up the Curators' Forum—not quite a trade union, but clearly a threat to the Met's established power structure. Then there was the fact that four times, in 1970, 1971, and 1972, he had written memoranda to the museum administration, calling for a change to its acquisitions policy in regard to antiquities, drawing attention to the fact that the Met was acquiring plundered and smuggled artifacts.

He had first been fired, by Thomas Hoving, in July 1971, ostensibly because he could not get along with colleagues and therefore was unable to excavate properly. He was given six months' academic leave to look for another position and was moved out of the Ancient Near Eastern Department. But Muscarella chose not to go quietly, hired himself a lawyer, and twice got the date for his departure postponed. In August 1972, he was fired again, and this time he was given just a month's notice, mainly because the museum had acquired extra evidence that he was, allegedly, difficult to work with on excavations. This time Muscarella obtained a temporary injunction. At much the same time, the American National Labor Relations Board was investigating the Met because it had fired a number of other people because of union activity. As a result of this investigation, several museum employees were reinstated. Muscarella was one of them.

When, in early 1973, the *New York Times* was investigating how the Euphronios vase had reached the Met, Muscarella said, to a *Times* reporter, that he was opposed to the purchase and expressed the view that the krater had been looted from Italy, not acquired, as Hoving and von Bothmer maintained, from Dikran Sarrafian in Beirut. He was also quoted as saying that he believed the museum trustees had not adequately questioned the provenance of the vase. "They have abdicated responsibility," he said. "They should have checked out every possible origin of the vase before it was purchased."

Muscarella's views were published in the *Times* on February 24, 1973. Four days later, at a staff policy meeting, Ashton Hawkins, a vice president of the museum and the Met's in-house counsel, discussed Muscarella's statements and announced, "We are definitely going to get rid of him now."[2] Muscarella later gave a television interview on the program *Straight Talk*, in which he again spoke against the purchase of the vase, and he wrote about "the curatorial role in plundering" in the *Association of Field Archaeology News*. At the end of 1973, Muscarella lectured to the Archaeological Institute of America, again on the curatorial role in looting, after which he was asked to give more lectures, on the same topic, to other organizations. In early 1974, his article in *Field Archaeology News* was reprinted in other academic journals.

Later that year, in October 1974, he was fired for the third time, accused—in a letter of three and one-half pages—of unprofessional conduct, the letter terminating his employment on December 31 that year. By this time Muscarella's attorney, Steven Hyman, a partner in the law firm of radical defense lawyer William Kunstler, was so dismayed by the Met's tactics against his client that he had agreed to waive his fee. Hyman obtained an injunction, a full one this time, and the court appointed a fact finder, a lawyer acceptable to both sides, named Harry Rand. The twelve days of hearings were spread out between September 11, 1975, and November 26. Four months later, in March 1976, the fact finder produced a 1,379-page verdict—in which Muscarella was totally exonerated. Rand concluded that *not one* of Hoving's allegations against the assistant curator "is sustained by the record."

That was not quite the end of the affair. Muscarella was reinstated, as he had to be, but the trustees didn't approve the action until December that year, and it was not until May 1977 that the museum put in writing that he was "an Associate Curator in the Department of Ancient Near Eastern Art in good standing." Moreover, the following March, in 1978, Muscarella was notified that he was being "promoted" to "Senior Research Fellow." He was told that this was the equivalent of being a full curator, but in fact he was being sidelined. Since 1978, Oscar White Muscarella has never received a salary raise, or any other promotion, except cost-of-living increases, and even those stopped in 2000.

Criticizing Thomas Hoving and his policies, in particular with regard to the acquisition of the Euphronios krater, has exerted a heavy toll. But Muscarella, like the vase, is still—as we write—at the Metropolitan Museum. Over two decades later, events in Italy are vindicating him, and in more ways than even he could think possible.

I

Operation Geryon

I T ALL BEGAN WITH A ROBBERY, deep in the south of Italy. Melfi is a small town in the mountainous Basilicata region—east of Naples and north of Potenza. It is a savage landscape, cracked with dried river beds, the scars of distant earthquakes, the soil baked pale by the Mediterranean sun. Though Melfi is sleepy and nondescript, its medieval castle is spectacular. It is said to contain 365 rooms—one for every day of the year—and its nine forbidding square brick towers, the oldest built in 1041, mark an imposing outline, like large jagged teeth, against the sweep of Mount Vultura, a looming mass of dark red rock that rises up more than 4,000 feet. In the time of Frederick the Second, Melfi was the Norman capital of the south (before Palermo assumed that honor), and it was from here that Pope Urban II called the First Crusade, to conquer the Holy Land.

Thursday, January 20, 1994, was a cold, brilliantly sunny day in Melfi. There was a faint smell of olives in the air, as the pickers in the fields below the castle ate their lunch in the shade of the trees. It was 1:45 PM.

There were no visitors to the castle that day. The building had been given to the Italian state back in 1950, and three rooms had been turned into an archaeological museum. One of the main attractions of the museum was the so-called Melfi vases. These are eight terra-cotta pots, each 2,500 years old, brilliantly decorated in white, red, and brown, with stories from the Greek classics—goddesses playing lyres, athletes being crowned with garlands, scenes of dancing and feasting.

Luigi Maschito was bored. He had been a guard at Melfi Museum for nearly three years now and he had often been bored, but on brilliantly sunny days like this one it was worse, and he would much rather have been out in the fields or exploring the lower slopes of Mount Vultura with his dog. Maschito had with him a new book of crossword puzzles that he had been given for Christmas. It was a gift he had asked his mother for, precisely to help relieve the tedium of just such a day as this. Even so, and despite the rudimentary wooden chair he was perched on, he couldn't help dropping off to sleep every now and then. He had already eaten his lunch and that invariably made him drowsy. His crossword book, open on his knee, fell to the floor.

He opened his eyes and bent to pick it up.

His forehead struck something hard—and when he looked up he gasped.

He was staring at the barrel of a pistol.

The man holding the gun didn't say anything but held a finger to his lips. Maschito knew what that meant—who didn't? He didn't resist as another man tied him to his chair. "*Merda! Cazzo!*" he thought. "Is this really happening?"

How had they gotten in unnoticed? The castle could only be entered via an old stone bridge, and it had not one but two protecting walls. The men must have known that at lunchtime the castle came to a standstill.

Maschito's shoulders were pulled back, hard, by rope. He sat mute, terrified, as three men, all dark-haired, all in their thirties, all wearing sunglasses, took a huge metal lug wrench and attacked the glass case protecting the Melfi vases.

The glass of the case shattered immediately and fell in a shower of fragments on to the tile floor. The sweat of fear ran down Maschito's forehead and into his eyes as he watched the three men reach forward and snatch at the eight precious vases. The men still didn't speak—the entire operation was carried out in complete silence.

One man took three of the smaller objects. The second man lifted the smallest vase, a jug, and placed it inside one of the others, a larger bucket-shaped vase with handles. He slipped these under the arm of the man with the gun, so he still had one hand free for his weapon. Then the second man took the remaining vases, one of which had a narrow neck, making it easier to hold, and hurried out of the room. They had obviously rehearsed this procedure beforehand.

The man with the pistol pointed it again at Maschito. The robber lifted the barrel so that it was vertical and touched it to his lips—another warning to keep silent. Then he too was gone.

Maschito was no fool. He struggled to free his hands before starting to shout and scream. In no time, two of his colleagues appeared. In fact, they had heard the alarm go off when the glass of the protecting case had been smashed but assumed that the alarm had malfunctioned. Never dreaming there was a real robbery in progress, they hadn't hurried.

Seeing Maschito tied to the chair, one guard ran toward him while the other, Massimo Tolve, turned and gave chase out of the room. He rushed from the building, through the two arches set into the two protecting walls, and out along the stone bridge, the only way in and out of the castle.

The road fell away sharply beyond the bridge, and there was a parking lot farther down. As Tolve turned off the bridge, he saw a car reversing in the lot. He watched it pause while it changed gear, and then it moved forward, accelerating down the remainder of the hill, heading west for the road to Calitri.

Thanks to that pause, he was later able to tell the police just two things about the car. That it was a Lancia Delta—and that its license plate was Swiss.

An ornate, four-story, ochre-and-white baroque palazzo, a small jewel on the Piazza Sant'Ignazio in the center of old Rome, lies just across from the Jesuit church of Sant'Ignazio, famous for its trompe l'oeil cupola painted by Andrea Pozzo (1642–1709). This splendid edifice is the public face and headquarters of the Carabinieri Art Squad, the Italians' way of showing the value they put on their heritage. The squad also has twelve regional units and one of these, in Naples, now became the operational headquarters for the Melfi investigators. One of the vases that had been stolen in the Melfi theft showed Hercules carrying a circular shield and in combat with Geryon, a three-headed monster. Because the monster with three heads resembled the antiquities underworld, which manifested itself in many different guises, Colonel Conforti—the man in charge of the Art Squad—code-named the Melfi investigation "Operation Geryon."

At the time of the Melfi theft, Roberto Conforti was fifty-seven and had been in charge of the Art Squad for a little over four years. He is old-fashioned, experienced, round faced, with a small mustache and the gravelly voice of a man who smokes two packs of Marlboros every day. He was born in Serre, near Salerno, and still speaks with a distinctive southern Italian accent despite his many years in Rome. His father was a civil servant, his mother was—and his sister still is—a schoolteacher, and his wife was in the same class as his sister at school. He grew up at a time when it was normal for him to address his father as *"voi,"* the Italian equivalent of the French *"vous."* In those days, the commander of the local Carabinieri would cuff children over the head if they were out on the streets too late, when they should have been home eating dinner with their parents. He studied law at Naples University but preferred law enforcement as a career and joined the Carabinieri when he was nineteen. In the nearly forty years between then and Operation Geryon, Conforti was involved in one tough assignment after another. He was in Sardinia in the late 1960s, the years of Sardinian banditry, during which time his wife and first daughter needed bodyguards. In 1969, he moved to Naples to become commander of the Poggioreale area, with its notorious Poggioreale prison. This area Conforti himself describes as *"fetente,"* fetid—nasty and stinking—a place where his wife had to lock herself and their daughter in their bedroom, with water and emergency medicines, refusing to come out until he arrived home. He was promoted to run the investigative unit in Naples, a critical time when the Camorra (the Naples region version of the Mafia) and the Sicilian Cosa Nostra were beginning to consolidate, as they began their foray into drugs. One of the main Mafia figures escaped from prison at that time and, as Conforti puts it, "Homicides just happened in repetition." It was gang war. His successes there resulted in further promotion, this time to Giuliano, probably the most Camorra-infested area in the Naples hinterland, after which he was given command of the entire Naples area. He was moved to Rome in the late 1970s and given command of the operational unit there, at a time when terrorism was growing, in particular groups like the Red Brigade.

Conforti has been involved in all the hard, intractable problems of Italian crime. He has learned the tricks of the trade, has spent long parts of his career working undercover, against the most formidable, well-equipped, determined, and *organized* criminals that Italy has produced. Despite the pressures on his wife and daughter early in his career, he and his wife had three more girls, and Conforti is now a grandfather five times over. Such is his commitment to law enforcement, and the need to uphold Italy's institutions, that it has rubbed off on two of his daughters, who are themselves magistrates and, moreover, are married to magistrates.

In 1990, Conforti was given command of the Carabinieri Art Squad. He was charged with "reviving" it. The squad then consisted of just sixty men, who occupied the palazzo in Piazza Sant'Ignazio—and nowhere else. Within two years, Conforti had established a branch in Palermo, two years after that in Florence. Next, newly opened at the time of the Melfi theft and Operation Geryon, came Naples. Bari, Venice, and Turin lay in the future.

Conforti himself had no special training in art. At his *liceo,* or high school, there had been a *Professoressa Prete,* an art teacher he always remembered because she wore a different hat every day and taught him that, in Italy, one is everywhere *surrounded* by art. So, for as long as he can remember, Conforti has loved Caravaggio as much as he has loved Beethoven and Chopin, the three artists he most admires.

He learned early in his time in the Art Squad that though Italian art museums are well guarded, their archaeological treasures are the poor relation. They have less money spent on them and rank lower down in the government's priorities. And so he took the theft at Melfi especially badly. There was only one aspect of the theft that gave him hope.

Spectacular thefts, like the one at Melfi, are always carried out with an international angle. The Swiss number plate in this case proved it but I would have suspected an international angle anyway. There is no need to risk an armed robbery just for a local theft. When thieves steal important, high profile objects, they do so either because they already have a buyer, or they think they have a buyer ready. Many times we have tracked thefts and lootings as far as the Swiss border, but usually our inquiries stop there. Our jurisdiction goes no further, the Swiss laws are helpful to the criminals and it was always my hope that one day we could extend our investigations beyond Italy's border, to show the international side of the traffic in antiquities. When the vases at Melfi were stolen, and we learned that the thieves drove a Swiss car, I remember thinking, "This could be the springboard that takes us into Europe."

But Conforti had no idea what was about to unfold.

Italian police (to use the term loosely, since the Carabinieri are in fact part of the army) have one advantage over similar authorities elsewhere. Because the looting of antiquities is such a widespread problem, at any one time the Art Squad has a number of people under surveillance. In particular, phone tapping is routine. The taps are voice activated, and the legal permissions to operate them have to be renewed every fifteen days. In the wake of a big theft like that at Melfi, however, they are essential, for the telephone traffic tells the police who to focus on.

Long experience had taught the investigators what to look out for. At the lowest level, the tombaroli, or tomb robbers, are invariably laborers or farm workers, who don't make many calls. Above them come those the tombaroli call the *capo zona*, the head of a region. The tomb robbers normally sell their finds to a capo zona, frequently a man with a white-collar job, meaning he has some sort of education, and whose telephone records as often as not show that he regularly makes calls abroad. In this case, following the Melfi raid, there was a burst of telephone traffic centered on the Casal di Principe area. Casal di Principe is a small town north of Naples, in the center of the region that produces the delicious buffalo-mozzarella cheese.

Analysis of the telephone records in Casal di Principe showed that four men in particular had recently been making a lot of international calls. One of these, a certain Pasquale Camera, was particularly interesting, for a check on his background produced the arresting information that he had been a captain in the Guardia di Finanza, Italy's finance and customs police. He was careful not to use his home telephone very much, but the calls that he did make were to Germany, Switzerland, and Sicily.

This early burst of telephone activity didn't last, however, and it seemed that the investigation had stalled. Spring came and went; so did summer. Then, quite by chance, Art Squad headquarters in Piazza Sant'Ignazio received a call from the German police in Munich. The Germans said they had received a request from the Greek police, asking them to raid and search the home of a certain dealer in antiquities who lived in Munich. This man was an Italian named Antonio Savoca, known as

"Nino," and he was believed to be involved in the illegal traffic of antiquities out of Greece and Cyprus. In view of the fact that Savoca was Italian, the Germans said, were the Carabinieri interested in taking part in the upcoming raid? Colonel Conforti didn't need to be asked twice. He selected two officers, a lieutenant and a marshal, who took the first Alitalia flight to Munich. The raid was scheduled for October 14, 1994.

At the briefing on the morning of that day, twelve people were gathered in Munich police headquarters—two Italians, two Greeks, the rest German. Savoca, they were told, lived in a three-story villa in the Pullah suburb of the city, a prosperous area in the south, wooded and quiet. The villa had been under discreet surveillance for some time, and the raiding party was shown a sketch of the house and its surrounding garden. There was a high hedge, enclosing some mature trees and a well-kept English-style lawn, bordered by flowers. Four people were detailed to surround the house, which left eight to take part in the raid proper. Each of these was given a room to inspect as soon as entry had been effected.

The squad arrived in Pullah at about seven in the morning. The weather was overcast and it was threatening to rain. Savoca's home was on a quiet, dead-end street and had a sloping Mansard roof. All the men were in uniform, which made them appear more intimidating. The villa was quickly surrounded, and the German captain in charge of the operation rang the doorbell. Savoca himself answered. A small, round-faced, dark-skinned man of forty-four, Savoca had spiky hair and was wearing a blue shirt and jeans. (His family originally came from Messina in Sicily, but he had been born in Cernobbio on Lake Como in the far north of Italy.) He was read his rights and told he could telephone a lawyer if he wished, though the police did not have to wait for the lawyer to arrive. He seemed nervous but was relatively calm in comparison with his wife, Doris Seebacher, a small blond from Bolzano. She was furious, which Conforti's men interpreted as an auspicious sign.

There were three other people in the villa besides Savoca and his wife: their two children, and Savoca's mother. She remained with the children while the police searched the rooms. The laws of evidence demanded that Savoca or his wife be with the raiding party at all times.

The search did not begin well. Just inside the front door, to the right, there was a huge study, with a central desk, bookshelves with books, and below them, a display cabinet with lights and antiquities on display. To the Italians this was no more than normal. People mixed up in the illicit traffic in antiquities often pose as collectors—they keep the loot in properly lit display cases, as a "collector" would, to deflect suspicion. The police spent several minutes tapping the walls and floors and ceilings for hidden compartments but discovered nothing. Beyond the study was a huge kitchen, and beyond that a monumental spiral staircase, made of marble, that led both up and down. They tried downstairs first.

The basement was divided into three sections. The first room they came to was a storeroom, a *magazzino* in Italian, which contained scores of boxes, each containing fragments of antiquities, many with dirt on them, and each carefully classified—"red-figure," "black-figure," "Attic," "Apulian," and so on. The police found this promising. There were also a few complete objects in this room, vases mainly. The second feature of the basement was a huge laboratory, spotless and laid out like a medical pharmacy, with scientific instruments, lancets, magnifying glasses, jars of chemicals, paints, brushes, and other equipment with which fragile antiquities could be cleaned and restored to their former glory. This was even more promising than the magazzino.

Beyond the laboratory, however, the raiding party was in for a real surprise, something that none of the police there that day had ever come across before—not the Italians, nor the Germans, nor the Greeks who had flown in from Athens. It was a pool. At first glance it looked like a swimming pool. It was five feet deep, more than sixty feet long, and some thirty feet wide. It was lined in tiles, with skimmers to ensure the efficient circulation of water. But this pool wasn't used for swimming. Standing in the water, in rows, like so many giant chess pieces, was a score or more of ancient vases and jars. This was Savoca's way of cleaning the bigger antiquities—they were dipped in the pool, then left for a few days, and the chemicals in the water removed the encrustations and other blemishes that they had acquired down the ages. The police were dumbfounded. This was restoration on an industrial scale. The great majority of the vases were of Italian origin, though there were some from Bulgaria and some from Greece. Next to the pool were a number of plastic vats, containing stronger chemicals used to clean the vases with really difficult encrustations. The smell from the chemicals in the vats was quite strong, and no one risked putting his fingers in the liquid to reach for the artifacts. Savoca was silent. There was no hiding what the pool room was used for.

For the Carabinieri, however, the pool and its contents were just the first of several surprises that day. Alongside the pool, standing in a neat row next to the vats, and in a very clean state, were three of the magnificent vases stolen from Melfi. They varied from about nine inches to more than two feet high. One showed a naked youth crowned with a diadem and holding a *phiale* (a plate) with sweetmeats on it. Another showed a woman with a crown, dancing and playing an ancient tambourine. A third showed a warrior, in armor, with a shield and spear, relaxing and talking to a maiden. They didn't seem to have been damaged during their journey north across the Alps.

So far as the Italians were concerned, their journey had already been more than worthwhile, but the day and the surprises weren't over. The raiding party climbed back up the marble staircase. Above the ground floor, on the first floor, were the bedrooms, but above them, there was another floor set into the mansard roof, a room with sloping walls. When the raiding party reached this top floor, yet another discovery awaited them. All around the walls there was shelving that, like the floor space in this room, was packed with antiquities—hundred and hundreds of vases and *stelae,* or stone slabs carved with inscriptions. There were bronzes, statues, mosaics. There were frescoes, jewelry, silver. The vast majority of objects were of Italian origin but here, too, there was Bulgarian and Greek material. And in the middle of the room were the remaining Melfi vases.

Also in the middle of the mansard room, next to the Melfi vases, was a small writing desk. On examination, this was found to contain Savoca's personal archive. And what an archive it turned out to be. Savoca had the meticulous—the obsessive—habit of recording every transaction he had ever made *on cards.* These five-by-eight-inch cards contained the name of every object he had acquired, the date of the transaction, the price he had paid, *and the name of the individual he had acquired it from—with their signature.* For the investigators, of course, this was pure gold.

The raiding party spent the rest of the day photographing the contents of Savoca's Pullah villa, and he was told that all those contents were being seized. The Italians identified the Melfi vases as stolen, as well as some others from a town called Scrimbia, another out-of-the-way place in the

deep south of Italy.* But the Italians also spent several hours that afternoon searching the card index archive for the name of the individual who
had supplied Savoca with the Melfi vases. At about 4:30 PM, they finally
found what they were looking for. The signature was unmistakable, and
it was a name they knew: Luigi Coppola. There were two things that Conforti's men already knew about Coppola, in addition to his name. First, he
came from Casal di Principe. Second, he was a capo zona who worked
alongside the man whose phone they had been tapping, Pasquale Camera.

▼

Back in Casal di Principe, the surveillance of Camera was stepped up,
and Coppola was added to the phone-tap list. But as often happens in investigations, the breakthrough in Munich did not prove anywhere near as
fruitful as it had promised to be at the time. Camera was still tight-lipped
on the few occasions when he did use his home phone, and Christmas
came and went without any further advances. Early in 1995, following a
certain amount of legal wrangling, the Melfi vases were returned and there
was an elaborate ceremony to mark the occasion, attended by the local
mayor, the local MPs, the local police chief, and Conforti. Luigi Maschito
briefly became a minor celebrity in his hometown all over again, photographed by the local paper.

The phone taps at Casal di Principe were left in place, but nothing
much was revealed, nothing that would enable Conforti to act. Once again
the investigation appeared to have stalled. Spring passed and summer arrived. Half of Conforti's men were on vacation when fate intervened.

Pasquale Camera was a big man, weighing in at a little under 400
pounds, and as this suggests, he liked his food and he liked his drink. On
August 31, a Thursday, he took his lunch at Luciano's Restaurant in Santa
Maria di Capua Vetere, a small town north of Naples and very near Casal

---

*This illegal dig had come to light when a building company had been clearing a road,
which had collapsed. It turned out that the road had collapsed because tombaroli had
built a tunnel under it, to get from a house on one side to a *stipe*—a room attached to
a temple—opposite. Votive objects galore had been smuggled out via this tunnel, but
once the road had collapsed, the very distinctive antiquities from Scrimbia had been on
the Carabinieri's watch list ever since. Dozens of objects in Savoca's mansard room
matched the style of objects typically found at Scrimbia.

di Principe. He then set out on the A1, the Autostrada del Sole, Italy's main north-south freeway, to drive to Rome.

The Carabinieri didn't follow him. They knew where he was headed—his apartment in Rome—and there was no need. Following people can be costly in terms of manpower and risky when using cars. Conforti had also learned long ago, when he was head of the investigative unit in Naples, that cars can be a giveaway. It happened the hard way when, one morning, he arrived at the scene of a crime, in plainclothes and in what he thought was an unmarked car, only to have someone approach him and say, "Ah, you came with the 820!" He didn't know what the man meant until he noticed that those were the last three digits of the license plate. Thereafter, in the Art Squad, Conforti only used rented cars for tailing jobs—from Hertz, Avis, Europcar—anonymous models that were changed every day. In undercover "sting" operations, he would rent more expensive models—a Mercedes, for example—when having his men pose as wealthy collectors. This helped them to look the part.

The August day was hot and sultry, though traffic on the Autostrada del Sole was light. Sometime between 2:30 and 3:00 PM, just as he was approaching the exit for Cassino, with the great stone hill of Monte Cassino and its historic Benedictine monastery looming above, Camera's car, a beige Renault 21, left the road, smashed into the guardrail at the edge of the autostrada—and overturned. Camera was killed instantly, pronounced dead by the side of the road by the paramedics without being taken to hospital. There were rumors, later, that his car had been interfered with in some way, but Conforti discounts this. He thought it more likely that Camera fell asleep at the wheel after a heavy lunch. He was too big to fit into his seat belt, which wasn't fastened around him, and the impact at speed—and when the Renault overturned—was fatal.

In Italy, road accidents are the responsibility of the Polizia Stradale, and they were brought in on this occasion. However, when accidents occur in small towns such as Cassino, the local Carabinieri are also informed. In addition to being told that a fatal accident had occurred, they were told on this occasion that a number of photographs had been found in the glove compartment of the car, showing archaeological objects. It so happened that the commander of the Carabinieri in Cassino at that time had himself been a member of the Art Squad not long before. On being told about the contents of the glove compartment, he immediately telephoned his former colleagues in Piazza Sant'Ignazio, who passed the message along the line to the men on the ground.

The information was timely. About an hour before, the men manning the phone taps in the *procura*, the prosecutor's office in Santa Maria di Capua Vetere, had begun picking up cryptic messages being exchanged between tombaroli to the effect that "The captain is dead," and they hadn't known what to make of it. The information from their colleagues in Cassino clarified the situation—Pasquale Camera had been a captain in the Guardia di Finanza, Italy's financial and customs police.

Conforti now saw his chance—an opportunity that might never come again. Within an hour his men had contacted a magistrate in Santa Maria di Capua Vetere and obtained a search warrant, in Italian a *decreto di perquisizione*, which entitled them to raid and search Camera's apartment in Rome.

Naples to Rome is normally a two-hour drive. That night, owing to traffic, they didn't reach Camera's apartment in the San Lorenzo district in northeast Rome until 9:00 PM. They had stopped to pick up the equipment that would enable them to break down the front door. In the event, however, a neighbor saw them as they huddled around the entrance, and when he understood who they were, he offered a key to the apartment. Even so, under Italian law the Carabinieri weren't allowed to search the premises until a relative had been contacted and given the chance to be present. The helpful neighbor had the phone number for Camera's mother in Naples.

It was an awkward call to make: Only hours after her son had been killed, the police were asking the old woman to be a witness, in a search of her dead son's apartment. Camera's brother-in-law agreed to drive up from Naples, and only after he had arrived could the search go ahead. It was by then after 11:00 PM.

It was a big apartment, located between the Piazza Bologna and La Sapienza, Rome's oldest university, an area with a mix of old and new buildings. The apartment, in a relatively new building, had a square-shaped sitting room, a large study leading off it, and a balcony running along the south side that looked down on streets crowded with students. Any one of the Carabinieri would have given his eyeteeth to be able to afford such an apartment. The furniture was a little on the flamboyant side, with the decoration—wallpaper, curtains, lampshades—in pastel shades. Beyond that, however, the contents of the second-floor apartment were incredibly untidy—papers were strewn all over, uneaten food was turning moldy, dirty laundry appeared to have been dropped anywhere. Eight men took part in the raid, and their first aim was to put order into the chaos. There were hundreds of photographs, Polaroids mainly, and pages and pages of documentation, together with scores of antiquities, some of which were genuine but many of which were obviously fake.

The investigators spent a few hours that night sifting through the contents of the apartment and then sealed the door. They called Conforti, who was at home but still awake. He is one of those people who needs little sleep, and they knew he would be anxious for news.

Over the next few days, as they assessed the material they had seized, they made a number of discoveries. First, they found phone bills for five different cell phones. These bills showed that they were *all* registered in the name of a certain Wanda d'Agata. Second, utility bills and mortgage payments further showed that the apartment was also registered in the same name, Wanda d'Agata. It didn't take the investigators long to deduce that Wanda was a convenient "front" for Camera. As he moved around, buying and selling looted or stolen antiquities, he and his contacts used only the cell phones registered to her. All that ever showed up on the official records, therefore, was that Wanda was calling herself. This is why Camera didn't appear to be using his own phone very much—he was using one of Wanda's. The apartment was in her name to keep him off the radar of all official bodies. This was a highly suspicious—and highly effective—modus operandi.

What really pushed the investigation forward and confirmed Camera's importance and involvement in trafficking antiquities were the photographs of the archaeological objects that had been found in the glove compartment of his Renault. They arrived at the investigator's offices a day after the raid on the Rome apartment. There were about fifty pictures, and among them was one of a calyx krater by Asteas, a fourth-century BC Italian vase painter, and another of a very striking statue of Artemis. In Greek mythology, and according to Hesiod, one of the earliest Greek writers after Homer, Artemis was the daughter of Zeus and the sister of Apollo. She loved hunting and dancing, and was one of the three virgin goddesses of Olympus. She was also notorious for her anger and jealousy, which led her to kill many others—humans, gods, and goddesses.

To Conforti and his men it was immediately obvious that this statue was an exceedingly rare and valuable object indeed. All investigators in the Art Squad are given lessons in art history—in painting, sculpture, and drawing—by the superintendency of Italy's Culture Ministry, and because they handle a lot of objects, and see a fair proportion of fakes, they quickly develop an "eye" for the quality of artifacts. The white marble Artemis was about four feet high and showed the goddess with hair braided across her forehead and falling down the side of her neck, striding out in a full-length tunic and sandals. The tunic fell down her body in triangular folds, and there was a hunting strap across her breasts. Her features showed a slight smile as she looked directly ahead. Her arms were cut off at the elbows, but otherwise she was intact.

The investigators knew she was Artemis for one simple reason—it was a classical image and three other near-identical versions were known, one in Naples, one in Florence, and one in Venice. All were in museums, and all were Roman copies, dating from the first century AD, of a lost archaic Greek original that dated to the fifth or sixth century BC. Since none of the statues in the three museums was missing, *this* Artemis was a major find. It might even be the original Greek Artemis. Given Camera's links with the Naples area, in particular with Santa Maria di Capua Vetere, the photograph found in his car strongly suggested that the statue had perhaps been excavated in that area. Who could say what else had been purloined during the illegal dig of what was clearly a very important site? And so recovering this Artemis now became a major focus of the Art Squad. The photograph recovered from the glove compartment had some meat hooks in the background—the Artemis had been transferred from the ground to a butcher shop. Shortly afterward, however, in Camera's apartment, the Carabinieri came across another photograph of the Artemis, against a different, and less striking, background. Clearly, Camera was intimately involved in trading this valuable and beautiful object.

The second breakthrough as a result of the raid on Camera's apartment came via the other names mentioned in the paperwork the Carabinieri confiscated. These names led the investigators in two directions. In the first place, they led eventually to no fewer than seventy other raids, which unearthed hundreds of looted vases and other objects—and to the arrest of nineteen individuals, all of whom were found guilty at their subsequent trials.

From our point of view, however, the second direction is more interesting. For among the names in the documentation in Camera's apartment was that of Wanda d'Agata's son, a man named Danilo Zicchi.

He was raided toward the end of September, still as part of Operation Geryon, and in his apartment two very important discoveries were made. First, from the furniture, wallpaper, and other decorations, Conforti's men realized that Zicchi's apartment was the very place where the statue of Artemis had been photographed after it had left the butcher shop. Faced with this evidence, and the threat of some very fulsome and unpleasant Carabinieri attention, Zicchi decided to talk—up to a point. He admitted that his apartment had been used "for years" as a "warehouse" for looted antiquities, many of them from Sicily. The objects would be stored in his apartment, he said, for months or longer, and then, acting on instructions, he would pack the antiquities into boxes and *mail* them abroad from the post office on the ground floor beneath his apartment. (The man in charge of the post office below confirmed later that Zicchi had indeed been sending packages abroad "for years.") The objects were almost always sent out in fragments, Zicchi said. That way they occupied less space, drew less attention to themselves, and should the package break open for any reason, a collection of untidy pieces looked much less suspicious. Zicchi also said that he had met Pasquale Camera when the latter had been a captain in the Guardia di Finanza and had been tipped off about him. Instead of prosecuting Zicchi, the two men had become close colleagues.

The second discovery in Zicchi's apartment was Camera's passport. Together with the fact that Camera's own apartment was in someone else's name, as were several of his telephones, this confirmed—if confirmation were still needed—the lengths to which Camera would go to hide from official notice. He kept his profile as low as he possibly could, consistent with being able to travel abroad to further his business interests, and to bank his profits from those interests. Otherwise, Camera didn't exist.

The investigators took away about sixty objects at the end of that first raid on Zicchi's apartment. They had in mind a second raid, on the grounds that, as Conforti pointed out, having been raided once Zicchi would think he was safe. Before they could do so, however, Conforti received a phone call from an archaeologist at the Villa Giulia, Rome's Etruscan museum. This was Daniela Rizzo, an archaeologist at the museum who worked closely with the Art Squad, verifying whether allegedly looted objects were genuine or not and, if genuine, where they had most probably been looted from. This time, she was calling to say that she had been contacted by an old woman who said that her son had just inherited a collection of antiquities and was anxious to have her—Rizzo—come and see them, authenticate them, and register them, so he could possess them legally (this is how the system works in Italy). Rizzo was being so pressurized, she said, with the old woman so adamant that she verify and register the objects "at once," that she was becoming suspicious.

What was the name of this woman, queried Conforti. More to the point, who was her son?

"His name is Danilo Zicchi," said Rizzo.

This was interesting. "How many objects does he want to register?"

"About eighty, I think."

Even more interesting. Sixty objects had been seized. Now, by some lucky "accident," Zicchi had "inherited" another eighty.

The upshot was that Rizzo agreed to pay Zicchi a visit the following day to "inspect" his objects. She was accompanied by a "colleague," who was of course an investigator from Conforti's Art Squad, in plainclothes. More investigators remained down on the street, ready to swoop once they got the word.

In fact, that day they discovered something incomparably more important than eighty looted antiquities, something that provided one of three starting points for the overall investigation that gave rise to this book (this was the second starting point, after the theft at Melfi). This discovery was kept top secret from everybody except Conforti and the Rome public prosecutor. In Zicchi's apartment, in a file on a desk, just sitting there, was a single handwritten sheet of lined paper, with two punched holes on the left-hand side so it would fit into a ring binder. The sheet was covered in Pasquale Camera's handwriting, and it was nothing less than an *organizational chart* showing how the clandestine antiquities network was arranged throughout Italy, Switzerland, and elsewhere. It revealed exactly who was in the entire hierarchy—from top to bottom, and everyone in between—and beyond that, how they were related to each other, who supplied whom, who was in competition with whom, which areas of Italy were supplied by which middlemen, and what their links were to international dealers, museums, and collectors. The chart was breathtaking.

The handwriting, in blue ballpoint pen, was quite clear. It was an educated hand, manifestly laid out with some forethought, and Zicchi confirmed it as Camera's script. Right at the top, in large letters, it showed "Robert (Bob) Hecht," with two small lateral arrows pointing to "Paris and USA—museums and collectors." Hecht's name was underlined, and from this line other arrows went to and from his name. The lines indicated that beneath him was a series of international dealers and collectors, scattered across Europe, whose names were also written in larger letters. These were, first, Gianfranco Becchina, of Basel, Switzerland, and Castelvetrano in Sicily, and the name of his firm, Antike Kunst Palladion. Next came Nicholas Goutulakis, of Paris, Geneva, and Athens, with a two-way arrow directly linking him to Hecht. The rest of the names were: George Ortiz, of Geneva and Argentina; "Frida," of Zurich; Sandro Cimicchi, a Basel restorer; and Giacomo Medici, of Rome, Vulci, Santa Marinella, and Geneva.

Below these were still more names, written in smaller letters. Below Becchina was Elia Borowsky, an M. Bruno, of Lugano, Cerveteri, and Torino, though with other words in brackets ("north Italy, Roma, Lazio, Campania, Puglia, Sardinia, Sicily")—indicating his areas of competence. Below him was Dino Brunetti of Cerveteri, followed by Franco Luzzi of Ladispoli, a small town on the coast, just north of Rome, and below him the words "*Tombaroli di . . .* " and then a list of places including Grosseto, Montalto di Castro, Orvieto, Cerveteri, Casal di Principe, and Marcenise. Also under Becchina was "Raffaele Monticelli (Puglia, Calabria, Campania, Sicilia)," and under him Aldo Bellezza ("Foggia," and elsewhere). Under Medici, dotted lines linked him to "Alessandro Anedda (Roma)" and Franco Luzzi (again), of Ladispoli, with a solid arrow linking him to "Elio—stab. of Santa Marinella" ("stab." is short for *stabilimento*, meaning "factory"), "Benedetto d'Aniello, of Naples," and "Pierluigi Manetti, of Rome." (See the Dossier section for a facsimile of the chart.)

By itself of course the chart proved nothing, and a number of people included worked in the business of restoring antiquities and may well have been doing no more than carrying on their lawful activities. But it was very circumstantial evidence against many of those cited. It contained some names that the Carabinieri knew, and a few that they didn't. But most important of all, the chart showed the various levels of involvement, the role of Switzerland in the clandestine trade, and the links between the various participants. In other words, *it was the underground network's view of itself.* Nothing like this had ever been found before. Within days, the chart was being referred to by the few aware of its existence inside the Art Squad—and in the offices of the public prosecutor—as the "organigram."

"The moment I saw that scribbled sheet of paper," says Conforti, "I thought back to 1977, in Naples, when we found in very different circumstances the organigram of the Camorra. Organized criminals are strange from this point of view—after all, the Red Brigade made the same mistake as well. And that is, they write about themselves, they put it on paper. So organized delinquency doesn't change, it merely varies. And this time it was the same. It gave us the chance to move into terrain where, although we weren't floundering, we didn't have certainties."

From the point of view of the Carabinieri, the organigram (see p. 362) was most immediately useful for its identification of the two most senior *Italian* figures in the network. Among the international dealers, Hecht was an American resident in Paris; "Frida" was Frederique Tchacos-Nussberger, an Egyptian-born Greek resident in Zurich; Nicholas Goutoulakis was Nikolas Koutoulakis, a Greek-Cypriot resident in Paris (now dead); George Ortiz was in fact an heir to the Ortiz-Patiño tin fortune, of Bolivia, not Argentina, and he resided in Geneva. Elia, or Eli, Borowsky was a dealer-collector of Polish origin who had lived in Canada for many years and by then was living in Israel; the network was nothing if not international. But the chart identified two Italians, Gianfranco Becchina and Giacomo Medici, as being senior figures, and the lines and linkages shown below their names made it clear that these two men were primarily responsible for bringing antiquities out of Italy.

Operation Geryon had recovered the Melfi vases and had resulted in nineteen arrests. It was therefore wound up in the fall of 1995. This allowed Conforti to turn his attention to what appeared to him to be the bigger fish—to Gianfranco Becchina and Giacomo Medici.

From Camera's organigram, the man whose name interested Conforti the most was Giacomo Medici. The colonel had known about the dealer for years, and the Carabinieri had even paid surprise "visits" to his houses several times. A property he had owned in Vulci, attached to a protected archaeological area, had been purchased compulsorily by the state, on the advice of archaeologists.

Naturally, Conforti started tapping Medici's phone. This eavesdropping proved enlightening because it quickly established that one of the capi zona (the senior figure among the tombaroli) in the Naples area, one of the men they had targeted after the Melfi theft—a certain Roberto Cilli—was observed from his phone calls to have particularly close links with Medici. Cilli was a gypsy, from a family of gypsies who had become Italianized. He lived in Montalto di Castro, a small town on the Via Aurelia, just north of Tarquinia, one of the most famous Etruscan centers, in a celebrated street of run-down shacks—the Via dei Grottini—to which the authorities turned a blind eye. Cilli's father had been a well-known tombarolo, and his wife was even better known, as a fortune-teller who numbered several rich socialites and TV stars among her clients.

Conforti's tried and tested procedure in the Carabinieri, when targeting a senior criminal, is to pressure first his less-important colleagues. If the Art Squad can offer inducements to persuade the supplier of a bigger fish— the less well educated, the less sophisticated, the less protected—to confess or give away crucial details, these details can be used against the more important figures.

Before the investigators could move against Cilli, however, another unexpected twist occurred. In London, Sotheby's catalog for its antiquities sale that year showed a photograph of a sarcophagus that was on the Art Squad's list of stolen works. It had been taken from the church of San Saba on the Aventine, one of the seven hills of Rome. For any investigator, a stolen object is always easier to deal with than looted works. There are records of stolen works, whereas looted objects almost by definition leave no trace when they are dug up in the middle of the night by a tombarolo. So, once Sotheby's had been presented with the evidence confirming that the sarcophagus was stolen, the company had no choice but to tell the Carabinieri that it had been put up for sale by a Geneva-based company called Editions Services and that the company was run by a French-speaking Swiss, Henri Albert Jacques. The address of Editions Services was given as 7 Avenue Krieg. An official request was immediately sent to the Swiss by the Italian authorities, seeking permission to question Jacques and to inspect the premises of Editions Services.

Since there was no question that the sarcophagus was stolen, permission was quickly granted. When approached, however, Jacques said that he was only the administrator of the company in question, a "fiduciary," in effect a minion who looked after the finances and acted as an official "face." Furthermore, he said, the address at 7 Avenue Krieg was little more than an accommodation address. The company was actually based at the Freeport, just outside Geneva, and the real owner—the "beneficial owner," in English legal terminology—was an Italian named Giacomo Medici.

Coming after the raid on Savoca and the accident that had killed Camera, together with the subsequent discovery of the organigram, this was an extraordinary stroke of luck, and for the moment, all thought of using Cilli to put pressure on Medici was put on hold. Another official request was dispatched to the Swiss, seeking permission to raid the premises of Editions Services in Geneva Freeport.

Geneva Freeport ("Port Franc" in French) is a massive set of warehouses to the southwest of the city, where goods may be stored without officially "entering" Switzerland, the point being that no tax is paid on these goods unless and until they do officially cross the border. The advantage for Switzerland is that the hundreds—if not thousands—of personnel associated with the Freeport, who live in Geneva, bring with them a busy commercial life and considerable foreign currency.

Once again, the Swiss complied quickly and, on September 13, 1995, the raid took place. Medici had been contacted, at the last minute, but was on holiday in Sardinia and couldn't get back that day. This time the raiding party consisted of a Swiss magistrate, three Swiss police, headed by an inspector, three of Conforti's men, an official photographer, and the deputy director of the Freeport. The offices of Editions Services were located on the fourth floor of the plain, steel-built warehouse, on Corridor

17, Room 23. Seventeen is an unlucky number in Italy, the tradition deriving from ancient Rome and its use of Latin numerals. In Roman numerals, seventeen is spelled XVII, which is an anagram of VIXI, meaning "I lived" or, in other words, "I am now dead." Medici's warehouse was henceforth invariably known as "Corridor 17."

The door to Room 23 was, like the rest of the building, made of anonymous gray metal. The deputy director of the Freeport had a key and, at the magistrate's instruction, let them all in. Room 23 in fact comprised three rooms. In the outside room—the first the raiding party came to—there was a settee, some chairs, and a glass table supported by an enormous stone capital. At the far end there was a frosted glass window, but the rest of the walls were lined with cupboards. At first sight, Room 23 was ordinary. It was a sitting room and not especially stylish, at that; there was a thin brown carpet covering the floor. However, when the Carabinieri started opening the cupboards, they quickly changed their minds. There was nothing ordinary about the room in any way. All the cupboards were shelved—and each and every one of the shelves was packed—crowded, teeming, overloaded with antiquities: with vases, statues, bronzes; with candelabra, frescoes, mosaics; with glass objects, faience animals, jewelry, and still more vases. Some were wrapped in newspapers; frescoes lay on the floor or leaning against walls; other vases were packed in fruit boxes, and many had dirt on them. Some had Sotheby's labels tied to them with white string.

But that wasn't all. In the outer part of Room 23, there was also a huge safe, five feet tall and three feet wide. Amazingly, it wasn't locked.

If the contents of the cupboards had been astounding, the contents of the safe were truly astonishing. One of Conforti's men whistled as he realized what he was looking at. Inside the safe were twenty of the most exquisite classical Greek dinner plates that anyone there that day had ever seen, plus a number of red-figure vases by famous classical vase painters. The Carabinieri immediately recognized one as by none other than Euphronios. Together, the objects in the safe must have been worth millions of dollars.

The plates and the Euphronios vase were taken out and placed on the glass-topped table. The photographer, as he had done with all the other objects in the cupboards, took several photographs from various angles.

Then the team moved on into the inner room, leaving the most junior of the Swiss police, the least experienced, to return the plates and vase to the safe. He replaced the plates without any difficulty, but when it came to the vase, he lifted it, naturally enough, by the handles. It simply never occurred to him that the vase was made of fragments that were only loosely glued together. A more experienced man—one of Conforti's men, for instance—would have known that the handles of the vase wouldn't bear the weight. And so the body of the bowl parted company from the handles and fell to the ground, breaking into pieces along the lines where the various fragments had originally been glued together to form the whole. The sound of shattering pottery ricocheted around the room and everyone froze. It later transpired that Giacomo Medici had paid close to $800,000 for the vase.

The Euphronios pieces were picked up and, gently, returned to the safe. Then the party again moved on into the inner room. This was no less astonishing, but in a different way. It was brimming, not with antiquities but with documentation. There were thousands of photographs (later estimates put it at about 4,000)—most of them Polaroids, others negatives, all pictures of antiquities, many of which had dirt on them. There were stacks of documents—invoices, consignment notes, condition reports, letters, and checks. The letterheads on some of the invoices and correspondence told their own story: Atlantis Antiquities, New York; Robin Symes Limited, London; Phoenix Ancient Art, S.A., Geneva; the J. Paul Getty Museum, Los Angeles.

It was clear that the outer room was where Medici received prospective buyers, and where objects for sale were displayed in secure and discreet circumstances. It was equally clear from the way the documentation was just scattered around the inner room that Medici had never expected anyone to come calling *here*—everything was just lying around, with no attempt at concealment.

Everything in the inner room was photographed as well—all the documents, the albums of photographs, the contents of drawers and cupboards, together with general views so that the authorities could be certain at a later date that nothing had been taken. The final move that day was to seal the outer door to Room 23. They locked the door, put police tape across the door frame, and fixed a large wax seal over the keyhole, with the Geneva magistrate's embossed badge pressed into it. From now on Medici couldn't get in, unless accompanied by someone from the Geneva court.

When Conforti heard about the contents of Corridor 17, even he was astonished. He loves to garden, and that evening, when the Carabinieri called him from the departure lounge of Geneva airport—it was after 8:00 PM—he was on his terrace watering his large array of exotic plants. "We had heard talk of the Freeport often enough—Freeport this, Freeport that, Freeport, Freeport, Freeport. But we had always thought of it as a place of transit and had never imagined whole warehouses—*what* a discovery. When I heard the news, in that moment I thought that perhaps—perhaps—the ball of twine would now be unraveled. In that moment, I felt that the work I had being doing since I took over the Art Squad in 1990 had come to fruition, had found a reason."

But—and it was a big "but"—the objects were on Swiss soil. Medici, on the other hand, was an Italian citizen. Would the Swiss want it known that the Geneva Freeport was being used as a way station for valuable and culturally important objects that had been looted from Italy and passed on to the salesrooms, collectors, and museums in London, the United States, and elsewhere? On this first visit of the Italian authorities to the Freeport, Medici had not been present. What arguments would he use, what arguments *could* he use, to make it appear that the antiquities in his warehouses were legitimate? Would the Swiss, in the interests of a quiet life, just let the matter drop, or might they choose to believe the man who was bringing in business to Switzerland? These were not trivial or rhetorical questions—a good lawyer could have a field day.

Back in Italy, and as a result of what had been found in Geneva, an investigative public prosecutor, Dr. Paolo Giorgio Ferri, was appointed to pursue Medici and his Geneva operation. It was clear from what the investigators had found in Switzerland that Medici was the biggest "catch'" the Carabinieri had ever had, so far as looted antiquities were concerned. How close would they get to him?

Paolo Giorgio Ferri, forty-eight when the investigation began, is a small, precise man. Bearded, with a soft voice and a ready smile, he had a law degree from La Sapienza, Rome's oldest university, and was a high-flier in the public prosecutor's office, having previously worked on heavy-duty criminal cases—mostly murder and drug trafficking. But as he set to work, thinking how best to pursue Medici, there was another twist of fate in store for him. While the Carabinieri had been at the Freeport, another set of investigators had also been there at the same time. Their paths had never crossed, but that was about to change.

2

SOTHEBY'S, SWITZERLAND, SMUGGLERS

THE OTHER INVESTIGATION taking place in the Geneva Freeport had its origin in the fate of James Hodges, an employee of Sotheby's, the international auction house established in 1744. Hodges, in his early thirties in 1995, had worked for Sotheby's in a number of capacities, which included being an administrator in the Antiquities Department. This meant that so far as antiquities were concerned, Hodges was in charge of the paperwork, in regard to buying and selling, and the transfer of funds in and out of Sotheby's—all the financial transactions between the company and its customers. He had access to the most confidential information.

In 1991, Hodges had stood trial, accused of stealing from Sotheby's two antiquities—a helmet and a stone head—of forging a release note purportedly giving him permission to have these objects at home, and on eighteen charges of false accounting. Essentially, in the false accounting charges, he had been accused of setting up two bank accounts in fictitious names and regularly paying himself small sums that no one else noticed for a while but which quickly added up. Hodges was found guilty of stealing the helmet and head and of forging the release note, but he was acquitted on the eighteen charges of false accounting. He was sentenced to nine months' imprisonment.

Before he was prosecuted, Hodges had photocopied or stolen a number of internal Sotheby's documents that, in his view, showed the company in a bad light, that it was behaving dishonestly or unethically in certain ways. His initial aim was to use these documents as a fallback, or bargaining tool, should his own dishonesty ever be discovered by Sotheby's. In the event, when he did get found out, Sotheby's refused to do any deal and insisted on a prosecution. Hodges therefore contacted one of the authors of this book (Peter Watson), seeing publication of Sotheby's own (and more widespread) wrongdoing as fitting revenge.

Whether or not Hodges deserved his jail sentence, and whether or not he should have stolen the paperwork that he undoubtedly did steal, these documents nonetheless appeared to show prima facie wrongdoing inside Sotheby's in a score of areas. Among the documents he had were a set showing that there were three men in Switzerland, who between them consigned thousands of antiquities over the years to Sotheby's salesrooms in London, none of which had any provenance whatsoever. These three men were Serge Vilbert, Christian Boursaud—and Giacomo Medici. In one notorious sale, Sotheby's offered "a whole batch of smuggled antiquities," according to Brian Cook, the distinguished keeper in the Department of Greek and Roman Antiquities at the British Museum, including a dozen Apulian vases.[1]

Sotheby's was pressed to withdraw the vases by a special representative of the Italian government, who flew to London for the purpose, and by Professor Felice Lo Porto, superintendent of antiquities in the Puglia region, who let it be known that a large, fourth-century BC tomb near Arpi (an old, rich settlement near Foggia) had recently been looted. He said he believed the Sotheby's vases came from there. Other British museums, such as the Royal Museum of Scotland in Edinburgh, joined the British Museum in calling for Sotheby's to withdraw the objects, and Lord Jenkins of Putney, a former minister of the arts, formally raised the issue in Parliament.

Despite the negative publicity, aired in the London *Observer*, Sotheby's took the view that there was "no evidence" that the vases it was selling were either looted or smuggled. When Peter Watson spoke to Felicity Nicholson, the company's head of antiquities, in preparation for writing an article on the subject, she said, "I don't think one ever knows where antiquities come from. We assume our clients have title to whatever it is they are selling." She went on to describe Cook as "fussy, someone who doesn't necessarily reflect the whole of scholarly opinion."

Despite the opposition, the sale went ahead and the vases sold quite well. The art world is nothing if not cynical, and maybe the publicity had even helped. After a fruitless few days in London, the Italian special envoy flew home and the scandal died down. But James Hodges, watching this exchange from his unique vantage point as administrator in the Antiquities Department, knew that *all* the Apulian vases that Brian Cook reckoned to have been illegally excavated and smuggled out of Italy had been consigned to Sotheby's by one man. This man, Christian Boursaud, was a Swiss dealer with offices in Geneva and a shop called the Hydra Gallery.

Furthermore, from his vantage point, Hodges was well placed to watch events unfold. A couple of months after the scandal, Boursaud wrote to Felicity Nicholson, announcing the closure of his gallery, an event he blamed on ill health. When Nicholson replied, Hodges noted the wording of her letter: "With regard to the property we have here, I understand that you have been acting *as the agent* for the owner and we will of course wait to hear from him regarding the disposition of the rest of the property we have here from him for sale" (italics added).

Mulling over this wording, and listening to Felicity Nicholson in conversation with other specialists in the Antiquities Department, Hodges came to believe that in fact Boursaud was merely a "front" and that the true owner of the Boursaud objects, the real force behind the trade, was a certain Giacomo Medici. And the reason Boursaud was backing out was not ill health but because he and Medici had fallen out after the publicity surrounding the Sotheby's sale.

Hodges, in his uniquely qualified position at Sotheby's, never heard from Boursaud again, but he later realized that the range of goods consigned by the Hydra Gallery was much the same as those now being offered by a new gallery: Editions Services. In the July 1987 sale, there was a marble pilaster that had hitherto belonged to Hydra, had failed to sell, and was now being sold as the property of Editions Services. So there could now be no doubt: The Hydra Gallery had reinvented itself as Editions Services. Whoever was behind the companies was a prudent man. And the person behind the Hydra Gallery and Editions Services was one and the same: Giacomo Medici.

Throughout the 1980s, Giacomo Medici probably sold more antiquities at Sotheby's than any other single owner. Over the years, thousands of objects from Medici had passed through the London salesroom and millions of pounds had changed hands. None of the antiquities had any provenance because all were illegally excavated and smuggled out of Italy.

There was more. The documentation supplied by Hodges showed that the registered address of Editions Services was 7 Avenue Krieg in Geneva, and that it was registered in the name of Henri Albert Jacques. The documents showed that these details—Avenue Krieg and H. A. Jacques—were also used by another company that consigned many unprovenanced antiquities to Sotheby's. This was a company called Xoilan Trader, Inc., the beneficial owner of which was Robin Symes. Other documents that Hodges took showed that Symes and Felicity Nicholson, boss of antiquities at Sotheby's, had collaborated to smuggle a statue of the Egyptian Lion Goddess out of Italy. It was a cozy, close-knit world, which was exposed in a British TV program only days after the Carabinieri raid on Corridor 17.

It was not long before Conforti got in touch with the British investigation.

Why was it that police in Italy and journalists in Britain were in the same place, at the same time, investigating the same people engaged in the same illicit practices? To an extent, of course, it was an accident, the result of Hodges's predicament at Sotheby's. But there was a deeper reason, too, which accounted for why Hodges was able to observe what he did observe inside Sotheby's. The fact is that attitudes toward, and laws about, dealing in unprovenanced (and therefore very probably illegally excavated and smuggled) antiquities have been steadily changing as views on morality have evolved over the years. Those countries that are the source of archaeological material—the civilizations around the Mediterranean, in Central and South America, West Africa, and Asia—have been taking an increasingly robust line to protect what they see as their heritage. This has partly to do with cultural identity in newly independent countries, in particular after World War II, and partly to do with tourism, because properly excavated archaeological sites can be major attractions, and therefore sources of revenue.

Isolated attempts to control the movement of cultural property date back to early laws in Greece (1834), Italy (1872), and France (1887). After World War I, the newly formed League of Nations held discussions on the imposition of controls over the illicit exploitation of cultural property—in particular antiquities—but the resulting Treaty of Sèvres was never ratified. Throughout the 1930s, action on this topic at the League was coordinated by the Office International des Musées (OIM). Although a draft "Convention on the Repatriation of Objects of Artistic, Historical or Scientific Interest, Which Have Been Lost, Stolen or Unlawfully Alienated or Exported" was prepared, there were strong objections from the art market countries (in particular the Netherlands, the United Kingdom, and the United States), and in 1939, with the outbreak of war, the initiative came to an end. After the war, in 1946, UNESCO took an interest in a convention to protect cultural property in times of war, which led to The Hague Convention of 1954 and, two years later, to a number of recommendations "on international principles applicable to archaeological excavations." This specifically proposed that the art trade should do nothing to "encourage smuggling of archaeological material." In the 1960s, as a result of initiatives by Peru and Mexico, UNESCO adopted stronger recommendations "to improve the international moral climate in this respect" and this led, in 1964, to a Committee of Experts being set up, from some thirty countries, whose task it was to prepare a draft convention. This body eventually produced, in 1970, UNESCO's "Convention on the Means of Prohibiting and Preventing the Illicit Import, Export and Transfer of Ownership of Cultural Property," adopted on November 14 that year, by the general conference of UNESCO at its sixteenth session. This is not the only law or regulation governing these issues; there are also a number of trade agreements relating to the import and export of cultural material. But the 1970 convention has generally been taken as a watershed in this field. Although many archaeologists are against the international traffic in *all* archaeological material, period, most now take what they see as a more practical, pragmatic approach—that one shouldn't deal in, or have anything to do with, antiquities that have no provenance and first came to light *since 1970*, the date of the UNESCO convention. Objects in collections formed before 1970, and which have no provenance, may have been illicitly excavated, but the main priority is to stop the looting now, and for this the 1970 date is sufficiently modern.

Not all states ratified the convention with equal enthusiasm. Here are the ratification dates for a variety of states, from which a pattern will be evident: Cyprus, 1980; Egypt, 1973; France 1997; Greece, 1981; Italy, 1979; Jordan, 1974; Peru, 1980; Turkey, 1981; United Kingdom, 2003; United States, 1983. Denmark, Holland, and Germany have still to ratify the 1970 convention. Switzerland did so in 2004. In other words, there is still a reluctance to do so on the part of most market states.

This is despite evidence that the world's archaeological heritage—the material remains of past human activities—is being destroyed at an undiminished pace. In 1983, one study showed that 58.6 percent of all Mayan sites in Belize had been damaged by looters. Between 1989 and 1991, a regional survey in Mali registered 830 archaeological sites, of which 45 percent had already been damaged, 17 percent badly. In 1996, a sample of eighty were revisited and the incidence of looting had increased by 20 percent. A survey in a district of northern Pakistan showed that nearly half the Buddhist shrines, stupas, and monasteries had been badly damaged or destroyed by illegal excavation. In Andalusia, Spain, 14 percent of known archaeological sites have been damaged by illicit excavation. Between 1940 and 1968, it is estimated that something like 100,000 holes were dug in the Peruvian site of Batan Grande and that in 1965 the looting of a single tomb produced something like ninety pounds of gold jewelry, which accounts for about 90 percent of the Peruvian gold now found in collections around the world. In 1997, in the Qinghai Province of China, the ancient tombs at Reshui, one of the country's "Ten Most Famous Archaeological Sites," were looted by more than 1,000 local people, "who 'excavated' the tombs with high explosives and bulldozers." In Inner Mongolia the government estimates that between 4,000 and 15,000 tombs have been looted, and overall, the Chinese authorities estimate that between 5,000 and 12,000 looted objects reach the market every year. He Shuzhong, of the National Administration on Cultural Heritage in Beijing, who provided these figures, told us that one Chinese tourist company even runs a course on illicit excavation. He himself was physically assaulted on one occasion when he chanced upon looters at a site. In Niger, archaeologists at the Abdou Moumouni University of Niamey estimate that in the Bura, Bangare, and Jebu areas of the country, more than 90 percent of the sites have been looted, and in other areas, such as Windigalo and Kareygooru, 50 percent have been destroyed. And this is nowhere near the end of it.

The looting of Iraq is of course well known—between the end of the first Gulf war, in 1991, and 1994, eleven regional museums were broken into and 3,000 artifacts and 484 manuscripts taken, of which only fifty-four have been recovered. Following the second Gulf war, in April 2003, at least 13,515 objects were stolen from the Baghdad Museum, of which, by June 2004, something like 4,000 had been recovered. Despite the Taliban's high-profile demolition of the Bamiyan Buddhas for "religious" reasons, most of the destruction of Afghanistan has been wrought by the search for salable antiquities and manuscripts; it has continued, if not actually worsened, since the Taliban's removal from power.

Further information about the material scale of the illegal trade can be extracted from official police statistics. In Turkey, for example, between 1993 and 1995 there were more than 17,500 official police investigations into stolen antiquities. In 1998, the Turkish Department of Smuggling and Organized Crime reported that in the previous year, 565 people had been arrested who had, between them, more than 10,000 archaeological objects in their possession. Greek police reported that between 1987 and 2001, they recovered 23,007 artifacts. In one year, 1997, German police in Munich recovered fifty to sixty crates containing 139 icons, sixty-one frescoes, and four mosaics that had been torn from the walls of northern Cypriot churches.

The Italian experience is just as bad. The Carabinieri Art Squad was founded in 1969—just as the 1970 UNESCO convention was being prepared—as a result of an upsurge in looting and black-market trading associated with the postwar rise in prosperity of the West and the increasing sophistication of the art market. The official title of this new unit was the "Comando Carabinieri Ministero Pubblica Istruzione—Nucleo Tutela Patrimonio Artistica" (Ministry of Education Carabinieri Division—Unit for the Defense of Cultural Heritage), or TPA for short. Italy at that point became the first country to have a police department specifically assigned to combat art and archaeological crimes. In 1975, the TPA became part of the new Ministry of Fine Arts and the Environment and moved into the fine building it still occupies, designed by Filippo Raguzzini (1680–1771). A computerized database was developed as early as 1980. Among the TPA's high-profile recoveries have been Piero della Francesca's *Flagellation*, stolen from Urbino in 1975 and recovered in Switzerland a year later; Raphael's *Esterhazy Madonna*, stolen in Budapest in 1983 and recovered in Greece two months later; in addition to the recovery of works by Dürer, Tintoretto, and Giorgione. The TPA has helped train the art squads of other nationalities, including Palestinians and Hungarians; following the second Gulf war, in 2003, the Italians were asked to help organize the security at Iraq's many archaeological sites. Since it was created, the TPA (today the TPC) has recovered more than 180,000 works of art, nearly 8,000 of them abroad, and more than 350,000 antiquities. It has exposed 76,000 forgeries and brought charges against nearly 12,000 people.

In the 1980s, dealers in the market countries introduced codes of ethics, and museums revised their acquisitions policies but, very often, it has to be said, these moves were not much more than window dressing. In the 1990s, UNESCO sought to tighten up the 1970 convention, in particular with regard to the level of "due diligence" that dealers, collectors, and museums must use when acquiring cultural property without a fully documented history. This resulted in the so-called UNIDROIT convention, which was adopted by member countries in 1995 and came into force in July 1998. This convention says, in effect, that dealers, collectors, and museums must take active steps, or "due diligence," to satisfy themselves that cultural property without an adequate documented history has not been illegally excavated or smuggled. In other words, the onus is on the "good faith" purchaser to prove his or her good faith. In the United Kingdom, a new law was introduced in 2004 that makes it a criminal offense to knowingly trade in illicitly excavated archaeological objects.

Thus, there was a crucial change in attitude in the 1990s, the fruit of what had gone before. And this formed part of the "deep background" to both the Carabinieri's investigations of the illicit antiquities trade in Italy and our own journalistic investigations. The Italian Art Squad recognized that, eventually, it would have to take on the source of the *demand* for antiquities—the auction houses, and the dealers, museums, and collectors in the market countries—which is what made the discovery of the organigram so important. And Hodges realized that, having been sent to jail and humiliated by Sotheby's intransigence, he was in a position to seriously embarrass Sotheby's *and* do irreparable harm to the illicit antiquities network. As administrator in the relevant department, he had been vividly aware of the background legal, law enforcement, and archaeological issues swirling around the lucrative business of unprovenanced antiquities and the routine need at Sotheby's for subterfuge and deception. Faced with his particular, personal predicament, he was in a unique position to do something about it.

3

CONNOISSEURS AND CRIMINALS—THE
PASSION FOR GREEK VASES

Sculpture has always been popular and has been created afresh throughout history. Its appeal and beauty are obvious. Vases are different. Like sculpture, ceramics have been produced throughout history and in many different locations. But Greek vases stand out, partly for the great variety of their shapes, but mainly for the drama of the paintings that grace those shapes and are so *different* from anything else. These factors have combined to produce in art lovers, connoisseurs, and collectors a greater level of *passion* for Greek vases than for any other kind.

Given the sheer numbers of vases that have been excavated, there can be little doubt about their popularity in antiquity. An Athenian fifth-century BC poet, listing the most noteworthy products of different peoples, praised Athens for its invention of the potter's wheel and "the child of clay and the oven, noblest pottery." Plato wrote that a fine clay vase can be "very beautiful" though "not when set beside maidens." Pliny observed that in his day (he died in AD 79, observing the eruption of Vesuvius), "the greater part of mankind uses earthenware vases." Some Roman graves have been found containing Greek and Etruscan vases, but not many.

In more modern times, however, the passion for collecting these extraordinary relics of the past did not really emerge until the middle of the eighteenth century. There *were* vases in Renaissance collections (for example, the Medici in Florence had a vase collection, according to Giorgio Vasari, who wrote biographies of many artists), and ancient vases are mentioned in five collections in a Roman guidebook of the time. But their eighteenth-century popularity followed the discovery—in the late 1730s and then throughout the 1740s—of the buried remains of Pompeii and Herculaneum, which had been overwhelmed in AD 79 when the volcano Vesuvius erupted, spreading ash over a wide range and completely obliterating whole cities across a large area. The excavation of entire towns—whose inhabitants had been so surprised at the suddenness of the eruptions that they had been trapped going about their everyday activities, with their bodies as it were "frozen" for all time—captured the imagination of Europeans and others and was one of the factors that made archaeology popular. It was a vivid episode with which everyone could identify. Whole rooms, whole houses, entire temples and tombs, rows of shops and villas, even complete theaters, were recovered over the decades, together with fabulous frescoes, important sculptures, hoards of silver, armor, and other objects, some of them luxurious, some of them common-or-garden variety, all of them fascinating for the vivid light they threw on the past.

The Dominican friar Antonio da Viterbo wrote of "Truscomania," but it was the German art historian Johann Joachim Winckelman who paid several visits to Pompeii and Herculaneum in the 1760s and helped establish what became known as the Greek revival in a book that took eighteenth-century Europe by storm, *The History of the Art of Antiquity*. In the text he said that the allure of Greek art, its defining characteristic, was its "noble simplicity and calm grandeur," a phrase that became famous, and is indeed still famous. Generations of Germans and others, such people as Herder, Goethe, and Byron, became obsessed with ancient Greek culture. During Goethe's Italian journey in 1787, he observed, "One now pays a lot of money for Etruscan vases, and certainly one finds beautiful and exquisite pieces among them. Every traveller wants one." There was an early collection of vases in the Vatican. Initially, they were regarded as Etruscan and played a role in establishing the view that a large and sovereign Etruria was the basis of Western civilization. Winckelman, however, argued for their predominantly Greek origin. Laws to control their export were introduced as early as 1624 and again in 1755.

The Etruscans were in fact a rather mysterious people, but they were important because they composed the earliest urban civilization in the north Mediterranean, flourishing sometime between the ninth and first centuries BC, being most dominant in the sixth to third centuries. Much of what we know about them comes from the early writings of the ancient

Greeks and Romans. According to the Greek historian Herodotus, for example, they originally occupied the land of Lydia—what is now western Turkey—but were compelled to disperse after a great famine, when half the nation moved on and half remained behind. Their leader at the time was Tyrrhenos, from whom they adopted the name Tyrrhenians (and hence the Tyrrhenian Sea, along the western coast of Italy). Another theory is that they left Turkey after the fall of Troy, but the most recent archaeology suggests that the Etruscans were actually descendants of the Villanovans, people who thrived in central Italy in the ninth and eighth centuries BC and had an active artistic tradition, especially in bronze jewelry and glass-paste beads. Etruscan cities began to arise in the seventh century BC where Villanovan villages had once been. During the 700s BC, the Etruscans developed into a series of autonomous city-states: Arretium (Arezzo), Caisra (Caere, or modern Cerveteri), Veii, Tarchna (Tarquinii, or modern Tarquinia), and Velch (Volci, or modern Vulci).

The first Etruscan pieces to be discovered were two bronzes, found as long ago as 1553 and 1556, that is, during the Renaissance. Etruscan excavations proper began in the late eighteenth century, and in the nineteenth century, major archaeological discoveries were made at several sites, including Tarquinia, Ceveteri, and Vulci, all cultures that feature in the discoveries made in the Medici warehouse at Geneva.

To date, some 6,000 grave sites have been examined by professional, authorized archaeologists. The Italian archaeologists who examined the objects in Medici's Geneva warehouse calculate that "thousands" of tombs must have been desecrated to provide his "inventory," suggesting that illicit digs have ruined as many tombs as have been excavated legally and scientifically. In other words, as much has been lost to looters as has been found by reputable archaeologists.

No Etruscan literary works or historical accounts have been found, but there are about 9,000 inscriptions in Etruscan writing carved mainly on tombs. The first to be found were the bilingual Phoenician-Etruscan Pyrgi Tablets, found at the port of Caere in 1964. They showed that the Etruscan writing system is unique in that its letters come from the Greek alphabet, yet its grammatical structure is unlike any other European language. What can be discerned from the records is that religion was at the heart of Etruscan culture. The Romans themselves depended on some Etruscan books of divination. It appears that the Etruscans followed three sacred books for predicting the will of the gods: One book was devoted to reading the entrails of animals, another interpreted the meaning of lightning, and a third dealt with the flight patterns of birds. The Etruscan myths were heavily influenced by the Greeks, mainly in the fact that their gods possessed human attributes and dispositions. In Etruscan religion, on the other hand, the realms occupied by humans and by the gods were very specific, and their ritual followed very exact procedures to avoid the ill will of the gods. The Etruscan religion was based on more or less complete submission to their deities—one had to watch out for signs as to how to behave. A number of divinities were borrowed from Hellenic culture, including Aplu (Apollo), Artumes (Artemis), Maris (Mars), and Hercle (Hercules). Unlike many ancient civilizations, there does not appear to have been a great deal of difference in Etruria between the status of men and women.

The Etruscans were farmers, but they had a militaristic side and fortified their cities. They were also great seafarers and had active trading links to Phoenicians and to Carthage, long before Rome did; and they were active miners of iron, copper, tin, lead, and silver—and these sources of wealth contributed to the success of their civilization between the eighth and sixth centuries BC. Their decline began in the fifth century, then accelerated in the fourth. The main weakness was the inability of Etruscan city-states to unite against Roman aggression, and in the third century they were taken over by Rome. Their language, practices, and culture were suppressed, and they disappeared as a civilization.

The Etruscans were very advanced in science, technology, and art. Much of what we consider as typically Roman technology was in fact Etruscan: such things as stone arches, paved streets, aqueducts, and sewers. They had their own strong tradition of painting and sculpture, and they are as much the founders of Western culture as the Greeks and Romans. They had what has been described as an "ephemeral" attitude toward life on earth, which led them to build their homes of wood or clay, whereas their tombs were built to last forever. This attitude comes home most clearly at Cerveteri, where the cemetery is also a real town with streets and squares, with massive tumuli and rectangular tombs cut into the rock. This city, in fact, shows in a funerary context the same town planning and architectural schemes used in a living ancient city—if it were not for Cerveteri, we wouldn't know what ancient architecture was like. The *tombe a camera* (room tombs) were for entire families and were used for generations. These tombs were furnished lavishly, with stucco and terra-cotta sculptures, bronze models of sheep's livers (for divination), frescoes, vases, reliefs, arms such as spears and swords, household utensils, and, because tomb contents reflected a family's wealth or social status, gold jewelry.

Cerveteri is massive, but there is an entire city, Tarquinia (further north still, and more inland near Lake Bracciano), that is much more fanciful. A thriving center of business and trade, it also housed 6,000 tombs reached by elaborate underground staircases. Two hundred of the 6,000 are particularly famous for being painted, the earliest of which dates from the seventh century BC. Officially, they are opened in rotation, so that the delicate wall paintings that adorn them will be better preserved. Without Tarquinia and its wall paintings, we wouldn't know what ancient Etruscan daily life was like.

Vulci is about twenty miles away, near Canino. This has more tombs but is better known for its ancient castle and its bridge, one of the first examples of the arch. Active as early as the eighth century BC, Vulci was famous in antiquity for its production of handicrafts and for its agriculture. Strengthened by the presence of Greek labor, Vulci became equally famous for its ceramics, sculpture, and objects in bronze, and for the quality of its workmanship, which reached markets throughout the Mediterranean. At least four necropolises were built at Vulci, where there was a practice of placing statues of imaginary animals to guard the tombs. Immensely rich burial treasures have been found in these tombs, in particular a large number of ceramics of Greek production and bronze objects of local production. Other tombs had paintings showing the Greek myths intermingled with Etruscan myths.

There are several reasons Greek vases are as esteemed as they are. In the first place, the making of ceramics—objects made of clay by firing in an oven—is one of the defining practices of civilization. In the Middle East, the first pots were produced around 6700 BC. They were simple at first, and undecorated, but they enabled dry goods like grain and other seeds to be stored away from rats or birds; they allowed liquids to be stored with a minimum of evaporation, encouraging the development of beer and wine; and they made the transport of goods easier, encouraging trade. As the centuries passed, ceramics grew ever more elaborate, in shape, function, and decoration. And it was in Greece in classical times that this area of human activity culminated.

Our word "ceramic" comes from the Greek *keramikos*, meaning clay. The area of Athens where the *ceramies*, or community of potters, lived was known as Ceramicus, occupying an area bordering the Agora, along the banks of the Eridanos River. The fine clay of Ceramicus, combined with the brilliant technique of many Greek potters, resulted in the creation of multifarious shapes for vases, according to their function. Scholars and collectors who share a passion for Greek vases now recognize about a hundred different shapes for them, each of which has its own name. An *amphora*, for instance, is a two-handled vase used for storage and transport. The word *krater*, meaning "mixing bowl," describes a large vase. An *oinochoe* is a small pitcher used for dipping into the krater and pouring the (watered) wine into a drinking cup, or *kylix*. The kylix is sometimes called a "symposium-vase" because it is often shown in the paintings on vases, being widely used in the evening dinner parties in classical Athens, where serious conversations were the main attraction. Other common names for Greek vases are *hydria*, which are three-handled vases that had a variety of uses: for drawing water, as ballot boxes in votes for the Assembly, and to hold the ashes of the dead. The word *psykter* means "cooler," and this vase, filled with water and wine mixed, would be placed in a krater that had been filled with cool water, thus cooling the wine in turn. A *lekythos* is a flask that was used for toilet oils, perfumes, or condiments. It was also used in a funerary context, to pour libations over the dead. An *aryballos*, a small circular flask with a narrow neck, was used to hold and pour oil. It is often shown in Attic vase painting as suspended from the wrist of an athlete. An *alabastron* is a small, ovoid jar for perfumes, no more than four to six inches high. Although about a hundred types of vase are known, in practice only about twenty were in constant use.

The third—and crowning—aspect of Greek vases is their decoration. Many archaeologists and art historians believe that after the very beautiful but very mysterious cave paintings produced by early man, mainly in Europe about 30,000 years ago, Greek vase paintings are the highest achievement of human art until at least the great cathedrals of the High Middle Ages more than a millennium later. It is one of the reasons the ancient Greeks are held in such esteem. As Sir Peter Hall puts it in his book *Cities in Civilisation* (1998), in a chapter on ancient Athens that he calls "The Fountainhead":

> The crucial point about Athens is that it was first. And first in no small sense: first in so many of the things that have mattered, ever since, to western civilisation and its meaning. Athens in the fifth century BC gave us democracy, in a form as pure as we are likely to see. . . . It gave us philosophy, including political philosophy, in a form so rounded, so complete, that hardly anyone added anything of moment to it for well over a millennium. It gave us the world's first systematic written history. It systematized medical and scientific knowledge, and for the first time began to base them on generalisations from empirical observation. It gave us the first lyric poetry and then comedy and tragedy, all again at so completely an extraordinary pitch of sophistication and maturity, such that they might have been germinating under the Greek sun for hundreds of years. It left us the first naturalistic art; for the first time, human beings caught and registered for ever the breath of a wind, the quality of a smile.

This is what evokes a passion for Greek vases in so many people.

Painted Greek vases are known from the second millennium BC until almost the end of the first century BC. In the beginning of the period there were many local styles, but by the middle of the sixth century the vases of Attica, in particular its capital Athens, exceeded in quantity and quality those of its nearest rival, Corinth. This Attic supremacy was never surpassed and lasted until the disastrous Peloponnesian War ended in 404 BC, which robbed Athens of its profitable markets. After this, Attic vase painting went into decline, though it survived in other parts of the Greek world, especially Sicily and southern Italy.

At first, the main motifs were taken from sea life. These works were followed by a period when orderly patterns were drawn on the surface of the vases with a compass or ruler (the "geometric" style). Human figures appear in the eighth century BC, together with ideas from the East—floral ornaments, exotic beasts, and monsters. At this time, however, in Corinth, a decisive breakthrough was made, in the establishment of the so-called black-figure technique, often enhanced with incised lines in red and white. In the second half of the seventh century, this style spread to Athens, where from the very beginning the skill demanded by the engraving encouraged artists to develop their own styles. It is from this period on that the personal variation of the artists marks their creativity and individuality and an emphasis on human figures becomes the overriding principle that governs vase painting in its highest stage.

Many of the scenes on these vases come from Greek mythology, though they are not "book illustrations" in the modern sense of that term—the artist was left free to create as he wished, and in this way the first of the really great painters emerged. Nearly 900 vase painters are recognized through connoisseurship, accounting for about half the surviving vases, but only forty have left us their real names, with the rest being identified by a particular masterpiece. Among the great masters of Attic black-figure vases were Sophilos, Kleitias, Nearchos, Lydos, Exekias, and the Amasis Painter.

It is at this point that the scenes on Greek vases begin to achieve the special quality of personal experience, which makes them so easy for us, 2,500 years later, to relate to. The painting on Greek vases is naturalistic. The individuals are dressed as ancient Greeks, they do the things that ancient Greeks did, but we recognize ourselves in them: They gossip at the well, their dogs are a nuisance, they smack recalcitrant children, old men lust after young women, young women smile shyly as young athletes pass by. These are real people, with their character showing in their expressions—slyness, embarrassment, sarcasm, disgust. We feel for the somber mourners at a funeral. The vases are often incomparably beautiful, but they are also documents, showing ancient life in all its glory but without pulling any punches. This is why these vases are important, and why it is important that we know where they were when they were found.

Toward the end of the sixth century, the limitations of the black-figure technique, with its unrealistic color scheme, began to circumscribe artists and the new technique of red-figure vases emerged: the figures were left the color of the clay (and so turned red when the vase was fired), and detail was indicated by fine lines drawn in black glaze or in lines of diluted glaze, which fired as dark brown or translucent yellow. The entire background was a luminous black. This gave the figures much the same appearance as if lit by modern theatrical lighting, making them more dramatic and far more realistic.

And it was now that the truly fine artists began to produce the really great masterpieces, with new subjects matching closely the contours of the vases, which themselves were developing new shapes as well, to match the sophisticated life that then obtained in Periclean Athens—its golden age under its great general and leader, Pericles (c. 495–429). The greatest generation of vase painters was known as the Pioneers (because they experimented with new techniques), and the three greatest names among them were Euphronios, Euthymides, and Phintias. Euphronios (fl. c. 520–c. 500 BC) signed eight Attic vases as painter and, later in his life, signed twelve cups as potter, decorated by other artists. He was particularly interested in showing the human body and experimented with foreshortening to give his compositions greater depth. He also produced a pillar monument on the Athenian Acropolis. Euthymides (fl. c. 515–c. 500 BC) signed eight Athenian vases, six as painter, the other two as potter. There is an inscription on an amphora by him in Munich that reads: "Euphronios never did anything this good," generally interpreted as a playful challenge to the younger artist rather than a taunt. But it shows that artists were aware of each other's work. Phintias (fl. 520–500 BC) signed six vases as painter and three as potter. The spelling of his names varies, as he was not especially literate.

This period has been described as a *primavera* (a springtime) that painting would not see again until the Italian Renaissance. In other words, Euphronios, Euthymides, and Phintias are rightly to be regarded as the equivalent of Raphael, Michelangelo, and Leonardo da Vinci: They established the definition of excellence.

The next phase of Attic red-figure painters opened with the Berlin Painter and the Kleophrades Painter. The Berlin Painter is named after a large amphora in the Anitkensammlung (the Museum for Classical Antiquities) in Berlin. His figures so carefully match the shape of his vases that many scholars believe he must have been the potter as well as the painter. Moreover, these figures have that clean simplicity and grace that we now call "classical." The Kleophrades Painter (fl. c. 505–c. 475 BC) is named after the potter Kleophrades, son of (the black-figure painter) Amasis, whose signature appears on a large red-figure cup now in the Bibliothèque Nationale in Paris. In this period, scenes are lightened in style, with playful borders, and there are fewer figures. It was also about now that cup painters begin to be distinguished from pot painters. Cup, or kylix, painting was perhaps the most intimate of all forms, given the vessel's use in symposia. The great cup painters were Onesimos, Douris (who produced 280 vases, signing forty), and the Brygos Painter.

Toward the end of the fifth century BC, vase painting underwent yet another change, in that there arose a predilection for new compositions and certain mythological subjects. Scholars now think this was as a response to a great efflorescence of wall painting in Athens, which has been lost. This is thus an added reason for the importance of vase painting of this late period. A favorite subject was the battle between the Athenians and the Amazons, a mythical precursor of the more recent victory of the Athenians over the Persians. In this new stylistic period, the human body is shown in very varied, but very loose poses; there is much more foreshortening and drapery folds lose their rigidity, to both conceal and yet reveal the body beneath. (Much the same was happening in sculpture.)

Following the defeat of Athens in the Peloponnesian War in 404 BC, Athens lost its market in the West. This marks the point when local vase painting began to flourish elsewhere. Apulian and Gnathian painting (Gnathia was a town in Apulia, in southern Italy) became briefly fashionable. By the end of the fourth century BC, however, red-figure vase production came to an end in all parts of the ancient world.

Pottery is the most important material for the study of antiquity because it was produced in great quantities over several centuries and survives in abundance.

Paintings on vases tell us more about the Greeks, what they looked like, what they did, and what they believed in, than any single literary text. Thus even a vase with poor drawing often times takes on a special significance because of a story told for the first time, or a detail illumi-

nated. . . . In this context the average does not take away from the best;
rather, like the broad base of a pyramid, it directs the gaze to its summit
and supports it.

This tribute to the "poorly drawn and average" vase was written by none
other than Dietrich von Bothmer.

Among the first connoisseurs to amass a major collection of vases was
Sir William Hamilton. A member of the Society of Antiquaries, he was appointed the British plenipotentiary at the court in Naples, where he
formed not one but two collections of Greek and Etruscan ceramics. The
first collection, which consisted of 730 objects, was sold to the British Museum in 1772 for £8,400. His second collection was even finer than the
first, consisting of vases recently excavated—and he sent it to England to
be sold. Part was lost at sea, but the remainder reached London and was
auctioned. This auction did much to influence taste in England, one man
who fell under the spell being Joshua Wedgwood. He developed a modern version of Greek and Italian vases (at his plant called "Etruria") that
became so fashionable that at times they sold for three times as much as
the real thing. Hamilton's main rival in Italy was the Frenchman Vivant
Denon, later to be instrumental in the creation of the Musée Napoleon,
now the Louvre. His collection of Greek and Etruscan vases comprised
520 pieces. A tourist guide published in 1775 listed forty-two collections
with vases around Europe, in eighteen cities.

The revival of interest in ancient Greece—stimulated by the excavations south of Naples and Winckelmann's writings—was one of the main
factors giving rise to the neo-classical movement in the arts that engulfed
Europe around the turn of the nineteenth century. Romantics, too, were
in thrall to the classical world, not just Byron but his fellow poet John
Keats, who famously wrote his "Ode on a Grecian Urn," containing the
lines:

O Attic shape! . . . Cold Pastoral!
When old age shall this generation waste,

Thou shalt remain, in midst of other woe
Than ours, a friend to man, to whom thou say'st,
"Beauty is truth, truth beauty,—that is all
Ye know on earth, and all ye need to know."

Thomas Hope, a Dutch connoisseur who settled in London in the late eighteenth century, had three rooms of his house in Duchess Street, Portland Place, filled with vases.

This interest continued to grow in the nineteenth century, fueled by excavations further north than Pompeii and Herculaneum. George Dennis's book *Cities and Cemeteries of Etruria*, first published in 1848, celebrated the "sublime" and "perfect" quality of the vases that the excavations had uncovered, and collections in other European capitals, after Paris and London, began to make their appearance—in Berlin, Basel, Copenhagen, St. Petersburg, Vienna. In Munich, the collection of Ludwig I was exhibited at the Pinakothek as a "Prologue to the Renaissance." The finds at Vulci, many of which were discovered on the land of Lucien Bonaparte, were exhibited with the inscription "The Raphaels of Antiquity." The discoveries initiated what has been called "the golden age of vase collecting." The collection of Marchese Gianpietro Campana was formed at this time and, at 3,791 pieces, was probably the largest ever assembled. The United States followed toward the end of the century. E. P. Warren was responsible for the vase collection in the Boston Museum of Fine Arts. He settled in Rome, one of several vase scholars resident at the end of the nineteenth century, where the Piazza Montanova became an antiquities market every Sunday. With the establishment of chairs of classical archaeology in universities across Europe and North America in the nineteenth century, many institutions acquired study collections. In 1898, Adolf Loos, the modernist designer in Vienna, wrote that "Greek vases are as beautiful as a machine, as beautiful as a bicycle."

In the early twentieth century, connoisseurship took another step forward when the British academic J. D. Beazley introduced so-called Morellian techniques into the appreciation of Greek vases. Beazley, an Oxford scholar, was "much involved" with the poet James Elroy Flecker. He became Lincoln Professor of Classical Archaeology and an honorary fellow of the Met in New York. Giovanni Morelli was an Italian art historian of the late nineteenth century (he was a big influence on Bernard Berenson) who adapted Freudian techniques to connoisseurship. Originally involved in trying to understand early Renaissance painting, where many pictures are unsigned, he formed the view that painters betray their identity in what we might call the "unconscious" parts of their pictures—those areas such as the ears, eyebrows, or ankles, where they are perhaps not paying full attention or which do not form part of the main message of the work. These features, Morelli said, are invariably highly similar from one painting to another by the same artist. Beazley adapted this method to identifying Greek vases, and it enabled him to group them together, either by attributing them to painters who had signed a few vases or by assigning such titles as the Berlin Painter or the Villa Giulia Painter where there was no signature. In these cases the painter was named after his masterpiece. Over the years, these painters could be credited with an oeuvre, even a career, in which his painting style developed, matured, and (perhaps) declined. In providing names and identities in this way, Beazley gave new life to the market in vases. His accomplishment was a perfect scenario for collectors and dealers, helping transform an anonymous mass of objects into the archaeological equivalent of, say, the market in old masters. Other scholars subsequently did the same for vase painters in other areas of the classical world. This approach was so successful that George Dennis's book *Cities and Cemeteries of Etruria* was republished in 1985.

Today, Greek and Etrurian vases still evoke great passion and are actively traded. Since World War II, seventy-one private collections have been sold at auction. In the United States, apart from Boston, the great vase collections are at the Metropolitan in New York (formed between 1906 and 1928 and added to in 1941 and 1956), the Duke University Classical Collection at Durham, North Carolina, and the San Antonio Museum (formed in the 1990s). Several major collections costing several million dollars each have been assembled since World War II. Among archaeologists the passions are no less strong, though they have to do with different matters—for example, with whether the vases in these collections have been illicitly excavated, and whether these vases were quite as valuable in ancient times as some people say. Either way, these ancient objects still have the power to evoke passionate emotions.

After Etruria and Greece, Rome. The Roman reverence for the Greek way of life, its thought and artistic achievements, was one of the dominant ideas throughout the long life of the Roman Empire. When we speak now of "the classics," as often as not we mean Greek and Roman art and literature. But it was the Romans who invented the very notion of the classics, the idea that the best that has been thought, written, painted, and designed in the past is worth preserving and profiting from.

Also, the Romans had a notion of *utilitas*—by which they meant utility, unsentimentality, and pride in Roman achievements—and this had a major effect on innovation in the visual arts. Portraits had become more realistic in Greece, but they were still idealized, to an extent. Not so in Rome. The emperor might want his likeness to echo the dignity of his office, but for other families the more realistic, the better. There was a tradition in Rome, among patrician families at least, of keeping wax masks of one's ancestors, to be worn by living members of the family at funerals. Out of this custom there developed the Roman tradition of bronze and stone busts that were, above all, realistic. This is why Roman sculpture is so vivid, valuable, and sought after.

In architecture the invention of cement made all the difference. Toward the end of the third century BC, possibly via Africa, it was found that a mixture of water, lime, and a gritty material like sand would set into a durable substance that could be used either to bond masonry or as a building material in its own right, and up to a point, could be shaped in a mold. This had two immediate consequences. First, it meant that major public buildings, such as baths or theaters, could be constructed in the center of the city. Large boulders did not need to be brought from far away. Instead, the sand and bricks could be brought in smaller, much more manageable loads, and far more complex infrastructures could be erected to accommodate larger numbers of people. Second, because bricks and concrete, when it was wet, could be shaped, they didn't need to be carved, as stone did. Therefore, building could be done by less-skilled workmen, and even slaves could do the job. It was, in consequence, much cheaper. All this meant that monumental architecture could be practiced on a much larger scale than before, which is one reason Rome is the city of so many classical ruins today, beautiful brickwork bonded by mortar.

There was in Rome immense respect for Greek culture. From the first century BC on, Greek sculpture and copies of Greek sculpture were found in many upper-class homes in Rome. Many of these copies were very good, and today much of Greek sculpture is known only, or mainly, through Roman copies that are, of course, now very valuable in their own right. At first, Roman generals plundered what they could: In 264 BC, a Roman general took 2,000 statues from vanquished Volsinii. Greek artists quickly adjusted, and a thriving art market grew up in Athens (the so-called neo-Attic workshops), catering to the taste of Roman tourists. Later still, Greek artists set up shop along the Tiber River. Rome itself, in a way, was an amalgam of Greek ideas and Latin ambition, but thanks in part to concrete, there is much more left of it than Athens.

The antiquities Giacomo Medici was trading in included some of the finest objects ever produced by humankind—important historically, aesthetically, and intellectually. Many aspects of these important epochs of our past are still clouded in mystery. Virtually half of the history of Greek, Etruscan, and Roman culture in Italy has been stolen from us. The intellectual and artistic damage done by the looters has been immense. And Giacomo Medici played a bigger part in that destruction than anyone else.

4

CORRIDOR 17

IT TOOK A YEAR TO LINK the two investigations at the Geneva Freeport. The prosecutor, Dr. Ferri, realized that in London there was vital evidence, in his words *proof*, that Medici was a—and perhaps *the*—central figure in the traffic of illicit antiquities out of Italy to the world's markets. He realized that if the internal Sotheby's documents, leaked to us by Hodges, could be matched with the photographs and other documentation in Corridor 17 in the Geneva Freeport, he could demonstrate beyond all doubt that much of the trade in the antiquities department of one of the world's leading auction houses was made up of objects looted from Italian soil. For Conforti, too, the Sotheby's link was all-important. He had hoped that the Melfi theft might unravel the link that led out of Italy into Europe and beyond: The documents Hodges had taken offered exactly that opportunity.

By March 1997, thanks to parallel investigations we carried out into smuggled antiquities from India and old master paintings from Italy (broadcast on television and published as a book), Sotheby's closed down three departments in London—Antiquities, Asian Antiquities, and Asian Art—and several specialists were "let go." The company also stopped holding antiquities sales in London.

Once Hodges's documents had been used to conclude the London investigations, the originals could be handed over to Conforti and Dr. Ferri. The fact that Sotheby's had stopped selling antiquities in London was perhaps the most powerful acknowledgment of all that this particular trade was suspect and unwholesome.

Certainly, the Italians found a changed attitude in Switzerland, which had been shown up as a staging post in the illicit trade from both Italy and India. In the spring of 1997, after months of prevaricating, and after the

Sotheby's documentation had been passed to Ferri, documentation that proved—in his words—that Medici operated out of Geneva, the Swiss began to talk about a second visit to the sealed warehouses, to Corridor 17.

This second visit eventually took place in July and was very different from the first encounter. The party was led by a Geneva judge, Dr. Bertani, and her assistant. Also present were two of Conforti's men, two Swiss police, and five Italian consultants for the prosecution, including three archaeologists, their assistant, and a document expert. There were two archaeological consultants for the Italian Ministry of Culture, who were civil plaintiffs in the case; a representative of the Freeport; and this time, Giacomo Medici himself, together with his lawyer, Cleto Cucci, an advocate from Rimini who had previously defended many tombaroli, and who doubtless for this reason appeared on Pasquale Camera's organigram. He had an assistant and two archaeological consultants chosen by the defense. That made nineteen people in all.

The meeting was tense, particularly among the archaeologists. In the intervening months, although it may have seemed nothing much was happening on the surface, in fact the photographs of the Geneva warehouse and its contents, taken by the Swiss police photographer, had been passed to Rome. There they had been examined, not just by Ferri and by Conforti's men, but by Daniela Rizzo, the archaeologist at the Villa Giulia Museum, and by the director of the museum, Anna Maria Moretti, who was also the head of the Superintendency (the archaeological administration) for Southern Etruria. Aware of the huge scale of Medici's activities, as they examined the photographs, they also appreciated the superior quality of many of the pieces under seizure. Moretti and Rizzo realized that the archaeological examination of the objects in the Freeport, when it came, had to be carried out by the best authorities available, the very best scholars that Italy could provide. There must be no room for doubt about the status of the objects Medici had. They chose three people whom Daniela Rizzo would later call *"mostri sacri,"* three sacred monsters, extremely distinguished scholars. They were all famous in their profession, all in their fifties or sixties, and therefore well established, all world authorities on the type of object that had been found in the Freeport, and all of such eminence that their conclusions regarding the material could not be questioned.

The three scholars chosen were Professors Gilda Bartoloni and Giovanni Colonna, both of La Sapienza, Rome's oldest university, founded in the sixteenth century, and both professors of ancient italic antiquities and Etruscology, and thirdly, Professor Fausto Zevi, also from La Sapienza and the foremost specialist in Roman archaeology and Magna Graecia. Of these, Professor Zevi was probably the best known and Professor Bartoloni probably the most experienced, in a forensic sense, because she had been involved before in giving evidence at trials of tombaroli.

That July day, as they all walked through the security checkpoint to enter the Freeport and crossed the small piazza inside, with its black imitation-Botero sculpture, and then rode the elevator to the fourth floor, the tension among the archaeologists was palpable. Appearing for Medici were two specialists, one Swiss, the other Italian. The Swiss archaeologist, Fiorella Angeli-Cottier, was less well known to the Italian scholars. But Medici's other expert, Teresa Amorelli Falconi, *was* known to Bartoloni, Colonna, and Zevi—she had been a professor at Palermo University in Sicily and before that a professor at Rome University—and this was the source of the tension. Amorelli Falconi frequently appeared as an expert for the defense in antiquities-looting cases. On some occasions she gave answers as to the provenance of archaeological objects that were quite at variance with the views of other scholars. Zevi refused to shake hands with Amorelli Falconi, and though Bartoloni did, she found it difficult. Having seen the photographs of the material Medici had in the Freeport—its quality, its extent, and the clear evidence of recent excavation—Bartoloni, Colonna, and Zevi wondered how a reputable archaeologist could even *appear* for the other side. "It was embarrassing," said Bartoloni. "We kept our eyes averted."

In Corridor 17, the Swiss judge took the wax seal off the lock and opened the door. Then he stood aside to allow the others to enter, one by one. His own assistant went first, followed by the Swiss police, the Carabinieri, the archaeologists, and the document expert. Eventually, they were all gathered in Medici's showroom.

It was an important moment, psychologically speaking, for Bartoloni and the other experts. Yes, they had seen the photographs taken by the Swiss police. Their quality was excellent and gave the Italian experts a good idea of what to expect. But seeing the objects in the flesh, so to speak, was different, a much more emotional experience for the three distinguished "sacred monsters."

The Swiss judge had told Medici that he could be present at the examination, provided that he did not interfere. However, as the experts began to move around inside the warehouse and discuss the objects among themselves, Medici found it hard to keep quiet. Bartoloni gasped when she saw the boxes from a Cerveteri fruit cooperative filled with antiquities wrapped in Italian newspapers. There were other boxes where fragments had been sorted by type and color. "It was like a supermarket in there," said Bartoloni. "And heartbreaking."

Medici wouldn't keep quiet. At one point, Bartoloni and her colleagues were discussing where certain objects appeared to have come from, waiting for Amorelli Falconi to agree or disagree. Whereupon Medici turned on the judge, "How can my experts know the provenance of something, if I don't tell them?" He perhaps didn't realize at first what exactly he was saying.

The judge insisted that Medici be silent, at which point the dealer went berserk, shouting words to the effect that "You can't forbid a citizen to reveal the origin of his objects." He claimed that all his objects in the Freeport had been bought legitimately. This was his idea of provenance. The judge, however, would not be intimidated by Medici and replied coolly, "You are not a citizen of Switzerland." In other words, Medici did not enjoy all the rights he thought he did.

The mood remained tense throughout the morning and during the lunch break, Medici decided not to return in the afternoon. From then on, Bartoloni and the others were left to themselves, able to inspect the objects in the Freeport without his constant interference.

Bartoloni says she touched every single object in Corridor 17. On their initial visit to Geneva, they stayed for three or four days, but they returned several times over the next months. "We worked like slaves and talked very little," she remembers. It remained an emotional experience for them all. At times, Bartolini says she felt ill, and she was constantly amazed at the quality of the antiquities Medici had. "My indignation grew . . . some pieces were *so* important, and *so* beautiful." She even came across some pieces identical to those she had excavated herself, at Cerveteri in the 1980s. "Where did Medici get these things? We didn't know about them until the dig I worked on. There was no way they could have left the ground before then."

She went on. "I grew up aware of the plague of tombaroli, but even I had never imagined the clandestine trade dealt in such quantity—and *quality*. From what I could see, Crustumerium was just then being raped, as Cerveteri was raped in the 1970s." On that first visit, she also noticed a number of fakes, or pastiches. Many genuine objects had fake inscriptions—because they added to the value.

But their scientific curiosity grew, too. Being so close to the material, seeing its quality, absorbing the sheer scale of the trade, seeing the dirt still attached to so many objects, that first visit to Corridor 17 was overwhelming for Bartoloni, Colonna, and Zevi. Never before had leading archaeologists been in the presence of so many looted antiquities—there was, as Conforti told us, no precedent at all for what was taking place that day in the Geneva Freeport. The Swiss realized it as well as the Italians.

The Italians also grasped that the Swiss had changed, because they now began to talk about future visits, making it clear that the experts, who would need to examine the objects in great detail, could come and go virtually as they pleased, that Corridor 17 would remain sealed to Medici but not to them.

The examination of the antiquities in Corridor 17, by professional archaeologists, would form a major element in the case against Medici, but it would also be much more. This was the first time *ever* that expert archaeologists had been anywhere near looted material in such quantity. As such, it became an exercise not just in law enforcement but in what was in effect a new branch of scholarship. It provided the opportunity for knowledgeable experts to examine illicit material in ways that had never been conceived before, and therefore to produce new insights into this aspect of human activity at a level and on a scale not previously contemplated. The investigations in Corridor 17 broke new ground in every conceivable way, and the results of the investigations carried out there will change the world of antiquities—and antiquities collecting and antiquities trading—for all time.

5

FORENSIC ARCHAEOLOGY

IN THE FREEPORT

IN ITALY, WITH ITS HUNDREDS of thousands of archaeological sites and with its history of widespread looting, a new specialty has grown up in tandem with Conforti's section of the Carabinieri dedicated to combating the illicit traffic. This is the specialty of forensic archaeology. Forensic archaeologists, in addition to their usual activities undertaking legitimate excavations in ancient cultures, also make it their business to keep up to date where possible on clandestine digs and the techniques of tomb robbers, on which areas are being heavily looted and which cultures are being forged, on which cultures and objects are popular with dealers and collectors, on what is passing through the salesrooms and what has been recovered. They work closely with the various prosecutors and art squads around Italy.

At the most basic level, they are called in when any seizure of looted antiquities is made, however small. It is their task to establish, in the first place, whether the objects that have been seized or recovered are genuine or fake. This is fundamental and clearly affects what charges will be brought.

The forensic archaeologists are far fewer than the specialist Carabinieri Art Squads, but where they do exist they are attached to the various archaeological superintendencies that excavate and preserve different areas of Italy—Etruria, Campania, Puglia, and so on. From the photographs that were taken in Medici's warehouse at the first raid, in September 1995, it was clear to the Italians that the material he had in Geneva consisted of many Etruscan objects and that therefore the Art Squad needed the help and advice of Daniela Rizzo, the forensic archaeologist at the Villa Giulia, Rome's great Etruscan museum, who was well known to the Carabinieri and to the public prosecutor, Paolo Ferri. Besides her other duties, Rizzo was head of the Ufficio Sequestri e Scavi Clandestini, the Office of Clandestine Excavations and Seized Objects, so she was familiar with tombaroli techniques and the damage they can do. Another graduate of La Sapienza, Rizzo—an attractive, lively brunette in her forties—had, in the past, helped Ferri and Conforti in their prosecutions. It was she who, in collaboration with Anna Maria Moretti, at the time the superintendent for southern Etruria, today superintendent for the Lazio region, had helped Ferri to choose the team of specialist archaeologists—Professors Bartoloni, Colonna, and Zevi—who, besides having the requisite academic qualifications, could make the time available to study the objects in Geneva and would if necessary make good witnesses in court when the time came.

On their first visit to Geneva, the Carabinieri had reserved rooms for the archaeologists at a hotel located between the city's main railway station and its red-light district. The middle-aged archaeologists found this unsuitable and relocated to a smaller establishment in the more appropriate old town of Geneva. Though they worked like slaves during the day and hardly talked, they spent their evenings at restaurants on the hill of the old town, where the rest of the party were regaled at every meal by learned discussions between Professors Bartoloni and Zevi who, it seemed, disagreed on everything.

The archaeologists visited the Freeport on six separate occasions, between July 1997 and April 1999, twenty-three days in all. They submitted their final report to Ferri on July 2, 1999, almost two years to the day since the Swiss had offered to make the material available. It ran to fifty-eight single-spaced typed pages.

Dr. Bartoloni and her two colleagues found that there were 3,800 objects in Medici's warehouse, either intact or in fragments. In addition to the actual objects found in Corridor 17, there was a mass of photographs—more than 4,000—that related to still more antiquities that had already passed through Medici's hands and had almost certainly been sold to museums and collectors across the world. Taking these photographs into account, the experts examined something like 7,000 objects that Medici had handled.

▼

This was the first time that reputable academic archaeologists had been able to examine the inventory of an antiquities dealer with so many unprovenanced objects. Academically, scientifically, legally, commercially—and even philosophically—it was a historic occasion, and Professor Bartoloni and her colleagues were anxious not to waste such a precious opportunity.

Their report was divided as follows. A preface was followed by a classification of "Antiquities Presumably Found in Italy." Next came a list of antiquities "Presumably Found in Countries other than Italy," and then a list of pastiches—that is, ancient objects that had been interfered with in some way so as to make them commercially more attractive. The most obvious examples of this were vases where the gaps between the fragments had been filled in by modern restorers or where inscriptions had been added to old vases by modern forgers. Next came a list of objects of "dubious antique production," that is, the experts could not be completely certain whether these objects were genuinely old or were instead modern fakes. This was followed by a much bigger group of antiquities that the archaeologists described as "modern-made imitations of antique objects"—in other words, out-and-out fakes. Next came a list of objects "not imitating antiques," a strange group that might take in an inexperienced collector but wouldn't deceive a professional dealer, curator, or academic archaeologist. The report concluded with a number of technical appendices providing scientific information on all 3,800 objects from the warehouse. It was a massive enterprise.

By far the largest group of antiquities was described as "Objects of Ancient Origin, from Prehistoric to High Middle Ages" and was itself divided into two: "(1a) Objects which can with certainty or very high probability be said to come from Italian territorial digs," and "(1b) Objects coming from digs presumably made in countries other than Italy." Category (1a) was clearly of the most immediate interest to the Italians, but Medici had some exceedingly interesting and significant non-Italian material in his possession.

But first, the list of objects in category (1a), the material from Italian digs. This category ran to forty-nine pages. No fewer than fifty-eight different types of antiquity were involved, from Iron Age ceramics and bronzes of the Villanovan culture (ninth and eighth centuries BC), to Etruscan, Lazio, and Campanian architectural terra-cottas of the sixth, fifth, and fourth centuries BC, to Attic black-figure and red-figure vases of every conceivable shape, to Apulian red-figure ceramics, Teano ceramics, votive terra-cottas of central Italy of the fourth and third centuries BC, Roman architectural elements, Roman wall paintings, Roman era silver, gold, gems, and ivories. Many other categories could be added, more technical but still very important, which mean a lot to archaeologists, museum curators, and experienced collectors—for example, Buccheri, geometric ceramics, owl skyphoi (a *skyphos* is a deep cup with two handles, usually standing on a low foot), reticulated lekythoi, and transport amphorae.

The sheer scale and variety of Medici's inventory was the first point that the experts' report stressed. They calculated that thousands of tombs must have been desecrated for so many objects—of such variety and quality—to have been sequestered in Geneva. Next came the geographical reach. Still sticking with the Italian antiquities, we are talking here of material from Genoa, Tyrrhenian Italy, central Italy, Vulci, Tarquinia, and Cerveteri, all in the heart of ancient Etruria; north of Rome, Lazio, Campania (the region of Naples), Calabria (the deep south of Italy), Sicily, Puglia, Sardinia, the central Adriatic region, and Taranto. Nowhere in Italy was immune to Medici's plunder.

The size and the reach of the looting are not negligible matters. Far from it, they are the very heart of Italy's attempts to draw attention to its problems in this field. But it was in regard to two other factors that the juxtaposition of Medici's holdings and the access provided to three experts could really break new ground. These were: to prove beyond all reasonable doubt (1) that this great swath of material really did come illegally from the ground of Italy, and (2) that the illicit trade, contrary to what commercial interests often say, is not inconsequential but does in fact involve very important objects. Medici's cache represented a unique historical opportunity that in scale may never be replicated.

The most vivid evidence, leaning against the walls of the warehouse, and in one case lying on the floor, was a number of frescoes, wall paintings in red, green, blue, and gray. Some of the paintings showed women, horses, vases of flowers, architectural features of one kind or another. To Zevi, it was obvious from the style of painting that these frescoes came from Pompeii or Herculaneum, or somewhere similar—but where exactly? It would take them a few weeks to find the answer.

No less vivid was the fact that in Medici's warehouse, 300 fragments were found, consisting among other things of architectural roof elements, decorated terra-cotta tiles, and small heads that fitted on the outside of buildings, all of which were discovered—still dirty with earth—roughly packed in Italian newspapers dating to between December 1993 and October 1994. Furthermore, they were kept together in a large wooden crate and in some red-and-gray plastic boxes, bearing the writing, "ORTO FR. CERVETERI," which stands for "Orto Frutticola Cerveteri," a well-known fruit and vegetable cooperative, from the town of Cerveteri, north of Rome, near the coast.

No less incriminating—when you think about it—was the fact that so many of the photographs in Medici's warehouse, showing archaeological objects, often with dirt on them, were taken using a Polaroid camera, in particular the popular SX-70 model (two Polaroid cameras were seized, plus a regular camera). Polaroid photography was not invented until 1948, nine years after the relevant Italian law restricting the export of antiquities came into force, and the SX-70 was not introduced until much later, in October 1972 in the United States and in Europe later still. By definition, therefore, Polaroid photographs of dirty, unprovenanced antiquities are themselves evidence of a kind that these objects left the ground illegally. Furthermore, the state of many antiquities as shown in the Polaroids is such that, as any reputable and experienced archaeologist could confirm, these objects were obviously *not* excavated scientifically or professionally. Objects excavated professionally (and legally) have a very different appearance; they are photographed in situ, showing their context, with a measuring tool to indicate size, and are properly dated.

The professional analysis that Professors Bartoloni, Colonna, and Zevi brought to Medici's objects was detailed and cumulatively devastating, remorselessly linking specific objects to specific localities inside Italy, artifacts found in Geneva twinned with those known either from legal excavations at a specific tomb or villa, or from seizures of illicit material in the recent past, as part of Carabinieri undercover "sting" operations.

Only with such a huge find were such telling comparisons possible. For example, among the objects seized in the Geneva Freeport was an Iron Age *fibula* of the ninth century BC. The fibula is aptly described as the "grandmother" of the safety pin, but its use was rather more dramatic in antiquity, being employed to hold together the drapes in clothing. It became a decorative object in its own right and often identified the social and economic status of the wearer. Part of this particular fibula was made from a twisted gold thread, which is very rare. The experts pointed out that this fibula was very similar to one legally found in Tarquinia in the necropolis of Poggio dell'Impiccato, which dates from the second half of the ninth century BC. Another fibula, decorated with a feline figure, was very similar to one found in the Tomb of the Warrior at Tarquinia. In hundreds of cases the experts were able to make specific matches (see the Dossier at the end of the book for a fuller list).

In another example, thirty-two miniature cups and twenty miniature *olle* (wine pitchers with fat handles) were "very similar" to a series of miniature vases (especially olle) found on an official dig at Bandinella, Canino, in 1992, after the discovery of an illegal dig.

In yet another example, five *kantharoi* (wide drinking vessels with high handles, like big ears) and three amphorae had what are known as "cusped handles." This is a highly unusual (and therefore valuable) design, in which the handles are embossed with small cones in a row. According to the experts, these "can be easily recognised as coming from Crustumerium," where cups and amphorae "became famously cusped." But more than that, they observe that Francesco di Gennaro, inspector of the Archaeological Superintendency for Rome, has reported widespread illegal digging in the Marcigliana or Monte del Bufalo area, where the necropolis of Crustumerium is located. In other words, the material in Medici's warehouse and the illegal digging reported by di Gennaro are an exact match. This plunder is heartbreaking in that the Crustumerium necropolis has proved very important in providing knowledge about Etruscan funereal customs and the development of architectural styles, and for the study of production techniques for vases. Yet its largest sepulchre complex, southeast of Monte del Bufalo, has suffered clandestine digging on such a scale that the experts calculate that

> half the overall number of burials have been plundered. . . . The overall number of the plundered sepulchral monuments . . . is now evaluated at not less than one thousand; there is carpet-destruction and plundering of the burials. . . . Archaeological material of unquestionable Crustumerium provenance has recently been seized (for example, in Monte Rotondo near Rome, photographs of objects for sale were circulated in Cerveteri and Ladispoli) but are also exhibited for sale on the American antiquities market where a large quantity of Crustumerium objects is on show in antiquarians' shops in Manhattan . . . .

The experts were thus able to use the cusped handles of the vases seized in Geneva to link Medici to some of the worst plundering of recent times.

Then there were 153 Etrusco-Corinthian aryballoi and alabastra. This number of objects, the experts say, can only have come "from the plundering of about 20–30 room-tombs of southern Etruria." And in this particular case the evidence for recent plunder was vivid. One of the small vases still had the remains of a dirt-encrusted iron nail with which it was attached to a wall of the room.

Other aspects of the experts' great learning were applied to the methods of manufacture. For example, Bucchero ceramics are a form of vessel invented by the Etruscans and are black inside and out. They are made by firing in an oven with no oxygen. "As is known," wrote the experts, "they were the 'national' ceramic of the Etruscans," being continually produced throughout Etruria and Campania from the mid-seventh to the beginning of the fifth century BC, with an early start in Caere around 675 BC. Bucchero have been widely studied, and the minute differences in the mineral composition of the clay have been associated with different specific sites. In Geneva, Medici had 118 *intact* vases. "With the knowledge we have today, the vast majority of the vases can be judged as coming from the 'botteghe' [workshops], active between 675 and 575 BC, of Caere or its cultural area."

The three scholars employed a different type of evidence in the case of ceramics produced in mainland Greece. As their report makes clear, the Greek colonies of southern Italy and Sicily, together with Etruscan cities, were primary commercial destinations for vases made in Greece—in Athens, Sparta, Euboea, and Corinth. Amphorae and perfume flacons in particular were traded. However, Etruria was obviously a special area for some reason, because only in Etruria "have objects of exceptional quality been found." Scholars believe that these exceptional objects were sent as examples, as "commercial propaganda," to show what various "botteghe" were capable of, to encourage international trade. For example, it is known that certain shapes of vase were produced in Greece *but solely for export to Italy or Sicily*. The so-called Nolane vases are a case in point: They have an Attic shape, but their most important excavation sites have been at Nola, northeast of Naples; Gela, a city founded in the eighth century BC on the southern coast of Sicily by ancient Greek colonists; Capua, situated north of Naples; and Vulci. In fact, statistical studies have shown that out of more than 800 objects known, *only one* has ever been found in Greece itself. As the experts conclude, "One can without doubt say that the material of the Medici seizure includes an almost complete exemplification of the above-mentioned workshops."

In addition, there was in the Medici warehouse at the Freeport another kind of evidence that the experts' scholarship was able to expose: Even on vases of a type that *could* have come from Greece, some had "hallmarks." These were inscriptions scratched on the vases *after* their arrival at their destination, for some as yet unknown commercial reason. The scholars referred in their report to a seminal study by Alan W. Johnston, *Trademarks on Greek Vases* (1979), which examined 3,500 vases of this type and concluded, "[U]p till now no vase found in continental Greece . . . bears hallmarks of this kind," which are "basically limited to vases travelling toward the west . . . Etruria, Campania or Sicily." Moreover, the hallmarks are scratched exclusively in the Etruscan alphabet. Some of these vases were those found wrapped in Italian newspapers.

Yet more support for an Italian provenance comes from the fact that many of these vases were intact. This all-important detail may not mean much to most of us, but to archaeologists and Etruscologists the fact that the vases were *not* broken is almost certainly due to the circumstance that in the Etruscan necropolises there were entities known as room tombs, which didn't exist in ancient Greece. Almost all vases that have been found intact on legitimate digs have been found in room tombs.

Not unnaturally, in view of the events described in the Prologue concerning the vase by Euphronios, the experts devoted no little attention to objects by famous artists that were found on Medici's premises in Geneva. In particular, they concentrated on Exekias and Euphronios.

As Bartoloni and her colleagues point out, J. D. Beazley, in his 1956 publication, *Attic Black-Figure Vase Painters*—still today a reference book for black-figure ceramics—identified sixteen vases by Exekias for which the provenance was known and another six for which the provenance was not known. According to Beazley, thirteen of the vases whose provenance was known came from Etruria—five from Vulci, five from Orvieto, one each from other places in Italy—whereas only three came from other countries (two from Athens, one from France). In the case of Euphronios, in a similar publication drawn up in 1963, *Attic Red-Figure Vase-Painters*, also by Beazley, there were thirteen vases for which the provenance was known and nine for which it was not known. For those vases of known provenance, nine came from Etruria (two from Cerveteri, two from Vulci, one each from other places), three from Greece, and one from Olbia on the Black Sea.

The experts then added that, in the case of Euphronios, there was an exhibition held in 1990–1991, in Arezzo, Paris, and Berlin, in which eighteen vases, or fragments of vases, not known to Beazley, had come to light (this is not counting the Euphronios vase at the Metropolitan Museum in New York). *Not one of these new vases, or fragments, had any provenance at all.* Of these eighteen, eleven were in American collections or museums, five in Switzerland, and two in Germany. As the experts drily remark, "Paradoxically, objects which are part of old collections yield far more scientific data than objects of recent purchase."

The role of J. D. Beazley was important in another way, too. His prestige and eye were such that, after he produced his books, even people with unprovenanced vases sought him out, because an attribution by Beazley was commercially valuable. At the back of subsequent editions of his book, therefore, Beazley illustrated these unprovenanced vases and gave them attributions. As the experts point out, the fact that Medici had in his possession vases that fall under the aegis of Beazley's publications but are not *in* it invites the conclusion that they were excavated *subsequent* to the appearance of Beazley's books—books that were published well after Italy's anti-looting and anti-smuggling laws came into effect.

This by no means completes the evidence amassed by the three experts. Their lengthy report contained many other cases in which they could, for example, recognize the hand of a particular painter or the style of a particular *bottega*, or workshop, whose work is known only from sites in Italy, and there were plenty of other cases where graffiti in the Etruscan alphabet had been scratched on to the vases. The evidence that the vast bulk of Medici's material came illicitly out of Italy was as varied as it was overwhelming.

"Medici had so many important things," says Professor Bartoloni, with a mixture of sadness and anger. "In any archaeologist's career, he or she can hope to come across, perhaps, one or two important tombs. There was material in Geneva from at least *fifty* important tombs. To know that Medici had been distributing all this material around the world . . . it was heartbreaking."

It is often said by those who oppose any restrictions on the trade in unprovenanced antiquities that the bulk of the material on the market is relatively unimportant and that therefore the world need not be too concerned, because the loss to knowledge from this international, illicit traffic is, in effect, incidental, inconsequential. There will be many opportunities to address—and to contradict—this point throughout the rest of the book, but here we confine ourselves to three preliminary observations. The first has already been alluded to in making mention of a number of published reports about the trading patterns of ancient Greece—for example, Alan Johnston's study of the export patterns of vases with and without "hallmarks." This report provides a great deal of information about trading patterns in antiquity, about economic activity in both the country of origin and the country of reception, and of the relations between the two. It also throws light on matters of taste—that is, which artists and designs were popular where. Then there was the case of the Nolane vases,

Greek amphorae made exclusively in Greece for export to Etruria, a survey of 800 of which, in 1991, showed that only one specimen has ever been found in Greece. Medici had several. Think how our understanding would be changed if *any* of these did not come from Italy. "Ordinary" vases—the "poorly drawn and average," to repeat Dietrich von Bothmer's phrase—can still tell us a great deal about history.

Second, there is the fact that the sheer scale of plunder of "ordinary" material has very serious consequences. One small bronze dagger among the Medici material dated from the fifteenth century BC. This period was characterized by the deposition of arms in water or near the summit of high places. But the meaning of these cult places is still obscure: Who can say if the exact location where this particular dagger was found might not have told archaeologists a great deal about this mysterious cult? Again, a small bronze boat, of slightly later date and seized in Geneva, was of a type always associated with Sardinian clan chiefs. This was likely to have been found with other belongings of the clan chief, all of which are lost. Medici also had five couplings from horses' bits: This means a chariot would have been part of the excavation, much more interesting and much more valuable (a bronze chariot was found on an authorized dig in Vulci). A number of eighth-century BC axes were found together. These, in all probability, were not found in a tomb but had been buried in accordance with a cultish ritual. Who knows how interesting and important the cult was, or what the ritual consisted of and meant? This potential knowledge has all been lost. The same argument also applies to six semicircular razors found among the Medici material. The kantharoi with cusped handles, which fit with material from known illegal digs in the Monte del Bufalo area in Crustumerium, are the fruit of an illicit network that has, over the years, plundered more than 1,000 tombs. How can anyone say that the plundering of 1,000 tombs does no damage to our knowledge?

Also among the Medici material were 153 Etrusco-Corinthian balm containers, the fruit, say the experts, of the plundering of about twenty to thirty room tombs of southern Etruria. Such looting must have uncovered much other important material—all missing. By the same token, the 118 intact Bucchero vases also indicate the looting of many room tombs, all coming from one "bottega," about which, in all probability, we shall now never know anything. A number of geometric ceramics found in Medici's warehouse, though not everyone's favorite—as they are rather plain— have nonetheless been of great scientific interest over the last thirty years, because of the light they may throw on the early Greek colonization of Italy and the possibility of pre-colonial frequenting, by the Greeks, of the Tyrrhenian and Sicilian coasts, while they suggest at the same time the possible early settlement of Greek artisans transplanted into Italy. The exact excavation locations and the accurate dating this permits are thus of crucial importance. Once again, "ordinary" objects are very important.

But it is also true that much of the Medici material wasn't "ordinary" at all. On the contrary, as the experts went through the objects in the Freeport, and as their report makes clear, they found much of it "important," "noteworthy," "unique," "rare," and "magnificent." As well as vases by Euphronios and Exekias and the Villanovan fibula with a twisted gold thread, there was a rare Etruscan *bacellata* (bas relief), of particular interest because it had a double inscription of ownership on both the interior and exterior of the base, giving both the first and last name, and this was very unusual. There was a very rare and important triple-handled bronze cauldron of the kind found in the antechamber of the Regolini Galassi tomb at Cerveteri and a tubular *askos* (a smaller vase, perhaps three inches long, used for oils or perfume and often fashioned in the shape of an animal) in laminated bronze decorated with small chains, only found elsewhere in the rich tomb of the Bronze Chariot at Vulci. There was a rare pilgrim's ceramic flask, of the kind that comes from Veio, two magnificent amphorae attributed to the Painter of the Cranes, active in Caere during the second quarter of the seventh century BC, plus a rare askos by the same artist. A red-and-white painted biconic vase from Cerveteri was equally impressive, together with a rare oinochoe with a frieze of ibexes attributable to the Swallows Painter, who was active in Vulci. Another Vulci figure was by the Feoli Painter, and Medici had a polychrome oinochoe by him—of which only one other example is known, say the experts. A large alabastron from Tarquinia was in a style similar to that of the so-called Three-Heads Wolf Painter but sufficiently different that this must have been by someone else, an unknown painter, possibly a pupil. There were also two large Etruscanized Campanian amphorae from a very rare bottega. Buccheri decorated with "fan" graffiti were unique so far as the experts were concerned, and there were many Cerveteri vases, goblets, ladles, and female-caryatid stands that were sufficiently rare or valuable as to be singled out—seventy-five in all. The same argument applied to the Etruscan archaic period bronze objects in Medici's possession and the seven pairs of rare Etruscan gold earrings and two house-shaped funeral stelae from Cerveteri "of which there is nothing similar known." Other rare items included a late proto-Corinthian figured vase shaped like an owl, a single-handled Laconian pitcher, and a krater with stirrup handles with meander decorations. One goblet by the entourage of the painter Naukratis and in the manner of the Painter of the Hunt was similar to only one other known, which appeared on the Swiss antiquities market in the late 1980s and disappeared. Various *lekythoi* were rare or noteworthy, as was a red-figure *hydria* (a water-storage vase), "the only known work in this technique by the Rycroft painter."

Medici's material was, therefore, as notable for its important objects as for its sheer size and variety. Not even these examples do full justice to the most significant artifacts he brought out of Italy—all of it looted.

That the experts found it relatively easy to link so many objects to specific cultures, necropolises, workshops, painters, and even individual tombs may seem odd until one realizes how unique this exercise was. Normally, archaeologists are able to examine only the photographs of objects in the catalog ahead of an auction; or via a brief examination on viewing days, when several or many others are doing the same, jostling for elbow room; or when an object is already on display in the museum or collection where it ends up. One might ask whether the fact that the photographs in auction house catalogs never show, for instance, the Etruscan "hallmarks" on many objects means that the salesrooms are complicit to this extent.

The experts' report clearly demonstrates that the vast majority of Medici's material, excavated by tomb raiders and fed to him by regional middlemen, comes illegally from Italy. By one route or another, it had reached the Freeport in Geneva, Switzerland. In this one warehouse there was enough to satisfy the international antiquities market for two years. The question its discovery inevitably raised was this: Where—until this discovery took place—was Giacomo Medici's treasure headed next?

6

The Paper Trail, the Polaroids,
and the *"Cordata"*

ALTHOUGH THE ANTIQUITIES themselves formed the most vivid and moving aspect of the seizure in Geneva, there was no less interest—for Conforti and for Ferri—in the documentation found in the back office behind Medici's showroom. While the three archaeologists concentrated on the objects, the paperwork became the responsibility of Maurizio Pellegrini, a photographic and document expert who had one foot in the public prosecutor's office and the other in the Villa Giulia. Pellegrini was not an officially trained archaeologist, but he had a great deal of knowledge in that field and his examination of the documentation was an exercise in detective work that was no less complex than the archaeologists' daunting task.

Of medium build, with wavy salt-and-pepper hair, spectacles, and a slightly academic temperament, Pellegrini was, on the surface, a gentle, reserved soft-spoken man, but he proved to be tenacious and strong-willed. He revealed the type of obsessive personality that provides the exacting attention to detail required to trace the hidden links among letters, invoices, and photographs, which did so much to reveal the clever subterfuges in Medici's business and in his relationships with others. On their trips to Geneva, Pellegrini worked shoulder to shoulder with Bartoloni, Colonna, and Zevi. He shared dinners with them and mainly listened in as Bartoloni and Zevi aired their academic disagreements.

The size of the task facing Pellegrini may be gauged from the fact that there were in Medici's warehouse thirty albums of Polaroids, fifteen envelopes with photographs, and twelve envelopes with rolls of film. Besides the albums of photographs, Pellegrini calculated that some 100 full rolls of exposed film were seized, making a total of 3,600 images. In addition there was enough paper to fill 173 *faldoni*, white legal binders, each about six inches thick and tied with white laces. In all, there were close to 35,000 sheets of paper.

His job was not made any easier by the fact that, to begin with at least, he could only consult the documents in Switzerland. He wasn't allowed to photocopy anything, so he was confined to taking notes and using his memory for matters that were of special interest to him. Then, when he returned to Rome, he would cross town and compare his notes with, for example, exhibition catalogs in museum libraries, or in auction catalogs at Sotheby's. It was arduous, but after he began to make progress and understand more fully Medici's business arrangements, he initiated through Ferri a formal request for some of the documentation from the Swiss authorities. This request was granted, and toward the end of 1998, he made a special trip, on his own, to photocopy what he needed.

Just as the three archaeologists had been in an historically unprecedented situation in their examination of the objects under seizure at the Geneva Freeport, so Pellegrini was also in a unique position, for in addition to the documentation seized from Medici, he also had access to the documentation from James Hodges and official Sotheby's records, both of which showed who bought and sold what at a number of Sotheby's sales in London. Pellegrini furthermore had access to scientific publications and to the public prosecutor's files for other ongoing cases in Italy. He therefore had an unrivaled vantage point from which to view the interconnections of the antiquities underworld in an unvarnished way.

The first thing that he observed was that some documentation was original, and other papers were photocopies. This was a simple point—obvious, you would think—but it would prove important in establishing the links between Medici and others in the underground network. The second thing of importance that Pellegrini observed was that the photographic material was of three kinds. There were regular photographs—both prints and negatives—and there were Polaroids. Professional archaeologists do not use Polaroids: The quality is simply not good enough for scientific recording. The use of Polaroid photographs, therefore, was strongly suggestive of clandestine activity, mainly because they offer the advantage that they are instant and do not need to be processed through an independent laboratory that might be a security risk. The third type of photographic material comprised official photographs published in scientific reports.

But there was another aspect to the photography, especially the Polaroid photography, which attracted Pellegrini's early interest. The Polaroids fell into distinct groups. First, there were photographs of objects that were encrusted with dirt or calcarious deposits, in which the antiquities were often broken and incomplete. In other words, these objects were photographed near where they were excavated, in nearby fields or farmyards, in the houses of tombaroli, even on the back of a truck in one case. Next, however, there were many Polaroids showing *the same objects* restored, with the fragments joined together. In many cases, although the fragments had been joined together, the joins of the fragments were still visible, as were the gaps (the lacunae) where parts of the vases, say, were still missing. In due course, Pellegrini pieced together why the objects had been photographed in this state—but not at first.

Next came a series of photographs—Polaroids again—in which once more the same objects were depicted, but this time they had been fully restored, with the joins covered over and repainted and polished to look almost as good as new. In some cases, as Pellegrini worked through the documents, he found that many of these restored objects were also depicted in auction house catalogs or in museum publications. Finally, there was a most interesting set of photographs in which Medici, and sometimes others, were pictured alongside antiquities that were *on display* in particular museums. Over the months, Pellegrini was able to sift the photographs in such a way that, for dozens of objects, he could reconstruct an entire sequence: from objects just out of the ground, dirty and broken, to being restored, to being on display in the world's museums. Medici, it turned out, was a stickler for keeping records, and it was the photographs that provided Pellegrini with the first inkling of the totality of Medici's involvement. Many of the photographs had writing on them that directed him elsewhere in the documentation, and no less important, many showed interiors that he began to recognize as the investigation proceeded. This also helped him to piece together the complex web of interrelationships that would in time be fully exposed.

Pellegrini had to start somewhere, so he chose what was far and away the most immediately shocking set of photographs. This was a folder with, on the outside, the words *"Pitture romane Via Bo."* It contained a number of transparent envelopes holding negatives, some travel documents that appeared to indicate that certain frescoes had traveled between Switzerland and the United States, and a handful of invoices that appeared to indicate that the frescoes were valued at $141,000. A "ProForma Invoice," handwritten but on Atlantis Antiquities–headed notepaper, at 40 East 69th Street, listed sixteen objects, including "Noir et jaune. Dessins géométrique," "Rouge, vert, brun. 5 figures encadrées," and so on. The list seemed to relate to the frescoes in the warehouse, or some of them, but all did not become clear for a few weeks. On a subsequent visit, Pellegrini had with him a special digital film camera that was able to convert negatives into positive images. He fitted the various negatives into the device and, eventually, reached the wall paintings.

"Mi é preso un colpo!" he breathed. "I was hit." He couldn't believe his eyes, and he called out to the professors.

Zevi, the first to reach him, took the camera. "He was speechless," says Pellegrini. "Scandalized."

What the images revealed was a dismaying sequence—"a real horror," as he wrote in his report—in which the first pictures showed three walls of what any expert could recognize as a Vesuvian/Pompeian villa. They could make this identification because the three walls were frescoed in what is called the Campanian II style. The decoration on Roman villas went through what art historians and archaeologists recognize as four styles, between the second century BC and AD 79. Campanian II comes second in this chronology, and decorations in that style differ from what came before and after in consisting of more panoramic landscapes, mythological scenes, and certain architectural features.

The photographs showed three walls partially cleaned of the lapillae filling the room. Two of them were in red, pale blue, and gray. These walls showed two female figures in the foreground with, below them, miniaturized masks and smaller figures. On the right wall was shown an architectural drawing of a two-story building, with a similar symmetric design opposite, on the left wall. In other words, in this first sequence of photographs, the room—or one end of it—is intact. "The frescoes are in an excellent state of conservation, both pictorially and structurally." However, besides the walls of the room, the photographs also showed a mass of earth mixed with *lapillae* covering the floor and filling the space to a depth of a few feet; lapillae also encrust the ceiling area. Lapillae are a telltale sign to any Italian archaeologist. They are small balls of volcanic ash, formed after the eruption of Vesuvius in AD 79, which buried so much of the surrounding countryside south of Naples. This was further confirmation, in addition to the subject matter and pictorial style of the frescoes, that this room had been part of a villa that was one of those overwhelmed by the eruption of the famous volcano, but not one known to the official archaeologists. The first sequence of photographs therefore confirmed that this had been a very important discovery, made in a clandestine "excavation" by some tombaroli. It was the next set of photographs, however, that constituted the "horror."

This second set showed the image of the central wall—the one with the two female figures and the figurines—*but laid out like a giant jigsaw*. The images had been cut from the original wall, in a number of highly irregular pieces, each in size about as big as a laptop, and then put back together again on panels that were framed—edged—in wood. The fresco had been taken off the villa wall, detached from its right and left companions, and cut up into chunks. That it was the same image was quite clear to Pellegrini, even though there were gaps between the separate pieces: The two females were clearly visible and recognizable. In his report, Pellegrini commented that this operation, normally highly technical (when done by archaeologists), was here done crudely and in a hurry, without any regard for the integrity or sanctity of the images but simply so that the fresco could be quickly and more easily smuggled abroad. This was not all. Other sets of photographs showed that the same procedure had been employed with both the right-hand and the left-hand walls.

Another fresco was shown to have been similarly brutalized. This wall, primarily ochre in color with dark green-to-black painting, showed different shaped vases surrounded by dark borders and, higher up, a rearing horse in a circle of leaves. These images too had been broken into laptop-sized chunks, and they were photographed in the process of reassembly, on a trestle table with brushes, jars, and other restoration implements in the shot. In the next photo, the pieces are shown roughly assembled, with about an inch between segments, then more closely aligned as the restoration is completed. It is almost as if the restorers have taken pride in the vandalism.

That was not all. Two of the walls depicted in the photographs were found in the Freeport, packed in bubble wrap and leaning against a wall, as though they were about to be shipped out. The third wall, however, was missing and had presumably already been sold. It has not been seen since. The same may apply to other photographs of other frescoes, which may have been subjected to the same treatment. They include one picture of a head in a semicircular lunette. This was just lying on the floor in the Freeport warehouse. In fact, the Italians don't know how much Medici had or what he sold. From the dimensions of the walls, it appears that the photographs relate only to the solid lines in the diagram below, and that the room could easily have been of the dimensions outlined by the dotted lines.

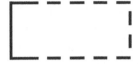

Possibly worse than all this was the final sequence in the horse and vases fresco. For, in the end, these images were *not reassembled together*. This time the pieces had been formed into single panels of smaller dimensions that, Pellegrini concluded, were more easily "placeable" on the market at more accessible prices and were worth more as individual pieces than the complete image if sold as "just one" fresco. In the paperwork, photocopies of two of the vases—inside the square boundaries—were included with a consignment note to an auction house, with the value "$10" attached, which, as Pellegrini noted, must have meant $10,000.

This, then, was the distressing starting point for Pellegrini. It revealed the scale of the traffic in illegally excavated antiquities, and the brutality shown by the tombaroli and those above them in respect to important and beautiful ancient objects, as well as the utter indifference to the archaeological importance of Italy's heritage, and it showed how inappropriate the word "excavation" is when applied to these activities. The frescoes of at least one important villa had been rudely and crudely ripped from their context and sold off to people ("collectors") who might profess to care about archaeological objects but obviously had no interest in the original and proper context. One wonders what else was found and looted from this villa, clearly no poor man's hovel. This indifference applied to everyone in the chain: from the tombaroli to the middlemen, the smugglers, and the restorers, to the auction house personnel, to collectors and to museum curators—wherever these objects end up. It was a matter of money and greed, pure and simple.

Pellegrini had copies made of the photographs of the Vesuvian-Pompeian villa and pinned them above his desk. They fired his indignation and spurred him to explore the paper trail with ever greater determination. For the mild-mannered Pellegrini, the next months would become a crusade.

Although Giacomo Medici was the main target of the public prosecutor, and despite the fact that the sheer quantity and quality of antiquities found in Geneva confirmed that he was indeed a major trafficker in the illicit trade, the Italian authorities knew that he was by no means the only important figure in the underground network. Many years of experience, Pasquale Camera's organigram found in Rome, and the Sotheby's documentation leaked by James Hodges all underlined that Medici was just one figure—albeit the most important—in a much larger network. From the start, therefore, Pellegrini was most concerned to sift the documents for other names, other powerful names, people who might link Medici with the international antiquities world: the great auction houses, dealers, galleries, collectors, and museums in Switzerland, Germany, Japan, Paris, London, and New York that as often as not seemed to turn a blind eye to the shady origins of this trade. Would the Medici documentation throw any light on this?

Spurred on by the evidence of the Vesuvian-Pompeian villa frescoes, Pellegrini's next move was to reexamine the documentation from London, reminding himself that Medici had consigned substantial amounts of unprovenanced antiquities to Sotheby's in London over many years; that other people, Christian Boursaud and then Serge Vilbert, had acted as "fronts" for Medici (although Medici was the beneficial owner of the antiquities, his name never appeared in the documentation or written record; the closest he came was to use the term "Guido's," Guido being his father's name). Pellegrini also recognized that Sotheby's personnel were aware of Medici's involvement and knew that he was the beneficial owner but that his name never appeared in their documentation and that he shared an administrative address in Geneva—7 Avenue Krieg—with another antiquities dealer, Robin Symes, who had earlier been shown to deal in both stolen and smuggled antiquities.

Pellegrini also discovered that the Hydra Gallery had discreetly morphed into Editions Services, not only because of unwelcome press coverage but because when Boursaud and Medici fell out over who owned what in Hydra, their argument led to a court case, held in 1986, over ownership of the Hydra Gallery, a court case that Medici won. The existence of the court case nicely confirmed Medici's interest in both Hydra and Editions Services.

Delving further into the documentation, Pellegrini found that the Hydra Gallery and Editions Services were not the only companies through which Medici consigned antiquities to Sotheby's. There were at least three others—Mat Securitas, Arts Franc, and Tecafin Fiduciaire, which each sold and bought unprovenanced antiquities at Sotheby's in London. Headed notepaper, consignment notes, and invoices for each of these companies were found among the folders seized in the Freeport warehouse.

Moving beyond Sotheby's, and Medici's Geneva-based companies, Pellegrini sifted another range of names, those of fellow dealers, well known in the antiquities world, all of whom seemed to have an especially close relationship with Medici. Besides Robin Symes and his Greek partner, Christo Michaelides, he found more names. Zurich-based dealers included Frederique ("Frida") Tchacos-Nussberger, an Alexandrian Greek, and Fritz and Harry Bürki, a father-and-son team of restorers. Also in Zurich were Ali and Hischam Aboutaam, of Lebanese extraction; it appeared they also had a warehouse in the Geneva Freeport. Finally, there were two men in Paris: Nikolas Koutoulakis, a Cretan dealer; and Robert Hecht, who was the joint owner of Atlantis Antiquities in New York, with his partner there, Jonathan Rosen.

Two other groups of people were also highlighted as Pellegrini went through the seized paperwork. One was a group of collectors, or collector-dealers, whose collections it appeared Medici had helped to form. These names included the Hunt brothers—Nelson Bunker Hunt and William Herbert Hunt. In the 1970s, this colorful pair had attempted to corner the world's silver market. They had begun buying silver in 1973, when an ounce cost $1.95; by 1980 it had reached $54.00, when the Hunts and their colleagues owned 200 million ounces, equivalent to *half* the world's deliverable supply. Then the government intervened and by March that year the price was down to $10.80. The Hunts (and many others) went bankrupt, in their case to the tune of $2.5 *billion*. Eight years later, in August 1988, they were convicted of conspiring to manipulate the world's silver market. During the 1980s, however, while awaiting trial, they had amassed a formidable collection of Greek and Roman coins and Greek and Roman vases. A second couple was Leon Levy and Shelby White, whose collection had been displayed in an exhibition called Glories of the Past at the Metropolitan Museum in New York, from September 1990 to January 1991. A third couple was Barbara and Lawrence Fleischman, whose collection had been displayed in the exhibition titled A Passion for Antiquities at the Getty Museum in Los Angeles, in 1994–1995, and at Cleveland, in spring 1995. There was Maurice Tempelsman, a Belgian-born mining and minerals magnate, chairman of Lazare Kaplan, the largest cutter of diamonds in the world, who was a Visitor in the Department of Classics at the Boston Museum of Fine Arts, and best known as the companion of Jacqueline Kennedy Onassis, the twice-bereaved widow of President John F. Kennedy and Aristotle Onassis. And there was George Ortiz, a collector-dealer who lived in Geneva, an heir to the South American Patiño tin fortune whose collection had been displayed at the Royal Academy in London in 1994 in an exhibition called In Pursuit of the Absolute. Finally, there was Eli Borowksy, a Pole, who had spent many years in Canada but by then had his own museum in Jerusalem, the Bible Lands Museum, filled with antiquities from the civilizations of the eastern Mediterranean. Pellegrini found it most interesting that this set of six names comprised the most valuable antiquities collections formed since World War II. If the documents were to be believed, Medici seemed to have had a hand in all of them.

Finally, Pellegrini came across a set of names that was the most surprising of all. This was a list of museum curators, as often as not professional archaeologists or art historians, who appeared to have been in regular touch with Medici. Among this group were Dietrich von Bothmer, at the Metropolitan Museum in New York; Jiri Frel, Arthur Houghton, and Marion True, all of the Antiquities Department of the Getty Museum in Los Angeles; Robert Guy, of Princeton and Oxford; Fiorella Cottier-Angeli, an archaeologist and art expert who worked for Swiss customs in Geneva; and Professor Jacques Chamay, head of archaeology at the Geneva Museum.

Some of the documentation was relatively easy to follow. For example, although the vast majority of the material seized in Geneva concerned unprovenanced material—that is, antiquities for which there were no records because they were discovered by tombaroli in the ground, Medici was also involved with several straightforwardly stolen objects. These antiquities had been stolen from specific sites, such as churches, archaeological displays, museums, or even private collections. This, of course, is how the Carabinieri had targeted Medici in the first place.* But, as Pellegrini was soon to find out, this was by no means an isolated instance. Among the masses of paperwork was a catalog, number thirteen in a series published by the Carabinieri Art Squad itself, showing objects that had been stolen from various locations in Italy. Medici's copy of the catalog had a bookmark in it, at a page reporting the theft of two Roman capitals (the decorated and carved top portions of stone columns) that had been stolen from the Villa Celimontana and from the archaeological site of Ostia Antica, the vast archaeological park covering the entire area of the ancient city of Ostia, Rome's onetime thriving port. The entry showed a photograph of one of the capitals.

Both the capitals were there, in the warehouse in Geneva, but—and this also incensed Pellegrini—they appeared to have been altered, by abrasion and other damage, in a crude attempt to disguise what they actually were. The bookmark, slipped in at the appropriate place, gave the game away and confirmed that Medici not only had stolen objects on his premises but that he must have known they were stolen.

In line with this was a folder marked "IFAR Reports," inside which was a set of magazines called *Stolen Art Alert*, the publication of the Interna-

*One such object was the sarcophagus stolen from the Church of San Saba in Rome, which had been consigned to Sotheby's in London by Editions Services (see p. 19).

tional Foundation for Art Research, a not-for-profit organization in New York. Each month, *Stolen Art Alert* publishes a list of photographs, a record of art that has been stolen. It is not unlike the Carabinieri list but covers thefts worldwide, not just in Italy. Medici not only had these records but some of the contents were marked with felt-tip highlighting. These included a second-century AD sarcophagus, stolen from the Villa Taverna in Frascati in 1987, and a second sarcophagus, undated but Roman, stolen in Rome in 1986. Pictures of both these objects were among Medici's Polaroids. He could not have been unaware that the objects he had were stolen.

Elsewhere, Pellegrini found a photograph of a marble head of Eirene, the Greek goddess of peace and wealth, on the back of which was written, in Italian, "Geneva 7/7/93—I hereby declare selling to Mr. Jacques Albert the object depicted in this photo exclusively owned by me and of legitimate provenance (*'di legittima provenienza'*). In faith Luzzi Franco. Received Fr 120." This marble head was stolen in 1993 from the archaeological site of Villa Adriana in Tivoli, Emperor Hadrian's haven near Rome, where he had a library and a theater and studied philosophy "in peace." Franco Luzzi was a well-known art and antiquities dealer, who, as Pellegrini, Ferri, and Conforti all knew, had close ties to Medici (he featured in the organigram). In fact, by the time Pellegrini came across this photograph, with the writing on the back, the marble head had already been recovered and was back in Italy. But it was another testament to Medici's involvement.

These stolen objects were few in number compared to the unprovenanced antiquities that were Medici's main line of business, but they were important for what they revealed about his attitude and the world in which he moved. Tombaroli, and even Medici on occasions, in the proceedings against him, like to portray themselves as lovers of the arts, as "experts" or professional archaeologists in a sense, helping to "preserve" material that would otherwise be "lost" to history. How plausible is that when the same people knowingly trade in openly stolen artifacts, and deliberately damage them to disguise where they came from? Instead, their real motivation now stands out. They deal in antiquities for one reason and one reason only: the money it brings in.

Pellegrini's main contribution to Ferri's investigation was the way he used the documentation to throw light on what we might call the *strategic* organization of the antiquities underworld. Indeed, Pellegrini's discoveries in this realm are a major contribution to the history of both archaeology and criminology.

His first insight was his identification of the existence in the antiquities underworld of "triangulations." A "triangulation" is a term originally used in arms dealing, when middlemen are trying to disguise who the ultimate "end-user" is for a particular set of weapons when general trading in them is, for one reason or another, forbidden. Or, more generally, when for political reasons one country tries to circumvent international sanctions. In this case, it is essentially a way of covering up who the real source of an unprovenanced antiquity is. "A," the real source (Medici, for example), wants to sell to "C," a museum or a collector. "C" does not wish to be seen buying from "A." In this case, "A" passes the object to "B," the "safe" intermediary (usually, but not always, a dealer in Switzerland), who then "sells" on to "C." Of course, the intermediary is recompensed in some way for his or her role in the transaction, but the chief purpose of the triangulation is deception.

However, the practice is less obvious, and more deceptive, than the simple triangle, because Pellegrini identified a form of antiquities traffic that was quite unknown before, except to its practitioners, and revealed a new level of organization and cynicism that will prove shocking to many people. This is the practice known to insiders as "the sale of the orphans." "Orphans" (or *"orfanelli,"* meaning little orphans) in this case refers to fragments of vases, in particular vases by well-known painters or potters, such as Euphronious, Exekias, or Onesimos. Fragments of their vases— small pieces of pottery—may be quite valuable in themselves, worth as much as several thousand dollars each.

When a vase by a well-known artist or potter is found in fragments, it is sometimes deliberately *kept* that way. The point of this tactic is that these fragments will be introduced on to the market one or two pieces at a time, over a number of years. The aim is twofold. In the first place, it is

to create, in the mind of a museum curator or a collector, a growing desire—a passion—to acquire or own a truly amazing work. By slowly building up the vase, the appetite of the collector or museum is whetted, and
this is another area where triangulation comes into play. To prevent naive
trustees from spotting what is actually happening, the fragments arrive in
the museum over several years but also via several different routes: They
may all start with person "A" and all end up with entity "C," but they
reach "C" via "D," "E," "F," "G," and so on. Trustees are expected to accept the (specious) argument that the subsequent fragments "turned up"
in a later dig and this explains how they reached the market by different
routes. In fact, the whole rigmarole is a setup.

A second function of fragments is to "sweeten" other acquisitions that
museums or collectors are thinking of making. Say a museum has three
or four pieces of a valuable vase and is anxious to acquire more, but is, at
one particular moment, thinking of acquiring something quite different,
a valuable stone head maybe, or a fresco. Should there be any problem or
delay with this larger acquisition, then a fragment of the vase that the museum already has part of will suddenly materialize on the market, in the
possession of the same dealer offering the larger piece to the museum. The
fragment will have surfaced via a triangulation, of course, one dealer doing
another dealer a favor, and the museum or collector will be offered the
fragment, or orphan, either as a gift, if the main deal goes through, or more
cheaply than would otherwise be the case (in the jargon "a partial gift").

The sale of orphans alerted Pellegrini to one final, more general and particularly cynical aspect of the antiquities trade. The phenomenon of triangulation shows that dealers operate together, do each other favors, cover
for one another, and the trading in fragments, in orphans, shows that these
triangulations can be quite widespread. Pellegrini asked himself why that
should be, and it was some time before he could answer his own question.
When he did, however, he surprised even himself. But his insight was confirmed by Ferri's later investigations.

Because he had access to so much documentation, Pellegrini was in a
unique situation to make an overview not only of what was *in* the papers
seized at the Geneva Freeport, but also what was *not in them*. And what
was not in them was an entire set of names—the names of Gianfranco
Becchina, who was based in Basel and carried out similar activities to

Medici; Sandro Cimicchi, a restorer also based in Basel; and Raffaele Monticelli, who worked in a similar capacity to Pasquale Camera. These names had all been in Pasquale Camera's organigram, but they weren't in the Medici documents—why was that? What Pellegrini deduced from this was that the illicit trade in looted antiquities out of Italy was actually divided into two broad groups. Both led to Hecht but by different routes. One led to Hecht via Camera, Medici, Bürki, Symes, and Tchacos. The other led to Hecht via Monticelli, Becchina, Cimicchi, and a Lugano dealer—the equivalent of Tchacos or Symes—named Mario Bruno.

Later, as Pellegrini delved deeper into the paperwork, he found the source of this divide. It lay in an intense rivalry between Medici and Becchina. They were competitors who disliked each other intensely and never passed up an opportunity to do one another harm. Their rivalry suited Hecht, of course: It fueled competition, which only added to the efficiency of the trade and, from Hecht's point of view, served to keep prices down. Later still in the investigation, Ferri discovered that this rivalry was real enough that the members of the different groups referred to each other as being part of a *"cordata."* In Italian, a *cordata*, coming from *"corda,"* the word for rope, refers to a group of rock climbers or mountaineers who are bound together on a mountainside for mutual safety. It was a vivid image, all too accurate.

Pasquale Camera's organigram had outlined the overall organization of the illicit traffic, but the triangulations and the two distinct *"cordate"* brought extra levels of sophistication. As with the triangulations, the main purpose of these cordate was to keep the end point of the chain—collectors and museums—"clean." The entire illicit trade out of Italy was organized so as to protect the sources of revenue.

It made cynical sense, but did the museums and collectors know all this? Pellegrini's next task was to try to find out.

7

THE GETTY—

THE "MUSEUM OF THE *TOMBAROLI*"

ANYONE WHO IS REMOTELY INTERESTED in archaeology or antiquities cannot have failed to have heard of the J. Paul Getty Museum in Los Angeles. Founded fairly recently, in 1954, by the oil billionaire, John Paul Getty, who died in 1976, the museum has made news time and again—sometimes for the right reasons, just as often for the wrong ones.

By all accounts, Getty himself was a fairly miserly and gloomy soul who only came alive when he was collecting art or antiquities (he famously said, "The poor shall inherit the earth—but not the mineral rights"). At Sutton Place, his house outside London, the hallway boasted a massive picture of a bull by Paulus Potter, the famous seventeenth-century Dutch animal painter, and a magnificent triptych by the British modernist Francis Bacon. Yet guests were expected to use the pay phone also installed there. He had begun collecting in earnest in 1938.

His first museum was housed at his ranch, his weekend house on the borders of Malibu. In 1974, however, he opened a brand new one near the beach at Malibu, on the Pacific Coast Highway, just north of Los Angeles, and this time he modeled the museum on the Villa dei Papiri, a rich Roman country house near Naples buried since the eruption of Mount Vesuvius and only partially excavated. The Villa dei Papiri had boasted a big library of scrolls, and scholars believe that the unexcavated part may still contain many originals of lost classics from the ancient world. The antiquities at Malibu were housed on the ground floor, paintings and decorative arts on the second floor.

After his death, the Getty Trust, formed to handle the impressive income from Getty Oil, had its own very special problems, one being that under U.S. law, in order to preserve its charitable status, it was required to spend a minimum percentage of the income from its $3 billion (now $5 billion) endowment within a specified amount of time. The museum was so cash rich there were fears it would distort the art market. That worry turned out to be exaggerated, and the Getty actually behaved quite discreetly on its way to acquiring a number of undoubted masterpieces in the realm of painting, including the *Adoration of the Magi* by Andrea Mantegna, *Portrait of Duke Cosimo I de' Medici* by Jacopo Pontormo, and *Irises* by Vincent Van Gogh. It was also decided to build an entirely new museum, on a hilltop above the Santa Monica Freeway, at Sepulveda Pass, overlooking both the Pacific Ocean and Los Angeles itself. Designed by the architect Richard Meier, modeled on an Italian hilltop town, and faced with Travertine marble, the new museum opened amid much fanfare in 1997. One of its inaugural exhibitions was Beyond Beauty: Antiquities as Evidence, a seven-part exhibition in which one section considered how scholars cope with antiquities when their origin is not known, and a second dealt with faking and how it can be identified. Irony has run through the Getty ever since the man himself modeled his first museum on the Vesuvian Villa dei Papiri.

Over the years since Getty's death, however, the museum has often been in the limelight for one controversy or another. Three have involved antiquities. The first was the case of Jiri Frel, an "electrically persuasive" curator who had once worked for Thomas Hoving and Dietrich von Bothmer at the Metropolitan Museum in New York. Frel considered the Getty trustees as no more than a raft of "intellectual cripples," and he was accused by Hoving in a book, *Making the Mummies Dance*, published in June 1996, of foisting "thousands of dubious works on the museum—for a tab totaling $14 million." Frel was in fact forced to retire in 1985 after disclosures that he had traded inflated appraisals for donated antiquities. He moved to Italy, where for a while he took up his legal residence in the house in Castelvetrano in Sicily care of Gianfranco Becchina, one of the senior Italian names on Pasquale Camera's organigram. At the Getty, Arthur Houghton took over as deputy curator and then Marion True was appointed to full curator.

Second, there was the matter of the Sevso treasure, fourteen magnificent pieces of Roman silver that appeared on the art market in London, via Switzerland, in mysterious circumstances in the early 1980s. These items were offered to the Getty in circumstances no less mysterious, in that the silver was purported to come from The Lebanon, but the export licenses turned out to be fake. The Getty played an active role in discovering that the export licenses were forged and did not acquire the silver, but neither did it alert any law enforcement or other authority as to what was afoot.

Two years later, in 1986, the Getty unveiled a new acquisition, a larger than life-size statue of a youth, known in Greek as a *kouros*. It had been acquired in Switzerland, the museum said, where it had been in a private collection since the 1930s. Stylistically, the statue appeared to date from the sixth century BC, but a controversy immediately erupted over its authenticity. As one scholar put it, "Why was the statue so pristine and white? Why did the style of the hair not match that of the feet? Would an ancient sculptor have mingled so many styles in one figure?" The discussion was not helped by the fact that most *kouroi* are in fragments; only thirteen are known that are as complete as the Getty figure (though it had arrived at the museum, in 1983, in seven pieces).

The Getty decided to have the marble tested, to see if it had come from one of the quarries known about in antiquity and to see whether the patina, or surface crust, was ancient or modern. The geologist asked to carry out the tests concluded that the marble was from the island of Thasos, in the north Aegean, an ancient quarry site, and that it had a "calcitic" patina that could have developed only over a long period of time.

Later, however, it turned out that the documents providing a Swiss provenance for the kouros were fake and that the surface patina was more complex than the original geologist had said and not necessarily ancient. It was also reported that the Getty was shown a marble torso, plainly fake, that had many similarities with the kouros. The Getty bought the fake, took the kouros off display, did more tests, and then transferred both statues to Greece in 1992, for an international colloquium to try and settle the issue. Despite this, scholars remained divided, though they were split along disciplinary lines: The art historians and archaeologists were convinced the kouros was a fake, whereas the scientists thought that the science proved it was genuine.

In Italy, it is fair to say, there was an added level of skepticism toward the Getty. This was for two reasons. In the first place, Italian archaeologists had not forgotten Dietrich von Bothmer, at the Metropolitan Museum in New York, for his role in the controversial acquisition of the Euphronios krater. In the 1970s and early 1980s, the curator of antiquities at the Getty was Jiri Frel, a former pupil of von Bothmer's. In addition, other curators at the Getty who followed Frel, in particular Marion True, had also been students of von Bothmer. The Italians asked themselves if these students shared the same rather cavalier attitude to provenance that their teacher had revealed in the Euphronios krater affair.

A second reason for the Italian wariness of the Getty was due to its publication of *Greek Vases in the J. Paul Getty Museum*. This catalog, published in six occasional installments, from 1983 to 2000, contained many vases that the Italians believed could only have come illicitly from Italy, and yet in the catalog they were given no provenance. This suggested, to the Italians at least, that the Getty curators did indeed share von Bothmer's attitude toward provenance. In short, they weren't overcareful about where their vases came from. Instead, they were busy making their mark, assertively acquiring and publishing their collection of Greek vases, intent on showing that the museum's collection was rapidly achieving distinction.

Thus, it would also be fair to say that when Maurizio Pellegrini began sifting through the documents seized in Medici's Geneva warehouse, he kept a special eye open for anything to do with the Getty Museum. He was not to be disappointed.

Section E of the public prosecutor's preliminary report to the Rome court ahead of Medici's trial in 2004 was devoted to Medici's relations with the Getty, and it was by far the largest section. It began: "In spite of the fact that Medici was found in possession of tens of thousands of archaeological objects, and in spite of the fact that he dealt with the most important objects purloined from Italian territory—to the point of making [Frida] Tchacos-Nussberger describe him as being the 'monopoliser' of the market—Medici never appears among the sellers [to the museum] and he is never mentioned in official certificates." Yet Pellegrini soon found that with no fewer than *forty-two* major acquisitions by the Getty, Medici was the source, and a number of the relevant people at the Getty knew it.

Among the documents that Pellegrini highlighted early on was a set of papers that had been drawn up in March 1986 by the legal firm of Piguet in Geneva as part of the court case between Medici and Christian Boursaud, when the two were contesting ownership of the Hydra Gallery. Among the documents listing the objects said to form part of the inventory of Hydra were a number concerning a bronze tripod. Pellegrini recognized this tripod: It was one that had once formed part of the Guglielmi Collection but had been stolen, together with a bronze candelabrum.

The Guglielmi is one of the most distinguished collections of antiquities ever formed. It was put together in the nineteenth century by the marquises of Guglielmi of Vulci from the fruit of excavations carried out at Sant'Agostino and Camposcala, which were part of the ancient city of Vulci. The collection was displayed at the Palazzo Guglielmi in Civitavecchia until the beginning of the twentieth century, when it was divided into two parts, between the brothers Giulio and Giacinto. The part belonging to Marquis Giulio, inherited by his son, was donated to the Vatican in 1937 and since then has been exhibited in the Gregorian Etruscan Museum. The other part, equally important, remained in the Guglielmi family until 1987, when it was purchased by the Vatican Museums, to be reunited with the other half. The collection consists of 800 objects and is especially strong in bronzes and Etruscan and Greek ceramics. Collections don't come much more important than the Guglielmi.

Concerning the tripod and candelabrum, the Medici-Getty papers showed that an Etruscan tripod, fifth century BC, and "an Etruscan candelabrum," also fifth century BC, had been sent to the Getty Museum in Los Angeles on May 25, 1987. The papers further disclosed that the objects had been sent via TWA and Mat Securitas of Geneva, a company that collected the rents at the Freeport and handled shipments for Medici's other company, Editions Services. However, in this case, the name on the accompanying documentation—all of which was found in Medici's offices in the Geneva Freeport—showed that the tripod and candelabrum were, purportedly at least, the property of F. (Fritz) Bürki & Son and that they had been sent to the Getty on the basis that they were a "loan possible purchase." According to a typed invoice signed by Bürki on May 20, 1987, the price attached to these objects was $130,000. Soon after, on June 2, a Getty Museum receipt was issued. This too was made out to "F. Bürki" for the receipt of the two objects, a bronze tripod and candelabrum. Again, this paperwork was sent to Geneva, to Medici, via Mat Securitas (Bürki lives in Zurich).

This was fairly transparent, but at that point, for some reason, Marion True, curator of antiquities at the Getty, wrote two letters to Medici, to two separate addresses in Geneva, one letter in Italian, the other in English. On June 10, she wrote to him, care of Mat Securitas, at the Route des Jeunes address. She began *"Caro Sig. Giacomo"* (Dear Mr. Giacomo), an unusual form of address in Italian. "The bronze tripod and candelabrum have arrived at the Museum. I hope to be able to purchase them within the next year; we shall keep you informed regarding the date of the presentation." It was signed, *"Cordialissimi saluti,"* which indicates an excellent personal relationship. Two weeks later, on June 26, she sent Medici another letter, this time written in English and beginning, "Dear Giacomo." At the end of this letter, sent to the Rue de l'Evéché, she wrote: "The tripod and candelabrum have arrived from Bürki, and they are quite beautiful. Slowly, we will work on John [Walsh, director of the museum] and try to persuade him to change his mind. With all best wishes to you and your son." In other words, in the less formal letter, she admits that the tripod and candelabrum came in from Bürki. Remember, we are talking here of stolen objects, stolen from a distinguished collection, part of which was already in the Vatican, with the other part about to join it.

The next move occurred when the Getty Museum wrote to Bürki, asking him to sign two loan agreements for the bronze objects, official documentation for the museum's files. Bürki did indeed sign these documents and returned them.

And so, as far as the written record was concerned, to begin with at least, these bronze objects had been sent to the Getty by Fritz Bürki. Unofficially, however, the curator concerned—Marion True—knew that they came from Medici.

But was this level of triangulation enough? Perhaps not, because the documentation also shows that some time later, Bürki's name on the shipping sheet was crossed out and instead, written next to it, in longhand, were the words "Atlantis Antiquities—Attn: J[onathan]. Rosen." According to the public prosecutor's report, "This [was] because of a letter which F.[ritz] Bürki sent to [the] P. Getty Museum, in which he declares that the objects belong to Atlantis Antiquities." From then on the annual update loan files were not signed by Bürki, but by Rosen, as president of Atlantis. When the letters were sent out from the Getty they were addressed to Andrea Hecht, daughter of Robert Hecht, who, with Rosen, was the proprietor of Atlantis.

What was going on? All became clear in February 1988 when the Getty asked Jonathan Rosen, at Atlantis, for permission to restore the objects. This was granted the same day in a fax signed by Andrea Hecht. Almost two years later, on January 17, 1990, the Getty informed Rosen of the museum's decision to purchase the tripod and candelabrum, for $80,000 and $65,000, respectively. Marion True's maneuvers had finally triumphed. But this necessitated an invoice, in which it was stated that the tripod's country of origin was Italy, that it had been bought from a Swiss antiquities dealer in Geneva in 1985 and legally exported "from its country of origin." Thus, Bürki's role now was to be the place where the tripod and candelabrum had first been seen, should anyone ask. Having two people between Medici and the Getty was judged safer.

Eventually, having been bought and restored, the tripod (but not the candelabrum) went on display and was published in the museum's acquisitions bulletin. Whereupon there was an immediate outcry in Italy, Conforti stepped in, and an archaeologist from the superintendency was dispatched to Los Angeles to inspect the tripod. It was established that the object had indeed been stolen from the Guglielmi Collection and, after a certain amount of to-ing and fro-ing, the object was returned to Italy on November 21, 1996. It is interesting that in the wake of the fuss, Marion True was interviewed by Richard E. Robinson, assistant U.S. attorney, and during the course of their conversation, she said that she had first seen the object in Switzerland and that it was owned by Bürki, or Hecht, who had acquired it from Mario Bruno, a dealer in Lugano who had since died. There is no mention of Medici. On the face of it, this seems to be contradicted by her letters of June 10 and 26, 1987, in which she reassured Medici that the tripod and candelabrum had arrived safely at the museum.

The matter has only recently been resolved. The documentation made it clear that a fifth-century BC bronze Etruscan *thymiaterion* (candelabrum or incense burner) was sent to the Getty at the same time as the tripod, and acquired in exactly the same way. But it was never displayed by the

Getty. Is there a reason only one of these objects was ever displayed? The Getty and Marion True may well not have been aware that the tripod and candelabrum were stolen but instead thought they had been illegally excavated and smuggled out of Italy—like so much else that they handled. Was it safer, more prudent, to put these objects on display one at a time, just in case? In fact, in November 2005, the Getty finally returned the candelabrum to Italy.

The tripod episode was fairly clear-cut, because the object had been stolen. But more instructive for showing the extent of the clandestine trade in looted objects was a whole series of photographs that were seized at the Freeport and that Pellegrini, despite having to work in Geneva, away from home and the resources of the Villa Giulia library, managed to match up with objects *in* the Getty.

In all that follows, the evidence unearthed by Pellegrini has a consistency that he never expected to find. All the photographs, including Medici's Polaroids, were arranged according to type, date, and location where the objects they depicted had been sold. They were not just a rough assortment but were kept in order. Medici's name never appears in the official Getty records concerning the acquisition of objects, though he kept plenty of the correspondence addressed to him, written on the museum's headed notepaper. And this is the point: Medici, it turned out, was a methodical man who took a misplaced pride in what he did.

In each of forty-two specific instances, Pellegrini found three sets of photographs in Medici's albums that were seized in Geneva. In the first set, the objects were shown, photographed by Polaroid, as they had left the ground. The objects were in pieces, in fragments, with soil and other encrustations adhered to them, and sometimes they were shown lying on Italian newspapers. In the second set of photographs—sometimes Polaroids, sometimes regular photographs (prints or negatives)—the objects were shown in various stages of restoration. The fragments were shown having been put together. Usually this was a preliminary restoration, in that the fragments were reassembled, and lightly glued, so that the vase took shape but the arrangement of fragments was still visible, the joins clearly indicated, and in several instances some fragments still missing, leaving gaps. In some ways, the third set of photographs was the most extraordinary of all, and very revealing, not just about the whole process but about Medici the man. In most cases, Pellegrini found photographs of the objects—vases, sculptures, other items—in the Getty acquisition catalogs. This completed the sequence from the ground of Italy, to Switzerland, sometimes to an auction house or a dealer's catalog, then finally to the museum itself. However—and this was the most vivid evidence of all, the most grotesque illustration of Medici's misplaced pride—there was also a fourth set of photographs, a small number of images in which Medici himself was shown *alongside* the totally restored antiquities, *on display in this or that museum around the world*. It was a form of pride or vanity that Medici wanted to be photographed with "his" objects at the end of their journey, as if this vindicated what he did, showing that he was the true "father" of these pieces that, having been found in the ground of Italy, were now on view all over the world in distinguished museum settings.

But, at the same time, Medici's pride or vanity gave the game away. The photographs, and the order in which they were kept, were by far the most psychologically convincing evidence that, by whichever route these objects reached the museums of the world, they had started out with Medici. The documentation showed that antiquities reached the museums via several roundabout routes, but the photographs proved that, in every case, Medici was the beginning of the chain. In all that follows, the reader should remember that a photographic paper trail exists for many objects that Medici handled and that ended up in museums or notable collections. It is as simple and as damning as that.

The first object of interest was a red-figure Attic neck amphora with triple handles and decorated with athletes. On one side was shown a *discobolus* (a discus thrower), and on the other side a spear thrower. The Getty's acquisition notes record that the discus thrower was in fact a famous athlete from classical Greece named Phaulos. The vase had been bought by the Getty in 1984, its manufacture was dated to circa 505 BC, and it was attributed to the Euthymides Painter. Euthymides, as Jiri Frel put it in his description and summary when the vase was being acquired, "is one of the three great masters of Attic r-f [red-figure] drawing, called Pioneers. There is no complete piece by him in the United States." At that stage, Frel said, the Getty had only fragments by Euphronios and "a controversial piece by Phintias" (the other two of the three great Pioneers). Frel said that the mouth of the vase was missing, but otherwise its condition was "perfect." He then wrote this: "In the twenties of this century [meaning the twentieth century] the piece belonged to Professor E. Pfuhl, the famous specialist of Greek art in Basel. It was sold last year by his great-granddaughter, Mrs. Lattanzi of Ascona, Switzerland, to the dealer. This information has been confirmed by Pino Donati, dealer in Lugano, Switzerland." Frel added that he considered the piece superior to the Euphronios cup that had been bought by Nelson Bunker Hunt in 1979, which had cost $750,000, and that therefore it was well worth the $400,000 that the Hydra Gallery in Geneva were asking.

All of this was most interesting, especially the fulsome details about the vase's provenance, in view of the fact that among the negatives seized in Geneva, there was one showing the Euthymides amphora broken in pieces and, as Pellegrini's report dryly comments, "not in an institutional setting."

Following the same methodology, Pellegrini next came across a red-figure Apulian *pelike*, attributed to the Darius Painter, which was acquired by the Getty three years after the Euthymides vase, in 1987. A pelike is a multipurpose amphora with a sagging belly, usually with a wide mouth. Ropes were passed through its handles for lifting. The Darius Painter of the late fourth century BC was active in Apulia, possibly in Tarentum, the modern Taranto, and he was the leading artist of his time. He is named for a monumental krater in the archaeological museum in Naples depicting the Persian king Darius. Instead of always depicting heroes, the Darius Painter was notable for frequently—and unusually—painting myths involving *heroines*. On this vase, a good example of his work, Andromeda sits on a throne while Cassiopeia kneels before her, entreating her pardon. Perseus stands on the right and Aphrodite looks on.

Pictures of this pelike were found among the negatives seized in Geneva. Again, in one of these the vase is shown in a showcase in the museum; it also appears in a Polaroid. The matching documentation, which Pellegrini also found, was particularly revealing. The pelike was apparently acquired from Fritz Bürki, via Atlantis Antiquities, and had never been published before. The paperwork showed that the vase was sent to the Getty together with another red-figure Apulian pelike attributed to the Gravina Painter and a black-figure Attic bowl, attributed to the school of the Lysippides Painter. This portrayed Dionysus and Hercules as revelers with drinking vessels, the latter wearing the skin of the Nemean lion over his shoulders. The presence of the drinking vessels and vines probably alludes to the best-known encounter between Dionysus and Hercules, the drinking contest that Dionysus won with ease. Although the supplier of the pelike was ostensibly Bürki, an error was made in the invoice regarding the price: Bürki had written $45,000, when it should have been $60,000. In order to straighten it out, however, Marion True wrote not to Bürki but directly to Robert Hecht. Much of this documentation, remember, was found in Geneva Freeport, on Medici's premises: a classic triangulation.

Still other documents showed that Bürki had "sold" to the Getty a Lucanian red-figure krater, showing Hermes, Apollo, and Artemis, and attributed to the Palermo Painter, plus a terra-cotta alabastron and an *ariballos* (a small flask for oil, often suspended from the wrist), both of the latter Corinthian. Yet all these objects were among the Polaroids seized from Medici.

More important still, a red-figure kantharos, with masks (of grotesque faces) attributed to the Foundry Painter and with pottery attributed to Euphronios, was also found among the Geneva Polaroids, showing the object before and after its restoration. This vase is a good example of the very high quality of the objects we are discussing in this book. It was the only known example of its type in North America and has no known parallel anywhere in the world. Curator Arthur Houghton, in his appreciation of this kantharos ahead of its acquisition, described it as showing athletes cleaning themselves after exercise. But on either side the kantharos was embellished, and embossed, with masks, one of Dionysus, the god of wine, and the other of a smiling satyr. These relief masks made drinking from the kantharos difficult (a kantharos is a luxury drinking vessel, but this one was probably never used, being intended instead to serve as a votive offering in a temple or tomb). The cup had been restored from many fragments, some of which were *already in* the Getty. The Foundry Painter, so named after the scene of a bronze foundry on one of his vases in the Berlin Museum for Classical Antiquities, was the strongest member of the workshop of the Brygos Painter.* The Foundry Painter favored just such scenes as were on this vase—symposia, athletics, or combat.

Marion True attributed the pottery of the kantharos to Euphronios for a number of reasons. His signature as potter is known long after he ceased to paint, perhaps after he went blind and instead concentrated on the more tactile potter's craft. Houghton added:

The attribution of the kantharos' potter is very difficult because there is no known parallel for this vase in any collection in the world except for that of the Getty Museum. We have fragments of at least two, and possibly three other kantharoi of the same type. . . . The fragmentary Getty vase has been attributed by Dyfri Williams of the British Museum to the painter Onesimos. Since the only potter who is known to link the work of the Foundry Painter and Onesimos is Euphronios, and we know also from other fragments in the Getty collection that he potted a number of hitherto-unknown unusual vase shapes, Marion True has attributed the manufacture of the kantharos to his hand. . . . As mentioned above, the only known parallels for this vase type are in the collection of the Getty Museum, and some of our fragments actually join this cup . . . In addition to its tremendous importance as a vase of hitherto-unknown shape potted and painted by two of the most respected artists of the late archaic period, this kantharos has a significance for the collection of the Getty Museum that it has for no other collection. We have the only other known vases of this type, and their condition is extremely fragmentary. . . . The Bürki kantharos has provided the key to the identification of the potter of this remarkable group of vases. . . . The cup presents no problem for export. It was in London from 1982 to 1984 with the dealer Robin Symes, then exported to Switzerland to Fritz Bürki and Son in Zurich. The vase is said to have been purchased originally from the

---

*The Brygos Painter flourished in Athens c. 490–470 BC and was a pupil of Onesimos.

Swiss market. . . . It was attributed to the Foundry Painter by Dr. Robert Guy of Princeton when it was in the possession of Robin Symes, and Guy has discussed with us the remarkable importance of the vase shape. . . . There is no market price that is truly comparable because there is no similar vase known. We purchased in 1983 approximately 2/5 of a large kylix signed by the potter Euphronios and painted by Onesimos for $180,000. Although the shape and decoration of the vase are quite different, the price gives a fair description of the value of an unusual vase from the artists of the Euphronian circle.

It was bought from Bürki for $200,000.

A tripod, a candelabrum, a red-figure amphora, an Apulian pelike, a black-figure Attic bowl, a Corinthian alabastron and a Corinthian ariballos, a red-figure kantharos—eight beautiful, rare, valuable objects, for each of which the documentation in the Freeport was the same: photographs of the antiquities at various stages of their journey from the ground of Italy to display in the Getty, from dirty and encrusted fragments to the restored and polished ensembles that the public sees in the showcases. The pattern was consistent for all of the forty-two objects the Getty acquired (see the Dossier for a full list).

Every single one of these forty-two antiquities was important, in the sense that they were all by definition of museum quality. Some of the vase shapes were unique, the only known examples of their kind; all were by major vase painters and were valued collectively at millions of dollars. Between 1983 and 2000, the Getty published six volumes of *Greek Vases in the J. Paul Getty Museum*, which purported to be a reputable academic publication. In fact, it was an ostensibly reputable academic publication that dealt in considerable detail with loot. There is probably no equivalent in the history of antiquities scholarship that has so betrayed its high ideals.

One of the most important objects in the Getty, which Medici handled and which reveals most about the activities of the Los Angeles museum in this field, was a splendid red-figure Attic kylix, made between 490 and 480 BC by Euphronios and decorated by Onesimos. Because these two artists were among the greatest known in the ancient world, this kylix is, therefore, directly comparable to the krater acquired by the Metropolitan Museum in New York in 1972 (see the Prologue). The subject of the Metropolitan's Euphronios vase was the death of Sarpedon. In this myth, taken from Homer's *Iliad*, Sarpedon, a hero of the Trojan War, is killed by the spear of an enemy warrior. The subject of the Getty's Euphronios-Onesimos kylix is a related theme, Iliupersis, or the sack of Troy, the central event in the Trojan War, and there are many scenes from this episode on Greek vases. The Italians had had their eye on the kylix for some time.

As Pellegrini pieced together the story, it emerged that the Getty had acquired the cup, in fragments, over a number of years in the 1980s. These fragments, it was said in the documents, were bought "on the European art market" and were published in the *Getty Museum Journal* as well as in *Greek Vases in the J. Paul Getty Museum*, which went through several volumes. By studying these publications, Pellegrini and others in Italy were able to establish that the first nucleus of fragments was bought in 1983, with others added in 1984 and 1985. In 1991, Dyfri Williams, head of the Greek and Roman Department of the British Museum and a noted expert on Attic ceramics, published the kylix in volume five of *Greek Vases*. Among other things, he said in an addendum that, in November 1990, he had seen a photograph of another fragment of the kylix. He said that this other fragment formed part of the edge of the vessel and was itself divided into three pieces. All this was, let us say, *untidy*. If three fragments existed—somewhere—and had been photographed, why were they not in the Getty *with* the rest of the object? What was going on?

Some light was thrown on the situation in 1993, when, in an official excavation, the Archaeological Superintendency for Southern Etruria discovered an impressive building for a cult in the S. Antonio area of Cerveteri. The cult was dedicated to Hercules and it was as certain as could be that the kylix (if not the Metropolitan's krater) had come from there. For a start, there was writing on the kylix that suggested this: a dedication, in Etruscan, to "Ercle," the Etruscan form of "Hercules."

Following this discovery, the Italians began to put pressure on the Getty to return the kylix, but the seizure of the Medici material in Geneva closed this particular circle. For among the photographs seized in Corridor

17, there was a whole raft of incriminating material. There was, to begin with, a color photograph of the *tondo*, the central round fragment that formed the base of the cup. There were also professional black-and-white photographs of the same piece, which may have been used to propose the object to the museum. Then there was a photograph of the last fragment that the Getty acquired and of the fragment(s) that the Getty never purchased but which Dyfri Williams wrote about. Finally, there was a photograph of the restored kylix *with* the last fragments that had reached the Getty. What was especially revealing about the Polaroid of the tondo was some writing on the margin, which read: "Prop. P. G. M." The object had been "Proposed to the Paul Getty Museum."

Then, and finally, to settle any doubt in the matter, Pellegrini discovered in Geneva a letter that Marion True wrote to Medici in January 1992, the main point of which was to thank him for the donation of a kouros head mentioned above (the one that "proved" the Becchina kouros was a fake). On the second page of this letter, True added: "I am enclosing, with this letter, with my compliments, a copy of Greek Vases 5. I hope that you enjoy it. I think that you will find many pieces included that you will recognize." *Greek Vases 5*, of course, contained the article by Dyfri Williams on the Euphronios-Onesimos kylix, with the note that he had seen a photograph of extra fragments.

Armed with this fresh documentary evidence, coming on top of the discovery of the cult building dedicated to Hercules in Cerveteri, not to mention evidence of the gradual acquisition of the fragments throughout the 1980s, the Italians now put still more pressure on the Getty. In the first instance, the museum was forced to open up its files and make their documentation available to the public prosecutor, Dr. Ferri. He also sent an international rogatory asking for all the museum papers on the forty-two objects that Pellegrini had identified, together with any documentation concerning a number of named individuals: Robert Hecht, Fritz and Harry Bürki, Robin Symes, Frida Tchacos, and of course Giacomo Medici. He also asked that the premises and offices of Marion True be searched and any relevant documentation surrendered. This latter request was not granted.

When they arrived in Italy, the Getty papers showed that the central part of the kylix—the tondo—had been acquired from the Galerie Nefer in Zurich, the gallery owned by Frida Tchacos-Nussberger. When questioned later, she said she had bought the tondo from Nino Savoca in Munich. According to the Getty paperwork, other fragments were allegedly acquired from the S. Schweitzer Collection, of Arlesheim, an old and mysterious Swiss collection often used to provide a false provenance for objects, because it had been donated to the state more than thirty years before and was difficult to cross-check. (Many museums in North America have a few items from this collection.) Still more fragments of the kylix were purchased from the Hydra Gallery in 1985 and originated, according to Boursaud, in the "Zbinden Collection." All this was disingenuous, yet more examples of triangulation, and nowhere more obvious than in the case of the Zbinden Collection. This is because, according to documents later supplied to Ferri and Pellegrini by Sotheby's, and unknown to the Getty and Boursaud, "Zbinden" often sold material at auction together with Boursaud. They were so close that they had the *same* account number with Sotheby's. This was yet more dissimulation and triangulation to protect Medici's involvement with the kylix.

Faced with this mountain of evidence, the Getty was forced to bow to the inevitable, and in February 1999, it did the decent thing and returned the Euphronious-Onesimos kylix to Italy. It may now be seen, on display, at the Villa Giulia Museum in Rome.

Medici also bowed to the inevitable. Knowing that the game was up, knowing what incriminating evidence was contained in the documentation that had been seized, he surrendered three more fragments of the kylix, three that fitted together to make one piece (as Dyfri Williams had exactly described them in his *Greek Vases* article), and which Medici had in his possession. He told the authorities that he was returning them "out of love for his country."

This episode had a happy ending—in a way. Ferri, Pellegrini, and Rizzo put the value of the Euphronios-Onesimos kylix at about $5 million. But it is even now not complete: There are some fragments still out there and the prosecutor is still looking for more.

One final set of objects—and their associated documentation—reveals the close links, even intimacy, between the Getty and Medici. On April

29, 1987, in a handwritten letter, on the headed notepaper of "Atlantis Antiquities, 40 East 69th Street, NY, NY 10021," was written:

> Received in commission for resale from Giacomo Medici at the price of $2,000,000.— (two million dollars) less 5% commission, payable to Mr. Medici after receipt of any payment from the J. Paul Getty Museum:
>
> 1) 20 Attic red figure plates ca. 490–480 BC
> 2) Various attic red figure fragments ca. 490–480 BC
>
> The above named objects have been delivered to the J. Paul Getty Museum with a receipt to Atlantis Antiquities, but are the property of Mr. Giacomo Medici.
>
> Geneva, Switzerland

It was dated and signed by Robert E. Hecht, Jr.

On the same day, John Caswell, associate registrar of the Getty, and Hecht jointly signed a loan agreement for "one year from the date of arrival," between Atlantis Antiquities and the museum, for three sets of objects. The loan agreement made it clear that the three sets of objects were twenty plates by the Bryn Mawr Painter, thirty-five fragments of a red-figure calyx krater by the Berlin Painter, and nine "Miscellaneous" fragments, though all were dated "ca. 500–490 BC/ ca. 490–480 BC." The entire group was insured for $2 million.

These plates were the same ones that had been found in Geneva, sequestered in the safe in Medici's outer office on Corridor 17. Besides the objects themselves, however, elsewhere in the warehouse three sets of photographs were also found relating to these objects. In the first set of photographs the plates were shown before restoration; they were in fragments. Each fragment was a few inches square, and it is hard to tell how beautiful or valuable they are, at least from the photographs. A second set showed the plates in the process of restoration. There were some gaps, but the figures on them can be identified. Third, the same plates were again photographed when their restoration had been completed. Pellegrini's conclusion was that this third set of photographs was the one that had been used for the presentation to the Getty, because there was a tag attached to one of the photographs, valuing them in shorthand at $2 million.

On this occasion, John Walsh, the director of the Getty, thought that it was an inappropriate use of museum funds to spend $2 million on so many works all by the same painter, and the plates were therefore sent back. Here too the transaction was revealing. The plates were returned not to Hecht, as the loan file in the museum showed the proprietor to be, but to Medici, the owner as Hecht's written note identified. The shipping receipts, kept by Medici and seized in Geneva, show that the plates arrived at the Freeport in December 1987. Medici kept the shipping documentation, opportunistic as ever, for use later as a provenance, to suggest that the plates originated from the United States, should he be able to sell them later on.

In fact, of course, the plates almost certainly came from Cerveteri. They are of such a quality and made on such a scale that if they *had* been excavated on an official dig, either recently or in the distant past, their importance is such that they would have been extensively written up, published, displayed, and discussed. The fact that the first set of photographs were Polaroids and showed the plates in fragments, and then being gradually restored, also confirms that they had come to light recently, having been previously in the ground.

Two other documents confirm the triangulation at work in this instance. Although the plates were notionally offered—loaned—to the Getty by Hecht-Atlantis, which is what appeared in the loan card (the Getty sent the Italian authorities no official documentation because they hadn't acquired the plates), they were also the subject of the two letters that Marion True wrote to Medici in June 1987, one in Italian, the other in English. On June 10, in Italian, she wrote:

Dear Mr. Giacomo, I am sorry to have to inform you that we cannot purchase the 20 plates at the moment on loan to the museum. I have spoken to the director who carefully examined the plates and has decided it is not opportune to purchase them now, for the following reason: the plates are all by the same artist and for a collection like ours it is preferable to spend 2 million dollars purchasing vases by different artists. I tried to convince the director of the uniqueness of this collection but he remained of the opinion not to purchase them.

On June 26, in English, she wrote:

I am terribly sorry about the plates myself, and I do hope that you will understand that the decision was certainly not mine. This is the first time that John has actually refused something that I have proposed. I should have mentioned the Berlin Painter fragments in my letter; naturally, we will return them with the plates as they were part of the Agreement. . . .

Evidently, as far as the Getty Museum is concerned, Medici was responsible for forty-two antiquities that the museum acquired, *all* illicitly looted from Italy and smuggled abroad, under his direction. In none of these cases is Medici's name mentioned in the official documentation that the museum keeps, but in the great majority, museum personnel—Marion True above all—must have been well aware of the origin of these pieces, as revealed by these letters to Medici. The tone of these letters, incidentally, is affectionate and almost intimate, as well it might be, considering what was going on. She is amazingly open in their correspondence. Medici seems never to have anticipated being raided in Geneva and perhaps True never imagined her correspondence with him would ever be seen by third parties. One of her letters, dated January 1992 and again written to him in Geneva, reads:

I was also very grateful to have the information on the provenance of our three fragmentary proto-Corinthian olpai [an *olpe*—plural *olpai*—is a medium-sized, single-handled wine jug]. To know that they came from Cerveteri and the area of Monte Abatone is very helpful to the research of one of my staff members. . . .

I intend to be in Rome together [with] John Walsh on February 19th through the 23rd. I will be back in Rome again from March 8th through approximately March 12th. During one of these visits, I hope that we will be able to get together and have some further discussion about future acquisitions.

It is hard to escape the conclusion, therefore, that the triangulations that Pellegrini identified were intended to protect the museum. If, for example, we did not have the material—and above all, the photographs—seized at

Medici's warehouse in Geneva, but just had the Getty internal documentation, it would only be shown that the museum had acquired a number of objects, mainly through the European market, over a number of years. The fact that the "European market" turned out to be mainly, but not exclusively, Swiss dealers would be suspicious to anyone knowledgeable about the traffic in illicit antiquities, but it would not amount to proof of anything, as is shown by the fact that the Getty maintained this acquisitions policy for so many years.

But the Medici documents now remove all doubts on this score. The J. Paul Getty Museum in Los Angeles is stuffed with loot, illegally excavated antiquities smuggled out of Italy. What is more, senior personnel know this, and have known it for many years. And they saw to it that the trade was so organized as to keep the museum's image "clean." The Getty well deserves the nickname that one of the dealers used during interrogation later in Dr. Ferri's inquiry. She said that the Getty was known in the Swiss trade as the "Museum of the *Tombaroli*."

In some ways, by getting involved with the antiquities underworld—the Medici conspiracy—the Getty Museum made a rod for its own back. The most obvious example is with the so-called Getty kouros. This was bought from Becchina, but the fake that was sent to the museum to *prove* that the kouros was not authentic was volunteered by Medici. Was he really trying to be helpful to the Getty, or was he settling old scores with Becchina? In dealing with such people as Becchina and Medici, how can one ever be certain—of anything? Medici claimed that *his* fake shared certain features with Becchina's kouros—but does that make the kouros fake? Who can be trusted when the cordate are bitter rivals?

8

The Metropolitan in New York

and Other Rogue Museums

THE GETTY MUSEUM IS A RELATIVELY new institution, but the same cannot be said about the Metropolitan Museum of Art in New York, which traces its origins to a Fourth of July party held in the Bois de Boulogne in Paris in 1866, when John Jay, a lawyer and grandson of the first chief justice of the U.S. Supreme Court, declared to fellow New Yorkers at the table that it was time for the American people to found their own gallery of art. The charter of the Metropolitan Museum was approved by the New York State legislature in 1870, and the building was inaugurated in 1880.

The museum has some notable coups to its credit. J. P. Morgan, the banker and financier who made a practice of collecting other men's collections, had an active association with the Metropolitan. Through him, and through Roger Fry, the scholar and art historian whom Morgan hired, the Met made some outstanding purchases: Leonardo da Vinci's *Head of an Old Man*, Renoir's *Madame Charpentier and Her Children*, and other masterpieces by Andrea del Sarto, Giovanni Bellini, and Botticelli. Benjamin Altman left his Rembrandt and Limoges enamels to the museum. In 1961, the Met paid a record $2.3 million for Rembrandt's *Aristotle Contemplating the Bust of Homer*, and in 1970 it acquired Velázquez's *Juan de la Pareja*, for a price that must have exceeded the £2.2 million that the Wildenstein Gallery had paid at auction shortly before.

From time to time, the museum has associated itself with lofty sentiments. Philippe de Montebello, the current director of the Metropolitan, lectures widely to groups across the United States, giving a talk titled, "Museums: Why Should We Care?" His lecture prospectus reads:

In the midst of global turmoil, why is art important? Is it indispensable? Does it bring order to the world? Does it give us the ultimate assurance of renewal and survival? How does one explain the sense of outrage and loss expressed by people worldwide over the destruction of treasures in Afghanistan and the subsequent looting in Baghdad? . . . In this new lecture . . . Mr. De Montebello . . . shows us how art is a tangible vestige of past civilizations. . . .

Given those sentiments and the museum's distinguished history, it is doubly regrettable that in the field of antiquities, the Metropolitan's record has been dismal. In fact, as the Euphronios krater affair showed, the Metropolitan's behavior on occasions can be positively lamentable. And it is not as if the Euphronios affair was an isolated case. When it comes to antiquities, the Metropolitan seems to lose its head.

The first noteworthy episode concerned the so-called Bury St. Edmunds Cross. This was an exquisitely carved ivory cross, a little less than two feet tall and just over a foot wide, and covered with tiny Romanesque figures and inscriptions in Latin and Greek. It was allegedly dated to the twelfth century, though there were scholars who doubted its authenticity. The cross appeared on the international art market, in a bank vault in Zurich, as early as the mid-1950s, but Thomas Hoving saw it in 1961, by which time it was already on offer to the British Museum for £200,000. The British Museum delayed, however, because it was concerned about whether the man offering the cross really had good title to it. His name was Ante Topic-Mimara and he was said to be a "former Tito partisan," a politically active Yugoslav, though according to two German journalists of *Der Spiegel*, Topic, alias Mimara, had been head of the Yugoslav intelligence services in Germany and then, because he was a "museum custodian" by profession, had become a member of the Yugoslav Restitution and Reparations Commission in the U.S. Zone. He therefore had wide access to artworks in the process of being returned to their rightful owners after World War II.

The British Museum asked Topic-Mimara to warrant that he had full title to the cross he was offering to sell, but this was something he steadfastly refused to do. In fact, he always refused to say where he had gotten the cross and for this reason the British Museum deal fell through. One evening, Hoving sat up drinking coffee with Topic-Mimara until, as midnight passed, the deadline expired. Thereupon, he paid over the $500,000-plus that was then the equivalent of £200,000, and the cross went to the Met.

The second episode, and conceivably the most outrageous antiquities acquisition of the Met, was that of the Lydian Hoard. In 1966, the museum had bought a treasure of gold, silver, bronze, and earthenware objects and wall paintings for $500,000 from the wealthy New York dealer J. J. Klejman, who said he had acquired it earlier from "ignorant" itinerant traders in Europe. He claimed the collection had been mixed with "junk" and was bought in at least two different European cities. Yet archaeologists who were able to see the treasure identified it as coming from ancient Lydia—the western part of modern-day Turkey, and the location of the kingdom of Croesus (as in "rich as Croesus")—and they believed it to represent the contents of four entire tombs that had been looted near Sardis where, as it happened, Harvard University archaeologists were conducting a legitimate excavation. The hoard sat in the basement of the museum, largely unseen except when Dietrich von Bothmer allowed in a few favored visitors. At one point, he and Hoving placed five silver vessels into an exhibition, wrongly labeled as "Greek," but no one noticed and they were returned to the basement.

Inside the museum, however, a memorandum was being circulated. Addressed to President C. Douglas Dillon, Director Hoving, Chief Curator Theodore Rousseau, and von Bothmer, it was written by Oscar White Muscarella, associate curator in the Department of Near Eastern Art (the man who complained about the acquisition of the Euphronios krater), and it was a passionate appeal against the destruction of burial mounds and against the purchase and display of objects lacking a scientific and secure provenance. Muscarella warned that if the museum were to risk exhibiting certain objects in its possession, it might trigger reprisals, "drastic action" against Western archaeologists in certain Middle Eastern countries. He also let it be known that a Turkish journalist had expressed to him an interest in inspecting the objects in the museum's basement.

The Turks knew that *tumuli* (tombs) in the Uşak region of west-central Anatolia had been broken into and looted by villagers. A number of objects were recovered by local police and the tomb robbers interviewed. Rumors about the Metropolitan's acquisitions began to circulate in the early 1970s, but although the Met's own documents reveal that the museum recognized the objects as among its greatest acquisitions, the purchase of the collection—essentially intact—was not announced. It was not until some of the pieces were put on permanent display in 1984, as part of the museum's so-called East Greek Treasure, that Turkish scholars were able to conclude that the objects *were* those looted from the Uşak tomb. At first the Turks tried to reach a negotiated solution, but their approach was summarily rebuffed. Later the museum tried to resist legal action by the Republic of Turkey, arguing in court that the statute of limitations had expired. This caused a three-year delay in litigation, but after that time the Met's arguments were denied and a trial was ordered. During the discovery process, the internal Met documents that were produced were damning. The most shocking were those of the Acquisitions Committee in connection with the second of the museum's three principal purchases, which noted, among other things, that the objects being acquired were said to come from the same part of Anatolia as those "acquired earlier." Another key aspect of the discovery process was the opportunity afforded to Turkish and American archaeologists to inspect at first hand the treasures in the Met's basement. Archaeologists who were familiar with the objects recovered from the tombs in Turkey were allowed to examine, close-up, the vast array of jewelry, ancient tools, wall paintings, silver oinochoe, and marble sphinxes. Among other things, from the measurements they took, they were able to match some of the frescoes in the museum basement to particular holes left on the walls of some of the tombs in Turkey.

Faced with such incontrovertible evidence, at the end of 1993 the museum caved in and agreed to return the treasure to Turkey without a formal trial. The treasure was returned the following year. But the way the museum had fought this case on a technicality and the fact that its own documents showed it was willing to acquire the objects even when its acquisitions committee knew it was loot left a bad taste. As one individual involved remarked, it was as if those at the Met were behaving like "pirates."

There is *still* a bad taste in many people's mouths in regard to a different hoard, this time a collection of fifteen pieces of almost priceless

Roman silver looted from an important site in Sicily in Italy. The silver includes beautifully decorated bowls, a silver ladle, two silver horns, and a magnificent gilt-silver emblem featuring classical gods in bas-relief. This unique silver is valued in the region of $100 million. The Italian government wants the silver returned, but the Metropolitan, for years, refused to recognize the Italians' claim, which was backed up by information from a Mafia "snitch" and by the discoveries of a well-known American archaeologist.

The Met took delivery of the first eight silver and gilt objects in May 1981, to be followed exactly a year later, in May 1982, by six more. The silver, said an official of the museum at the time, came originally from Turkey and had been legally imported from Switzerland. The pieces were published in the museum's own *Bulletin* in the summer of 1984.

Having studied the 1984 bulletin, the Italian archaeological and law enforcement authorities became more and more convinced that the silver had been illegally excavated and smuggled not from Turkey but from Sicily. Conforti felt so strongly about this that he had a series of "Wanted" postcards made, one of which depicted some of the silver pieces. Others in the series depicted the so-called Morgantina Venus and the Acrolytes at the Getty (an acrolyte is the marble head—or hands, or feet—added to a statue). Each was laid out like an old-fashioned Wild West "Wanted" poster, reflecting Conforti's opinion of the morality of certain U.S. museums. His conviction was supported by information obtained by a Sicilian magistrate who, while investigating another case entirely, received the confession of one of the accused, a mafioso called Giuseppe Mascara. Mascara, who had decided to turn informer, described himself as "head" of the Sicilian tombaroli. He confessed that he himself had seen and tried to buy the silver in question but had not managed to clinch the deal. According to him, the Morgantina treasure had ended up on the U.S. market.

Morgantina, with its beautiful Greek theater, its colonnaded temples, and acres of ruins, is a classical site dating from the third to the second century BC, situated in the very heart of Sicily, in the province of Enna.

When faced with Mascara's accusation, the Met responded through its vice president (and in-house lawyer), Ashton Hawkins, that it was "perplexed" that the Italians should rely on the testimony of a mafioso, guilty of other crimes. The Italians countered that the Americans ought to know from their own experience that when a mafioso decides to turn state's witness, he has nothing to gain and everything to lose by lying.

Then, in 1997 Professor Malcolm Bell entered the story. Bell, professor of archaeology at the University of Virginia, had been excavating at Morgantina for many years. He arrived at the conclusion that the silver in the Metropolitan Museum came originally from Morgantina because of two pieces of archaeological evidence he discovered. In the first instance, he found a coin that, in style, decoration, and silver content, he says came "from the same nucleus" as the silver in the Metropolitan.

In July 1997, he was asked by the Archaeological Superintendency for Enna, instigated by Dr. Raffiotta, to dig at Morgantina once again, this time in specific areas of Aidone indicated by the mafia "snitch" as possible sites for the provenance of the silver. There Bell discovered a house, already looted by tomb robbers, with two holes in the floor where he believes the silver was hidden: "When the Romans conquered Morgantina, a city already at the time famed for the quantity of its art works, the population panicked and many masterpieces were buried or hidden in cisterns or deep crevices." The two separate holes, says Bell, would explain why the silver was brought to the market in two different lots.

Back in 1993, Bell had applied to the Met for permission to examine the silver, but strangely enough, and contrary to their usual courtesy toward senior scholars, the Met had categorically refused. Now, after Bell's new discoveries, the Italians insisted that the Met allow him to examine the silver. Later, the FBI, as part of a new agreement between the United States and Italy, which guarantees that Americans will not be allowed to import illegally excavated material, said it would put its secure labs at Bell's disposal for the examination. Again the Met refused, describing Bell as "biased" and his arguments as "untrustworthy." Its spokesman said that it could not be proved that the silver came "exclusively" from Morgantina. Once again, stalemate. The FBI offer was not taken up.

Finally, however, and with the ignominious return of the Lydian treasure to Turkey in mind, the Met relented and in the spring and summer of 1999, Bell was allowed to examine the silver. The occasion produced its own drama. On four of the silver objects he read the name "Eupolemos," a name already found in Morgantina. The Met's Greek and Roman expert, Dietrich von Bothmer, had translated these inscriptions rather differently. The inscription, which von Bothmer interpreted as meaning "from the war," was based on his reading of the relevant part of Greek as "ΕΚΠΟΛΕΜΟΥ" Instead, in Bell's opinion, the letters read, "ΕΥΠΟΛΕΜΟΥ," one character different, but critically different, because it means the genitive case of the name Eupolemos, which translates as: "Of Eupolemos."

Although the Met, when it first acquired the silver, announced that the pieces came from Turkey, the Turks have never claimed it, despite their success over the Lydian hoard. Moreover, the Carabinieri Art Squad pieced together the chain of events since the silver left the ground. This information was made available by the Carabinieri at a special conference on the illicit traffic held at the McDonald Institute for Archaeological Research at the University of Cambridge, England, in 2000. The route was as follows: Vincenzo Bozzi and Filippo Baviera, tombaroli in Enna, sold the silver for 110 million lire ($27,000) to Orazio Di Simone, a Sicilian middleman based in Lugano in Switzerland, who sold it for $875,000 to Robert Hecht, who sold the silver to the Metropolitan Museum for $3 million. A not unfamiliar sequence.

Given these antecedents, perhaps we should not be surprised to find that the Metropolitan consorted with Medici almost as often as the Getty did.

There can be little doubt about this, for Maurizio Pellegrini found almost exactly the same kind of paper trail leading from Medici to the Met as he had found with the Getty. The evidence was there, in the Polaroids and other photographs seized in the Geneva Freeport. Antiquities would first be photographed while they were dirty and in fragments, before restoration. Then they would be restored, photographed again, sold to the Met—again through one or other of the various "front" outfits—and, finally, Medici would visit New York and have himself photographed with "his" object on display. Pellegrini isolated this paper trail in seven cases.

The first case concerned a red-figure Attic amphora. This was first shown dirty and unrestored in one of the photographs seized in Geneva. Another seized photograph showed the same object, now restored, on display in a case in the Met. A second instance relates to a Laconian kylix, which is depicted in the Polaroids as being made up of fragments with many gaps. A separate photograph shows the same object, now restored, in its showcase in the museum on Fifth Avenue. The third case concerns an oinochoe in the shape of a Negro's head. It too is shown in a Polaroid, and in a separate photograph appears in its showcase in the museum. Fourth, a red-figure Apulian *dinos*, attributed to the Darius Painter, was found in the photographs seized in Geneva. A *dinos*, also known as a *lebes*, is a deep bowl, usually rounded at the bottom so that it has to be set on a stand. It was used as a container, or for cooking or, when made of bronze, as a prize in athletic games. One set of photos shows this red-figure dinos in fragments; a second set shows it partially restored—with the fragments reassembled but the joins still visible; a third set shows the dinos, now fully restored, on display in its showcase at the Met.

Photographs of a red-figure psykter with figures on horseback were also among those seized in Geneva. One shows several fragments partially restored, but still with gaps. A separate fragment was photographed on its own. This object, too, was bought by the Met.

Then there were the photographs of a red-figure Attic amphora by the Berlin Painter. Among the photographs seized was one showing this in the early stages of restoration, with the fragments crudely assembled but with many gaps. A second photograph shows the amphora after complete restoration, "in near perfect conservative condition thanks to expert restoration which completely eliminated the traces of breakage." It too was shown in its showcase in the museum.

The seventh example is, of course, the Euphronios vase, discussed in the Prologue. Among the photographs seized in Geneva was one that appears from a covering note to have been taken in May 1987, when Medici was in New York. This photograph shows Giacomo Medici himself, standing proudly next to a large krater, showing the death of Sarpedon. It is indeed the Euphronios krater, and Medici's proud pose, with chest out, chin thrust forward, depicts him as a victor, as having won some kind of race or contest. There is no mistaking the message. A second photograph shows Robert Hecht on the same occasion next to the same object. Why were these photographs taken? Pellegrini, Conforti, and Ferri all realized that, by themselves, these images didn't constitute *proof* of anything. Taken in context, however, alongside all the other photographs—at the Met, at the Getty, and at other museums—in which Medici liked to be photographed with "his" objects, it was extremely revealing, and damning.

This does not complete the case against the Met. There were other tantalizing documents found in Geneva that provided more questions than answers. For example, there was an air-mail envelope, stamped December 14, 1990. At top left was the name and address of the Metropolitan, "1000 Fifth Avenue, NY NY 10028-0198," and typed below, Medici's name and address in Switzerland. Pellegrini never found out what had been in this envelope. As with the Getty, the Metropolitan had a very close relationship with certain antiquities collectors whose holdings were also stuffed with loot. As with the Getty, the Met associated itself with these collectors, adding the institution's considerable prestige to the collection, when it must have known that the objects it was putting on display had been illegally dug up and smuggled out of Italy.

Although the extent of the Getty's acquisitions earned it the title among the initiated of the "Museum of the *Tombaroli*," and although the Met's acquisition of the Euphronios krater and its behavior over the Lydian hoard and the Morgantina silver earned it the special opprobrium of the Turks and the Italians, these two museums were by no means the only ones that Medici and the rest of his network dealt with. It was impossible for Pellegrini to check all the documentation seized at the Geneva Freeport since many objects acquired and displayed in the world's museums are never published, so that good images, dimensions, and other details are not available for study and comparison. Nevertheless, some incriminating details are in the public domain.

According to Pellegrini, Medici was the origin of quite a few objects in the Ny Carlsberg Glyptotek in Copenhagen. Just two give a flavor. The first is made up of two antefixes showing Maenades and Silenus. An antefix was a roof decoration in antiquity, usually an upright ornament, and it was intended to conceal the joints between rows of tiles and to protect the gaps from the weather. A maenades was a female satyr, and a silenus a male one.¹ These antefixes, which are now in several museums of the world, not just Copenhagen, are much better than anything in the Villa Giulia, for example, and all appear in the Polaroids seized in the Geneva Freeport. The fact that the antefixes in Copenhagen and the Getty, and in Medici's Polaroids, show the ceramics to have been burned in part, may indicate that the temple was attacked or abandoned, possibly an important event in antiquity that, now, we shall probably never know anything about.

The second set of documents relates to parts of an Etruscan chariot— in particular, some incised bas-relief plates with sleeping lions, together with parts of the bridles and the wheels. The documentation shows that Medici sold these to Robert Hecht, possibly in the 1970s, for $67,000. Hecht then sold them on to the Copenhagen museum for 1.2 million Swiss francs (approximately $900,000).

Pellegrini's detective work also showed that in terms of sheer numbers, the Museum for Classical Antiquities in Berlin was just as bad as the Met. From the photographs found in Medici's possession in Geneva, there was a series of seven vases that originated with him that were acquired by Berlin.²

Robert Hecht, in highly unusual and revealing circumstances, subsequently admitted to having sold looted material to several other museums besides the ones considered so far. These others include the Glyptotek in Munich, the Museum of Fine Arts in Boston, the Cleveland Museum in Ohio, the Harvard Museum system in Cambridge, Massachusetts, the Campbell's Soup Museum in Camden, New Jersey, the Toledo Museum of Art in Ohio, the Louvre in Paris, and (once) the British Museum in London. We do not have the same level of detail for these acquisitions as we do for the acquisitions reported so far, but we see no reason to doubt what Hecht says: Most of the material he placed with these museums came from Medici (or possibly Becchina), in which case it will, almost certainly, consist of loot. At the same time, in the absence of detailed internal documentation from these museums, it is unclear who knew what and at what time in these institutions concerning the origin of these items.

You might think that it would be good practice for the network of dealers that surrounded Medici, based as it was in Switzerland, to steer clear of Swiss museums when it came to trading in illicit goods. Not at all. The head of archaeology at the Geneva Art and History Museum, Jacques Chamay, for instance, was involved with the Medici vases sold to Berlin.

Furthermore, from the material seized in Geneva, but in this case also from additional material seized at Medici's homes in Santa Marinella, north of Rome, and from his apartment in Geneva, the Carabinieri discovered that Medici received assistance from an unusual source. She was Fiorella Cottier-Angeli, a Swiss archaeologist who, ostensibly, worked for Swiss customs. It was she who, beginning in 1980 and continuing certainly until Medici's trial in 2003, authenticated thousands of objects. Acting in an official capacity, it was her job to issue certificates of authenticity and provide evaluations for tax purposes should the objects be imported permanently into Switzerland. She also issued *passavant* documents, essentially temporary import certificates that enabled, for example, an antiquity to be restored at the Bürkis' Zurich laboratory and then returned to the Freeport without requiring any payment of duty. In the first instance, Pellegrini found that some of her descriptions of objects were so vague that one could never be certain that the object returned to the Freeport was the same as the one that had left. Her expertise enabled Medici to show that the objects he was dealing in were genuine and not fakes. It seems she must have turned a blind eye to where these objects were coming from. The fact that these antiquities—or most of them—were genuine satisfied the Swiss concern that the Freeport might be being used in some sort of widespread antiquities faking operation. But of course Cottier-Angeli's certificates of authenticity doubly suited Medici because, besides authenticating the objects, she provided documentary proof that the objects had been in Switzerland, and exported from there, ostensibly legally.

Over the years, however, Cottier-Angeli became rather more than a consultant on behalf of Swiss customs. Frida Tchacos told Ferri that Cottier-Angeli had the keys to Medici's warehouses and that she herself was dealing in objects acquired from him. (Cottier-Angeli later denied this.) Among the documents, for instance, Pellegrini found an envelope marked "111," inside which was a small handwritten exercise book "in which Medici indicates a deposit (in the sense of a warehouse) in which two objects were being kept—a bronze candelabrum with a youth and a small pig, and a stamnos attributed to Kleophon." Elsewhere in the documents, Pellegrini found a photograph of a candelabrum with the same subject (a youth and a small pig), bearing the words: *"venduto C.A."* ("sold C.A.")— C.A. here being Cottier-Angeli. The same candelabrum was depicted in the photographs relating to the inventory of the Hydra Gallery during the 1986 proceedings, drawn up by the law firm of Piguet.* In Medici's note-books, many objects were sold to "Madame," a term that was inter-changeable with "C.A."

The closeness of the relationship is further underlined by the fact that Pellegrini found that Cottier-Angeli was a member of the scientific direc-tors for an exhibition held in Jerusalem in 1991, titled Italy of the Etr-uscans. She was listed in the catalog as one of the organizers for this exhibition, and she contributed to the text. Pellegrini established that var-ious objects displayed in Jerusalem were once in Medici's possession. Sev-eral of them are to be found in the seized photographs, many in a state prior to restoration. Once again, among these objects is a bronze cande-labrum, with a youth and small pig, where it is indicated as belonging to a Swiss collection, "A. P." This, Pellegrini discovered, refers to Alain Patry, a man who audits the accounts for the "Hellas et Roma" Associa-tion in Geneva. This association was founded by Cottier-Angeli, and its coordinator is—or was then—Pierre Cottier, her husband. A second exam-ple concerned an exhibition, Homère chez Calvin (Homer in the Land of Calvin), held at the Art and History Museum in Geneva in 2000–2001, cosponsored by the Municipal Department for Cultural Affairs of the City of Geneva, and the "Hellas et Roma" Association. Among the illustra-tions in the catalog of this exhibition is a photograph of an Apulian chal-ice-krater showing an episode from the Trojan War, a scene outside the walls of Troy, with many episodes of battle, men with shields and spears, and women watching. The caption lists the krater as belonging to a Swiss private collection, yet this same object is depicted in the photographs seized from Medici, where it is shown in fragments before being restored.

This is enough about the exhibition at the Art and History Museum in Geneva for the moment. But as with the Getty, as with the Met, as with the German museums, we are not yet quite finished with Fiorella Cottier-Angeli or Jacques Chamay.

*See p. 73.

9

"COLLECTORS ARE THE REAL LOOTERS"

IN 1993, RICARDO ELIA, an archaeologist from Boston University, wrote a book review in the pages of *Archaeology* magazine, the forum of the Archaeological Institute of America, the institution to which most U.S.-based professional archaeologists belong. The review was titled "A Seductive and Troubling Work," and its subject was a catalog that had just been published, *The Cycladic Spirit: Masterpieces from the Nicholas P. Goulandris Collection,* by Colin Renfrew, Disney Professor of Archaeology at Cambridge University in England. Cambridge boasts the oldest archaeology department of any university in Western Europe or North America, and Colin Renfrew was (and is) probably the greatest archaeologist of his generation.

Born in 1937, Renfrew is the author of at least three seminal works in archaeology. The first was *The Emergence of Civilisation,* an examination of the Cyclades in the third millennium BC, which challenged accepted notions of how civilization developed. The second was *Before Civilisation,* an analysis of the radiocarbon revolution in the subject, which challenged the assumption that prehistoric cultural innovation originated in the Near East and then spread to Western Europe. And the third was *Archaeology and Language,* which examined the notion of whether there has ever been a "mother tongue," a proto-language spoken by most of mankind's early peoples, before the evolution of the languages we speak today.

Renfrew was made a member of the House of Lords in Britain in 1991 and so was, without question, just about as distinguished and successful as an archaeologist could be. Nonetheless, in "A Seductive and Troubling Work," the much younger Ricardo Elia criticized him—and criticized him robustly. In his review, Elia's argument was drawn from the fact that Renfrew had lent his considerable name to a collection of Cycladic antiquities in which *none* of the objects had any secure provenance whatsoever. Renfrew, Elia said, had written about the collection as a jewel, as a wonderful aspect of Cycladic art—and yet, archaeologically speaking, it had no meaning. Because these objects had been looted, no one could have any real idea which island they had come from, what age they were, what their function was, what their relationship was to one another, whether they had been painted over in antiquity, and so on. For Elia, the Goulandris Collection barely deserved the name: It was booty rather than a proper collection, which ought to tell us as much as possible about the past. He regretted that a distinguished professor had lent his name and prestige to such an enterprise. "Collectors," he said, "cause looting by creating a market demand for antiquities. Looting, in turn, causes forgeries, since forgeries can only remain undetected where there is a substantial corpus of antiquities without proper archaeological provenance. These two problems—looting and forgery—fundamentally corrupt the integrity of the field of ancient art history." Elia ended his review with a phrase that was to cause much controversy, but would stick. "The truth is," he said, "Collectors are the Real Looters." Without their money, and their demand, there would be no market.

No one likes being criticized, but Renfrew took Elia's attack in good humor—and on the chin. He replied in the next issue of *Archaeology*, and in doing so he substantially accepted Elia's point. He agreed that in lending his credibility to the Goulandris Collection, he had, however inadvertently and indirectly, added to the risk that more antiquities would be looted, because collectors would believe that they could gain—socially, intellectually, financially—by becoming involved in such affairs. He added: "I was certainly shocked, on visiting the exhibition of the collection of Leon Levy and Shelby White at the Metropolitan Museum of Art in New York a couple of years ago, to find the most extraordinary treasure store of looted antiquities from all over the Ancient World."

It took Renfrew a while, but having familiarized himself with the problem and having been satisfied that the looting of antiquities had reached unprecedented and unacceptable proportions, he set up the Illicit Antiquities Research Centre at Cambridge, a special unit dedicated to academic study of the problem, to draw attention to the seriousness of the situation and devise methods to combat the crisis.

The Renfrew–Elia debate lasted, roughly speaking, from 1993 to 1997. Neither man could have known, going into this standoff, that the Medici seizure was about to take place and would throw an immense amount of light on the subject. For the truth is that, museums apart, Giacomo Medici supplied most, if not all, of the main collections of classical antiquities that have been formed since World War II. All modern postwar collections—and there are five of them, in the United States and Europe—are stuffed with loot, loot that has been acquired largely through Giacomo Medici and, for the most part, the collectors know it, or knew it if they have since died.

In a very hard sense, when you consider the sums of money involved, Ricardo Elia is right, perhaps more right than he himself knew at the time of his review: Collectors are the real looters.

Besides being president and CEO of the Kennedy Galleries in New York, Lawrence Fleischman was widely known for his philanthropic activities. Born in 1925 in Detroit, he studied at the Western Military Academy in Alton, Illinois, at Purdue University and the University of Detroit, from which he graduated in 1948, the year he married his wife, Barbara. He first became interested in antiquities during World War II, when he was a soldier stationed in France and visited the Roman ruins at Besançon. In 1963, he purchased several Greek vases from the collection of William Randolph Hearst. In 1966, he and his family moved to New York, where he became a partner in the Kennedy Galleries. His wife and he were supporters of many art institutions, including the Met, the Detroit Institute of Art, the British Museum, and the Vatican. Mr. Fleischman served on a White House advisory committee during the Kennedy and Johnson administrations and was cofounder with the art historian E. P. Richardson of the Archives of American Art. He founded the *Art Journal* and was a fellow of the Pierpont Morgan Library. With his wife, he formed an important collection of American art and he was asked by Pope Paul VI to help form a collection of modern religious art for the Vatican. In 1978, the Pope named Mr. Fleischman a papal knight of the Order of St. Sylvester, and in 1986, he was named a knight commander of that order by Pope John

Paul II. During this period, he met Dietrich von Bothmer, who advised the Fleischmans to sell the antiquities they then had, and according to a catalog written about their subsequent acquisitions, "He introduced them to dealers who specialized in ancient art."

In 1996, the Getty Museum acquired the Fleischman Collection of classical antiquities. The collection, which numbered some 300 objects, was valued at $80 million. The bulk was donated to the museum, the remainder—about $20 million worth—being purchased. How much the Fleischmans kept back isn't known.

This acquisition aroused concern among archaeologists for two reasons. First, as various studies have shown, 92 percent of the collection had no provenance, with the remaining 8 percent having been in other recent collections; in other words, they probably had no real provenance either. Second, the Getty Museum itself, in the form of Marion True and a colleague, published the Fleischman Collection, in a catalog for an exhibition in 1994 and then, immediately following its purchase of the collection, announced a new acquisitions policy—that objects would now not be purchased unless they were shown to be in established, published collections. Because the Fleischman Collection was now published (by Marion True, no less), this maneuver enabled the Getty to acquire its 300 objects "legitimately."

This was disingenuous, if not downright cynical. Being in a "published collection" does not somehow, as if by magic, make illicit objects licit. Such a maneuver may put a name between the museum and the soil of whatever country the antiquities have been looted from, but that is all. Moreover, where records exist and are available, and despite the Fleischmans' undoubted distinguished background, their antiquities collection was almost entirely made up of loot, and they and the Getty knew it.

Between the fall of 1994 and the spring of 1995, A Passion for Antiquities: Ancient Art from the Collection of Barbara and Lawrence Fleischman was on exhibit, first at the Getty in Malibu, and then in Cleveland. In the foreword to the catalog, John Walsh, director of the Getty, and Robert P. Bergman, director of the Cleveland Museum of Art, had this to say, among other things: "Unlike museum collections that generally try to provide the public with as complete and representative a view of an artistic period or medium as possible, the private collection knows no such restrictions. The only consideration for the collectors are, Do I like it? Can I afford it? Can I live with it? . . . The guiding factor in the selection of these pieces has been their exceptional artistic quality, not their archaeological interest." These words are as interesting for what is not said as for what is. Surely, being aware of the widespread looting taking place in many countries that are home to ancient civilizations, one question *any* private collector should ask (as should a museum curator) is this: Is it ethical to acquire the objects I am intending to buy? These sentiments of Walsh and Bergman (particularly the comment about acquisition for reasons of artistic excellence, not archaeological interest) were reinforced, to an extent, in the body text of the catalog where Lawrence Fleischman was quoted as follows: "When you are collecting for an institution, you are always influenced by what the collection needs; in commerce, you are motivated by what sells; but in forming a personal collection, you know that you will have to live with the object twenty-four hours a day, so you buy only what you react to most positively." In other words, there was a sense here that the Fleischman Collection was an entity personal to the Fleischmans rather than a collection more suited to a museum.

This is of interest here because the documents that Pellegrini found in Medici's warehouse in Geneva caused Paolo Ferri, the prosecutor, to ask several searching questions of the Getty. In turn, this produced a number of internal Getty documents to be made available. Though these were partially "redacted"—edited, because the Getty said certain parts were not relevant—the picture they reveal is clear enough.

In a note Marion True wrote to John Walsh, dated January 30, 1992, that is, two years *before* the exhibition of the Fleischman Collection, she wrote:

On September 21, 1991, Lawrence Fleischman telephoned to ask if the Museum would be interested in purchasing nine of the major pieces, including one group of 41 individual objects, in his collection.

True said that Fleischman's reason for selling was "apparently" personal financial difficulties due to the weak market in property and American paintings.

> The list of objects was drawn up by Mr. Fleischman himself, but he carefully selected objects that he knew would be of major importance for our collection.

The terms of purchase were straightforward: The group would cost $5,500,000 to be paid by February 15, 1992 and the price and the choice of objects were not negotiable.

> The total figure was principally the sum of the pieces paid for the individual objects by the Fleischmans. The group includes—

The list was redacted at this point, save for one object, a red-figured calyx krater signed by Syriskos. Then the memorandum continues: "As several of these pieces were offered to me at times when we were unable to buy and one was sold at auction, I can confirm that their prices are basically original cost."

She goes on:

> We were offered the calyx krater, the Corinthian aryballos, the bronze helmet and ankle guards; the snake-legged giant was sold at auction; Mr. Fleischman provided the purchase price of the silver amphora-rhyton. The other objects' original prices are not known but their present prices reflect fair market value. As you know from having seen the collection, there is no question that each of these objects is of exceptional quality and importance, and as the attached acquisition proposals explain, any one of these pieces would be a welcome addition to the collection. The possibility to purchase all together is an extraordinary opportunity. Following our discussion in mid-November, we arranged to bring the pieces to Malibu for study and photography in preparation for their presentation at the January meeting. Our inquiries to IFAR [the International Foundation for Art Research, based in New York, an organization that kept records of stolen art] and the governments of Greece, Italy and Turkey are not likely to be answered before the payment on the collec-

tion is due, because of both the shortness of time and the intervening holidays. As the pieces have been for some time in an American collection, however, and as scholars from all over the world have studied them, I think it is unlikely that the inquiries should raise any problems.

As other Getty documents make clear, Deborah Gribbon, associate director and chief curator, wrote to Fleischman on February 4, 1992, confirming that the purchase of the nine pieces for $5.5 million had been approved and that payment would be made on February 15, the deadline Fleischman had stipulated.

On the basis of this exchange, therefore, there would appear to be little difference between the Fleischmans' collection and that of a museum. Each of the objects was "of exceptional quality and importance." We may seem to be splitting hairs here, but the point will become clearer—and sharper—later on.

In the Dossier section we give full details of the eleven objects for which Pellegrini established a paper trail from Medici to the Fleischmans. Here, we concentrate on four, which between them underline the sheer quality of objects Medici and the cordata handled, and which pose awkward questions about the Fleischmans, and for Getty staff, most especially Marion True: Just where did they think this material was coming from?

We begin with a marble statue of Tyche that was acquired in this instance, according to the documentation, from Robin Symes. The heavily draped female figure is identified as Tyche by her turreted crown, which probably also identified the city she was meant to protect. Once again, this statue is depicted in the photographs seized in Geneva, where it is shown before it had been cleaned of the dirt that was encrusted on it. It was an important object, being purchased by the museum from the Fleischmans for $2 million. In antiquity the Greek word *tyche*, meaning chance or fortune, with its inherent mutability, applied to both men and cities. The great centers of Antioch and Alexandria both established cults to the goddess Tyche, but smaller towns would have worshiped her, too.

Had a statue this important been excavated legally, articles would have been written about it and published in scholarly journals. The fact that so little was known about the statue should, in itself, have been a tell-tale sign that the object's provenance was suspicious.

More damning still was a Roman fresco, a lunette showing a mask of Hercules and valued at $95,000, which was acquired by the Fleischmans from Bürki. On this occasion, however, the fresco was associated with Medici not because of any photographs but because, in dimensions, subject matter, and condition, in Ferri's words, it "would appear to be a twin to another fresco" seized in Geneva from Medici. In the photographs taken in Corridor 17 by the Swiss police, in the raid on September 13, 1995, the "twin" is shown just lying on the floor.*

No less revealing was a black-figure amphora attributed by Dietrich von Bothmer to the Three Lines Group (a group where the distinguishing characteristic was a motif of three short lines). This amphora can be seen in numerous regular photographs and Polaroids seized from Medici in Geneva. It was offered to the Getty by the Fleischmans, having been sold to them by Fritz Bürki in June 1989. From other documentation, we find that "RG" (Robert Guy, an archaeologist from Princeton and Oxford who advised several members of the cordata) said that this object had been "found together with" another object with gigantomachia (the revolt of the Giants against the gods, and their consequent slaughter, a favorite theme in the Classical and Hellenistic periods) that was still in the possession of "REH" (Robert

---

*In the catalog of the Passion for Antiquities exhibition, in relation to catalog number 126, the text of the Hercules reads as follows: "The superb illusionism of Second-Style Roman wall painting is brilliantly in evidence in this fragment from the upper zone of a Pompeian wall." It continues: "The upper portion of the fresco matches precisely the upper portion of a fresco section in the Shelby White and Leon Levy Collection. . . and is from the same *room* as catalogue number 125" (italics added; see the Dossier section). Catalog number 125 was in fact another fresco fragment, consisting of two rectangular panels and showing landscape scenes bathed in a light blue-green hue. The text argues that, based on the right-to-left orientation of the shadows on the columns, "this was part of the right-hand wall upon entering the room."

These two items recall the frescoes from the Pompeian villa that Pellegrini first encountered when delving into Medici's documentation—they too were of the Second-Style (see p. 69).

We know that three walls were photographed by the tombaroli, but it is not clear if they are from the same villa. Only *parts* of three walls were recovered in Corridor 17, but if the building had dimensions as hinted at in the diagram on p. 71, many frescoes might still be missing.

Emmanuel Hecht), and a third vase, a hydria of the Würzburg Painter, "still in the possession of" Robin Symes. How did Guy know that these objects had been found together? This is a clear sighting of the cordata.

Now we turn to one final object, in relation to the Fleischmans. Among the documents seized in Geneva, Pellegrini found photographs of a red-figure chalice (calyx) krater, which was part of the 1992 sale from Fleischman to the Getty. This was a vase by Syriskos. The Geneva photographs showed the krater "during different stages of restoration." The Getty's acquisition notes, compiled by Richard Neer, emphasize that the vase was "one of the most exciting and important to come on the market in recent years." It was valued at $800,000 and had been acquired from Robin Symes in London in 1988. One reason for the high value was that the iconography on this vase was exceedingly unusual. It showed Ge, the goddess of the earth, sitting on a chair, wearing a petal crown. She is flanked by her son, the beardless Titan named Okeanos (the Titans were the mythical race of giants, predecessors of humankind), and the bearded Dionysus, god of wine. On the back of the vessel, a goddess is again flanked by two males, but this time it is Themis, Ge's daughter. Themis is flanked by Balos and Epaphos. Epaphos was the son of Zeus and Io, born on the banks of the Nile. Marrying Memphis, he had a daughter named Libya. As a result of a union with Poseidon, Libya gave birth to Balos, who was in turn the father of Aegyptos and Damno, and also father of Danaos, the ancestor of Homer's Danaans. This highly unusual arrangement therefore seems to be about the birth—or at least the early days—of the gods and the nations they gave rise to.

But the vase was more important than even this might indicate, for the graffito under the foot showed that the vessel in antiquity cost one *stater*, the equivalent of two days' pay for an Athenian soldier. As the Getty report notes, "Prices are very rare on Greek vases. . . . The cost of quality vases in the ancient market is a critical issue, especially for studies concerning the relationship of this medium to society as a whole. Furthermore, this graffito is the first to use the *stater*, a large denomination, for pricing." (Usually it was the smaller-denomination *obol*.) The signature on the vase, Syriskos, means the "Little Syrian," and he was certainly, at one point, a slave. Other vases in the same hand are signed "Pistoxenos Syriskos" and still others, dated later, just "Pistoxenos." The Getty report continues, "It has been concluded that the slave Syriskos changed his name at some point to Pistoxenos, probably on gaining his freedom; the vases with the double signature are transitional pieces, marking the change." Nor is that all. "The style of the drawing is unquestionably that of the artist previously identified as the Copenhagen Painter. . . . This krater identifies the Copenhagen Painter as Syriskos himself. . . . It therefore provides a valuable clue to the interrelationships of this important group of artists."

The acquisition of this vase, and the analysis of its features, convey something of the excitement of classical scholarship—the sense of discovery and of interrelationships. This is also what justified the high price of $800,000 and confirms once more the sheer importance of the objects that Medici and the cordata traded in. But where was this important vase found? We know nothing about that.

The full list of objects acquired by Fleischman—depicted in the Polaroids seized in Geneva, given in the Dossier—shows that he almost invariably acquired his antiquities from either the Bürkis or from Robin Symes. Did he *never* ask himself where Fritz Bürki or Symes got these objects from? Were none of them troubled by the silence surrounding these rare and important antiquities?

There were two final pieces of paper that Pellegrini unearthed at Geneva in relation to Fleischman, but they weren't Polaroids. They were checks. One was dated July 20, 1995, number 116, made out for $100,000 and drawn on the Republic National Bank of New York, 452 Fifth Avenue. The other was dated March 20, 1996, was numbered 4747, made out for $550,000, and was drawn on the Chase Manhattan Bank, 11 West 57th Street. But the curious thing about both checks is that although they were found in Corridor 17, on Medici's premises, they weren't made out to him but to "Phoenix Ancient Art SA." Why would Medici have in his possession at the Freeport in Geneva checks made out to someone else? And why would one of the checks be postdated March 20, 1996, when it was seized during the raid that took place on September 13, 1995? Was it to be honored *after* the sale of the Fleischman Collection to the Getty? This was all partly explained, and amplified, by other documentation Pellegrini discovered. One was a note, on Phoenix Ancient Art–headed paper, dated Geneva, May 5, 1995, which read:

> This letter confirms that Phoenix Ancient Art S.A. will be responsible for paying to the bearer of the following two checks, made to us, the same amount at the same date that appear on them if any problem in clearing them occurs:
>
> 1) check nbre 116, Republic National Bank of New York, dated July 20, 1995, in the amount of US$100,000.—
>
> 2) check 4747, Chase Manhattan Bank, N.A., dated March 20, 1996, in the amount of US$550,000.—
>
> Total . . . . US$650,000

It was signed "Hischam Aboutaam."

This seems a clear example of triangulation. This was still further underlined by another document in the same file. It was a "Contrat de Partenariat," a contract of partnership, between Editions Services and Phoenix Ancient Art. Dated "Genève le 8 Juin 1994," it outlined an arrangement confirming that at the sale of the Hirschman Collection of Greek vases, held at Sotheby's on December 9, 1993, the two parties spent £1,953,539.39, in the proportions two-thirds by Editions Services and one-third by Phoenix Ancient Art. The two parties agreed that this sum was the equivalent of US$3 million and that in the future resale of the objects, the two partners would be reimbursed in those proportions—two-thirds to Editions Service and one-third to Phoenix.

Still more documents testified to the close association between Medici and Phoenix—transport notes for Editions Services goods, written on Phoenix notepaper, monthly invoices (signed) from Medici to Phoenix for "services" ("expertise, consultation," and so on), in sums ranging from 9,500 Swiss francs to US$30,000.

Some idea of the overall importance of the objects in the Fleischman Collection may be had from Pellegrini's calculation that the average price of their objects was in excess of $100,000. Nonetheless, the most troubling aspect is that so many of these unprovenanced objects came from Medici, and therefore out of the ground of Italy illegally. The Getty's own documents make it clear that the museum knew that most of the objects had surfaced via such figures as Robin Symes and Fritz Bürki. The checks show that Fleischman dealt directly with the Aboutaams. Everyone knew what was going on. Yet in the Getty's acquisition documentation, the "Provenance and Exportability" section never queries where these objects come from.

That makes it regrettable—more than regrettable—that the Getty, and Marion True in particular, saw fit to begin acquiring the Fleischman Collection and then had the gall to declare a new acquisitions policy at the museum, affirming that it would only acquire objects that had been in published collections. Marion True was well aware by then that many if not all the modern collections of antiquities have been acquired in exactly the same way as the Fleischman Collection.

The checks were a bonus, a vivid reminder of how close the glitzy world of the collector is to the underworld. But it is Medici's bread-and-butter records that are truly shocking: remember that every object discussed in this chapter is represented in the incriminating Polaroid collection in Corridor 17.

Maurice Tempelsman, the Belgian-born diamond merchant and chairman of the largest diamond cutters in the world, was a visitor to the Classics Department of the Boston Museum of Fine Arts, a member of the Council on Foreign Relations, and was perhaps best known for being the companion of Mrs. Jacqueline Kennedy-Onassis. During the 1970s and 1980s, Mr. Tempelsman acquired a major collection of Egyptian, Near Eastern, Greek, and Roman antiquities, mainly sculpture. According to the documentation, most of the objects were acquired through Robin Symes.

Fairly early on, however, Mr. Tempelsman was seeking to sell his collection, and, in fact, his antiquities were offered to the Getty on no fewer than four occasions beginning in October 1982, when Jiri Frel was curator, and when Tempelsman approached the museum through Robin Symes, who offered *en bloc* twenty-one of his most important objects, including a number of Egyptian and ancient Near Eastern antiquities. The asking price was $45 million, and it was refused. In the summer of 1985, after two other unsuccessful approaches, Symes made a fourth proposal, this time offering eleven of the most important Greek and Roman objects, for $18 million. On this occasion, the relevant curators recommended acceptance, and the eleven items were officially acquired in 1985.

The documents concerning this matter, which the Getty made available to Dr. Ferri, were redacted to an extent, and they identified only three of the eleven pieces, one a marble sculpture of two griffins attacking a deer, the second a marble bowl, a footbath with painted Nereids on Hippocamps (sea horses), and the third a marble Apollo. As it happened, however, all three of these important marble objects were found depicted in the seized Polaroids in Geneva. There were three Polaroids of each object, "clearly photographed with the same camera and at the same time, so much so that the lot numbers on the back of the photographs are the same (00057703532)." Each object was shown in fragments, encrusted with earth, and photographed on an Italian newspaper lying on a table with a multicolored tablecloth. Because they all shared the same batch number in the photographs, Pellegrini concluded that they were all found on the same site at the same time. And in time they became the subject of an article in the Getty *Journal*, number fourteen, for 1986, where it was hypothesized that in antiquity the objects came originally from the same geographical area "if not from the same site." The author speculated that the original location was perhaps Macedonia and that they had been shipped to Taranto and then to Etruria. How much did the author know?

To cap it all, Pellegrini found among the documents negatives of a visit Medici had made to Los Angeles. Among these negatives was a photograph of the man himself standing next to the three marble objects from the Tempelsman collection, "almost as if he was claiming their paternity."

The sheer quality of the Tempelsman material is attested to by Dr. Cornelius Vermeule, curator of the Department of Classical Art at the Museum of Fine Arts, Boston: ". . . its condition, quality and aesthetic importance are supreme." David G. Mitten, Loeb Professor of Classical Art and Archaeology at Harvard, said that "the objects in the group are of consistently outstanding quality" and that several "rank among the masterpieces of the art of their period anywhere." They were, he said, "hallmarks in the history of art." Jerome J. Pollitt, professor of classics and classical archaeology at Yale, said that if acquired, "the Tempelsman objects would substantially raise the level of quality of the Museum's antiquities collection and provide it with material which in some areas has no known parallel." Finally, John G. Pedley, professor of classical archaeology at the University of Michigan and director of the university's Kelsey Museum of Archaeology, also agreed that some of the objects were without parallel and were of great scholarly importance.

The notes compiled about individual objects amplify this. The marble group of griffins attacking a deer (valued individually at $5.5 million) was "a stunning *tour de force*, unparalleled anywhere in Greek art. . . . This group is unique; there is simply nothing else known like it . . . this piece also provides one of the finest examples of colored marble sculpture to survive." Of the marble bowl, with paintings on the inside (valued individually at $2.2 million), "No other such object is known to me. . . . The painted scene and its rich polychromy make the basin unique, a precious example of the almost completely vanished classical Greek monumental painting, the art which was most praised by ancient Greek and Roman writers on art . . . This piece is of the highest possible importance. . . . As an exquisite example of Greek painting at its finest, as well as its fundamental importance for our understanding of late classical Greek polychromy, pigments, and the techniques used to apply them to marble surfaces, the basin is of unique importance." And for the statue of Apollo (valued at $2.5 million), "This statue may well be the finest and most accomplished piece of its kind in North America."

So far as classical art is concerned, these pieces are as important as can be. There can be no more talk in the trade that unprovenanced antiquities are humdrum, ordinary objects. Yet in the acquisition notes, written by Arthur Houghton, under "Provenance and Exportability," here is the *entire* entry: "The collection represents a selection of objects from a larger collection formed by Maurice Tempelsman, a diamond merchant resident in New York, over the past twenty-five years. The individual pieces come from a variety of sources, although the largest number were provided directly by, or were bought through, Robin Symes of London. All have been legally imported into the U.S. The collection is currently in the Museum."

And that's it. These were objects of immense importance, yet they had no history before Symes or Tempelsman—*and no one chose to ask ques-*

tions. Not the Getty staff or the experts who inspected the material. Did no one ask where such important material came from and why the objects had not previously been published? Did no one ask Robin Symes where he had acquired such wonderful material? Had no one any idea where they probably came from? Were they frightened of the answer? Or, did they already know?

In many ways, Shelby White and Leon Levy parallel Barbara and Lawrence Fleischman. As a rich couple, they have devoted their lives to the arts. As Fleischman served on a White House advisory committee in the Kennedy and Johnson administrations, so Shelby White served on President Clinton's Cultural Property Advisory Committee, albeit controversially. (Since the aim of the committee is to help stem the flow of ancient foreign artifacts into the hands of private collectors, Nancy Wilkie, president of the Archaeological Institute of America, said of Shelby White, "It's like putting a fox in charge of the chicken coop.") Just as the Fleischmans helped kick-start the Archives of American Art and supported many art institutions, so Shelby White and her late husband provided funds for a "Shelby White and Leon Levy Court for Roman and Etruscan Art" at the Metropolitan in New York. And just as the Fleischmans built a collection of ancient art, which went on display at the Getty and was then acquired by the museum, so the Levy-Whites acquired an equivalent collection, which was displayed in an exhibition with a title no less grand than the Fleischmans': Glories of the Past ran from September 1990 to January 1991 at the Metropolitan Museum. Since 1999, some of the Levy-White objects have been on permanent display at the Met.

And, as with the Fleischmans, the Levy-White Collection is stuffed with loot.

In a way, this should not come as a surprise. Two of the items in the Fleischman Collection, two Pompeian frescoes, not only have their "twin" in Medici's warehouse in Geneva, but actually fit together—like a jigsaw puzzle—with frescoes in the Levy-White Collection.*

---

*See the Dossier section.

Given all this, and what has gone before, it comes as no surprise, therefore, to find that Pellegrini's familiar paper trail also leads from Geneva to the Levy-White Collection, just as it led to the Fleischman Collection and to the Tempelsman Collection. Besides the Polaroids in Corridor 17, showing many objects that would end up with the Levy-Whites—broken, dirty, just lying around—there was quite a bit of correspondence. There was, for example, a group of invoices sent from Robin Symes to Leon Levy; no doubt Symes had to copy Medici on his invoices to prove he was charging what he said he was charging. There were also invoices from, and correspondence about, the Aboutaams.

The Dossier section gives full details on ten valuable and important objects in the Levy-White Collection in which the documentation shows that they originated with Medici. In every case, the paper trail is familiar and comprehensive, and just three examples will illustrate the overall quality of the material.

A black-figure Attic amphora attributed to the Bucci Painter (540–530 BC), number 106 in the catalog for the Levy-White Collection, appears in the seized photographs and was also sold at the notorious Sotheby's sale in London, on December 9, 1985. It is actually a vase the British Museum would have bid on, had it had a proper provenance.*

Pellegrini's report draws particular attention to two Caeretan *hydrie,* water storage vases from Cerveteri. Pellegrini found it especially interesting that the two vases were used to explain an article in the journal *Greek Vases in the J. Paul Getty Museum,* volume six, for the year 2000. The two vases in the Levy-White Collection were very distinctive: One showed a panther and a lioness attacking a mule, and the second showed Ulysses and his companions fleeing from Polyphemus's cavern (Polyphemus was the one-eyed giant in Homer's *Odyssey* who refused hospitality to Ulysses and his cohort). Both these vases were shown in the seized photographs, where each is broken and in fragments, with sizable gaps. In this case, however, the photographs also consisted of a number of enlargements, showing the fragments close up. What struck Pellegrini was that, in the Getty article, in discussing their construction and method of manufacture, various drawings of the vases were used, and these show the vases

---

*See Note, pp. 384–385.

with the original break lines *as revealed in the seized photographs*. In other words, Peggy Sanders, who made these drawings, must have seen the vases either in the stages of restoration, when the joins between fragments were still visible, or she must have seen the photographs of the fragments that were eventually seized in Geneva. Where did Getty personnel, not to mention Shelby White and Leon Levy, think that these vases, and the fragments that composed them, had come from?

In this case, that was not the end of the matter. Further awkward questions are raised by certain letters that were found among the documentation obtained from Corridor 17. This correspondence was between the Levy-Whites (in fact the curator of their collection) and a Dutch authority on Greek vases, Professor Dr. Jaap M. Hemelrijk, of Wanneperveen in Holland. Professor Hemelrijk was interested in publishing the hydrie and in the course of his letter asked if he could include the photos (which, from his phrasing, he had evidently seen) "taken before restoration of the vase." Alongside this, someone has written in hand: "Aboutaam?" The date on this letter is May 16, 1995, just over a year after the Phoenix Ancient Art invoice to the Levy-Whites. In other words, it was obvious to everyone that these hydrie had only recently been put together.

One final, but very important object links the Levy-Whites with the Hunt brothers, whose collection is considered next. This was a fragmentary red-figure calyx krater signed by none other than Euphronios. This krater—at eighteen inches by twenty-two inches, a good bit smaller than the Met's—was the star in the sale held at Sotheby's in New York on June 19, 1990, which saw the dispersal of the collection of Greek and Roman vases and coins amassed by the Texan oil billionaires (or former billionaires), Nelson Bunker Hunt and William Herbert Hunt.

The Hunts were in fact originally from Illinois, where their ancestors had moved after the Civil War. One son of these ancestors preferred to make his money by gambling on cards, and he was successful enough to start drilling for oil in Texas. He was dogged for years by rivals, who claimed he had cheated them, but he came out on top and his eldest son, Hassie, built on his fortune. However, Hassie developed a mental condition that necessitated a frontal lobotomy. Bunker, being the next oldest, took over. He extended the oil business into Pakistan and Libya, where the world's largest oil field was discovered on the tract of land licensed to the Hunts. This was an oil prospector's dream come true. In 1961, Bunker's half interest in this tract was valued at about $7 billion, making him the richest private individual in the world—at age thirty-five. During the 1970s, the Hunts diversified, adding to oil an interest in real estate (5 million acres at one point), cattle, sugar, pizza parlors—and silver. Inflation was high in the 1970s and gold could not be held by private citizens at that time, so the Hunts began to buy silver in enormous quantities.

Prior to their bankruptcy in the early 1980s, the Hunts had built up extensive holdings in Greek and Roman coins and vases. The collection was cataloged in 1983 under the grand title, The Wealth of the Ancient World, but was dispersed in 1990 as part of their efforts to straighten out their affairs in the wake of their bankruptcy and subsequent conviction. At that June sale, the Hunts' Euphronios kylix, albeit only one-fourth complete, became the first Euphronios to be sold at auction in the twentieth century and, fittingly, it fetched a record price for a Greek vase, outdoing even the Met's krater, with a hammer price of $1.76 million. It was bought by Robin Symes, who was bidding on behalf of the Levy-Whites.

Now there were four notable features about the sale of this krater. In the first place, the Hunts' collection of Greek vases and coins was acquired though the Summa Gallery in Los Angeles. The public face of Summa was a controversial figure in his own right: Bruce McNall. McNall is another of those colorful figures—like the Hunt brothers—who populate the edges of this story. Born the son of a University of Southern California biochemistry professor in Los Angeles, McNall developed an early passion for ancient coins. This led him as a young man to the antiquities shops and bazaars of Turkey, Egypt, Italy, and Algeria. In 1974, he paid a record $420,000 at a Swiss auction for the world's rarest coin, a fifth-century BC Athena decadrachm, and six years later he sold the world's first $1-million coin. As he rose in a financial and social sense, McNall bought himself a hockey team, the Los Angeles Kings; and a football team, the Toronto Argonauts; and financed a number of films, including Blame It on Rio and The Fabulous Baker Boys. He owned a horse that won the Prix de l'Arc de Triomphe and a stable with 100 thoroughbreds, and numbered among his friends Goldie Hawn, Michelle Pfeiffer, Michael J. Fox, and Ronald and Nancy Reagan.

In 1974, he formed a partnership with Robert E. Hecht, who became the éminence grise in McNall's Summa Gallery, located prominently on Rodeo Drive in Beverly Hills in Los Angeles. Widely ridiculed for embellishing his background (he invented bogus graduate work at Oxford, England, and a partnership with J. Paul Getty), McNall was twice forced to return antiquities to Turkey because they had been illegally excavated and smuggled out of the country. One involved a Roman sarcophagus that had been stripped by thieves of a series of carved scenes depicting the labors of Hercules, concerning which some of the panels were recovered in Turkey—and the matching ones turned up at Summa. The second involved eight marble sculptures stolen from the famous Roman city of Aphrodisias; and here, too, four turned up at Summa.

Later on in his career, McNall admitted his role in the widespread smuggling of illegally excavated coins and antiquities (80 percent of the ancient coins on the market, he said, are "fresh," meaning fresh out of the ground), but by then his association with the Hunts was long over. They had met in 1978, at the Santa Anita Race Track, when Hunt had asked McNall two questions. First, "What was the relationship between gold and silver in the ancient world?" McNall had replied, "Twenty-four to one, about." And second, "What would it take to form the biggest coin collection in the world?" Hunt was, of course, then in the middle of trying to corner the silver market, but over the next few years he and his brother used McNall, and the Summa Gallery, to acquire not just coins but antiquities as well. McNall later told journalist Bryan Burrough that he charged "close to a million" for a Euphronios cup that was "probably bought from the same tomb robbers who allegedly supplied Hecht's Euphronios vase."

The second noteworthy aspect about the smaller krater by Euphronios is that it wasn't the only Euphronios vase in the Hunt sale. There was another, a kylix, that was bought for close to $800,000, by none other than Giacomo Medici. It was this kylix that was discovered during the first raid on Corridor 17, on September 13, 1995, and then dropped and broken by a Swiss policeman.*

*See p. 22.

The third noteworthy aspect about both the Leon Levy-Shelby White Euphronios and the one found in Giacomo Medici's possession in Geneva was that both featured Hercules in the iconography. This one showed Hercules straining and struggling, locked in battle with Cycnos, one of the primordial Titans, son of Ares, the Greek god of war.

The fourth noteworthy aspect of the Levy-White krater was that Polaroid photographs of it, dirty and in separate fragments, before it was put together as a vase, were found among Medici's documentation in the Geneva Freeport. In other words, the full route of this Euphronios was: Medici to Hecht to Summa Gallery to the Hunt brothers to Robin Symes to the Levy-Whites.

Nor was this all. In 1991, some months after they bought the smaller Euphronios krater, the Levy-Whites sent it to the Getty Museum conservation department to have the vase examined and re-restored. The ostensible reason for this was that the Levy-Whites had two extra fragments that were allegedly by Euphronios and formed part of the krater, and they wanted the Getty conservation people to add the new fragments. The documentation unearthed by the Italian public prosecutor showed three relevant points about this episode.

In the first place, it turned out that the two fragments *did not* fit with the krater. Second, an addendum to a letter written by Dr. Anne Leinster Windham, curator of the Levy-White Collection, to Maya Elston of the Getty's Antiquities Conservation Department contains the following: "2 fragments (probably not numbered) are in Livingroom. Case A. They were thought to fit with krater, but don't. Fred Schultz told me (6/95) that he had owned them, and given them to Hecht as a 'gesture of good faith.' Then Hecht turned around and sold them! . . . Date purchased: 06–25–90." In other words, the Levy-Whites acquired the fragments six days after they bought the vase at auction. This is the very same date as Robin Symes's invoice to Leon Levy for buying the krater at Sotheby's.

Finally, here are some excerpts from the examination of the krater by Maya Elston, of the Getty Conservation Department, written on July 23, 1991.

Initially the body and the lips were thrown as one piece, while the foot and the handle were made separately. . . . The krater has been previously restored. 75 fragments comprise the preserved one quarter of the original. Most of them are located on side A [the principal scene], whilst the rest are dispersed over the entire surface. . . . STRUCTURAL CONDITION OF THE TWO ADDITIONAL FRAGMENTS. . . . Partial cleaning had been carried out although encrustation and soil deposits are still dispersed over the surface, mostly located on the broken edges . . . In addition to [the] initial damage in antiquity, *some fresh surface damage can be observed on the larger shard (perhaps these are traces from an excavation tool . . .).* (italics added)

This vase too is among the Polaroids in Medici's Geneva warehouse. Indisputably, both these Euphronios vases started out with him. This, of course, is not without significance in regard to the provenance of the Metropolitan's Euphronios krater. Finding fresh tool marks on the fragments, did conservator Elston not ask herself what was going on?

Quite apart from the two vases by Euphronios, Pellegrini found two other objects of very great value that were once in the Hunt Collection and which were sold in the great sale of their collection at Sotheby's in 1990. These were a black-figure Attic kylix and a red-figure Attic *stamnos* (a large amphora with handles on the shoulder) showing figures bathing in a fountain. The documentation showed that both of these had passed through a gallery and an auction house: They had both been first sold at the Summa Gallery in Los Angeles and then been put on auction at Sotheby's in 1990.

However, in Medici's warehouse, besides the kylix and the stamnos themselves, he also found *photographs* of both objects, *but*, in both cases, they were fragmented, dirty with soil, "summarily reassembled" but with many gaps and altogether in the state normally associated with recently excavated material. There were three photographs of the stamnos, "with clearly evident missing parts," though its provenance from Italian territory was made obvious by the fact that under the foot of the vase there was some writing, partly in Greek and partly in the Etruscan alphabet (the letters HE were in Greek, the letters CA in Etruscan).

So, a new but simple question arises. How could Medici have bought the kylix and the stamnos at the Hunt sale in 1990 *and* have in his archive photographs of these self-same objects *before* they were restored? The answer was that he acquired them as soon as they came out of the ground, had them restored, passed them on to Hecht, for sale at the Summa Gallery, and then he *bought them back*. Why? To manipulate the market for his business.

Another six objects—all part of the Hunt Collection—appear in the seized photographs. Two were red-figure Attic amphorae, one was a black-figure Attic amphora, each shown in the photographs as "recomposed" in a preliminary way, with many gaps between the fragments and with the photographs evidently taken in a house. By the time they were sold, in the Sotheby's sale in New York, each was in perfect condition, with the gaps filled in and properly colored.

The pattern is wearily familiar.

●

In January 1994, the Royal Academy in London hosted an exhibition with a grand title, In Pursuit of the Absolute: Art of the Ancient World. This was in fact the George Ortiz Collection. The lack of provenance of many of the objects in the exhibition was criticized by archaeologists on BBC TV a few days after the show opened. Ortiz defended himself robustly, arguing that 85 percent of all antiquities on the market are "chance finds." On the same program, Professor Colin Renfrew disagreed.

Ortiz was one of the names in Pasquale Camera's organigram. He himself has admitted that he bought much of his material from Gianfranco Becchina and from Koutoulakis, other names in the organigram. But he clearly didn't buy everything from them, because in one of the boxes of documentation seized in Geneva, among photographs depicting archaeological material "taken during or immediately after their removal from their original context," Pellegrini came upon a Polaroid photograph of a sculpture in *nefro*. Nefro is a form of stone specific to the Vulci area of Italy. The photographs Pellegrini found had clearly been taken on the site where this sculpture was discovered, "still dirty with earth and not yet restored." It depicted a horse with rider and was typical of Etruria, in particular the markers used for Vulci burials. This horse and rider, shown in a farmyard in the Geneva photographs, was identical with one displayed in the Royal Academy exhibition. Pellegrini adds: "We must point out that in the catalogue file there is no mention whatsoever regarding the acquisition of the piece, evidently recent and through Medici, who had a copy of the [Royal Academy] volume in his small Geneva library."

To take these collections at their own estimation of themselves, you would think that these are present-day marvels, jewels of collecting by people who care deeply about the past. Look through the catalogs for the exhibitions based on the collections and there are thousands of objects, worth millions of dollars. And yet, *not one* of these objects has a provenance and, we now know, they comprise mostly loot. These collections of statues, vases, and items of jewelry in fact tell us next to nothing about the past because the great majority of the objects have been ripped from their context by tombaroli, at times motivated (they say) by a misplaced "passion" for archaeology but always interested in money, and brought to market by Medici and his surrounding network, who, to judge from the markups *they* place on these objects, are even more interested in money, and exclusively so. It is these collectors whose funds and cavalier collecting habits, without thought for where these objects come from or how they were ripped from the ground, sustain the looting that does incomparable damage to the heritage of Italy and—without doubt—elsewhere.

THE LAUNDRIES OF LONDON

AND NEW YORK

ECIPHERING THE PAPER TRAIL that has been the subject of
the previous four chapters occupied Maurizio Pellegrini for
many months. It was a fascinating and important piece of
detection, but from Paolo Ferri's point of view, it had one serious, indeed near-fatal flaw. The original documents they were dealing
with were in Switzerland and the batch that Pellegrini had brought to
Rome were photocopies. The information in the photocopies might be
just as good as the information in the original documents, which were still
sequestered in Geneva, but they were no good *as evidence*. Any court,
anywhere, would insist on the documentation being original. The same
argument applied to the objects themselves that were under seizure in
Geneva. They were evidence, and if Ferri was to produce this evidence in
court, in Rome, he had to get the vases and statues and bronzes themselves out of Switzerland and into Italy.

But, by early 2000, the Swiss still hadn't made a move, nor had they indicated whether they were likely to be proceeding against Medici. Time
was passing. Medici was claiming that his business activities were being
unreasonably disrupted, and he tried time and again to have the warehouse and its contents de-sequestered. He insisted on his innocence and
that the charges against him be dropped.

But then, in early 2000, two occurrences came together. In 1997, it had
emerged that a number of Swiss banks held many accounts belonging to
victims of the Holocaust that had remained dormant since World War
II, accruing interest but not being used. Many people—Jewish and non-
Jewish alike—were outraged by this and felt that these monies should be

used to benefit Holocaust survivors. In 1998, a conference was held in Washington, D.C., and despite opposition from the Clinton administration, hundreds of state and local finance officials across the United States decided to implement sanctions against Swiss banks in their respective states, states that included California, New Jersey, New York, and Pennsylvania. Initially, the Swiss criticized the boycott and threatened to sue. The three main Swiss banks—Credit Suisse, Union Bank of Switzerland, and the Swiss Bank Corporation—all resisted any payout. Just over a month later, however, and a matter of days before the sanctions came into force, the Swiss banks backed down and agreed to start payments to Holocaust survivors. Between then and the summer of 2000, an overall figure for repayment was worked out: $1.25 billion. This was settled by a judge in July 2000, and at the beginning of August that year, the three big Swiss banks agreed.

This was all happening at the time Pellegrini was working on the paper trail and while Ferri was waiting for the Swiss to decide on whether to prosecute Medici. The Holocaust survivor issue would prove crucial.

The second event was that Pellegrini finally sorted out a pattern in the documents that had been troubling him. He had been worrying away at the documents and had begun this part of his investigation by trying to find out exactly what Medici had sold at Sotheby's, and where these antiquities had ended up, after they passed through the London auction house. That was necessary if the objects were to be recovered. Ferri had officially asked Sotheby's in London for help, and the salesroom had sent him *some* documentation, but it wasn't complete—so they felt in Rome—and was consequently not as helpful as it might have been.[1]

So Pellegrini drew up a comprehensive list of what Medici had *consigned* to Sotheby's. Next, where he could, he matched this to photographs found in the Geneva warehouse. Finally, he did what he could to match these two sets of records with what was actually *sold* at Sotheby's. This exercise produced a confusing picture, at least to begin with. Some of Medici's objects were sold, and when they were, Sotheby's refused to say who had bought them. That was their commercial right, they said. But quite a few of Medici's objects did not sell and were included in later auctions—where, again, some sold and some did not.

Many objects were included in three or four auctions before they were finally sold.

But, and this is what was confusing to begin with, some of the objects seized in Geneva had Sotheby's labels on them. These small white cards, tied to the objects with thin white thread, had written lot numbers on them and dates from the sales where they had been sold. So Medici was buying as well as selling at Sotheby's. Ferri and Pellegrini asked themselves why he would do that when he made his money by acquiring illicitly dug vases and other antiquities from tombaroli in Italy, where the markups were so much greater than they ever could be with objects bought openly at auction, where anyone interested could look up the prices paid.

It was late one afternoon in November 1999 when Pellegrini finally saw the light. He was sitting at his desk in the small office he shared with Daniela Rizzo, chief investigative archaeologist, on the second floor of the administration building at the back of the Villa Giulia Museum, in Rome's elegant Parioli district. It was drizzling and already dark, and the only light came from his Anglepoise lamp. He was looking at the Sotheby's catalog for its auction of antiquities in December 1994, five years before. There are usually 400–600 lots in an average sale, and as he leafed through that particular volume, he had reached Lot 295, a Gnathian-style hydria. This object, he knew by then, had been sent for sale by Medici some two to three years before, and it had been in other sales but hadn't found a buyer. That November afternoon, however, Pellegrini had a strange sensation: He had seen Lot 295 before, and very recently. But where? It could only have been among the objects seized in Geneva. The vases and statues themselves were of course still in Switzerland, but good-quality photographs had been taken of everything. So Pellegrini found himself back among the photos. And what he found was that Lot 295 featured in the photographs not once *but twice*. It was shown in the Polaroids, as dirty and fragmented, before restoration; and it was shown in the high-quality photographs taken by the Swiss expert—*with a Sotheby's label attached to it.*

The penny dropped. Lot 295 had been sent to Sotheby's for sale by Medici and, after one or two unsuccessful sales, *it had been bought back.* This explained the odd pattern that had been haunting them all—Paolo

Ferri, Conforti's men, and Pellegrini himself. It explained how Medici could have in his possession in Geneva many objects that, according to the records, he had sold.

Armed with this insight, Pellegrini now looked at Medici's documentation under a new light. It didn't take him long to find other examples. In the Dossier section, we give the complete and detailed list he prepared for the prosecution against Medici. In each case the pattern was the same. In the first instance, Pellegrini identified twenty-nine objects, in four sales between 1987 and 1994, in which Medici bought back objects he had sent for sale at Sotheby's in London. There was, for example:

- A black-figure Attic amphora, which was sent to Sotheby's by Editions Services. It was taken into Sotheby's under the account number 216521 and was Lot 283 in its antiquities sale held on December 14, 1987, when it sold for £17,000.

- A terra-cotta head was sent to Sotheby's by Editions Service on September 13, 1989, number 50 in the consignment note. It was taken in by Sotheby's with the property number 1002611 and was Lot 100 in its antiquities sale held on December 11, 1989, when it sold for £2,200.

- Four Apulian terra-cotta vases were sent to Sotheby's by Editions Services on 2 March 1990, numbers 51 and 57 on the consignment note. They were taken in by Sotheby's with the property number 1012763, and were Lot 319 in its antiquities sale of December 8, 1994, when they sold for £1,100.

Each of these objects—twenty-nine in all—was received at Medici's Geneva warehouse, where it was originally dirty, incomplete, and fragmented, as the seized Polaroids confirm. Later, these same objects, now restored, were sent to Sotheby's for sale, and after sale they were returned to Medici's warehouse, bearing Sotheby's labels.

In other words, this was an extensive laundering operation, "extensive" because Ferri and Pellegrini had documents that related only to the 1987–1994 period, and Sotheby's, though cooperative to an extent, did not cooperate fully. Even so, the documentation that Pellegrini did manage to trace showed that, in one sale, dated December 8, 1994, Medici bought back twenty-four objects, paying £34,250 for the privilege. Except that he didn't have to pay all that since he was, for the most part, paying himself. What he actually had to pay was the commission on the sales, twice over—once as seller, and once as buyer. Assuming the commission was somewhere between 10 and 15 percent, both on buying and on selling, the December 8, 1994, sale would have cost Medici between £6,850 and £10,275. To this would have to be added the cost of shipping these goods to and from London, and costs for illustrations in the catalog, but the above sums are almost certainly exaggerations since Medici, as a valued and regular customer of Sotheby's, would have been able to negotiate rates more favorable to himself. (Different documents show that, on other occasions, Medici paid Sotheby's between 6 and 10 percent commission, which means that this particular transaction probably cost him between £4,110 and £6,850—hardly bankruptcy level.) But obviously, whatever the cost, the existence of the objects back in Geneva showed that Medici judged it worth his while.

Ferri asked Sotheby's for its cooperation, which it offered, providing information only in regard to Editions Services, and concluding that, between 1985 and 1994, each of the few clients who bought large numbers of Editions Services goods "were established and well known dealers, who generally bought large numbers of items at Sotheby's. We do not believe that there are any grounds for believing that any of them was buying on behalf of Editions Services. To have been laundering any significant number of works of art, Editions Services would have needed to use dozens of different agents and/or pseudonyms none of which were known to us. None of the information we have suggests that this was the case."

Sotheby's did, however, identify what it called "two areas of difficulty." The first was a small number of instances (fewer than ten), all relating to pre-1986 sales, when Boursaud appeared to have been buying items he was selling. "This practice is (and was at the time) forbidden by Sotheby's contracts and internal policy but can be difficult to spot, prove and/or prevent." Second, Sotheby's established that at the December 1994 auction, "a known and, so far as we are aware, legitimate Geneva based transportation company, Arts Franc, purchased 14 of the 34 items sold by Editions Services . . . we have now identified circumstantial evidence to indicate that this company may have been acting on behalf of Editions Services in making these purchases."* Finally, Arts Franc had acted for Editions Services "in relation to the transportation of and payment for" certain items purchased by Editions Services in relation to an earlier sale, in London on July 7, 1994, and subsequently, in a Sotheby's sale in New York on June 1, 1995.

Sotheby's was adamant that it was not aware of these practices until after the Medici investigation was begun, and that it would not have permitted them had it known. The company did admit, though, that such practices were difficult to identify and to prevent. This seems to be confirmed by the fact that Sotheby's own inquiry identified an "area of difficulty" with fourteen items in its sale of December 8, 1994, whereas Rizzo and Pellegrini found twenty-four items in that sale that had been bought back. In other words, not only Arts Franc was acting that day on Medici's behalf—at least one other buyer or company was as well. To that extent, the laundering was a sophisticated conspiracy.

It seems then that *some* buying back, or laundering, did occur and is accepted by all sides. The list originally given above (and completed in the Dossier section) refers to five separate sales, which all took place at Sotheby's in London. But Sotheby's in London may not have been the only laundry for antiquities. Sotheby's, in its report, mentioned a suspicious sale at its own New York branch.

During the raid on Phoenix Ancient Art, Jeffrey Suckow, the manager for Inanna Art Services, the company that owns the warehouses at the Freeport where the seized materials were being held, handed over photocopies of auction house catalogs relating to fourteen other sales between June 1995 and October 2000 in which objects seized from Medici had been sold and bought by the Aboutaams. These sales took place at Sotheby's and Christie's, both in London and New York, and at Bonhams in London. In at least two of these cases, the objects had started out with Medici, as proved by the Polaroids. They had then been "sold" at auction, bought by

---

*The circumstantial evidence was that the buyer lodged a bid just above the reserve on each item and did not bid on any other items. Furthermore, the commission bid was lodged just minutes before the sale, and afterward, Sotheby's shipping department was instructed to send the purchases of Arts Franc together with the purchases of Editions Services to Arts Franc's address in Geneva.

the Aboutaams, and ended up back with Medici. That confirms laundering in seven sales, and possibly as many as twenty-one, stretching from
1987 until 2000.

What was the purpose of these activities? Since they occurred on such
a scale, it was obviously worth Medici's time and trouble—but how, and
in what way?

There are three possible answers, though one does not rule out the others. First, and most obviously, the fact that some of the antiquities on display in the outer room in Corridor 17 at the Freeport had Sotheby's labels
tied to them gave them a spurious provenance: The labels were visible
"proof" that these objects had been bought on the open market and were
therefore "safe," or "clean," and could be sold—even in Italy—because
at this point they had an "official" provenance. The paper trail put together by Pellegrini in this case (paragraphs 1 to 20 in the relevant section
of the Dossier) proves that such a presentation was totally misleading. But
even without that, wasn't Medici's practice in itself curious, even suspicious? A moment's reflection will show what we mean. A good proportion
of the art, furniture, and jewelry on sale at dealers' galleries around the
world—in New York, Los Angeles, London, Paris, Milan, Munich, Zurich,
Hong Kong, Sydney, Rio de Janeiro—has been bought at auction, but the
dealers never advertise that fact, for the simple reason that, were they to
do so, enterprising prospective customers or collectors would simply look
up the records of the sale at which the painting or necklace or vase had
been auctioned and find out what the dealer had paid for it. This would
give them an inside track in any negotiations when it came to a potential sale. Therefore, Medici's behavior, in advertising that a good number
of his objects for sale had passed through Sotheby's—even to the extent of
showing the lot number—was a giveaway, evidence of a kind that what he
was offering for sale in Geneva was, in fact, the very opposite of what he
was pretending. The objects were not "clean"—far from it: A minority
was stolen, the rest looted.

A second reason for the Sotheby's rigmarole was revealed by Medici's
selling pattern. That is, he would submit things for sale and buy some

of them straight back, but with others he would leave them at the auction houses, to see how well they sold—or didn't sell. Those that didn't sell immediately were reentered in subsequent auctions; in some cases, he bought them back after repeated failures. This suggests that he was using the auction houses to rig prices. When he consigned material to Sotheby's, he naturally had some idea of what he wanted them to fetch. The consignment notes invariably had reserve prices attached, the minimum sum a consignor will allow an object to be sold for. If they fetched that price, all was well and good and he would let them go. However, if they didn't sell at the price he wanted, and if they didn't sell after being offered at auction several times, that could only mean either that they were on the market at too high a figure or that for some other reason the demand for that type of item simply wasn't there. In either case, buying back a certain proportion of his own objects helped resolve the problem. To the uninformed observer, the vases or statues had "sold" at the target price, "confirming" their value. If enough of a certain type of object "sold" in this way, that must mean there was a healthy taste for it and other collectors would take note.

There was a third way in which Medici would have benefited from his "buyback" operation in the salesrooms. In fact, the whole antiquities trade would have benefited, in an indirect way. An argument often heard from those who oppose any stringent restrictions on the trade in unprovenanced antiquities is that when you look at the auctions, much of the unprovenanced material that passes through the salesrooms is neither very rare nor very important. Therefore, this argument runs, the whole problem is much less grave than the archaeologists say it is. As far as Medici's deception is concerned, one aspect of his behavior was to "salt" the salesrooms with less-important material. In the list above, and in the Dossier section, the highest price that any "laundered" object sold for was £17,000 ($30,600) and the average sum was £2,105 ($3,790), considerably below the average price of the antiquities the Fleischmans sold to the Getty, which was more than $100,000. In salting the salesrooms with less expensive items, Medici accomplished two important objectives. By buying back—and therefore propping up the price of—basic objects (ordinary vases, routine marble heads, not uncommon capitals), he maintained the gold standard in antiquities. Provided that ordinary, garden-variety objects have a certain minimum price level and can be seen to have that price level, everything else above them will be multiples of that basic value. At the same time, by ensuring that the auctions were salted with "ordinary" material, he could help maintain the fiction that the antiquities market is primarily made up of such items.

There are two responses to this theory. First, as was explained in detail,* it does not follow at all that "ordinary" material is necessarily unimportant. Its distribution, context, dating, and material of construction, along with any inscriptions it may bear, can all affect its importance. The second response is of course that Medici's main concern was with important objects—museum-quality objects worth at least $100,000 each and crafted by the most important and accomplished artists of antiquity, objects he was so proud of that he crossed oceans to have his photograph taken with them on display in museums, objects so important he had to hide behind a whole network of fellow conspirators so he couldn't be linked directly with major museums.

This puts a new light on the antiquities auctions in London and New York. All the people mentioned in this book—Medici, Symes, Hecht, Koutoulakis, Tchacos, the Aboutaams—use the auctions. No doubt they provide a bread-and-butter income, but most of the objects they deal in at the salesrooms are relatively unimportant (not invariably, but mostly).

Critics say that if the auctions of unprovenanced material are abolished, as many would like, the trade will go underground. But what the Medici material shows, in particular the laundering activity through London and New York, is that it is *already* underground. The important material never comes anywhere near the salesrooms. This is another sense in which the antiquities trade is organized. The organization of the salesrooms— whether the salesrooms themselves realize it or not—is designed to mislead.

Pellegrini's identification of the London and New York laundries was, perhaps, the niftiest piece of intellectual detective work connected with

*See p. 62.

the Medici documentation. As it happened, it also proved to be the exercise that broke the logjam with the Swiss.

Pellegrini had had his first inkling of what was going on in London back in November 1999, that drizzly, gloomy afternoon sitting at his desk in his office in the Villa Giulia. By the time he had tracked all the other examples and had gotten some replies from Sotheby's, it was well into 2000. But that was precisely the time when the Swiss and the U.S. courts were agreeing on the massive liability of Swiss banks to Holocaust victims. When the Swiss learned that Medici's warehouse in Geneva was in part a repository of *laundered* antiquities, their attitude changed, and changed rapidly. In addition to the Holocaust business, Switzerland was sensitive to being a conduit for drug-trade money laundering. And so, in the second week of March, the prosecutor general of the Geneva canton finally ruled that there was sufficient evidence to consider Medici guilty of receiving and thus causing "damage" to the Italian state. Two days later, on the 15th (the "Ides") of March, the Swiss Embassy in Rome made a formal request to Italy to proceed against Medici for the crimes of *"appropriazione indebita"* ("undue appropriation," or "receiving") and theft, committed in Switzerland. Exactly a week later, the Italian Ministry of Justice formally initiated proceedings against Medici for his crimes committed in Switzerland, and on June 2 the entire contents of Corridor 17—all of the documents, the Polaroids, the prints, the negatives, and the seized objects, with and without Sotheby's labels—became available to Conforti, Ferri, and Pellegrini.

At last. Within ten days, a firm of removal experts was found and hired, and two trucks were dispatched to Geneva with a ten-man crew. Supervised by Conforti's Carabinieri, it took them two whole weeks to load the contents of Medici's warehouse into crates and then on to the trucks. But by the end of June, it was done. There was a last-minute glitch at the barrier of the Freeport. Since September 1995, when Corridor 17 had been sealed with wax by the Swiss magistrate, no rent had been paid. The management of the Freeport would not let the trucks leave until the rental arrears had been cleared. Fortunately, Ferri had foreseen this problem and had issued the Carabinieri the authority to pay the bill.

When they reached Rome, the trucks separated. The one carrying the archaeological objects made for the Villa Giulia, where the antiquities were unloaded and stored in a reconstructed Etruscan temple, situated in the gardens of the museum. The other truck, with the documents, went to Piazzale Clodio and the Palazzo di Giustizia, where Ferri had his offices.

Finally, the evidence was on Italian soil. Pellegrini's elucidation of the paper trail was as convincing as it was shaming of so many figures. But now that Ferri had the originals under his control, he had some real muscle. Now the interrogations could begin. And there was no question about where he would start—with a visit to Paris to meet Robert Hecht.

11

Phone Taps and the Great Rumor

I T WILL NOT HAVE GONE UNNOTICED that several earlier investigations into the illicit traffic in antiquities by the Italian authorities had foundered because, once the alleged tombaroli or smugglers had been arraigned in court, they denied what they had earlier told undercover police, confided to journalists, or admitted on arrest. In most cases, the Italian authorities were unable to make the charges stick because, as Hecht—among others—noted several times, it was always impossible to prove that the objects under scrutiny really had been excavated illegally inside Italy. Independent and incontrovertible photographic or other documentary evidence didn't exist.

But in Medici's case, of course, all that had changed. This time there was an amazing richness of material: some 4,000 photographs, tens of thousands of documents, 4,000 looted antiquities. Not only was this material evidence invaluable in its own right, but it also gave Ferri a crucial advantage over some of his earlier colleagues: It provided him with ammunition he could use to search and interrogate other suspects in the Medici network. It was clear that Medici was the biggest quarry the Italian authorities had ever had in their sights in this particular area of underworld activity and that the biggest trial of its kind was envisaged. Serious resources were being thrown at the problem. The photographs, invoices, and letters, not to mention the spread of Italian antiquities in the museums of the world, meant that Ferri could confront a whole raft of tombaroli, dealers, auctioneers, academics, and curators with hard evidence of their culpability, something no one had really been able to do before in this field. The situation was unprecedented.

Conforti recognized it. "After the material arrived from Switzerland, I took satisfaction in holding the Polaroids in my hands. The pleasure of finding myself with something solid, something substantial . . . knowing that we could now put the prosecutor to work on *real* evidence, on *proof*." But Conforti wasn't going to sit back. He recalled his time in Naples, fighting the Camorra. Then there had been a special Carabinieri unit, battling against the Red Brigade. Conforti had learned a thing or two from these operations, and he now adapted those earlier tactics in the field of antiquities looting.

"I said to the chief public prosecutor, look, at this moment we have 270 proceedings against various individuals. They are all separate. Why don't we create a pool of magistrates, just as there is with the Anti-Mafia Pool in Palermo, the Clean-Hands Pool [anti-corruption] in Milan, a pool of magistrates who will deal with this kind of criminality, who can work together, exchange information, and become expert in the field they are prosecuting. And so, over time, the same thing was done—in Bari, Turin, Florence, and Palermo." Paolo Giorgio Ferri, part of the Rome pool, became expert in the laws, not just of Italy but of Switzerland, Britain, Germany, and the United States. Between them they worked out the order of trials, designed to put increasing pressure on the culprits, beginning at the bottom and working up. This book appears partway through that process, and readers may judge for themselves how successful the Italian tactics have been.

We have said that the turning point in the investigation, so far as the interrogations were concerned, came when the Swiss decided to take no action against Medici but instead turned all the evidence over to the Italians. That is true. However, for a variety of reasons, Ferri was able to conduct *some* interviews before the Swiss decision. For example, the documentation taken from Sotheby's by James Hodges was not in Switzerland and, as soon as we realized that Sotheby's was not going to take any legal action against us, we made our material available to Ferri. He was able to act on this well before 2000.

In fact, he was able to interrogate Henri Albert Jacques as early as September 11, 1995, two days before the raid on the Freeport. He could do this because Editions Services—for which Jacques was the administrator—in addition to consigning for sale at Sotheby's a stolen sarcophagus from the

San Saba church in Rome,* had also handled an object stolen from an Italian citizen living in the Latina area, a few miles south of Rome. The movement of stolen objects that have crossed international borders has always been easier to investigate than the smuggling of looted antiquities.

In his interrogation, Jacques confirmed that Editions Services was a Panamanian company created in 1981 and bought in 1986 by Giacomo Medici. In 1991, he said, the company had rented rooms in the Geneva Freeport, from Mat Securitas SA. He said that "the only purpose of the company was that of collecting the proceeds deriving from antiquities sales at Sotheby's in London, and that purchases were made exclusively through Sotheby's." It was Medici, he said, who managed these sales and kept the proceeds, and he observed that "no bookkeeping of any kind had ever been maintained." He also gave it as his view that "very many objects, also of great value, had been handled through Sotheby's." He insisted that he was only the administrator and that Medici had all the "economic rights" in the company. But Jacques did admit that he was the administrator of other companies, including Tecafin S.A. and Xoilan Trader, Inc. He had administered Xoilan since 1976. He himself had started this company for an English citizen, Robin Symes.

Danilo Zicchi, of course, was interrogated immediately after his premises were discovered in February 1996. He fleshed out the general picture given here in two ways. He confirmed—and this was very important as evidence—that the organigram was indeed in Pasquale Camera's handwriting, and he revealed that sometime around the end of 1994 or beginning of 1995, Camera had told him about a treasure of more than 100 Roman silver pieces that had been found in the Vesuvian area. (This is by no means improbable. In July 2005, a 2,000-year-old silver dining service—twenty goblets, plates, and trays—buried in volcanic ash in Pompeii when Vesuvius erupted, went on exhibit at the archaeological site, after being unearthed by workers digging a new highway that will pass near the Pompeii ruins.) Zicchi said the treasure was of such a quality that it could only be compared to two similar ones, the Pisanella Treasure at the Louvre (this 109-piece silver hoard was excavated in 1895 at the Villa Pisanella in Herculaneum and given to the Louvre by Edmond de Rothschild), and that

*See p. 19.

of the House of the Menandro, discovered in the basement of the home of the Pompeian poet Menandro, in 1930, and now at the National Archaeological Museum in Naples. Together with the clandestine silver, Zicchi said that a few hundred gold and silver coins had been found, also from the Roman era, of the Julius Claudian dynasty (which ruled in the first century BC and the first century AD). This treasure, "found in about 1990 by an elderly person," had, he said, been bought by a Benedetto D'Aniello of the Naples area (named in the organigram), who had sold it to Giacomo Medici. Camera had revealed all this to Zicchi because he was furious that the treasure had been "dismembered." This had happened, apparently, after Medici took the hoard to Switzerland and sold part of it to "the Symeses." Other parts had been sold to a Persian (whom Zicchi named), a man living in Switzerland but with a warehouse in London.

Then there were a number of tombaroli whom Ferri interrogated as part of Operation Geryon. On occasion, their information—backed up by phone taps—confirmed the emerging picture of the organization of the cordate. One was Walter Guarini, interrogated several times in March 1999. Guarini was a tombarolo from Puglia who had stepped up the ladder and become an important middleman-dealer in his own right. The Carabinieri had had their eyes on him for some time, and Guarini, no fool, had several times given them tip-offs and information when—of course—these didn't directly jeopardize his own activity. Guarini confirmed that Hecht has "always been Number One in the world, for many years." Here is the next exchange:

PUBLIC PROSECUTOR [DR. FERRI]: Do you know if Hecht is the person to whom all of Europe turns to launder these objects, or not?

GUARINI: A large part turns to him.

P.P.: To launder them?

G.: Yes, to sell them. But not only Italians, also foreigners: Turks, Lebanese, Syrians . . .

P.P.: "Launder" is quite a scientific term in this field. You see, I wanted to be precise about this.

G.: Put them on the market.

P.P.: And why did he [Medici] not, for example, go directly to the Paul Getty Museum?

G.: I think that the Getty uses a filter to buy certain artifacts.

P.P.: Why do they use a filter?

G.: Because I believe Bob Hecht is highly accredited for his profession, which he has been practicing for forty years, almost fifty years.

P.P.: So this filter is in charge of buying and selling?

G.: He's certainly the reference point.

Guarini also set down the names of those in the various cordate, specifying who was linked to whom. He listed a raft of tombaroli names from Puglia, Sicily, Campania, and Lazio who supplied Savoca, including [Vincenzo] Cammarata; he listed the people in Naples and Rome who supplied Frida Tchacos, including Pasquale Camera; he said that "Frida's contacts abroad are [Michael] Steinhardt [a New York dealer], Leon Levy, Jiri Frel, and Marion True."

Then came this next exchange. It appears that during Ferri's discussions with Guarini about Robert Hecht, Guarini happened to mention a *memoria* (memoir) that Hecht was writing. (Remember that this interrogation took place in 1999.)

Ferri leaped on this reference because in their phone taps, the Carabinieri had more than once heard mention of a *"memoria,"* yet hadn't been able to make sense of what they heard. Was it something written? A tape? And what was its purpose?

P.P.: What is this *memoria* of Bob Hecht? Bob Hecht's *memoria*—what is it?

G.: I heard about it in Savoca's house, at Nino's . . .

P.P.: In what year?

G.: Last year, or two years ago.

P.P.: And where is this *memoria*?

G.: This *memoria* is . . . it appears that Bob has it, that he wrote all . . . all his trafficking [*"traffico"*] in the last years with all the characters . . .

P.P.: It's not that Nino Savoca had the *memoria* of . . .

G.: No, no. He didn't have it nor did he know . . . in fact, at the time he was afraid of this *memoria.*

P.P.: Savoca was afraid of this *memoria*? Why?

G.: Probably because they too were in this *memoria*.

P.P.: Of course, I imagine so . . .

G.: Just as all the dealers who had anything to do with . . .

P.P.: I understand . . .

[deletion for legal reasons]

P.P.: . . . in the end I suppose I'll have to say thank you to good Mr. Guarini, but at the moment I can't say thank you, because the members of your cordata have not emerged. So, this *memoria* of Bob Hecht's?

G.: If I had it, Doctor, I'd give it to you immediately . . .

P.P.: And Savoca hasn't got it by any chance?

G.: No, no. They're all so afraid, Doctor . . .

P.P.: Who?

G.: Savoca also is afraid of the . . .

P.P.: They haven't got it, no . . . ?

G.: . . . of the direct contacts . . .

P.P.: . . . in some floppy disk?

G.: No, no, absolutely not, because when . . . the guy who died [Savoca died in 1998] was telling me, that when this subject was touched, Bob Hecht became secretive, and then without putting . . . without recording please . . . Can I say something without recording?

P.P.: Oh no, you can't. Better that you keep it to yourself. Not to me. Nothing doing.

G.: No, well . . . It concerned Bob, who is an extremely dangerous man. Absolutely.

P.P.: Oh, I imagine so; he's central to international trafficking [*"traffici internazionali"*] for the past twenty years.

G.: Yes, but apart from this, he's dangerous.

Another tombarolo was Pietro Casasanta. Among tomb robbers in Italy, Casasanta is notorious. A rough, portly chain-smoker in his late sixties who lives in Anguillara, north of Rome near the shores of Lake Bracciano, he began digging in 1960 and told us that he has discovered "about a hundred villas" (he does not, he says, "plunder tombs"). He is notorious for making three extraordinary discoveries. In 1970, he found L'Inviolata, a large settlement, a temple cult that he says contained sixty-three statues, twenty-five of them life-size. Many of these, he says, he sold to Robin

Symes. He returned to L'Inviolata in 1992 and discovered the famous Capitoline Triad, a six-ton marble statue of three seated gods—Jupiter, with a sheaf of lightning in one hand and an eagle at his feet, Juno, with a scepter and a peacock, and Minerva, with a shaft and an owl. Made of Lunense marble, this sculpture is unique, the only example depicting this triad that is intact. After a two-year Operation Juno, the piece was recovered by the Carabinieri and is now displayed in the Palestrina National Archaeological Museum in Palestrina, a town southwest of Rome (L'Inviolata is in Palestrina municipal district). Casasanta was jailed for twelve months. Then, in 1995—that is, within a year of his release from prison—he discovered an ivory head of Apollo, dating from the fifth century BC, and three Egyptian statues of goddesses, two in green granite and one in black. He found these, he says, in a field not far from a well-known archaeological landmark, the Baths of Claudius, and he believes he discovered a luxurious villa that belonged to the family of the first-century Roman emperor Claudius.

The ivory mask in particular was very valuable. Ivory sculptures, even in antiquity, were extremely rare. They were known as Chryselephantine sculptures, after the Greek for gold and ivory. (Great sculptures—such as the Athena Parthenos in the Acropolis in Athens, had their head, hands, and feet made of ivory, and their wooden or stone bodies covered in gold leaf.) Ivory was so expensive in antiquity that only emperors and other important figures could afford such statues. They were so rare that only one other life-size figure is known to have survived in Italy, found at Montecalvo (again, near Rome) and now in the Apostolic Library in the Vatican. And only one set of life-size Chryselephantine sculptures survives in Greece.

Casasanta smuggled the ivory and the three statues out of Italy himself and sold them to Nino Savoca. They agreed on a fee of $10 million.

Casasanta admitted to knowing Medici, having met him once in the "antiquities warehouse" (as he put it) of Franco Luzzi in Ladispoli. (Luzzi, it will be recalled, was mentioned in the organigram, where his area of influence is given as Ladispoli, on the coast north of Rome.) Casasanta said he had never done business with Medici—he didn't like to deal with "Roman" dealers—but he had always known his name "because in their world he is a well-known figure." He said that he had on a couple of occasions met Robert Hecht in Basel but that he'd not had "work" dealings with him, nor with Gianfranco Becchina. He had instead concluded a few "deals" with Ali Aboutaam abroad, for which he had "undergone penal procedures." Casasanta's problem was that the market "relative to his activity" was dominated by groups (the "cordate"), so he couldn't even approach "certain milieus." Casasanta, whose interrogation overlapped with Guarini's, was the first person to use the word "cordata," and he indicated that, for him, there were three groups, not two—one out of Italy via Savoca in Munich, one via Becchina in Basel, and one via Medici in Geneva. In his milieu, he said, "it was commonly believed by all that Medici was '*il boss dei boss*' [the boss of bosses]," even though he, Casasanta, had no knowledge of specific facts. Casasanta believed that it had been Medici who had gotten him into trouble, putting the Carabinieri on to him when he had found the Capitoline Triad (and had left Medici out of the deal). Casasanta said it was rumored that "Medici was at the head of traffickings, a 'general' both in Italy and abroad, in London just as in Basel and Cerveteri." (He meant Geneva, not Basel; it was all the same to him—Switzerland.) In particular, Franco Gangi, to whom Casasanta had sold the objects he dug up for fifteen years—from the end of the 1960s to the end of the 1980s—had told him that when he came into Etruria, "he would find 'Giacomino' Medici, because everything in Etruria went through Medici and one could not 'work' because Medici would always take everything and controlled the market through his many contacts and relations in the area."

Casasanta gave an interesting account of Medici's early years—how, for example, his parents had a stall at the Fontanella Borghese, where they sold small objects. For many years, Casasanta said, Medici had a man, Ermenegildo Foroni, known as "Scotchwhisky," who acted as his shipper and sold goods abroad for him. This name, Ermenegildo Foroni, was of course one of the names on Pasquale Camera's organigram. (Casasanta didn't know about the organigram at the time of his interrogation.) It was common practice, he said, to use Swiss shippers to temporarily store objects on their way abroad. He confirmed that Pasquale Camera would organize thefts from museums and churches and that he had a close relationship with Nino Savoca in Munich—he was part of that cordata. To quote the official record of the interrogation, "Right back at the time when Camera was a lieutenant of the Finanza [Guardia di Finanza], Savoca and his wife would come to Etruria and would sleep at Casasanta's house because they didn't want to go to hotels [where they would have to register, showing their passports], thus avoiding being noticed and leaving their names around; then they [Casasanta and Savoca] would go together with Lello Camera [Lello is a nickname for Pasquale]—it was the early sixties—to get frescoes in Paestum."

Broadening out, Casasanta said that the Euphronios krater had been found by a certain Renato, whose nickname was "Roscio." He had been identified but had died. "Franco Gangi used to say he had given 180 million [lire, or $150,000] to Giacomo Medici to buy the Euphronios krater and Medici had 'nicked' the money and had sold the vase to others." Through Nino Savoca, Casasanta had met a "lady, about 35–40 years old in 1995," introduced as the deputy director of the Metropolitan Museum in New York, who had come to see a Roman head at Casasanta's home; afterward Nino Savoca had bought the head "following the indications of the woman." In 1970, he had made a fabulous find, much more important than the Capitoline Triad; he had found over sixty sculptures. He had sold them for not very much to Roman dealers, and the greater part of these had later been bought by Robin Symes and Christo Michaelides. In the autumn of 1970, they came to Rome and often bought objects excavated by Casasanta.

Mario Bruno, he said, was a friend of his, a dealer who operated in Etruria and Puglia, where everybody worked, and he would sell the archaeological material abroad. "He lived in Lugano where he had a villa on the lake. He knew Giacomo Medici and Bruno used to speak badly of him since they were competitors in trafficking archaeological material from Italy, both busy trying to buy the best objects that came to light." He (Casasanta) had given the Triad to Bruno. Becchina had a fabulous gallery in Basel. It was some years since he had retired to his villa in Sicily, though he had been very active for fifteen or twenty years before. "Becchina used to buy archaeological material principally in Sicily where he had some good suppliers who had also got him some valuable pieces. In Etruria he used to buy from tombaroli who would bring him the merchandise to Basel. Becchina, from being absolutely nothing, from being an emigrant with a small suitcase, had gone to Switzerland, had in some way begun his work in Basel and had become a multimillionaire. Becchina bought himself a large estate in his hometown, he bought a baronial palazzo where he lives alone with four to five servants. . . ." Casasanta knew Frida Tchacos well. He'd also sold her a small head in Zurich in 1990–1993. "Tchacos was powerful and tied to the Symeses and had noteworthy means at her disposal."

The fact was, the paperwork discovered in Geneva was beginning to work. The details revealed in the Freeport, plus the organigram, convinced the smaller fry at least that their interests lay in cooperating with Conforti and Ferri. The public prosecutor was encouraged. But he would be much more encouraged if he could find that memoir by Hecht that Savoca had mentioned to Guarini, and which had been referred to, so tantalizingly, in the phone taps. Did the memoir exist?

12

THE PARIS RAID ON ROBERT HECHT

I N THE NEXT PART of the investigation, Ferri relied initially on what are known in English as "letters rogatory." These are, essentially, requests for help in investigations from the judicial authority in one country to the judicial authority in another country. They are cumbersome and unwieldy. A public prosecutor like Ferri will prepare the paperwork, showing the legal grounds and a prima facie case for the investigation, which is passed from the Italian Ministry of Justice to the ministry of justice in France or Britain or the United States. The ministry in the receiving country then passes on the written request to whatever judicial office or police force the proposed investigation might concern. Any reply goes via the same route in reverse. Such a rigmarole can and does take months. It is not unknown for answers to be more than a year in coming back. Often, there is no reply at all. It was a matter of considerable regret, on Ferri's part, that while he secured prompt and willing cooperation from the French, slower but still willing cooperation from the Swiss and Germans, and grudging cooperation from the Americans, the British and the Danes were totally unhelpful.

Fortunately, the man whom Conforti and Ferri were interested in above all others, Robert Hecht, now lived in Paris and the French police were more cooperative than most. Following the arrival of the material from Geneva in Rome at the end of June 2000, Ferri immediately issued a letter rogatory for a raid on Hecht's apartment in the Boulevard Latour Maubourg, in the Seventh Arrondissement of Paris, near the Invalides and Napoleon's tomb. Even though the French were totally cooperative, permission for the raid didn't come through for some months. The raid was finally scheduled for February 16, 2001.

Two of Conforti's most experienced men and four French police officers took part. Hecht, they knew, had an apartment in New York. The Americans had already denied them permission to raid that address because, the Americans said, the information the Italians had about him was "not recent." The fact that the Swiss had held on to the documents for so long was already taking its toll. Furthermore, technically the Paris apartment was in the name of Hecht's wife—in other words, it wasn't his. Fortunately for the Italians, the French were not as persnickety as the Americans. "In Paris, we had zero difficulty," says Conforti.

Robert Hecht's family founded the Hecht chain of department stores and he grew up in Baltimore. Born in 1919, he attended Haverford College, outside Philadelphia. He learned Latin in high school, started Greek at college, and had begun graduate work in archaeology when he was called up in World War II. After serving in the navy, he spent a year at Zurich University working on a Ph.D., then won a two-year fellowship at the American Academy in Rome. In 1950, he turned from the academic life to dealing art and made his first sale, an Apulian vase of the fourth century BC, which he sold to the Metropolitan in New York. Balding, with a fringe of white hair, Hecht walks with a limp now, though he has never allowed an artificial hip to stop him from playing tennis, one of his passions. The others—besides antiquities—are his two daughters, claret, and backgammon. He is an inveterate gambler.

The Paris apartment was on the second floor. The senior French officer knocked on the door. Hecht's wife, Elisabeth, opened it. At first she tried to resist the incoming policemen. She said Hecht wasn't there and, moreover, that he did not live there, and hadn't for fifteen years. The police—both French and Italian—were expecting this (it was a familiar delaying tactic) and presented her with a simple ultimatum: Either she could let them in willingly, in which case they promised not to enter her own bedroom; or they could do it the hard way, break down the door if she barred them, when they would go through the entire apartment.

She let them in.

Inside, it was "[n]ot luxurious, but elegant," says one of the men who was there. A spacious hallway featured an impressive chandelier, and the apartment had two bedrooms. The furniture was antique rather than modern. There was a study on the left, but Elisabeth led them to one of the bedrooms, which, she indicated, was Hecht's. The two Carabinieri in the raiding party had often enjoyed a joke that in the movies, police searching an apartment always look first under the bed. In real life, no one ever hides anything under the bed. Well, on this occasion—at the very moment they entered the bedroom, they could see some white plastic shopping bags *wedged under the bed*. They placed them on top of the covers, and reached inside. The first things they took out were some ancient vases— Attic, Apulian, Corinthian—full of earth. Then they found a bronze helmet, and a bronze belt, both dusted in soil. Next they came across a number of vase fragments, in the same dirty condition.

The rest of the discoveries that day were mixed. There were several folders with photographs packed inside. One contained thirteen Polaroids, all marked with the same serial number. These showed an oinochoe with a wild boar, the base of a large vase, possibly Apulian, a bronze mirror with two warriors, a winged figure—and one showed a sculpture-antefix with two horses' heads. Polaroids of an identical object were found among Medici's documents in Geneva (which by now, of course, were in Rome).

Another file had fifteen color photographs showing female busts, "very dirty with earth," according to the official report on the raid. They were ready to be cleaned and restored. Then there were photographs of the twenty red-figure Attic plates, the same as had been found in the safe at Geneva, and exactly the same set of photographs as Medici had, including the one with the tag on it that said "21 pieces 2,000."* These were in a folder with a copy of the letter that Hecht had sent to the Getty in which he informed the museum that he had the plates on consignment from Medici. A final folder of photographs showed twenty-three objects, each of which had been found in Medici's photograph albums seized in Geneva.

Among the letters was one dated April 18, 1991, from Felicity Nicholson, director of Sotheby's Antiquities Department, to Editions Services at 7 Avenue Krieg, Geneva. It included this paragraph: "We also have an Attic black-figure Panathenaic Amphora which Bob Hecht asked should be put in your name. This we intend to include in our July sale." Sotheby's, or at least Felicity Nicholson, was perfectly aware of the Medici-Hecht cordata.

In a sense, however, these photographs and letters, though very use-

*See pp. 96–98.

ful as corroboration, only confirmed what Ferri and Pellegrini already knew, that Medici was responsible for bringing illicit material out of Italy and that Hecht was the main conduit between him and the world's collectors and the great museums. And that members of the cordata traded antiquities in each other's name. In contrast, the other documentation found in Hecht's Paris apartment was much more interesting for the *fresh* light it threw on the world inhabited by him and Medici.

The most dismaying was a series of letters that General Conforti, writing in his capacity as head of the Carabinieri Art Squad, had sent to William Luers, the president of the Metropolitan Museum of Art in New York, about the Morgantina silver.* In his letter, dated November 15, 1996, Conforti referred to some letters rogatory that were being prepared in relation to the silver that, he said, had been "unlawfully excavated," but he raised the possibility that the Met might want to return the treasure voluntarily "with adequate publicity." Ashton Hawkins, executive vice president and counsel to the trustees, replied, saying that the museum "remained convinced of the facts as they were given at the time of the purchase." Hawkins was polite but firm, and Conforti was rebuffed. One is prompted to ask *why* Hecht had been sent this correspondence. What interest did Hecht have in the Morgantina silver? According to the museum's official account, the silver pieces came from Turkey and were acquired legally, in Switzerland. What role had Hecht played in the museum's acquisitions of them? The suggestion that arises from this scenario, that the Metropolitan Museum in New York is in a closer, cozier relationship with the antiquities underworld than it is with the legitimate police authorities, is disappointing, to say the least.

The nature of Hecht's close relations with museums—and theirs with him—was further reinforced by two other documents found in Boulevard Latour Maubourg. These were notices, sent to two museums and signed by Conforti, that announced that the Carabinieri was putting on its Web site 500 images of archaeological objects that had been stolen or illegally excavated in Lazio, Puglia, Campania, and Sicily; in other words, these objects had been looted and Conforti was asking the museum directors to look out for them. What did the directors do? They sent the information to

*See pp. 103–106.

Hecht. Why? Could it be they were warning him? Once again, it seems that some of the world's museums are on more intimate terms with the sources of illicit antiquities than they are with the legitimate police authorities. One of the museums was the archaeological museum in Geneva, the other had its name obscured with white-out. One of the Carabinieri lifted the page up to the light. Held in that way, the name of the second museum was clearly visible: the Archaeological Museum in Munich (the Antiken-sammlung). Why did the museum want its name covered up?

There was one other document of consequence that the Carabinieri came across that February day in Paris. Ever since the discovery of Pasquale Camera's organigram in 1995, the Italian authorities had realized that Hecht was the main figure, the top man at the head of the cordate that smuggled material out of Italy. But, more than that, during the subsequent investigations, discussed in the previous chapter, they had picked up from various sources the fact that many of the lesser figures were frightened of Hecht and intimidated by him. The main reason for this, as Ferri was told, was that Hecht had let it be known—among those he dealt with regularly—that he was writing a book about the antiquities underworld. Although Hecht never actually said so (he was too clever), the implication of this was that anyone who stepped out of line, anyone who crossed him, anyone who tried to bypass him, anyone who tried to usurp his role, anyone who tried to poach his contacts would be named in the book and exposed. It was never made clear whether Hecht would publish the book in his lifetime or, as some sources appeared to have been told, after his death, to provide funds for his wife to live on. Each time Ferri, Pellegrini, or any of Conforti's men heard about this "book" or "memoir," the more intrigued they became. By the time they obtained permission to raid Hecht's flat, on that February day in 2001, it was the main thing they were looking for.

Naturally, the discovery of the letters and Polaroids at Boulevard La-tour Maubourg provoked much discussion among the raiding party, especially the Italians. Besides discussing the decoration on the vases that had been found, they naturally referred to other, related documentation found in Geneva that fitted with what they were uncovering in Paris. At this point, however, one of Conforti's men noticed Elisabeth Hecht listening in on what they were saying. This was odd because when they had entered the hallway to the apartment, at the beginning of the raid, she had spoken French to the French policemen and, in response to a direct question, had denied being able to speak Italian. Neither of the Carabinieri gave it a thought to begin with. But then one of them recalled that among Hecht's correspondence was a letter to his wife at Via di Villa Pepoli—she *had* lived in Italy. And so he gave her a fresh ultimatum. Either he and his colleague would step away and discuss their next moves out of earshot, or they could all speak Italian.

Mrs. Hecht—wrong-footed—now admitted that she understood Italian.

Eager to press their psychological advantage, Conforti's men immediately said they were less interested in dirty antiquities than in the memoir that they had heard on the underworld grapevine that Hecht was writing.

Elisabeth Hecht stiffened but said that she knew of no memoir. Her slight hesitation was picked up on by Conforti's men.

The French policeman leading the raid also noticed. "Right," he said, adopting the Italians' tactics, "either you lead us straight to the memoir, or we turn over the whole apartment." He made it clear that there would be serious disruption to Mrs. Hecht's routine and that her own bedroom would no longer be off-limits.

Without speaking, she turned on her heel and led them into the study. And there, in the middle of the room, was a desk, and in the middle of the desk, just sitting there, for all to see, was a plain, buff-colored folder. Inside, when they opened it, was a manuscript, its pages handwritten on lined legal-size paper, on plain paper, and on graph paper. The pages were covered in rows of untidy handwriting that, upon closer examination, the Carabinieri could see was in English. There and then they couldn't understand it, but flipping through the pages, they saw a number of names, abbreviations, and initials they recognized—Vulci, Montalto di Castro, R. Symes, Euphr., "G.M."

This was it.

The rumors had been true, the gossip on the grapevine had been accurate, Savoca and Guarini had been telling the truth. Hecht *had* written a memoir and now—at last, at long last—they had it.

The memoir was seized but, of course, it was seized on the authority of the *French* police. It would be some time before the Italians could get their hands on it. Meanwhile, realizing how serious the raid was turning out to be, from her husband's point of view, Elisabeth Hecht now called him, in New York. She spoke to him, and he said he would leave for Paris immediately. He was, he said, anxious to speak to the law-enforcement authorities.

A day or so later, while the Carabinieri were still in Paris, seeing to the paperwork necessary if the objects and documentation found in the raid were to be transferred to Italy, Hecht got in touch. He had flown in from New York, he said, and was anxious to see the Carabinieri, not the French police. He asked for a meeting.

Ferri authorized a brief meeting, and one of his men met with Hecht the following day. Hecht chose the meeting place, in front of Notre Dame, the great cathedral of Paris, on the Ile de la Cité. Hecht said he would be there, at four o'clock in the afternoon, "on the left-hand corner as you look at the church."

At four o'clock it was raining hard. But Hecht was on time, wearing a fawn coat, but with no hat and no umbrella. The lieutenant almost felt sorry for him. Hecht led the way to a nearby café, where the meeting lasted barely twenty minutes. Hecht wanted to know what had happened during the raid, why he had been targeted, what they thought they had found. The lieutenant was under strict instructions from Ferri to give nothing away. All he did say was to advise Hecht to "get a lawyer."

It may have been a short meeting and next to nothing may have been said, but it had been important, Ferri felt. Hecht had asked for the rendezvous, and during it he had asked all the questions. Despite everything that had happened, it appeared that he had not been expecting the raid, and now—and for the first time, so far as Hecht was concerned—the boot was on the other foot. Hecht wasn't frightened exactly, but he was certainly nervous. That hadn't happened before.

Ferri planned an interrogation of Hecht, but before that, he needed to get his hands on the memoir in Italian. Ferri speaks some English but not enough to cope easily with a long, handwritten document in a scrawl that isn't always easy to decipher even for a native English speaker.

The French provided the memoir quickly enough, but when they did, for evidential reasons (that is, to prevent pages from being deleted or new ones added), when the document arrived in Rome it was held together by a special binder—a hole had been pierced through each page and they had been laced together with twine—and the pages were numbered. This was all reasonable, except for the fact that the Italians quickly found that the pages were not in the right order—they didn't all read on from one page to the next. Whatever had happened after the raid in Paris, the pages had been jumbled. Therefore they had to be photocopied and rearranged in their proper sequential order, and only then translated. All of which took time.

But eventually it was done, and at last Ferri and the others could read what Hecht had written.

Written in English, the memoir was eighty-eight pages long and appeared to have been compiled over several months and years. There are one or two idiosyncracies in the text—for example, instead of "with," Hecht usually writes "c" or "c̄," shorthand for the Italian (or Latin) *con;* "C.C." is the common Italian abbreviation for Carabinieri; "Æ" is silver; "Au" is gold, and so on. There are many references to food and drink, tennis and his family, but none at all to his gambling. The tone is self-confident, even self-righteous throughout, cocky in places. The narrative, which ranges from the 1950s to 2001, is divided into eight sections. It begins with the early years—the 1950s and the 1960s—in Italy, Turkey, and Greece. It gives—perhaps significantly, and certainly most interestingly— *two* versions of the Euphronios krater affair. There is a section devoted to the acquisition by the Getty of the Euphronios-Onesimos kylix, followed by a more theoretical section in which Hecht argues that his activities have benefited archaeology and in which he defends himself against the charge that he and his kind have desecrated the archaeological heritage of several civilizations.

In an early section, referring to 1961, he describes returning to his Rome apartment after a trip to Sicily with a miniature altar, or *arula,* that he had bought in Gela, a city founded by the Greeks in the eighth century BC. The very next morning he was raided by the Carabinieri, but they didn't find the arula. Instead, he showed them some cheap archaeological items he kept in the apartment for just this sort of occasion, and to deflect suspicion.

At that time, the Carabinieri were carrying out one of their irregular sweeps on the antiquities trade and, by chance, stumbled on the Swiss dealer, Herbert Cahn, who was in Rome on a visit. Interviewed at Carabinieri headquarters, one of the people he admitted knowing in the Italian capital was Robert Hecht, but Cahn said that he did no business with the American expatriate because he was "a competitor." However, he did name two Roman dealers he had bought from over the previous few years—Renzi and Pennacchi.

> When I was told about this I couldn't believe it. I called up Cahn and asked him if this was true. He replied, "Ja. Ich habe es aber minimal gehalten." (Yes, but I kept it at a minimum.) Cahn did not realize or want to realize that he was dealing in contraband and that in this activity it is ignoble to inform against your collaborators.

This was an interesting sighting of the word "contraband."

That wasn't all. Cahn was carrying his address book on him and the Carabinieri seized it. In addition to the names and numbers of his contacts, the address book included a record of what he had bought and from whom.

> These notes included a letter from Mr. Sabatini, a school teacher in Canino (near the site of Vulci—the biggest source of fine Greek pottery) agreeing to Cahn's offer for two vases, one of which was a Rhodian oinochoe and saying that he awaited Cahn's visit.

Then, without warning, Hecht completely changes the subject—to George Ortiz, a man he had dealt with over the past forty years. After first describing Ortiz's background, he discusses his collecting, how he developed a passion for Greek art especially, starting with visits to museums, then using dealers on both sides of the Atlantic, buying mainly bronzes, usually of very good quality. But then, after familiarizing himself with the main dealers in Rome and Athens, Ortiz soon made contacts with grave diggers and traffickers in the countryside, especially in Southern Etruria. . . . George became well known among the villagers and in their investigations the Carabinieri found correspondence and evidence of payments by George in houses they searched. They even found evidence of checks on Swiss Credit Bank which he had given to a gentleman in Montepulciano.

In the autumn of 1961, charges were brought against the Rome dealers Renzi and Pennacchi, against Cahn, Ortiz, and Hecht, who were accused of receiving stolen property. All were acquitted. On appeal, all were found guilty. Finally, in 1976 (yes, fifteen years later), Cahn and Ortiz were found guilty and given brief suspended sentences, while Hecht was acquitted.

The memoir, which was to become of considerable importance in the subsequent criminal trials, is full of interesting tidbits about the history of tomb-robbing. For instance, Hecht records how in 1963, a Swiss dealer went so far as to equip the looters in Tarquinia (well known for its painted tombs) with electric saws, with which they could more easily strip frescoes from the walls of tombs and villas. Ironically, when the police discovered what was happening, they decided that only Americans would risk and finance such flamboyant looting techniques and Hecht's residence permit was revoked. He was expelled, as a result of which he missed the birth of his daughter.

It is known that Elia Borowsky bought several frescoes from Tarquinia at this time.

In another vignette, Hecht was shown some beautiful silver figures in Pandrossan Street in Athens. The Armenian dealer insisted on cash so Hecht prevailed on a female friend to fly in to Athens from Zurich for a short holiday—provided she brought with her forty one-thousand-dollar bills. That seems to have done the trick for, a few days later, she flew back to Switzerland—with the silver figures. These figures, Hecht says, are now in Copenhagen.[1]

Beginning in 1963, Hecht was allowed back into Italy, though at first his residence permit was for one month at a time, then three months, and finally, by 1965, it was for a year at a time. He had by now renewed a relationship with one "GZ," George Zakos, a Greek who had grown up in

Istanbul, whom Hecht had known since 1951. After a number of small deals, mainly having to do with coins, the bigger transactions commenced.

One involved the British Museum and began when Zakos produced three silver cups with floral designs and a scene from Iphigenia among the Taurians (an episode from Homer; Tauris is today's Crimea). Hecht was in London the following weekend, ahead of a visit to Sir John and Lady Beazley at their home in Oxford. Not wanting to traipse the cups all the way to Oxford, Hecht asked Dennis Haynes, the British Museum keeper of antiquities, if he could leave the cups with him for safe keeping. Hecht's initial thought had been to sell the cups to the Boston Museum of Fine Arts, because a friend of his, Cornelius Vermeule, had just been appointed curator. However, to Hecht's considerable surprise, Haynes inquired after the price of the cups. Wrong-footed for once, Hecht said he would think about it and, after he returned from his visit to the Beazleys, gave Haynes what he described as a "defensive" price of $90,000. What he meant by this was that he thought such a figure would be well beyond the British Museum. In fact, Haynes didn't turn a hair and Hecht was paid by the end of the month. In this way, Hecht identifies loot in the BM.

There are several episodes such as this one. Hecht is "brought" material, which he describes in detail, though the routes out of Italy, Greece, or Turkey are only rarely specified.

And so, vignette by vignette, the years elapse in Hecht's narrative, before Medici ("GM") is introduced. It was early 1967 and Hecht was out of Italy, when his wife told him on the phone that a middle-man called Franco Luzzi (mentioned in the organigram) had been offered a good-quality kylix but his suppliers, the tombaroli, wanted what was then a high price. His appetite whetted, Hecht returned quickly to Rome and met with Luzzi near the Campidoglio [Rome's capital, today the seat of the municipality]. Hecht is usually very coy in his memoir about these meetings, and he makes it clear that he went to considerable lengths to avoid being seen with such middlemen by anyone in authority. At the rendezvous, he had Luzzi make a pencil drawing of the kylix, which showed that on each outside surface there was an owl between olive branches. In the central round part, the tondo, there was a youth with a vase. Hecht must have liked what he saw for he told Luzzi to buy the cup, whatever it took. Luzzi complained that the tombaroli were asking 1,800,000 lire (then equivalent to $3,000). Hecht said that he would guarantee Luzzi at least 2,500,000 lire, ensuring a tidy profit. However, when Luzzi went back to his tombaroli suppliers they countered by saying that Medici had already told them he would beat any offer Luzzi made. And in fact, on that occasion, Medici bought the kylix and sold it on to the man he then mainly supplied. According to Hecht, this was Eli Borowsky.

But Hecht wouldn't be beaten. Medici had bought the kylix for 1,500,000 and sold it to Borowsky for only a hundred thousand lire more. So Hecht told Luzzi to go back to "GM" and offer him 2,000,000 lire. Although these sums are paltry by today's standards, at that time such differences in price were significant and as a result of Luzzi's improved offer, Medici got back the kylix from Borowsky and sold it to Hecht.

So, in the evening on the Lungotevere [the boulevard that runs alongside the River Tiber in Rome], in front of the [old] Palace of Justice, in my car, parked behind theirs, Luzzi and GM showed me the cup and I asked GM if he would be content with 2.2 [million lire]. He jumped with joy and said "yes" . . . I gave Luzzi a commission of 800,000 lire, so both were happy. Later, I sold this to Dr. Hirk, a Basel chemist, for 60,000 Swiss Francs (= ca. 8,500,000 lire).

Hecht was obviously a bit of a show-off, who liked people to know how clever he was and how readily he could read character. He certainly seems to have understood Medici very well, right from the beginning. In a passage which, as the judge noted in Medici's trial, was confirmed by other tombaroli, Hecht wrote:

Up to this time GM (in his 20's) had been the purveyor to a pharmacist in Rome. GM's father and mother had a stand at the open air market at Piazza Borghese and sold minor objects from excavations to tourists. GM was more ambitious and having bought a second hand Fiat 500 for $400, rose early each morning and toured the villages of Etruria visiting all the clandestine diggers. Each evening he returned with his booty to the pharmacist, who gave him in cash a small profit, but bought everything. The sale of the kylix was an eye opener for GM. He saw that quality had a high premium.

This proved to be an understatement. As we shall see, this episode had pivotal consequences for Medici's career. From now on the objects he provided to Hecht began to rise markedly in value. Moreover, in Hecht's text the prices of their deals are from now on recorded in dollars, not lire. The sums involved rise over the years from $1,600, to $6,000, to $63,000. In each case, Hecht is careful to tell us what happened to these objects, which collectors or museum they ended up with and, of course, what handsome profits he made. For example, a set of Etruscan silver chariot fixtures, which he says he bought from Medici for $63,000, he sold on to Mogens Giddesen at the Copenhagen Museum for $240,000.

"G.M. soon became a faithful purveyor," he records, and indeed the list of objects Medici provided Hecht with is impressive. But of course, this background, though very vivid, is also very incriminating. And then, without any preamble or any other sort of warning or change of pace, halfway down page fourteen of this section of the memoir, Hecht broaches the subject of the infamous Euphronios krater.

In preparation for that, however, we need to consider one other matter.

In 1993, just before the investigations that are the subject of this book began, Thomas Hoving published his own memoirs. Since he had left the Met, he had become a journalist, among other things editor-in-chief of the magazine *Connoisseur* (now defunct), and had written at least one art book and a novel. His 1993 memoirs were entitled *Making the Mummies Dance*, a reference to his brand of showmanship when he was director of the Metropolitan, and chapter 17 was titled, characteristically, "The Hot Pot." It began typically enough. "I have fallen in love more often with works of art than with women," and it concerned the Met's acquisition of the Euphronios krater. This version differed in some interesting ways from the earlier version, as given here in the Prologue.

His most important revelations this time were:

- He had first been alerted to the existence of the vase by a phone call from Hecht's wife, directly to him, in September 1971; she said that her husband had "just" been consigned "a startling piece";

- During subsequent negotiations Hecht constantly referred to the "dollar situation," because that currency was weakening progressively at that time against the Swiss franc;

• Hecht was aware that the Metropolitan Museum was considering selling its coin collection and offered a swap;

• In a preliminary letter to the museum, Hecht said that the price of the krater would be comparable to that for an impressionist painting (the Met had just paid more than $1 million for a painting by Monet);

• The first photographs of the krater showed it recomposed but with the joins visible.

Hoving also said that in July 1976, he had received an unsolicited letter from Muriel Silberstein, in Chicago, in which she claimed that she had met Dikran Sarrafian in Beirut in 1964, when he had shown her some cylinder seals and a box containing shards of an ancient Greek vase by the artist Euphronios. Hoving never explained why it had taken her so long to come forward, but she stuck to her story, which she had independently told to several others.

For Hoving this didn't clear up the matter—he was too experienced and canny for that. But, putting all he knew alongside Mrs. Silberstein's information, Hoving in his 1993 memoirs came up with a new theory—that there were *two* kraters and one cup, all by Euphronios and all on the market in the early 1970s. The second krater, Hoving said, was the fragmentary one owned subsequently by the Hunt brothers, sold in their sale in 1990 and acquired by Leon Levy and Shelby White.* Both this second krater and the kylix, Hoving said, were acquired by the Hunts from Bruce McNall. Again according to Hoving's new theory, the whole business had begun when Hecht had sold to Munich's Antikensammlung in 1970 (actually 1968) a fragmentary Euphronios krater (a third one) for $250,000. Where this came from Hoving didn't say, but he added that "it seems likely" that Hecht, in concluding this deal, recalled Sarrafian's fragmentary krater, which he claimed to have seen in Beirut in 1965, and persuaded him to sell. And it was *this* that Hecht originally intended to offer to the Met.

"Then a miracle took place." An Etruscan tomb near San Antonio di Cerveteri was found by tomb robbers and the complete krater was discov-

*See p. 129.

ered in December 1971. According to Hoving, Hecht simply switched the two kraters, in the sense that he attached the Sarrafian provenance to the Cerveteri krater. This, Hoving says, would explain the various mix-ups: in the dates, the mix-up over whether Sarrafian's krater was complete or not, the mix-up over when the Sarrafian's krater left Lebanon, the mix-up in regard to the chronology of the invoices, the mix-up over when the krater reached Bürki for restoration. It would explain what Mrs. Silberstein saw in Beirut in 1964 and why Sarrafian did not receive all the monies he should have.[2]

So much for Hoving's updated account. We return to Hecht's memoir. The judge at Medici's trial, in announcing his verdict, compared this "true story" with Hecht's later "sweetened" version (see below, this chapter). Both accounts give key insights into the operating methods of these antiquities dealers.

GM was loyal and one morning in December 1971 he appeared at our apartment in Villa Pepoli shortly after breakfast with Polaroids of a krater signed by Euphronios. I could not believe my eyes. B. L. [Hecht's wife] exclaimed "Can this be true?" Within an hour we flew to Milan, had a vinous lunch at the Colline Pistoiesi [Cuisine from Pistoia] and took the train to Lugano where GM had the krater in a safe deposit box. The negotiations did not take long and we agreed on 1,500,000 Swiss Francs on the instalment plan. That same evening I went on to Zurich, left the krater with Fritz Bürki, paid GM all the liquid cash I had at the time ($40,000) and went back to Rome to take the family to Courmayeur for a ski vacation. And a happy vacation it was.

I owned in partnership with GZ a lifesize bronze eagle with which I had had no success, either with Fort Worth, L. A. County Museum, or the Metropolitan. To pay for [the] Euphronios I got GZ's permission to sell it to Robin Symes for $75,000 (we had paid $40,000). So, here was some more $ for GM. I had thought of giving the krater to Sotheby's but Felicity Nicholson's $200,000 estimate was a bit low. M Gyp [?] tried to get a Danish shipowner to buy it for the Glyptotek in Copenhagen but without success.

I had written a letter to DvB mentioning a r/f krater like the one in ARV page—[*Attic Red-Figure Vase Painters*, by J. D. Beazley] but virtually complete and with an appealing mythological scene. Shortly thereafter DvB replied that both his and his director's appetites were whetted and asked the price.

Hecht told them—cheekily—that the price would be at the same level as an impressionist painting, because the draftsmanship on the vase was the equal of the Monet that the Met had itself just bought, for $1.4 million. Hecht waited for Fritz Bürki to complete the restoration of the vase, which he did but still left the jumble of joins showing in red glue, so that the people at the Met could see what was old and what was new. Then Hecht flew to New York with some good-quality photographs. Von Bothmer, who lived on Center Island, had invited him to stay for part of the weekend. On the Sunday morning, Hecht was picked up by von Bothmer's car, but on the way to Center Island the driver hit a dog and Hecht was forced to cradle the animal—bleeding and whimpering—as they sought out a vet. The vet told Hecht the dog would live but the delay meant that Hecht, covered in blood, didn't arrive at von Bothmer's until well after he had planned.

DvB opened the door in the company of his son Bernard, then about seven years old. DvB: 'Bernard, ask Mr. Hecht if he knows the name of Herakles' brother.' I replied: 'Bernard, you tell me.' Bernard: 'Iplikles.' I replied: 'Bernard, you are half right—they were half brothers.'

Von Bothmer was very impressed by the photographs and so everyone relaxed. Hecht played some tennis with the curator's "beautiful stepdaughter," they all swam in the family pool and ate dinner. The next morning, the two men were driven into Manhattan together and showed the photographs to Tom Hoving and Ted Rousseau, curator of paintings and Hoving's deputy. They were no less impressed than von Bothmer and the four men agreed to reconvene in late June, at Fritz Bürki's in Zurich, to view the vase itself.

Dietrich von Bothmer, Thomas Hoving and Theodore Rousseau all came and looked at the krater in the garden under the sun. Tom Hoving pulled me aside & said that this was the finest work of art offered to the museum since he had become director. . . . Lunchtime was approaching, so we drove into Zurich to the Rotisserie de la Muette for grilled steaks and a discussion of the krater.

Hoving opened the negotiations suggesting some kind of annuity to be paid over several years. I replied that the price could be negotiated but that I wanted a lump sum and reasonably soon since the dollar was very weak. (At the time the $ had fallen from 4.30 Swiss Francs to 4.05 Swiss Francs.) Then I mentioned the ancient coin collection to be auctioned by Sotheby's.

Some time before, Hecht had been told by von Bothmer that the museum was intending to sell its collections of ancient coins and that the curators had been conferring with a bank and a particular coin dealer to hold a joint auction.

Hecht suggested at the meeting that the Met might get a better deal on the coins with Sotheby's, and Hoving quickly made some calls to Peter Wilson, chief executive of the auction house, and flew off immediately to London. Sotheby's did offer a higher estimate, cheaper terms, *and* advanced the museum some money.

Rousseau paid a second visit to Bürki's for another look at the vase, at which time he suggested that the restorer cover over the red joins with black paint. The Met was obviously moving toward a deal and, sure enough, in mid-August, Hoving called Hecht in Rome and offered exactly $1 million for the vase. Hecht accepted.

The following day he traveled to Zurich, where he found that Fritz Bürki had almost completed his restoration, covering over the red joins.

I reserved two first-class seats on the TWA flight, Zurich-to-New York [one first-class ticket then cost $450]. On arrival at JFK [airport] I was met by Mr. Keating, the MMA's shipping agent and an armed museum guard. . . . When we arrived at the loading platform at the south end of the museum, my wife Elisabeth and our two daughters were there to meet me. . . . When I showed Hoving the invoice stating that the krater came from Dikran, he laughed and said "I bet he doesn't exist."

This narrative, of course, totally contradicts the account originally given by the Metropolitan Museum of Art at the time of the krater's acquisition.

On the following day, Hecht flew to Malaga in Spain for a holiday at Lew Hoad's tennis camp, and a couple of weeks later von Bothmer got in touch to say that the museum's trustees had approved the purchase of the vase.

. . . the check for $1000000 was sent September 11 to Zurich. I immediately changed the check into Swiss Francs at the rate of 3.91 Swiss Francs to a dollar. By May 1974 the $ had fallen to 2.40 Swiss Francs and now is worth about 1.30 Swiss Francs.

Note his recollection of the exact date the money was paid and the specific exchange rates, down to two decimal places, that seem to be engraved on his memory.

At this point, Hecht's memoir mentions the *New York Times Magazine* article on the krater and the subsequent investigation by Nicholas Gage, referred to in the Prologue of this book. Finally, Hecht discusses the fact that Sir John Pope-Hennessy, then director of the Victoria and Albert Museum in London, and later director of the British Museum, expressed reservations that the krater was a fake. Hecht reports that this was also the view of Robin Symes and his partner Christo Michaelides. The criticism evidently got to him, for a whole page of the memoir is taken up with the plaudits the krater received from other experts.

Until this point, the account has been seamless. The Euphronios story is the culmination of a section of the memoir, fourteen pages long, beginning in 1967, and devoted almost exclusively to Hecht's dealings with Medici. The *New York Times* involvement in the story doesn't occur until page ten of this section and then occupies only a few paragraphs. After this, Hecht then returned to a fuller account of the *New York Times* and London *Observer* investigation of the provenance of the krater. This starts on a fresh page, in slightly different pen. (Hecht used several pens, and several inks, for the memoir, including a fountain pen.)

In a fourteen-and-a-half-page section, he recalled Nicholas Gage's investigation, and the way the Carabinieri pursued him, the prosecution in Italy, his eventual acquittal, and an attempt in 1977 by the Italian authorities to have the New York police put him before a grand jury. He was eventually acquitted there, too, but during his cross-examination before the grand jury, he was characterized as being little more than a "street peddler." This got to him, and, to the jury's great amusement, he tells us, he read off an impressive list of institutions to which he had sold material. These institutions included the British Museum, the Louvre, the Glyptothek in Munich, the Glyptotek in Copenhagen, the Museum of Fine Arts in Boston, and museums in Toledo, Cleveland, at Harvard University, the University of Pennsylvania, and the Campbell Soup Museum in New Jersey. With the grand jury's dismissal of the charges against him, Hecht noted that the "harassment ended."

His memoir then switches to more historical material. Thirty or so pages later, however, he returns once again to the Euphronios affair. This time there are crucial differences in his account. This section is dedicated solely to the affair and is physically separate, not part of a seamless narrative exploring other deals and other times. Moreover, the paper is not lined but is either plain or graph paper, and the manner of writing is somewhat different. Notably, there are far more abbreviations. It begins in this way, for instance, describing the situation when Tom Hoving first saw the krater in Zurich:

> Hvngs spont. react. revealed the sensitive art lover. "Ths s t gtst̶e̶ wrk f art offrd t th mus sns I'v bn there!" I replied, "how abt t Bury St. Ed. X?" "As a work of art this is mch fnr." For 1½ hrs. they inspected th pt. glued together from abt 100 pieces.

As before they went to the Rotisserie de la Muette for lunch and discussed price, where, on this occasion, he says that Hoving told him about the coin auction (in the earlier account, and in Hoving's own account, it was the other way around and Hecht had mentioned the coins to Hoving). "Hoving wanted to pay some in the fall and some in the coming year." Then this: "I̶ ̶m̶e̶n̶t̶i̶o̶n̶e̶d̶ ̶t̶h̶a̶t̶ ̶I̶ ̶w̶o̶u̶l̶d̶ ̶p̶r̶e̶f̶e̶r̶ ̶e̶a̶r̶l̶y̶ ̶p̶a̶y̶m̶e̶n̶t̶ ̶a̶n̶d̶ ̶a̶l̶t̶h̶o̶u̶g̶h̶ ̶I̶ ̶w̶o̶u̶l̶d̶ ̶b̶e̶ ̶w̶i̶l̶l̶i̶n̶g̶ t reduce the price in order t mk early payment poss." This was changed to read: "I said that I would ask t owner t reduce the price in order t mak early payment poss."

He goes on: "July & Aug wer spent finding a solution agreeable both t mus and m̶e̶ the owner." Later, after flying the krater in its box on the

TWA flight, "I was mt at Kennedy by an armed museum guard, Mr.—and Mr. X, the museum's customs brkr." As before, when he reached the museum his wife and two daughters were there, B. L., as he called his wife, dressed in a dirndl skirt and his daughters in colorful jeans. "My wife now saw the crat, for t 1ˢᵗ tim & exclaimed, 'I could almost cry, it's lk a Rembrandt!'" Afterwards Hecht and his family crossed Fifth Avenue, to the Stanhope Hotel, and had a drink at the pavement café there.

> We felt relaxed. Why not? A great museum had just received one of the few finest archaic Greek ptngs surviving and we had steered it there. Mainly we were happy because Dikran was now assured of securing his old age.

He then proceeds to repeat the details of the Sarrafian story, which explained the origins of the krater as having been acquired in London in the 1920s and Sarrafian's decision to sell before moving abroad. In this account, Sarrafian finally contacted Hecht in early 1971 to say that his agent would be in touch in Zurich in August that year.

"The teleph rang at about 7 A. M. & a voice w/ a typ. ME Fr. accent sd: 'Iz thees Mr. ~~hecht~~ Edge-te.'" The man came, Hecht showed his passport to prove who he was, then they both went to Fritz Bürki's to give him the vase to restore. Hecht took the agent to the station and himself caught the evening flight to Rome "and stayed up late c B. L. telling her the Sarpedon story." He stayed in Rome for a wedding, then again went off to Lew Hoad's tennis camp in Spain, while his wife and daughters went to America. While his wife was in America, he asked her "t cal DvB & mention that he should prepar for a bombshl."

The rest of the account is almost word for word what Hecht maintained in 1972, though at the time none of the above was made public.

One of the most arresting features in this part of the memoir is the severe abbreviation of the words. Are they incriminating? Does the truncated nature of so many words suggest perhaps that Hecht had written them before, that he was slightly bored with them so he couldn't be bothered to write them out in full and was now coming up with an amended version? And do the crossings-out signify slips of the pen that in fact reveal the real truth, as when he uses "I" or "me," then changes it to "the owner"? Why, in this latest account, can he not remember the name of

Mr. Keating, the museum's broker at Kennedy Airport, yet he can remember what his wife said, on seeing the krater, that it made her want to weep and reminded her of a Rembrandt? Is it likely that if she really did make such a stagey remark, he would have overlooked it in the other account? Isn't his account of Sarrafian's agent's arrival in Zurich—referring to him as "~~hecht~~ Edge-te" equally stagey? In this version, Hecht told his wife to alert von Bothmer to a bombshell. How does this square with the other account, that he sent von Bothmer a letter, and with Hoving's account, that Hecht's wife called *him*? Isn't the level of incidental detail in this second account much less than in the "Medici version"? There is no mention of a wounded dog, no talk of tennis with von Bothmer's beautiful stepdaughter, no exchange with von Bothmer's son about Herakles' half brother? Most important of all, if Sarrafian's agent didn't bring the vase to Zurich from Lebanon until August 1971, as Hecht says here, how can Dietrich von Bothmer have seen it at Bürki's, as he said he did, in *July* 1971?

The very fact that there *are* two accounts is of course curious. The eighty-eight pages of the memoir contain no other example where Hecht describes events twice and gives different versions. Then there is the fact that there are several parallels in the first "Medici version" that fit with Hoving's account and not with the other one. These include Hecht invoking the sale of the museum's coins to pay for the vase, Rousseau's second trip to Zurich, the fact that the first photographs of the vase showed it with a "spider's web" of cracks, the comparison in price to the painting by Monet, and Hecht's worry about "the dollar situation." Ferri later found out, in his interrogation of Robin Symes, that the London dealer confirmed he had bought a bronze eagle from Hecht, for $75,000, in the early 1970s.

The judge in Medici's trial was in no doubt about this second version. He said it was "sweetened" and "contains blatant corrections aimed at avoiding possible demands for reimbursement from Museums which had, at very dear prices, purchased objects such as the Euphronios krater." Just how prescient the judge was, we shall see.

Hecht's memoir is remarkable, too, for the candid light it throws on other aspects of the antiquities trade. In one section he describes how art and antiquities can be used to obtain highly questionable tax breaks from the Internal Revenue Service.

In the mid-1970s, Hecht crossed paths with Bruce McNall.* They met in May 1974, at a coin auction in Zurich, when McNall, using funds from one of his backers—whom Hecht names—paid the then-record price for a coin, 850,000 Swiss Francs for an Athenian decadrachm.

On that same trip, McNall showed the backer "four fresco panels of the fourth century B.C. ~~with a horse race scene~~ which decorated a tomb at Paestum, an ancient Greek city about 50 miles south of Naples." The backer bought them from McNall for $75,000 and later gave these same frescoes to the Getty where they were valued at $2,500,000. Hecht observes dryly at this point that the backer was in the 50 percent tax bracket, and so, by deducting this from his taxable income he saved $1,250,000 in taxes, in effect a profit of $1,175,000. Later, Hecht says, this backer told him that he "collected" antiquities only in order to make donations to museums and it wasn't worth his while unless he could get them valued at five times what he had paid. Hecht gives two other detailed accounts of "collectors" who acquired antiquities simply to take tax breaks.[3]

In the spring of 1975, McNall proposed that he and a certain Sy Weintraub become full partners in Hecht's holdings and they set up two businesses in Los Angeles, the Summa Gallery and Numismatic Fine Arts. These enjoyed mixed fortunes—which Hecht explores in his memoir.

A late episode in Hecht's memoir reveals perhaps more than he intended. Here he is describing the process by which the Princeton Collection acquired a psykter from him. Proud of his connoisseurship, his guard slips just a little.

Calls from Mauro [Moroni, a well-known faker of antiquities] were rare because of my relationship with Giac. [Medici] and because of his relationship with Fried [Frida] Tchacos who daringly went to Cerveteri and

*See pp. 129–130.

paid cash on the spot. [But] in June 1984 came a call from Mauro telling me to come to Rome for a sensational r/f vase [with black decoration].

Mauro met me at the airport and we drove directly to his home in Cerveteri to show me the vase. It was a psykter, a vase used for wine cooling, decorated with reclining banqueters drinking from various vessels. . . . Within a few days Mauro delivered the psykter to Zurich and we concluded the deal at $225,000.

Hecht immediately called Robert Guy, at Princeton, and even over the phone he was enthusiastic. Guy said it sounded to him that it was not unlike a particular vase in one of the other main reference works, on south Italian vases, compiled by an Australian scholar, A. Dale Trendall and updated by Professor Alexander Cambitoglou. Based on the description Hecht gave him, Guy made a preliminary attribution to the Kleophrades Painter. Re-assured, Hecht sent photographs to Marion True at the Getty. She was enthusiastic, too, becoming even more so after she showed the photos to Dyfri Williams at the British Museum. Hecht was asked to bring the vase to Malibu as soon as it had been cleaned "and she did not find unreasonable the price of $700,000."

With the vase cleaned, Hecht hand-carried it personally—aboard Lufthansa, he tells us—just as he had done with the Euphronios krater. With ceremony, he unwrapped the psykter in the library of the Greek and Roman department of the Getty. To his great consternation, however, Marion was not impressed by the real thing. In fact, she was rather cold and asked that the museum's chief restorer be sent for. All became clear the next morning, when Hecht met True in her office. She told him that the museum would not be buying the psykter because they thought it was a fake. Hecht was incensed.

Some time later, he saw the Getty's restorer and asked him what had made him suspect the vase was not genuine. The restorer replied that some of the black figures, instead of being bluish black, as was normal in a vase of that kind, had a greenish tinge. Hecht was having none of it.

Actually, the occurrence of greenish figures adjacent to black figures is not unusual and could be caused by the vase breaking in the kiln because of the heat. . . .

From Hecht's point of view, however, the episode ended happily, because the vase was acquired by the Princeton Art Museum—on the recommendation of none other than Robert Guy. Despite this satisfactory outcome, Hecht couldn't quite let the matter drop entirely. He had been told, he said, that the doubts that had been sown in Marion True's mind about the psykter had come from Britain, and he thought the skeptic was Martin Robertson, former professor of Ancient Archaeology at Oxford.

Still he wouldn't let go.

Shortly after the acquisition by Princeton, Marion True admitted in a telephone conversation that Robert Guy had persuaded her of the psykter's authenticity.

Now, besides what this reveals about the provenance of Princeton's red-figured psykter, which the Italian authorities will no doubt be addressing in due course, this episode is also most interesting for the way in which it echoes Hecht's first account of the Euphronios krater affair (the "Medici version"). It is a straightforward narrative, obsessed with flights and sums of money; it gives bare details about seeing the object in Italy at first; then in Switzerland, dwells on the object's reception in the United States, shows off his scholarship and learning, and ends with Hecht triumphant in his claims about the authenticity of the object. In tone, details, and style it is a parallel narrative.

In a final part of the memoir, in which he comments on a series of articles in the 1990s about antiquities looting and smuggling in the *Boston Globe*, by the journalist Walter Robinson, Hecht sets out what we might call his archaeological philosophy. He says he told Robinson, who had telephoned him when researching his articles, that he had never smuggled objects, nor "instigated" the smuggling of objects. He did write that he was "not averse" to buying an antiquity without a pedigree "unless it was demonstrably stolen." But he went on to insist that "unprovenanced" objects (his quotation marks) are of "more use" to the world if they are in public museums and private collections, rather than in "obscure local salons." He also claimed that many objects stolen from Italian museums and private collections had been returned through his "agency," though he did not give any details.

This was, at the least, an interesting use of the verb "instigate." At several points in the memoir he meets middle men, either in Rome or Athens, is shown antiquities of one kind or another (at discreet venues where he avoids the limelight), discusses their value, or at least their price, and then takes possession of them in Switzerland, from where he sells them on at a handsome profit. Does this not classify as instigation? When he prevailed upon his "respectable" Swiss girlfriend to fly in to Athens, with forty one-thousand-dollar bills, to pay for some silver figures which he had been offered by an Armenian dealer on Pandrossan Street, and then fly out again, taking the figures with her, did this not count as instigation? When he met Mauro Moroni at the latter's home in Cerveteri and was shown the psykter that was brought to Zurich "within a few days" and which Hecht eventually sold to Princeton, did this not count as instigation? When he demonstrated to Giacomo Medici, in the matter of the kylix with a youth in the tondo, that "quality had a high premium," did that not count as instigation? He himself said the sale of the kylix was an "eye-opener" for Medici and that, following the incident, "G.M. soon became a faithful purveyor." We shall encounter similar idiosyncratic use of language again in this book—in Giacomo Medici's defense at his trial.

Hecht's interrogation on March 10, 2001, in Paris, took place twenty-five days after the raid in Boulevard Latour Maubourg. It was classic fencing match. From Ferri's point of view, Hecht was a difficult nut to crack at first, though gradually he did admit some things and contradicted himself several times, so that the overall picture came slowly into focus. Hecht said that he had written the memoir some four or five years before, in 1996 or 1997 (in other words after Hoving's memoirs), and that it contained only fantasies and things that he had heard. He had wanted to write a fascinating book, he said, that would sell well. He said that the first account of the Euphronios krater affair was the version "the Italians wanted" (even though it had been written four or five years before), that he "only hoped that Medici would give him the vase." He declined to expand on what, exactly, this meant, though it appears to confirm that Medici had *a* Euphronios vase in December 1971. He admitted that he knew Marion True but denied, at first, that he had ever sold anything to the Getty Museum. Then he changed his story and said that "maybe" he had sold them a bronze figure in the Attic style that he bought in a Swiss collection, and a black-figure cup, and some red-figure vases.

He could not (or would not) explain why True and Medici didn't deal directly, "seeing that they knew each other well." He did sell to the Getty the bronze tripod of the Guglielmi Collection (which turned out to be stolen) but didn't remember a candelabrum. When challenged that it was in Boursaud's inventory and shown a photograph, he recognized it and confirmed it had gone to the Getty. He also agreed he had "given" "a few" Apulian vases to the Getty but claimed not to remember the details. He did not remember the name of his suppliers, then named Medici (though he said he bought little from him) and Savoca, from whom he remembered receiving an archaic Greek bronze vase. Hecht remembered buying some coins from Monticelli, and he admitted receiving a small terra-cotta from Scrimbia from Orazio Di Simone and buying two bronze handles and a Greek vase from Becchina. He admitted knowing Sandro Cimicchi, a restorer who had lived in Borowsky's house. He insisted that he "generally bought unimportant bronzes and vases."

Regarding the Pompeian frescoes, Hecht said Medici had them in Geneva and had shown them to him, in the Freeport. He sent them to Bürki in Zurich to be restored. He had bought them from Medici and had paid him—the invoices made out to Bürki were what he called "courtesy invoices" for Medici to render importation possible. This was a polite way of saying the invoices did not give the true picture. He agreed that "[h]e lent himself to appearing in place of Medici." The frescoes were returned to Medici when "the illicit provenance of the frescoes had been pointed out to him."

The reader can judge for him- or herself as to what weight to attach to Hecht's replies in his interrogation and how they compare with his written memoir. The other raids and interrogations carried out by Conforti's men and by Dr. Ferri would confirm certain aspects of Hecht's memoir but would vividly contradict other parts.

13

RAIDS IN ZURICH AND GENEVA,
ARREST AND INTERROGATIONS
IN CYPRUS AND BERLIN

BOUT A MONTH AFTER THE RAID on Hecht, in the second
week of March 2001, a Swiss magistrate, two Swiss police,
together with two investigators from Conforti's Art Squad
and Public Prosecutor Ferri himself, raided the premises of
Phoenix Ancient Art, S.A., at 6 Rue Verdaine, in Geneva, and also the
premises of Inanna Art Services at the Freeport.

Of course, the Italians were already aware of the close links between
Medici and Phoenix Ancient Art because of the documentation found in
Corridor 17, including checks made out to Phoenix by Lawrence Fleischman, a partnership contract with Editions Services, and a series of
monthly invoices made out to Phoenix by Medici, for his expertise.

At the premises on Rue Verdaine, only the manager of the company,
Jeffrey Suckow, was there, so none of the Aboutaams were interrogated,
either then or later. Suckow handed over to the Italians a list of auctions
at which the Aboutaams had bought objects being sold by Medici and in
which, in at least two cases, those objects had ended up back with him
in Corridor 17. Apart from this, five vases were seized, all of which had
been temporarily imported into Switzerland by Ariss Ancient Art and
which, Suckow said, were owned by Noura Aboutaam, sister of Ali and
Hischam. Two of these objects came from Medici, as shown by the seized
Polaroids.

The details about the laundering, and about Noura's involvement, were
steps forward, but small ones, so far as Ferri's investigation was concerned.

He had higher hopes for what he might find later that day in their warehouse in the Freeport.

The Carabinieri, of course, were by now more than familiar with the Freeport, its gray-painted structures, its green stairwells, its forbidding metal doors. After lunch, as they reached the doorway to Inanna, there was a slight hiccup when the Swiss judge expressed reservations that Inanna actually had anything to do with Phoenix Ancient Art and the Aboutaams. Ferri explained again the links between Medici and the Lebanese, and the references in the seized documents to Inanna. The judge remained doubtful, but after still more discussion in the corridor outside the offices, she agreed to let one of the Swiss police go inside the warehouse and see who was there. He came back to say that inside were Jeffrey Suckow, whom they had met earlier, and Ali Aboutaam. Reassured, the judge allowed the raid to go ahead. Whereupon Ali Aboutaam—six foot three, balding, heavily built—left.

As they had approached the Inanna warehouses, on the floor directly below Medici's, there had been nothing to suggest that the rooms inside would be any different from his. The gallery at Rue Verdaine was plush and elegant.

Not at the Freeport. There is a word in Italian—*"raccapricciante"*—which is not easy to translate but means, basically, "it makes your flesh crawl." And this was the universal reaction of the Italians as they entered Inanna's offices. "There was a sea of objects everywhere," says one of Conforti's men. "It was distressing to see so many objects of culture treated with such violence." What he meant was that, far from being packed away in cupboards, as Medici had done with his objects in Corridor 17, at Inanna there was absolutely no respect for anything to be found there. "There were gold rings strewn on the floor, in envelopes; there was a wooden Egyptian sarcophagus that had been sawn into pieces; there were glazed ceramics just lying everywhere, jumbles of coins, glass and jewelry; there were mummies leaning against the wall, even mummies of cats; there was material from Iraq, Iran, India, and South East Asia—all scattered over the floor in a huge mess."

In the outer rooms, most of the material—the objects just lying around—were not of Italian origin. But in the room farthest away from the door, there were some cupboards, and all the material inside them was

Italian. And what did they find among these objects? Two boxes of ceramics from Scrimbia.*

The Italian objects were photographed, replaced in the cupboards where they had been found, and the cupboards—but not the warehouse—sealed with wax. Whatever their personal opinions of where the non-Italian material had come from, the Carabinieri had no professional interest, and no competence or jurisdiction to take any action in connection with it. When the Carabinieri returned two months later, with the archaeologists, for the technical assessment of the Italian material at Inanna, the rest of the warehouse was empty. Everything else—the Iraqi, Iranian, and Indian material—had all been removed.

As the Italian cupboards were unsealed and opened, it was now the archaeologists' turn to feel *"raccapriccio."* On closer examination, one of the boxes in the cupboards was found to contain gold rings *with the finger bones of the dead still attached to them.* Clearly, when the tombs had been looted, the hands and fingers of the long-dead had simply been broken off by the tombaroli, to save time. To Conforti, nothing in his long career showed the sheer barbarity of Medici's cordata so much as this.

Suckow said that the warehouse had existed since 1992 and had been created by Sleiman Aboutaam, the father of Ali and Hischam. Suckow had been employed as manager after he had worked on the computers at Phoenix. Suckow said that, in fact, neither Inanna nor Phoenix owned any of the objects in the Freeport warehouse. He said the company existed solely to buy and sell on behalf of others. Its most important clients, he said, were Ariss Ancient Art, Tanis Antiquities Ltd., Sekhmet Ancient Art, and the Galerie Weber of Cologne. Many objects, he said, were sent to Inanna for restoration. The company issued passavants and would send material principally to two restorers in London, Martin Foster and Colin Bowles, and one in New York, Jane Gillies.

Suckow said he had continued to manage the warehouse even after Sleiman Aboutaam and his wife had been killed in the SwissAir plane crash off Nova Scotia in 1998. Ali Aboutaam came to the warehouse once a week to view the objects that had arrived in the interim and to give instructions about sales. The Italian objects found in the Freeport belonged, he said, to Ariss Ancient Art. He said he knew the names of Fritz Bürki,

*See p. 10.

Giacomo Medici, and Editions Services but had never worked for them. He knew the name of Marion True at the John Paul Getty Museum but couldn't remember if he had ever met her. He didn't know the names Christian Boursaud, Hydra Gallery, or Xoilan Trader.

The raids on the Aboutaams had, in reality, raised more questions than they had answered. What, actually, *was* their business? If Suckow was to be believed, they owned nothing but just operated a holding company. As the Fleischman checks found in Medici's warehouse seemed to indicate, they were in reality just a convenient "front" for other people. Their part in the laundering of objects at auction seemed to support such a role, too. The state of their warehouse, and the grisly business of the finger bones inside the rings, seemed to show that they had no real regard for art or ancient artifacts. In their exploitation of the archaeological world, the Aboutaams were just about as cynical as you could get.

Ferri was aware that the role of the Aboutaams was mysterious, and all the more interesting for that. But, as he put it, "There was no time to follow all the rivers." He had his priorities and time was passing. His next target was Fritz and Harry Bürki, the restorers in Zurich.

The raid on their premises took place some months later, in October 2001. This time there were present two of Conforti's men, four Swiss police, and a Zurich magistrate. The Bürkis' apartment was on the fourth floor of a tall anonymous building near the main railway station. Once the raiding party had gathered outside the apartment, the senior policeman rang the bell. No reply. They rang again. Still no reply. It was decided not to bludgeon the door open, but instead to send for a locksmith. One of the local Zurich police pulled out his mobile phone and dialed someone the police had used before. As he was dialing, however, the door to the apartment suddenly opened, and Harry Bürki—tall, thin, pale, with black hair and a black mustache—stood there. Had he been listening just inside the door, waiting for them to go away, only to realize that they *weren't* going away?

"Yes?" he said.

Inside they found a restorer's laboratory, "even more technological than Savoca's," says one of Conforti's men, who had seen both.

But what caught the eye of the investigators was a bag, a battered sports bag. It was tall, made of some kind of canvas, and it had a false bottom—it was less deep inside than it was outside. When they opened up the false bottom, the compartment below was found to contain crumbs of soil. No less interesting, the bag was decorated with the emblem for an Italian football team, Mondragone, a town very near to Casal di Principe. Casal di Principe, it will be remembered from Chapter 1, was where the burst of telephone activity occurred among the tombaroli after the theft at Melfi. Casal di Principe was where Pasquale Camera had a house.

Was this bag the device used to smuggle objects out of Italy?

Harry Bürki shrugged his shoulders. He said he didn't know what they were talking about. He didn't know what the bag was used for.

He was asked who lived in the room where the search was taking place.

"I do."

"Where is the bed?"

He had no answer. There was none.

At this point, one of the raiding party noticed a room off the entrance hall. It was small, just big enough for a spiral staircase made of wood. "Where does this lead?" asked Conforti's man, mindful of where the (marble) spiral staircase in Savoca's house had led.

"Nowhere," replied Bürki.

"We'll take a look anyway," said the senior Swiss policeman.

Upstairs, there was another huge apartment. It had bookshelves with many books. Conforti's man pulled out one and, by a stroke of luck, it fell open to reveal a passport, Robert Hecht's passport as it happened, albeit out of date.

Conforti's man looked at Harry Bürki, who now admitted that this apartment belonged to his father, Fritz, who was abroad.

They thereupon thoroughly searched the upstairs apartment, finding many archaeological objects, some with Becchina tags on them. They were all photographed and seized and, somewhat later, the photographs were sent to Rome. There they were examined by Daniela Rizzo so that she could identify whether they had in fact come from Italy. Armed with this information, Ferri and Rizzo returned to Zurich some weeks later to interrogate both Bürkis, father and son.

Neither was very helpful at first. The interrogations, which lasted three hours, took place at their laboratory.

Fritz Bürki began by conceding that he knew that most of the objects he had been asked to restore in his career came from illegal digs, even though everyone pretended such antiquities were part of their "family heritage." When shown photographs of the Guglielmi tripod,* he said he had never seen it, only heard about it five or ten years before. After being shown the J. P. Getty documents relating to the acquisition of the self-same object—which he had signed—he immediately changed his account and said that Mario Bruno had asked him to sign the document as "lender" (by the time of the interrogation, Bruno, the dealer from Lugano described in Chapter 11 was dead). Fritz Bürki didn't know why Bruno used him as a "front," he said, but speculated that since Bruno was known as a receiver of stolen goods, perhaps the museum didn't wish to have direct contact with him. He didn't know how Bruno had come into possession of the tripod, he said, and later on informed the Getty that Hecht and Atlantis (and not he himself) were the true owners of the object.

He said he knew Medici, but the latter had never been to his laboratory and he, Bürki, never bought anything from Medici, nor did he restore objects for him. Ferri then showed him some photographs of vases before restoration that had been found in Medici's Geneva warehouse. Fritz Bürki claimed not to recognize them. Ferri paused, for effect, then pointed out that the furniture and the wallpaper shown in the background of the photographs *were exactly the same* as that in the room where the interrogation was taking place.

Grudgingly, Bürki admitted to having some dealings with Atlantis Antiquities and to having restored the Euphronios krater, for which he'd made out a regular invoice, but he refused to answer further questions on the grounds that he had already been questioned (thirty years before, however). Ferri noted that there was a photograph of the Euphronios krater on Bürki's desk. Bürki could not explain how Medici's name and details were in his agenda, or why his were in Medici's. He claimed that what Medici said with regard to his—Bürki's—delivery of objects to the Freeport for sale was untrue; Medici was lying. He had no memory of specific antiquities or what he might have been paid for working on them.

*See p. 84.

He did admit to having acted as a "front" for Hecht, who was his most important client, but denied acting as a "front" for anyone else. He knew Becchina but said he had never been to his laboratory, and Bürki could not explain why some of the objects in his laboratory at the time of the raid had tags with Becchina's name on them.

He admitted that his son and he had restored the Pompeian frescoes, of which he was shown photographs. He said that he had never seen the photographs of the frescoes on the clandestine dig, but that the frescoes themselves arrived cut into eleven pieces. The restoration had lasted twelve to eighteen months, and the objects were on his premises for at least three years.

His son was no more forthcoming. Harry Bürki knew Medici, he said. He had seen him at Sotheby's auctions but did not store objects in Medici's warehouse, did not buy anything from him, and claimed that where his name was included in Medici's documentation, it was false. But he did admit that in restoring the Pompeian frescoes with his father, he had seen the photographs taken *in* Pompeii by the tombaroli and admitted it was possible Marion True might have seen the frescoes in the Bürkis' laboratory. He knew Becchina, he said, but the objects on the Bürkis' Zurich premises bearing Becchina tags had been bought in Munich about five months previously, from someone now dead. He too could not explain why the tags were there and had Becchina's name on them.

He admitted that "[p]erhaps he sold some objects to the Getty but he does not remember." Harry Bürki did not remember from whom he had bought the Etruscan tripod, sold to the Getty for $65,000, but he excluded Medici. Over the years, he said, he sold about ten objects to the Getty, using Hecht as intermediary.

The Bürkis admitted as little as possible, but even so their dissembling was quite obvious.

Frida Tchacos was interrogated in rather dramatic circumstances that came about partly by accident. The route to her went via the statue of the Artemis, a photograph of which had been found in the glove compartment in Pasquale Camara's Renault, the one that overturned on the Autostrade del Sole near Cassino and killed him. The Artemis was important partly because three other versions of it were known, all of which were in Italian museums, and partly because it might be the Greek original of those Roman copies. Even if it were a Roman copy itself, it was still valuable and it would be important to find out where it had been excavated.

Danilo Zicchi, Camera's colleague, in whose apartment the Artemis had been photographed after it left the butcher shop, said that he thought Frida Thacos was involved with the statue. Walter Guarini, the Puglia tombarolo we met in Chapter 11, was known to be one of the main suppliers to Frida, so pressure was now put on him to help with the return of the Artemis.

Sure enough, the statue was returned. It was left in a field near Bari and the local police alerted by an anonymous telephone call. That seemed to have concluded the matter—except that one day while going through the transcripts of some telephone taps, Ferri happened to notice that members of the cordata were *still* referring to a statue of Artemis. A frightening thought occurred to Ferri: Was the statue that had been returned a fake? The sculpture returned in Bari had been examined by experts and declared genuine, and its measurements conformed exactly to the other three known works. But still . . .

Ferri had other experts look at the Artemis, and they made an unusual observation. The measurements of the "Bari" Artemis, if we can call it that, were indeed exactly what they should have been, except that in the case of the recovered statue, its height was the same as all the others *including the base*. Clearly, the forger had designed his work using good photos and had been given the dimensions. However, he had misunderstood that the height of the statue referred to the Artemis *without* its base. The Bari *figure*, if not the entire ensemble, was a good few inches shorter than it should have been.

It was clear that the Bari statue was a serious attempt to mislead the law enforcement authorities—it took money, time, and not a little skill to create such a forgery. All this was confirmed when Conforti found the forger and he confessed. Conforti and Ferri were both incensed. Yet more pressure was put on Guarini, and he admitted that the real Artemis was *still* with Frida Tchacos in Switzerland, whereupon Ferri issued an international warrant for Tchacos's arrest and initiated the legal process for her extradition to Italy. Now she couldn't travel—the minute she crossed any international border, she would be arrested and held.

While the extradition process was working its way through the Swiss legal system, Ferri received a visit in Rome from Tchacos's lawyers, seeking agreement. After several hours of discussion, Ferri agreed that he would drop the charges against her *if* she complied with two demands. First, the real Artemis must be returned, and second, she must write a detailed memoir, setting out what she knew about the antiquities underworld in general, naming names and giving particulars about Medici's and Hecht's and Symes's operations. And here there arose a misunderstanding that, eventually, would work to Ferri's advantage.

Tchacos agreed to Ferri's conditions and, before long, the Artemis was returned to Italy. At this point, Ferri rescinded his extradition request. But Tchacos never complied with the second request, and never sent Ferri a memoir. Maybe she didn't think it mattered, that what Ferri really wanted all along was the Artemis. But the public prosecutor is a stickler for the rules of fairness, and to him a deal is a deal. And so, although he withdrew the extradition request, he did not withdraw the international warrant for Tchacos's arrest.

Therefore, when Tchacos—believing that there were no legal impediments hanging over her—next took a trip abroad, she was in for a surprise. She had a brother who lived in Cyprus, and in the second week of February 2002, she landed at Limassol airport. At passport control, she was recognized, arrested, and held. The Italians were informed, and she was kept in jail overnight, before being placed under house arrest at her brother's. It took three or four days before Ferri and two of Conforti's senior men could get to Limassol, and the intervening period was clearly a distressing experience for her and may help explain why, during her interrogation, when it came, she was so cooperative. It may also have had something to do with the fact the Ferri, normally so mild-mannered, now saw his chance and, sensing Tchacos was vulnerable in Cyprus, agreed to hurry only if she agreed, in his words, to "amply cooperate." She agreed, he hurried, and she was interviewed over two days on February 17 and 18, 2002.

What he wanted from her was what he had originally asked for—a memoir, her view of the way the underworld really worked, and the part played in it by Medici, Hecht, Symes, and the others. She did not disappoint this time, immediately confirming the existence of the cordate. She said Symes had told her Hecht was a dangerous man, that she too found him "vindictive" and was afraid of him. She confirmed that Medici was Hecht's "right-hand man," that Hecht was writing a book to be published after his death, for the benefit of his wife, and that he had once photographed Symes when he was holding something "compromising"—in other words, looted.

She went on to say that the Aboutaams were replacing the older dealers. In 2001, Harry Bürki had told her he no longer restored—only traded. Medici was not an expert, she said: "[H]e really couldn't recognize one painter from another, just as I can't." But he was well aware of when he was selling fakes. The Symeses (i.e., Robin Symes and Christo Michaelides) had sold a marble Venus by Doidalses (one of the more famous classical Greek sculptors) to Jiri Frel at the Getty. It was fake and originated, she thought, with Medici. She had met Medici in the 1970s "and at that time he was already a person of intres . . . an important person." He already had premises in the Freeport in Geneva and asked her there to see some marbles. Among these marbles was a Venus by Doidalses (a Venus *"acoupis,"* crouching), but most of the objects there that day were fake. She said the Getty had already bought one like it: "It was already known that these fake Venuses were on the market."

She confirmed that Medici was known as the biggest dealer, "that he had contacts with all . . . with all the big dealers, the biggest dealers . . . with Hecht mainly, [but] not with Gianfranco Becchina—they hated each other." She knew that Medici had the Hydra Gallery and that Christian Boursaud fronted for him. Then this exchange followed:

FERRI: Was Hecht already famous at that time? [They were talking about the 1980s.]

FRIDA TCHACOS: He was already famous. Hecht was in Paris, he was known to be the biggest, he always lost money on . . . on . . . the Casinos. Then . . . yes, of Medici I can say that once I'd been struck by him when I saw him at Sotheby's, this in '85 . . . in '90, when he was buying vases, red-figure or black-figure vases, but at very high prices and I didn't understand how someone like Medici could have the money to buy these vases. And I tried to find out, but no-one could tell me why he bought these vases. At the time I thought he bought them to have . . . to have a collection of vases for himself, then I understood . . . that he did . . . did all these movements with Sotheby's, to put vases . . . to sell his vases and then buying them so as to have a provenance, which I didn't know at the time. And in the last . . . in the last years I learnt that he was in partnership or worked with the Aboutaams, the Arabs of Freeport, Geneva.

FERRI: These last years, what does this mean?

FRIDA: Hmm . . . since they opened at Freeport, it's not yet ten years . . .

FERRI: Yes.

FRIDA: And first there was the father . . . and also on the Aboutaams, afterwards I'll repeat this, that at a certain point at Sotheby's the Aboutaams were seen buying vases next to Medici. They were both standing at the back, they weren't sitting down, and the Aboutaams were buying very important vases at very high prices.

She further confirmed that Medici sold "quite a lot" to Robin Symes, that Symes "undoubtedly" bought vases from Medici, and she agreed that Symes bought the Morgantina Venus from Orazio Di Simone. "That was what was always said."[1]

Returning to Hecht, she said that "he was a scholar, but a terrible character, who made one afraid . . . he was an old man, an old nasty man. I was always afraid of him . . . What else can I tell you? Hecht was called 'Mister Percentage' . . . because he took a percentage . . . I think from Medici as well . . . his great clients in Los Angeles were the Hunts, the Hunt brothers . . . I knew though that Medici was behind him . . . yes, yes."

She confirmed that there was "a precise triangle"—Hecht, Becchina, Monticelli—and that the latter mainly supplied "[e]verything that could be found in the south of Italy; I think Apulian [vases], I think terracottas, I think bronzes. . . ." She later amended this cordata to include George Ortiz and Mario Bruno. She said that Mauro Morani was part of the Savoca cordata, and he had provided the kylix by Onesimos, or at least some of it. She met Morani through Guarini and knew him to be "a very able creator of fakes."

She gave evidence that before Marion True was married, she had a lover in Rome in the early 1990s, one Enzo Constantini.

Aha, aha. She frequently went to Italy to see this lover. And it was interesting because after the visits of Marion True in Italy, in Rome, the Romans knew a lot more about the Getty—the Romans in general knew more than the Paul Getty itself . . . all the Italian market knew that the Getty was buying or not buying, from whom. . . . And every time I showed her something she . . . she said to me: "Beautiful, interesting, I can speak to Fleischman about it. . . ." So, later we understood how the Fleischman-True things went. . . . Dealers offered Marion True some things, and she, just as with me, refused or bought, I don't know. But with me she refused and then she received a phone call from Fleischman who said to her: "What have you got for me?" and then, after you'd waited many months, perhaps years, reserving something for Marion True, Fleischman would come into the game . . . Fleischman was in relationship with Medici. . . . But it was Marion True who got them together . . . Fleischman was a dealer, Tempelsman was not.

Tchacos confirmed that the Levy-White Collection was purchased from Symes, and the routing was: "Mainly from Hecht; I don't know if from Medici but if we say Hecht we say Medici; recently she [Shelby White] was buying a lot from the Aboutaams."

She described von Bothmer and Robert Guy as academic "enemies," that if one attributed a vase to one painter, the other would attribute it to someone else. She said that George Ortiz was the biggest collector in Europe and that his collection was made by Becchina but that he also had links with Savoca. She confirmed that Becchina sold a great deal at Sotheby's and that Borowsky had had contact with German museums.

One of the things that came over strongly in Tchacos's interview was how bitter the rivalry was at times between the different cordate. She herself heartily disliked Hecht. Elsewhere in her interview, she referred to an occasion when several of the Swiss-based antiquities dealers were on the same plane, traveling to Japan for the opening of the exhibition of the George Ortiz Collection at a museum there in 1993. During the flight, she said, Becchina had come up to her and said, as she put it, "We mustn't allow certain people to work." When asked who Becchina meant, she replied that he had been talking about Savoca.

Tchacos also confirmed that Fiorella Cottier-Angeli, the Swiss expert and customs official who "has this collection of Etruscan vases," had told her that she had a key to Medici's warehouse. After beginning as an adviser to Medici, for customs appraisals, "there began this activity of knowing Swiss collectors, to whom she then also supplied objects, which undoubtedly came from Medici . . . she was connected to the Director of the Geneva Museum, who was a rather weak character and did what she wanted of him."

Ferri asked: "Which means?"

". . . means that if she wanted to do . . . to sell something to a collector, she had an expertise drawn up by this guy of the Geneva Museum, this . . . [Jacques] Chamay."

Tchacos was astonishingly forthcoming. Perhaps it was her character, perhaps it was the fact that she was, at the time, under arrest in Cyprus.

Ferri's instincts about Tchacos's mood in Limassol were correct. While they were there together, they arrived at a deal. There were certain objects that the Italians were anxious to recover, and chief among them was the ivory head discovered by Casasanta and sold to Savoca. The life-size head of Apollo, which had once formed part of a Chryselephantine statue in antiquity, was quite possibly the most important archaeological object to be unearthed since the Euphronios krater in 1971 (many people think it is even more important than the vase). In Limassol, Tchacos let it be known—without actually saying so—that she could help in the recovery of this object. In view of her cooperation, Ferri now let it be understood that in return for her help with the ivory head, he would limit the charges he would bring against her. He said the charges would be confined to offenses that carried penalties of two years or less (with a good chance that the prison terms would be suspended) and, most important, Tchacos would not be joined in the conspiracy charges that he was planning to bring against Medici, Hecht, Robin Symes, and perhaps Marion True.

Frida Tchacos agreed to this deal and, on September 17, 2002, she was convicted of handling stolen and smuggled goods, and of failing to notify the authorities of the antiquities that came her way. She was given one year and six months' imprisonment, suspended, and fined 1,000 euros (approximately $1,000). But, so far as Ferri was concerned, there was more to it than that. Tchacos, he knew, was very friendly with Robin Symes—and the public prosecutor was anxious to interview Symes. Symes had residences in New York and Greece, and businesses in Switzerland, but he spent most of his time in London, where the police and judicial authorities did not cooperate at all well with the Italians. Thus, Ferri's deal with Tchacos was more than it seemed: It was designed to put pressure on Symes. He knew that Tchacos would discuss her treatment in Limassol with Symes, for the unvoiced subtext to the encounter was that Ferri believed that Symes had the ivory head, bought from Savoca. He therefore believed that what Tchacos had in fact promised, without actually saying as much, was that she would put pressure on Symes to return the head.

So far as Ferri was concerned, Symes was a much more important link in the chain. He shared the same address with Medici at Avenue Krieg in Geneva, he was an active member of the cordata that supplied the Getty, the Levy-Whites, Maurice Tempelsman, and several others. So Ferri wasn't about to do a deal with Symes, as he had done with Tchacos, *but he was prepared for Symes to think that he might.* Because of the poor cooperation offered to the Italians by the British (more like noncooperation, in fact), there was little chance that Ferri would ever be able to raid Symes's premises in London, or interrogate him there. The deal with Tchacos, therefore, had as one of its aims that it would lure Symes to Rome, in search of something similar.

It took a year, but it worked. At the end of March 2003, Symes offered to travel to Rome voluntarily to be interviewed at the Palazzo di Giustizia by Ferri. He had with him his Italian lawyer, Francesco Tagliaferri. (This name was a source of much amusement for everyone: in Italian "Tagliaferri" means "cut Ferri," in the sense of a "shortened Ferri" or "Ferri cut down to size.") Tagliaferri was also Tchacos's lawyer.

Unsurprisingly, Symes was uptight about everything and Ferri had to squeeze information out of him. It was like being with the Bürkis all over again. Symes said he had known Medici for a very long time, since the 1980s, when the Italian would go to London for Sotheby's sales. However, at the time he was interviewed, Symes claimed that he and his partner, Christo, hadn't met Medici in more than ten years. Symes insisted that Medici was an expert in vases, that he had a very important collection and that "since they were famous and published vases, he did not need to certify their origin." In particular, Symes confirmed that Medici could distinguish the painters who had painted particular vases. This was of course in direct contradiction of what Frida Tchacos had said and what others would say.

Xoilan, Symes said, was the company in whose name objects that he intended to collect (keep) were purchased, whereas for dealing he used another company, Robin Symes Limited. (This is directly contradicted by evidence we detail in Chapter 15.)[2]

Symes claimed there was nothing unusual or incriminating about the Polaroids found at Medici's warehouse, even though they showed objects in fragments and covered in dirt. "Conserving the photos of an object which still has to be restored is simply to show the client the original condition of the object and how much and what kind of restoring work had been done. Many dealers give the purchaser the photos of the object before its restoration." (Again, this is directly contradicted by Ferri's later interrogations.) He confirmed that Felicity Nicholson was a great friend of his (he found her "molto simpatica"), and they frequently went out to dinner together. "She was incredibly honest and reserved in her work at Sotheby's," a description that hardly squares with her behavior in regard to the Lion Goddess, Sekhmet,* when she had asked Symes to smuggle it out of Italy. In fact, Symes rather spoiled his argument by admitting it was Nicholson who had prevailed on him to take part in the exercise.

Symes knew Hecht and had visited him when the latter lived in Rome. He had never visited him in Paris, and although he hadn't done much business with him, Symes did confirm that in 1971 or 1972, he'd purchased a large bronze eagle from Hecht for $70,000–$75,000, then sold it to the Getty Museum. This, of course, is an important confirmation of an episode that Hecht had mentioned in his memoir, in his first "Medici ver-

*See p. 26 and the Notes, p. 386.

sion" of the route by which the Euphronios krater had arrived at the Met. Symes also said that an acquaintance of his, Peter Wilson, CEO of Sotheby's, had shown him a photograph of a Euphronios vase that had been offered to Sotheby's at that time, and Symes had noticed that it was identical to the one purchased by the Metropolitan. This too confirms the "Medici version" in Hecht's memoir, where he said that he had considered selling the vase at Sotheby's but had been disappointed by Felicity Nicholson's estimate of $200,000. Felicity Nicholson, who had no professional training in antiquities but had begun life at Sotheby's as a secretary, was a protégé of Peter Wilson's, who took a great interest in her department. She would certainly have shown Wilson any photographs of a major vase that Hecht sent in. This is presumably how Wilson (who died in 1984) came to show the photographs to Symes. Symes also said that he had thought the Euphronios was perhaps a fake, without knowing that in the "Medici version" in his memoir, Hecht had written about just this—that Robin and Christo (and Sir John Pope-Hennessy) had cast doubt on the authenticity of the vase. So, in at least three ways, and without realizing it, Symes confirmed the "Medici version" of the way the Euphronios krater had reached the Metropolitan Museum in New York.

Symes said Hecht had told him, twenty-five years earlier (not five or six years before, as Hecht said to Ferri), that he was writing a book for his wife. He thought that Hecht was an excellent scholar but an unstable character, saying he drank too much and was unreliable, the "proof" being that he had sold a statue to Symes only to tell the Getty—to whom Symes had sold the statue—that it was a fake.

Symes had bought fragments of Greek vases from Medici. Medici had given him some fragments to donate to the Metropolitan since, as an Italian, it might raise a few eyebrows should he donate them directly. At the Getty, True could not purchase from a person like Medici, otherwise the object could not have a valid provenance. Symes said he would have been "amazed" if Marion True had ever purchased anything directly from Medici. Here then, from the horse's mouth, is confirmation of triangulation and the reasons for it.

Both Symes and Christo had excellent relations with Marion True, "more personal on the part of Christo since he did not sell objects," whereas Symes did. Marion True, Symes said, had a house near his in

Greece, and they would see each other during the summer. Symes said he had met Jiri Frel when the latter became curator at the Getty, meeting him in London, in Los Angeles, and also in Greece. He considered Frel a bit crazy and not entirely reliable. He (Frel) had gone to Symes in Greece to show him photographs of a kouros that he wished to purchase, and Symes told him that he thought it was fake and had said the same thing to John Walsh, director of the Getty, who had consulted him in London before the purchase. Medici had told Symes in London that he owned something "very similar to the Kouros," and Christo had told Marion True.

This fitted with one set of Getty documents we haven't yet mentioned in any detail. It will be recalled from Chapter 7 that the Getty acquired a kouros in the mid-1980s but that when it was unveiled, the statue provoked a furor over its provenance (or lack of one) and over its authenticity.* This kouros was sold to the Getty by Gianfranco Becchina, following which Medici sent to Los Angeles a statue that, he said, was fake and yet had very many features similar to the kouros.† Here then, the two bitter rivals, members of different cordate, were attacking one another.

Lawrence Fleischman, Symes said, had put together a collection in a very short time, in order to sell it to the Getty. He had heard from an American dealer, he said, that in order to sell an object to the Getty, one had to sell it to the Fleischmans.

Symes confirmed that he had sold various objects to Tempelsman, who had sold them to the Getty, and that he had sold various works to Shelby White, "who would never have bought directly from someone like Giacomo Medici." This is yet another confirmation of triangulation, again from the horse's mouth. Symes confirmed that Koutoulakis was supplied by Medici "since at Koutoulakis' he had seen objects he'd previously seen at Medici's." He had bought the ivory head from Savoca for $850,000.

Ferri's final "encounter" in this phase of the investigation was an international rogatory for an interrogation carried out by one of Conforti's men, directed at Professor Wolf Dieter Heilmeyer, the director of the Museum

---

*See p. 82.
†Again, see p. 99 and 209.

for Classical Antiquities in Berlin. This rogatory concerned the museum's acquisition of seven vases, all of which were among the photographs seized in Geneva.

In May 2003, at an international conference in Berlin, titled "Illegal Archaeology," Heilmeyer, organizer of the conference, announced that Berlin State Museums would no longer acquire, display, or restore any objects that did not have clear provenances. "If there is any doubt about provenance," he said, "we don't go further." Archaeologists have been watching.

According to Professor Heilmeyer's response to the rogatory, the seven vases in Berlin were acquired on four different occasions. The first acquisition concerned a skyphos of the Trittolemos Painter, which had been sold to the museum in 1970 by Koutoulakis, in Geneva, for $60,000. The curator for the purchase was Dr. Adolf Greifenhagen, now dead. In addition, four fragments of the skyphos were later donated by Robert Hecht, who said he had purchased them in Geneva.

The second acquisition was made in 1980. This was an Attic kylix, bought for £16,000 from Robin Symes. Heilmeyer went to London to view this acquisition and said he couldn't remember whether he had seen a photograph beforehand or not. He added that no investigation was made into the provenance of the kylix.

The third acquisition was the most important and took place in 1983. It concerned four Apulian vases. They came from a much larger group of twenty-one vases, all acquired at the same time, but Polaroids of only four of them were found in Medici's albums. All twenty-one had been offered to Berlin by one Christoph Leon of Basel on behalf of a Basel family, the Cramers. Professor Heilmeyer examined the vases on the premises of the head of archaeology at Geneva Museum, Jacques Chamay. "Chamay had pronounced himself to be the discoverer of the vases, specifying that his research had begun after he had examined a fragment of one of the vases in the Cramer family's old library." Professor Heilmeyer had spoken to the person who declared she had restored the vases, Fiorella Cottier-Angeli, who told him that the vases had been in very old chests and had reached Geneva "in the nineteenth century." Cottier-Angeli also said that she did not wish her name to appear in the museum's publications. All the vases came from Puglia, and the museum officials had believed what Leon, Chamay, and Cottier-Angeli had told them about the provenance. The overall price of 3 million marks had been paid to Leon. The fourth acquisition, an Attic krater, had been left to the museum in 1993 as an inheritance from the Brommer Collection. In the donor's documentation there was no indication of provenance.

In other words, in this case too, the usual suspects—in the usual triangular relationships—are in evidence. And the usual falsehoods were told about provenance.

Conducting interrogations through cumbersome letters rogatory, in foreign languages, with suspects who have the opportunity to be as uncooperative as possible and the time to decide what they will do with any incriminating evidence in the months before they are interviewed, is far from ideal from the point of view of the law enforcement authorities. Almost all the cards are stacked against them from the word go. In this instance, however, Dr. Ferri had quite a bit to work with, and perhaps the single most important result to come out of these raids and interrogations was that he discovered nothing to refute or contradict the picture that Pellegrini, Rizzo, Conforti's team, and he himself had been able to build in the months and years since the discovery of the organigram and Medici's first arrest. Indeed, they had added considerably to their understanding, despite the reluctance of some witnesses to be fully open. And on the all-important role of Medici, Hecht, Symes, Becchina, and Savoca, the picture had been amply corroborated. The existence of triangulation and the cordate was confirmed, together with the fact that it was "business as usual." Hecht's memoir really existed, it contained a version of the Euphronios krater story that was very different from that given at the time (that is, in 1972), and yet was itself corroborated by some of the new information vouchsafed by others who were in a position to know.

There remains one raid to mention, the second one conducted on Medici. This time, however, the location was not the Geneva Freeport but Medici's house at Santa Marinella, north of Rome, near the coast. It took place in 2002, and by far the most interesting discovery was an album of photographs in which one of the most prominent images was the Euphronios krater. The album, a ring binder, contained not one but several images of the krater. But on closer inspection, when the photographs were back at his office in the administration block of the Villa Giulia Museum, Pellegrini observed that two of the images of the krater were in fact fake. The main scene of the genuine Euphronios krater—the one in the Met— is of the dying Sarpedon with blood flowing from three wounds on his body. He is held by the gods of Sleep and Death, each of whom has wings, beautifully rendered, that stick out at either side of the composition. On either side of this main motif are guards, each man holding a spear.

These spears are important. Both are held upright, and the tip of the left-hand spear touches the tip of the god's wing. The right-hand spear, in contrast, is held a short distance away from the tip of the wing belonging to the god on the right. In the fake vases, or copies, the arrangement is dif- ferent. In one, the tip of the spear is *behind* the wing of the god on the left-hand side of the composition, covered by it, and in the other the spear is *behind* the wing of the god on the right-hand side. At first sight, the im- ages are the same, but on closer inspection the fake images are in fact very obvious—no connoisseur or professional archaeologist or art histo- rian would be taken in for long. On a subsequent visit to Santa Marinella, Ferri actually saw one of these fakes or copies—the one where the spear was behind the wing of the right-hand god—and he says this vase was about half the size of the real Euphronios krater, and much less moving. "It was cold and stiff," says Ferri.

But the quality is not really the point. The existence of the two other kraters—whether they were copies or deliberate fakes—doesn't prove any- thing, one way or the other, about Medici's involvement in the Met's con- troversial acquisition of the original vase, any more than the organigram proves that the people named in the document are members of the organ- ization that is suggested. But, as with the organigram, these images are highly suggestive. When asked why he had them, Medici said that he was fascinated by the Euphronios krater, by its quality and iconography, and the copies were merely a measure of that fascination and passion for vases by masters such as Euphronios. But why this vase and no others, why two copies rather than one, why were there deliberate mistakes introduced?

He had no answer.

Ferri asked who had made the copies, but Medici wouldn't answer that question either. The prosecutor paid a visit to the most prominent faker of Greek and Roman vases, but he denied having anything to do with Medici. Stalemate.

It was frustrating, but it only made Ferri more certain that he had the right man in his sights and that the Metropolitan's acquisition of the Euphronios krater marked a turning point in the whole underground trade of looted antiquities.

Across a twenty-year period, from the late 1960s to the late 1980s, no fewer than *five* vases by Euphronios surfaced on the market. Prior to that, nothing new by him had been discovered for more than a century. In terms of classical archaeology, this was a miracle. Miracles of this kind inspire some people but they don't satisfy the methodological skepticism of scientists. The five objects comprise the fragmentary vase which Hecht sold to the Munich Antikensammlung in 1968, the Sarpedon krater which Hecht sold to the Metropolitan Museum in 1972, the Euphronios and Onesimos kylix which Frida Tchacos sold to the Getty in 1983, the krater which the Hunt brothers bought from the Summa Gallery (owned by Bruce McNall and Robert Hecht) in the 1980s, and which was bought by Robin Symes for Leon Levy and Shelby White in 1990, and the kylix bought by the Hunts from the Summa Gallery in the 1980s, and which was acquired by Giacomo Medici at the Hunt sale in 1990. We now know from Pellegrini's paper trail that four of these vases involved Robert Hecht, and that three involved Giacomo Medici. The appearance of these five vases on the market so close to one another is either a freak coincidence or, to more skeptical minds, an indication of a sudden epidemic of fakes in the art world.

Put all that alongside the fact that Medici had, in his house at Santa Marinella, near Cerveteri, a photograph of the Met's Euphronios krater, photographs of two copies or fakes, and one of the copies or fakes itself, and then put all *that* alongside the fact that a cult building dedicated to Hercules—the iconographical subject of many of these vases—was discovered in Cerveteri in 1993, and the suggestion becomes overwhelming that the five Euphronios vases scattered over Europe and north America came from this one source—Cerveteri, via Medici and Hecht.

All of which only made the prosecution of Giacomo Medici more urgent.

At that point, only one aspect of the investigation remained to be completed: the interrogations in the United States.

14

INTERROGATIONS IN LOS ANGELES

AND MANHATTAN

I F GIACOMO MEDICI WAS enemy number one in the eyes of Conforti and Ferri, and if Hecht was number two, it was debatable who was number three. There was no shortage of candidates: Becchina, Fritz Bürki, Symes. And then there was Marion True. Medici referred to Symes and Christo as his "diaspora," meaning that as Hecht began to age, they were the main conduit in spreading his objects around the world. In reality, of course, they were all part of a much bigger diaspora—the spread of antiquities out of Italy and throughout the world—to the United States, to Britain, to Germany, to Japan, to Denmark: all of it illicit.

It was inevitable that Conforti's and Ferri's investigation should lead to the United States. No sooner had the Swiss decided not to proceed against Medici—and the documentary and photographic evidence, together with the 4,000 or so antiquities, had been transferred to Italian soil—that True's lawyer proposed a meeting with Ferri. This interview was not as quickly accomplished as Hecht's but still occurred a great deal earlier than some of the others. Ferri, Rizzo, Pellegrini, two of Conforti's men, and an official—an archaeologist from the Italian Ministry of Culture—flew to Los Angeles in June 2001 to interview her. The Alitalia 747 landed at Los Angeles Airport on a baking hot day, the smog haze over the downtown skyscrapers visible from the aircraft's final approach.

The Italian team was staying at a hotel in Santa Monica, a pretty town on the coast just south of where the new Getty is located. They had no chance to enjoy its amenities, however. After the long, twelve-hour flight they were all tired, and Ferri had ordered a meeting at eight the next morning, before they boarded their people-carrier for the rendezvous at the museum. The reason for Ferri's strict regime was a response to the way those on the American side had conducted themselves. Eleven months earlier, the Italian public prosecutor had issued letters rogatory, asking for several documents, to interview True, Dietrich von Bothmer, and Ashton Hawkins. Ferri had been told that von Bothmer was "not available" unless the Italians decided to bring charges against True, and he never received any response at all to his request to interrogate Hawkins. In addition, the U.S. attorney involved, Daniel Goodman, had argued that Ferri's original request to the Getty was "too vague, too wide" and that unless he could be more specific, the museum could offer no assistance.

Then, ten days later, a knock was heard on Ferri's door at the Palazzo di Giustizia in Rome—and there stood Richard Martin, the Getty's lawyer. He had with him a bunch of documents.

By handing over some of the paperwork voluntarily, the Getty was not compelled to provide all of the pertinent documents, and it faced no penalty for what looked like cooperation. The Getty knew that letters rogatory are cumbersome instruments and Ferri would have little choice but to accept what was offered. The Getty also knew that its voluntary gesture would avoid the formal process of discovery, which would have compelled it to reveal all.

And so, that morning in Santa Monica, Ferri wanted one last meeting to make sure his people were all on their toes ahead of a crucial encounter. They would get only one bite from this particular apple. It was June 20.

The meeting began at 9:30 AM in the conference room of the museum, which rests on the top of a hill overlooking the Sepulveda Pass and Highway 405, the San Diego Freeway. The meeting room is large, with windows along one side and a long, oval-shaped, blond-wood table. The Italians sat down one side, the Getty people down the other, with Ferri directly opposite Marion True. On the American team, besides True herself, there were ranged: Daniel Goodman, the U.S. attorney, representing the U.S. Department of Justice; Deborah Gribbon, then director of the Getty, representing the museum; Richard Martin, the Getty's lawyer; Lodovico Isolabella, True's elegant Italian lawyer; and interpreters and official stenographers, there to record proceedings.

True is a handsome woman who, over the years, has been both

brunette and blond. She spent her early career at the Museum of Fine Arts in Boston, in the Greek and Roman Department. She transferred to the Getty Museum in 1983 and became curator two years later.

The interrogation lasted for two whole days, and at first, the meeting was tense. True was being interviewed on serious charges in front of her colleagues and superiors; there was bound to be a fraught atmosphere.

Ferri's aim was to relax True, and to get her talking—at least to begin with—about others. If she would incriminate others, he could use that against them, perhaps to get back at True. It was a classic fencing match, but carried out via the unwieldy form of translation. Ferri had mixed feelings: He was angry at what True had done, but he was also fascinated by a woman who was undoubtedly strong, was well versed in her subject, and had, he felt, been led astray.

During the course of her questioning, True said she had first met Giacomo Medici in 1984 in Basel, Switzerland, at the sale of the Bolla Collection of Greek amphorae. (The Bolla family lived in Lugano.) They had been introduced by Robert Hecht and Dietrich von Bothmer. Later, she said, she saw Medici in Geneva, Rome, and Malibu, California. In Geneva in 1988, she saw him together with Robert Hecht, at the Freeport. On that occasion, she was offered a bronze Etruscan tripod and a candelabrum, and at the same time Medici showed her some photographs of a collection of red-figure Attic plates attributed to the Bryn Mawr Painter. They were intact and not in fragments, she remembered, though one plate had an edge missing. She met Medici again one or two years later in a bank in Geneva where he showed her, among other things, a late-Hellenistic sculpture of the Goddess Tyche, already cleaned. (This was the statue eventually sold by Symes to the Fleischmans, who then sold it on to the Getty.) Later still, Medici came to see her in Malibu, when again he was with Hecht. It was a courtesy visit and Medici had his son with him. True, crucially, contradicted Symes, insisting that she did not consider Medici an expert.

True said she knew that certain things purchased by her predecessor, Jiri Frel, had been acquired from the Hydra Gallery, and she knew that both that gallery and Editions Services were owned by Medici. Through Frel she had also met Gianfranco Becchina, in his case at the Getty in 1983–1984, "when there was beginning to be talk of the statue that was to become known as the Getty Kouros." She confirmed that, so far as she knew,

Becchina and Medici hated each other. Becchina, she said, had at that time already sold the Getty a dinos krater and some fragments of frescoes.

She had known Robert Hecht since 1972 or 1973 when she worked at the Museum of Fine Arts in Boston. "He was a good friend of the curator of the museum, Cornelius Vermeule and his wife, Emily." (Emily Vermeule had been Marion True's professor.) True confirmed that Hecht was in partnership with Bruce McNall in the Summa Gallery but that he had also been in partnership with Fritz Bürki in Zurich and kept various objects in Bürki's shop. This contradicted Bürki's testimony.

She was, she said, good friends with Dietrich von Bothmer at the Metropolitan. He too had been her professor. True's nerves seemed to intensify when the subject of von Bothmer was raised, and she asked for a break. Daniela Rizzo noticed that the heel on one of True's sandals was broken and, after the break, she had changed her shoes.

The interrogation proceeded, and Ferri returned to the matter of Dietrich von Bothmer.

FERRI: Did he ever confide— Did he ever confide in you? I'm insisting on this particular point.

TRUE: Yes, I think it's fair to say he did.

FERRI: When?

TRUE: In terms of important confidences, sort of at the end of his position when he was retiring around, say, must have been 1990, that time.

FERRI: He confided in you in a major way, and I have the same information, I have information about a major—that he confided with you in a major way. Can you tell me what that is?

TRUE: Just to put it in perspective, Mr.—Professor von Bothmer wanted me to be his successor at the Met. And at one point I was in his office, and he had a photograph, an aerial photograph, which showed the necropolis of Cerveteri. And looking at the necropolis, he pointed to a certain spot on the photograph and said this is the place where the Euphronios krater was found.

FERRI: Did he show particular tombs?

TRUE: Yes.

FERRI: Where was that tomb, was it Sant'Angelo?

TRUE: I don't know. I honestly— It was just this photograph and I—

FERRI: Did he tell you why he was able to point out that tomb?
TRUE: No. Just said he'd been given the information that that was where
the krater had come from.

This was sensational testimony, of course, and Ferri would dearly have
loved to take a break there and then, to savor what Marion True had admitted. But, for the moment, he kept going. He then read the relevant ex-
tract from Hecht's memoir, the "Medici version" that related how Medici
had turned up one day at Hecht's Rome house with photographs, how
they had flown to Milan and taken a train to Lugano, and so forth. But
Marion True said she knew nothing of this. She was aware of the Dikran
Sarrafian version she said, and that was all.

She described Hecht as a very intelligent and fascinating man, but an
"incurable gambler" and a "chronic alcoholic." She confirmed that Robin
Symes had confided to her Hecht's threats to libel his rivals in a book after
his death.

She agreed that Hecht specialized in selling fragments of vases that had
already been bought by museums. Hecht was still active, she thought. She
had bumped into him in Athens about two years before, when they were
staying in the same hotel, and he was trying to sell something to the Benaki Museum (a museum of Greek culture, from antiquity to the present
day, part of which is in the Kerameikos district). She confirmed that although he could be charming, he "could also turn, be very hostile, very sar-
castic, very sinister. He was a person who had a very peculiar personality."

FERRI: Do you know if Hecht— Did Hecht ever threaten to slander
against anybody if you didn't go along with what he wanted or you
rebelled against what he wanted to do?
TRUE: I have heard threats of that kind reported.
FERRI: Who told you this?
TRUE: I think it was Robin Symes.

Later:

FERRI: . . . What were the threats that Symes referred to from Hecht?
TRUE: Just— I just remember something, and I can't tell you specifically
what it was, but it was a suggestion that Robin made— I mean that

he—Just trying to reconstruct what happened. It may have been at the anniversary party that Robin had in London. And it was like a— I think the 25th anniversary of his gallery and he had a big party. And I wasn't there, but he told me that Bob got very drunk and made some statements like, you know, I can destroy you all, or—Something very unpleasant but not specific.

She confirmed—and this was important—that when objects were offered to the museum, Polaroid photographs were never sent by the vendor, since they lacked the precision to show the real quality of the object on offer. This did not fit with the claim by Robin Symes that Polaroids were used, routinely, to show prospective clients the original state of an object.

She also confirmed that she knew all the key figures in the cordata. She said she had met Bürki many times in Zurich (Fritz Bürki, remember, could not recall having many dealings with the Getty.) Then came this exchange:

FERRI: Fritz Bürki is a restorer of art objects. Did he—Has he sold any objects directly to the J. Paul Getty?

TRUE: I think he is represented as the owner of objects that we bought. And this was a situation, as I told you, I knew that he worked together with Bob. And either one or the other of them owned the object. And sometimes an object would come under Bürki's name.

FERRI: I see. So they would exchange—One was an intermediary for the other?

TRUE: Yes. I mean one had the feeling with Bob Hecht that he—he worked with various people, depending on people who were really able to provide funds.

She said she could not really explain why she had written the letter she did, on June 10, 1987, to Medici, telling him that the two objects would be bought by the museum, since according to her, she knew that the bronzes belonged to Bürki and then Hecht.

FERRI: So you knew that the owner was Medici?

TRUE: Medici was the person who had showed them to me. As I told you, whether the objects were owned by Bürki or Medici, I couldn't tell you.

FERRI: Why did you accept documentation coming from Bürki?

TRUE: Because, as I told you, Bürki frequently worked together with Bob and Bob worked together with Giacomo.

The museum bought several objects directly from Medici, she said, including fragments of the Onesimos kylix and the Caeretan Hydria, "so there was no reason why Medici's name should not appear in the museum's documents." Challenged with the fact that, despite this statement, Medici's name does *not* appear in Getty documents, she answered that some objects were in the name of the Hydra Gallery, though she admitted that the words "Editions Services" do not appear in the Getty archives. Asked about the letter she wrote to Bürki, concerning the ongoing investigation, in which she said she had seen the tripod in Geneva at Medici's, and not in Zurich at Bürki's, she answered that her memory was faulty and that she had only remembered the true course of events when prompted by Hecht. When the museum returned the tripod, it did so on the basis that it would not be returned to Guglielmi because he "had probably smuggled it out only to then report the theft once it had been discovered." She admitted sending verbal guarantees to Medici concerning the arrival of the tripod even though he didn't appear to be the owner. She said that the confidential, intimate tone of her letters to Medici was due to the fact that she and the museum needed him because of the case of the kouros, the fake they had bought from Becchina, after Medici sent proof of its falsity. In addition, letters exchanged with Medici concerning three olpai were indicated by Medici as coming from Monte Abatone in Cerveteri. Medici had told her whence the objects came. She said, "Evidently he was in relation with whoever had excavated them."

True said she was present at an argument between Robin Symes and Robert Guy, in which the latter, while examining objects of Symes's collection, had pretended not to have ever seen them before, whereas she knew that he had seen them at Medici's and kept this fact secret. "It was therefore obvious that Symes' objects came from Medici."

Regarding the Onesimos kylix, the initial purchase was made by Jiri Frel from the Galerie Nefer (Frida Tchacos's gallery). Then the fragments of the central tondo were bought by Arthur Houghton (the museum did not ascertain its provenance, but True agreed that the fragments came from the Hydra Gallery), and one fragment was donated in 1986 or 1987 by von Bothmer—it was a fragment that Dyfri Williams had recognized among those of von Bothmer's collection. The fragment had a sticker on it, which read "RH '68," which she understood to mean "Robert Hecht 1968." She recognized among the photos seized from Medici—including a Polaroid—the fragments of the tondo of the kylix, and she confirmed that, in 1991, Williams published this object, reporting that he had seen a fragment of the border that, she confirmed, was in Medici's possession. She had received from Christo Michaelides a photocopy of a photograph that showed the fragment. Michaelides said that the piece was on the market (more triangulation), but she was never offered it. (It was this fragment, indicated by Dyfri Williams, that had been handed over by Medici when he knew that the game was up.)

True said that she knew at least some of the Levy-White collection came from Tchacos, Hecht, Symes, the Aboutaams, and Becchina because several objects had first been offered to her by these people. She admitted that the Hunt Collection was gathered through Hecht, McNall, and the Summa Gallery—and she confirmed moreover that when she first went to the Getty, Jiri Frel had told her about "the sodality between Hecht, Bürki and the Hunts."

She described Ortiz as "an exceptionally unpleasant human being. He— he lives outside of Geneva, has his collection in a vault underground. I think his closest connection is with Becchina and with— He was close with Nikolas Koutoulakis. He seemed to have a love-hate relationship with Robin Symes, who threw him down the stairs once."

Regarding the Attic plates, she said that when the museum decided not to buy them, Medici refused to sell the accompanying fragments, which had been offered for about $125,000.

Shown the photographs of the Pompeian frescoes, she confirmed that she had seen the real things in Zurich—where she remembered there were three walls (which means that at least one is still missing). In her opinion they would be impossible to sell, and in fact she said she was so worried by the offer that she had someone accompany her—professor Michael Strocka, an expert in frescoes from Freiberg University—as a witness. She added that there was "part of the cornice" that reminded her of a fragment in the Levy-White Collection and that there was a fragment in the Fleischman Collection that "could be part of the same" and, if so, perhaps it should be returned. She said she was shocked by the frescoes: "It is impossible to remove architectural objects like these without destroying the structure."

This was an important moment. During the lunch break on the second day, Maurizio Pellegrini had been shown around the museum by True herself. He found her much more sympathetic than he had expected and far more so than anyone else on the opposing team. They stopped in front of the Griffins and Pellegrini looked from the beautifully displayed loot toward True. "I felt that, in that moment, True was *'dispiaciuta'*" (sorry). Not so much sorry for being guilty, which he felt she was, but because she was an archaeologist and was betraying her profession.

Ferri was tougher. His heart had begun to harden against True when he had heard what Tchacos had to say about the Fleischmans and the way the Getty curator had used—and abused, as he saw it—her relationship with them. As True talked about being "shocked" by the frescoes she had seen in the Bürkis' workshop, he also recalled the fact that it was written in the catalog to the Fleischman Collection that their fresco, the lunette of Hercules, "came from the same room" as one in the Levy-White Collection and, as Ferri now knew, had its twin in Corridor 17. He felt that Marion True was appealing for sympathy here when she didn't deserve it. It is fair to say that, from that moment, Ferri was determined to bring True to trial.

After lunch, proceeding to other matters, Ferri next tackled an example of the trade in fragments, or orphans. The kantharos with masks was first offered—to Jiri Frel—by Symes. To begin with, it was turned down, then sold to the museum in fragments, first by Fritz and Harry Bürki, "who said they had got it from Symes, partially put together." Other fragments came in 1988, from Symes, then another eleven fragments in 1996, from Brian Aitken, a North American benefactor of the arts.

And in regard to the Douris Phiale, described by True as an "exceptional object," she said that it was acquired in fragments "from various provenances"—Tchacos, Symes, Bürki, Werner Nussberger (the husband of Tchacos). She tried hard to get all the fragments, negotiating "with everyone—Hecht, Tchacos, [Herbert] Cahn."

More generally, True agreed that in acquiring fragments, most of the edges were sharp, meaning that they had been broken recently. "I would say in most cases they were sharp joins that were close. They allowed for a tight join." She said there was at times "weathering" on the surface. "But they were not worn."

She also confirmed that a certain vase that was in the Getty was shown in Medici's Polaroids. This was important because the Polaroid showed the vase with a hole punctured in it. Daniela Rizzo explained that the hole had been made by a *spillo*, a long metal spike used by tombaroli to thrust in the ground, searching for buried tombs. From time to time, the spike punctures the vases of a very full tomb—so this type of hole betrays that the vase has been illegally excavated. True responded, "I know. I understand."

Finally, Dr. True was able to render Dr. Ferri a service. He showed her a sequence of photographs, including Polaroids, and she was able to confirm not only which objects were in the Getty's collection but, in some cases, in which other museums certain objects could be found. True confirmed nineteen objects that were in the Getty, though two others—fragments of vases by the Kleophrades Painter and the Berlin Painter—could have formed part of incomplete objects they already had. She pointed out one or two fakes, as she saw them, but she located a Laconian kylix and two more objects at the Metropolitan Museum in New York; another object in Toledo, Ohio; a lekythos "in Cleveland or Richmond Museum"; a *situla* (a bronze vase with handles, like a bucket), "perhaps in Richmond"; a vase at the Museum of Fine Arts in Boston; and a Sabene statue, also in Boston, acquired through Hecht. Other objects she identified as being in Minneapolis, at least one object that she knew was in the Levy-White Collection, and a third at the Japanese museum in Koreshiki Ninigawa.

From the cumbersome bilingual interviews, nothing had been unearthed during the two days with True that seemed to contradict Ferri's case. On the contrary, much had been confirmed and amplified. Medici's role, together with Becchina, as being the major source of illicit objects out of Italy, had been reinforced. The triangulations—involving Hecht, Symes, Bürki, and Tchacos—had also been underlined. And of course, most notable were the close links between True herself and von Bothmer on the one hand, with the underworld on the other. As curator of antiquities at a major museum, True—like von Bothmer—had shown herself perfectly prepared to be part of this clandestine network, and well aware of where the objects her museum acquired had originated. She confessed herself "scandalized" at the damage that must have been done in excavating the Pompeian frescoes, but apart from that she seems to have had little compunction or regret about her part in driving other acquisitions. Certainly, during the course of her interview, she expressed no remorse. All this only confirmed for Ferri that he would, eventually, bring charges against the Getty's curator.

Ferri's primary "target" was, of course, Medici. At the same time, he couldn't ignore the fact that he now had two important pieces of evidence that changed utterly the status of the Euphronios krater at the Metropolitan Museum. He had Hecht's memoir, which said that it had been Medici—and not Dikran Sarrafian—from whom von Bothmer had acquired this object. And he now had Marion True's testimony that von Bothmer, no less, had identified the very tomb in Cerveteri from which the krater had come. (Third, of course, though this wasn't conclusive, he had another Euphronios vase, taken from Medici's safe in Corridor 17 in Geneva, now safely under lock and key at the Villa Giulia in Rome. Moreover, with linked iconography—this is the kylix in the photograph that Hoving saw.)*

And so Ferri now set out to see von Bothmer. In fact, in this part of the investigation he teamed up with a colleague, Dr. Frank di Maio, a Sicilian public prosecutor investigating the Morgantina silver.† Obviously, the Italians thought they would strike a more reasonable and responsible bearing if they made these two inquiries at the same time. Also, the two inquiries fed on each other, together putting pressure on the Americans

*See the Prologue, p. xvi.
†See pp. 103–106.

to cooperate. Therefore, in the first week of August 2002, the Italians sent off an "Urgent Request for Judicial Assistance," addressed to "The Competent Judicial Authority of New York, USA." This followed up rogatory letters of June 2000 (immediately after the documents and antiquities had been transferred from Switzerland)—the Italians could not be accused of dithering.

The objects of their inquiry were accused of contravening, in the case brought by Ferri, four articles of the Italian penal code—neglecting to report archaeological discoveries, illegal export, receiving contraband, and conspiracy. In the case brought by Dr. di Maio's investigation of the Morgantina silver, there were three indictments—neglecting to report archaeological discoveries, illegal export, and the receiving of contraband.

The documents the public prosecutors sent to the Americans outlined succinctly why the Italians were so anxious to interview two U.S. citizens—both former employees of the Metropolitan Museum of Art in New York, former curator von Bothmer and Ashton Hawkins, formerly vice president of the museum and in-house counsel.

The document began by setting out clearly what had been discovered at Medici's warehouse in Geneva and identified the seven objects at the Met that, the Italians said, had come from him, including the Euphronios krater. The Italians pointed out that Hecht's memoir, seized in Paris, gave an account of how the krater had left Italy, that Marion True had testified that von Bothmer had pointed out on an aerial photograph the tomb in Cerveteri where the krater came from, and that when Hecht was asked during his interrogation which of the versions of the Euphronios krater was correct, he requested a break in the questioning so that he could consult his lawyer, "thus giving us to understand, with good reason, that the official reconstruction of the affair of this important archaeological find, was nothing else but a story told to hinder penal and civil actions in Italy." The document also referred to the kylix by Euphronios that ended up with the Hunts.

The Italians believed that von Bothmer could help them sort out the exact acquisitions trail not only of the seven objects in the Met but also of many objects in the Getty and in the Levy-White Collection, for which he had, after all, compiled the catalog.

They were also concerned with two other matters. Ferri and Pellegrini had, over the months, examined the *Getty Museum Journal* and noted that von Bothmer had been very active in donating fragments to the museum, in particular as follows:

• in 1984, one fragment of an Euaion kylix;

• in 1986, forty-seven (unspecified) fragments out of 810, by different artists, purchased by the J. P. Getty Museum;

• in 1987, four fragments of a Douris kylix and, on a separate occasion, one fragment of a Douris kylix;

• in 1987, eleven (unspecified) fragments out of 189, by different artists, purchased by the J. P. Getty Museum;

• in 1988, thirteen fragments of an *Astragal* by the Syriskos Painter;

• in 1989, one fragment of a goblet krater by the Berlin Painter;

• in 1993, eight fragments of a *Skyphos* by the Kleophrades Painter;

• in 1993, one fragment of a kylix by the Brygos Painter;

• in the years 1981–1982–1987–1988—a total of thirty-two fragments of a Douris kylix.

That made 119 fragments in all. How had von Bothmer come by these orphans, as fragments are known in the trade? What was going on?

Ferri was also interested in von Bothmer's attitude. When, in 1985, he had been sent Sotheby's catalog for its July antiquities sale, he had spotted that Lot 540, an Attic black-figured amphora, had been identified in an Italian magazine as having been illegally excavated by a tombarolo from Tarquinia. His reaction had been to alert Felicity Nicholson at Sotheby's, and not the Italian authorities.

This pattern of behavior was not dissimilar to that encountered by General Conforti of the Carabinieri, whose letter to the Met (and to Munich) about illicit objects had found its way to Robert Hecht's apartment in Paris. In Ferri's view the episode needed following up.

▼

At the same time, Frank di Maio was on the trail of the fifteen pieces of Morgantina silver. In the mid-1980s, when doubts had first arisen about the provenance of the silver, which was announced in the museum's summer bulletin of 1984, the Metropolitan had given contradictory accounts of how the treasure had reached Fifth Avenue. It had first said that the silver was acquired on two separate occasions, in 1981 and 1982, purchased from a certain Nabil el Asfar, a dealer in antiquities from Beirut. According to this account, Asfar had acquired the silver pieces from his father sometime after World War II and in 1961 they had been sent to Switzerland, where they had remained until the Metropolitan Museum decided to buy them. However, the museum had not actually bought them until the silver pieces were *in* the United States.*

The invoices actually produced by the Met itself didn't match the museum's own account or the import documentation provided by U.S. Customs. We have been here before, of course, more than once. This scenario is more than a little reminiscent of the Euphronios krater affair and the fuss over the Sevso silver, when the export licenses, purportedly from Lebanon, turned out to be forgeries. Once again, Lebanon is the putative country of origin; once again, a father has left his son some valuable antiquities; once again, though very beautiful and rare, they have been stored for years without anyone knowing about them; once again, they have been brought to the United States, from Switzerland, by Robert Hecht.

In December 2000, di Maio questioned Vincenzo Cammarata, a well-known Sicilian "collector" of archaeological artifacts, and a coin collector, too, well known in the international traffic of these artifacts.† During questioning, Cammarata said: ". . . regarding the silvers, I heard they had been discovered, or rather found, as a result of a fortuitous archaeological finding at Scillato [a small town of 750 inhabitants, in the remoter part

*See p. 104.
†See Chap. 16.

of Palermo province, known for its oranges]. In particular, I know all this because of some persons who asked me how much the pieces were worth. I understood the pieces to have come from Morgantina." Cammarata also showed di Maio some newspaper cuttings he had that referred to the silver pieces, and he said another man, Vincenzo Arcuri, had also seen them. Arcuri was interviewed the following month, on January 4, 2001, when he said: ". . . in the first years of the eighties, two persons that I did not know came to look for me in this centre, in Piazza Garibaldi, where they made me look at some silver archaeological items and they asked me how much they could make. . . ."

Arcuri recalled that the people said they were from the Palermo area and they showed him four objects, "among which I remember a round pyxis 7–8 centimeters [2–3 inches] high, with a partially gilded lid, representing 'Scilla,' placed frontally, two silver glasses twelve centimeters [4–5 inches] high, however higher than the pyxis, and a small silver bowl. On that occasion, these objects were particularly dirty and partially covered with mud. . . . Upon my request for knowing the provenance of this material, I was told they all came from the area between Caltavuturo and Scillato." Shown sixteen good-quality unmarked photographs of Hellenistic silver, four pieces of which were from the Met and twelve of which were not, Arcuri immediately identified the Met silver pieces as the ones he had been asked about.

The American authorities had not been especially helpful to Ferri, or to di Maio. Yes, True had been interviewed, but permission to raid Hecht's New York apartment had been denied, permission to interview von Bothmer had been declined, for the moment anyway, and no reply was ever forthcoming about Ashton Hawkins. Investigations are difficult under such circumstances, to say the least.

But the Italians plugged away and eventually Judge Muntoni managed to obtain further interviews, though not until almost another three years had elapsed. In September 2004, he was able to interview Barbara Fleischman, John Walsh, and Karol Wight.

The questioning of Barbara Fleischman took place on September 20,

2004, at One St. Andrew's Plaza, in New York City. Thirteen people were present. Besides Judge Guglielmo Muntoni, Ferri, Rizzo, and this time just one of Conforti's men, there were: Richard Martin for the Getty; Lodovico Isolabella for Marion True; a representative of the U.S. Department of Justice; and two attorneys on behalf of Barbara Fleischman. Hecht had been invited to send a legal representative, but he declined.

The main thing that came out of the encounter was that Barbara Fleischman confirmed that she and her husband bought most of their objects either through Hecht-Bürki or Symes or Tchacos. She understood Hecht and Bürki to be partners and, though she and her husband bought a few things from the Aboutaams, she understood them to be mainly an outfit that sold on other people's behalf.

She said that the Fleischman collection was exhibited at—and then offered to—the Getty because their early good relationship with the Metropolitan Museum in New York had been damaged when the Met told them that they would have to pay for an exhibition at the Fifth Avenue museum that had been planned for several months *and* they would have to donate twelve objects to the Met. This had made Lawrence Fleischman very angry, so he had withdrawn his offer and all cooperation. Barbara Fleischman denied absolutely that she and her husband ever acquired anything as a way for the Getty to acquire it later. No one ever influenced them, she said, or was able to influence them.

She then told a story about Robert Hecht that, she said, showed his character. At one point her husband (who died in January 1997) was ill in the hospital and was visited by Hecht. She thought that was a civilized gesture—until Hecht took from his pocket a small bronze to see whether Fleischman wanted to buy it.

She said she never met Medici but always suspected he was a big figure in the background. She was at a loss to explain how two checks had found their way to Medici's warehouse but speculated that the Aboutaams were "factoring" them—again, that they were acting as agents. She conceded that when the Fleischman Collection was transferred to the Getty all the financial information was left behind, but that was just an accident, she said. All the paperwork about provenance *was* included with the objects. She and her late husband only bought works of art in the United States or in London, never Switzerland or anywhere else.

John Walsh, director of the Getty between 1983 and 2000, was interviewed in the same place on the following day. He came out strongly in support of Marion True, arguing that when she and he had arrived at the museum, the Getty's policy on the acquisition of unprovenanced material was "rather loose" and that she began to tighten things up. He said that they began to sound out governments from what he called the "archaeological countries" about which objects might have come from there; they speeded up publication, so that scholars could form a view about their acquisitions sooner rather than later; and they expressed a greater willingness to return objects that had been looted, "regardless of the statutes of limitations."

Marion True, he said, was the main force in all this, but although they notified governments of potential problems, the response was disappointing—in fact, they got very little response from the archaeological countries. There were no lawsuits and no formal claims, he said. Later still, in the mid-1990s, they tightened up even more, trying to collaborate still more closely with the archaeological countries. Walsh said that this made True, and the Getty, very unpopular with other American museums. He said that True's new polices were considered "too generous" in the eyes of the Metropolitan Museum, the Cleveland Museum of Art, the Fort Worth Museum—he said that the richer museums didn't like True's policy at all. In his eagerness to support True, and his own Getty, of course, he perhaps didn't realize what he was saying about American museums in general.

Walsh said he knew Symes, Hecht, Becchina, and a few of the other antiquities dealers, but in most cases he had met them just once and the relationship was confined to a handshake. He had heard of Bürki but had never met him, and the same went for Medici—he had heard the name but never met him, not even on the trip with Marion True to Rome when she had sent Medici a letter arranging a meeting. He said he had no idea how important Medici was.

Walsh said he had introduced the Fleischmans to True, in 1991. He had known them for years, since he was himself at the Met. This was well after the late 1980s, when Tchacos had said True was acquiring for the museum through Fleischman.

The following day—again at the same place—it was the turn of Karol Wight, Marion True's assistant curator at the Getty. Wight had actually been at the Getty since 1985, at first in a part-time capacity, and had been an associate curator since 1997. She was a confused witness, who seemed not to understand many questions, and the U.S. attorney overrode Judge Muntoni and allowed her to confer with her attorneys during the questioning, which was unusual.

On one matter, however, Wight's behavior was just bizarre. She was being questioned about the Fleischmans' decision to sell their collection to the museum and Marion True's role in that. She had said that True had no part in persuading the Fleischmans to choose the Getty, so Judge Muntoni asked her what it was that convinced them to dispose of their collection and sell it to the Los Angeles Museum, to which Karol Wight replied: "Is this the time for the story?"

Quite who this question was addressed to was unclear, but she quickly went on to describe an episode when Barbara and Lawrence Fleischman and Dr. True were walking through the museum, while their collection was still on display, and they came across a group of schoolchildren who had prepared reports on various of the objects. They had stopped to listen and became charmed by what the children had to say. After the children had finished their presentations, the Fleischmans introduced themselves and allowed the children to ask them questions. It was after this encounter, Wight said, that they had decided to sell their collection to a public institution and to the Getty museum. This was interesting of course because, only two days before, Barbara Fleischman herself had made no mention of such a motive for selling or donating their collection to the museum. In fact, she had said that she and her husband had opted for the Getty only after they fell out with the Metropolitan. She had made no mention of any schoolchildren.

Karol Wight said one other thing that drew Ferri's attention. Asked directly if there existed a "privileged" file of information in the museum regarding the provenance of antiquities, she replied that she knew of nothing like that. In his account, John Walsh had said that the Getty had tightened up considerably under Marion True and no longer took a dealer's word for it, that objects someone was offering to the museum were legitimate. One would have thought that if the museum had indeed done its own research into the provenance of the objects it was thinking of acquiring, then there would have been a record somewhere of the results of those inquiries.

In some of the U.S. sessions, there were as many as fifteen people in the room at any one time. This is a far cry from the image we all have of police interrogations taking place in small confined spaces, where one or two law enforcement officers spar with suspects on a one-to-one or two-to-one basis, where the exchanges can be rapid and tension-filled. In addition to the sheer size of the meetings—almost a crowd scene—there was the language barrier. This was to be expected. However, Pellegrini sensed something else, something he hadn't anticipated but maybe should have. "There was an element of competitive nationalism in the encounters," he said. Instead of being law enforcement *versus* suspects, it had become—to an extent—Italy *versus* the United States.

15

The Puzzle of the "Orphans"

IN THE COURSE OF THEIR VISIT to the United States, which had been so successful in some ways, despite the cumbersome nature of the interrogations, Ferri, Rizzo, and Pellegrini had cause to wonder if there wasn't at least one aspect of their investigation that was still beyond their full understanding. One way they glimpsed its elusive quality was in the activities of Dietrich von Bothmer. Over the years, between 1981 and 1993—in other words, over more than a decade—von Bothmer had donated no fewer 119 *fragments* of vases to the Getty. Why? Museums do not normally acquire fragments, at least not in any quantity. For example, Daniela Rizzo told us that the Villa Giulia Museum in Rome, where she works, never acquires fragments. It once *swapped* some fragments with the Metropolitan Museum in New York, because the Villa Giulia had some pieces that fitted a vase in the Met and the Met had fragments that fitted a vase in the Villa Giulia. But that was the only occasion. Professor Michael Vickers, at the Ashmolean Museum in Oxford, told us that he had recently acquired some twenty-odd fragments from Romania, but they had been legally excavated by reputable archaeologists and had been approved for sale and export by the relevant government authority. They were wanted in Oxford not to reassemble into a vase but for the study collection—as examples, for students, of certain types of ceramic manufacture and decoration techniques.

Thus, the Getty is already unusual in that (1) it acquires many fragments, and (2) it does so in order to reassemble these fragments into vases. Several prominent archaeologists we talked to have confirmed that this behavior by the Getty *is* unusual and that they have been aware of it for several years.

Just *how* unusual the Getty's behavior is may be seen from the following figures. In the ten-year period that the Italian investigators looked at, that is, 1984–1993, the museum acquired at least 1,061 fragments, of which von Bothmer accounted for 119. This is already seriously at variance with, for example, salesroom experience. We looked at twenty-three antiquities auctions held at Bonhams, Christie's, and Sotheby's between December 1996 and October 2005, almost ten years. During that time, 1,619 Greek and Italian terra-cotta vases were put up for sale. In those same sales, only twenty-four vase fragments came on the block (plus one fresco fragment and one fragment of a Roman wall relief). In fact, the figure of twenty-four fragments actually exaggerates the picture. In fifteen of the twenty-three sales of antiquities, no vase fragments at all were sold. Just three sales accounted for eighteen of the fragments (five, five, and eight). In most years, no vase fragments are traded.

Why and how should the Getty acquire, over ten years, 1,061 fragments, *fifty times* the number on the open market?

Fragments, or shards, can be important to scholars who specialize in ancient vases. However, ever since the eighteenth century, when Sir William Hamilton initiated the craze for vase collecting, it is whole vases that have been preferred, not fragments. Flinders Petrie (1853–1942), a British archaeologist, excavated at Naukratis and Daphnae, in the Nile Delta in the late 1880s, and used his discovery of pottery fragments to prove that these sites were ancient Greek trading posts, and he developed a sequential dating method by comparing pottery fragments at different levels. J. D. Beazley paid some attention to fragments when he was developing his method of attribution—but all that was in the early part of the twentieth century. Some dealers do trade in fragments even now, but more recently, for example, in Martin Robertson's *The Art of Vase-Painting in Classical Athens*, published in 1992, he included illustrations of 219 complete vases—and only twenty-one fragments. In Sir John Boardman's *The History of Greek Vases*, published in 2001, he included photographs of 234 different vases—but only nine fragments. Obviously, some painters, and some decorative techniques, are known only from fragments, but as the above figures show, the numbers are very small.

There is, however, a *commercial* factor in attributing fragments to the hand of known artists. According to museum scholars we have talked to, a fragment that might ordinarily be worth about $400 unattributed can be worth as much as $2,500 if attributed to a recognized painter. In the United States, therefore, attributed fragments may be attractive for the tax breaks attached to them. Both Dietrich von Bothmer (a student of Beazley) and Robert Guy are known among their colleagues for their skill and propensity to attribute fragments to recognized vase painters. Of course, it is much more satisfying—for both scholars and museums—to acquire vases, even in fragments, that are by recognized painters, so this is a situation where commercial and academic values are in line. And all this supports the idea, which Marion True admitted in her deposition, that the Getty acquired fragments in order to reassemble them into complete—or as complete as possible—vases.

But is there more to it than that? Is the fact that the Getty is so out of line with other museums a matter for concern, given all the other shortcomings in that museum's behavior described in this book?

There were four other pieces of evidence that caught the attention of Rizzo and Pellegrini. The first was the fact that many of the fragments, as True said, had sharp breaks, so that adjoining fragments fitted together very snugly: "I would say in most cases they were sharp joins that were close. They allowed for a tight join." She said there was at times "weathering" on the surface, "[b]ut they were not worn." She accepted that this must mean that at least some of the breaks were recent.

A second piece of evidence that caught the Italians' eye was a document released by the Getty in relation to the krater by Euphronios that the Levy-Whites had bought at the Hunt sale in 1990, and then sent to the Getty conservation department to see whether two other fragments, sold to them by Robin Symes, fitted. It will be recalled from Chapter 9 that the fragments did not fit but that during the course of her examination of the krater and the fragments, Maya Elston, of the Getty's conservation department had said, of the two fragments, "some *fresh* surface damage can be observed on the larger shard (perhaps these are traces from an excavation tool)" (italics added). Here then was another suggestion that fragments had been excavated only recently.*

A third instance was an exchange during Marion True's deposition at the Getty, when she said that the museum owned a cup by the Brygos

*See p. 131.

Painter and Hecht had once called and offered a fragment, which joined the cup, and that he had asked an "outrageous" price, as she put it. The final instance occurred during the negotiations over the acquisition of the twenty Attic plates that, in the end, the Getty did not buy. Medici, angered by the Getty's refusal, as a consequence withdrew the thirty-five fragments of the Berlin Painter krater that he was offering at the same time, for $125,000. Why? Why would Medici cut off his nose to spite his face? Why refuse $125,000 worth of business just because a bigger deal had fallen through? Why risk spoiling his relationship with the museum over some bits and pieces? Beyond that, why was this vase in fragments in the first place? Why had Bürki, or someone like him, not reassembled the vase? This is interesting behavior in itself, but what in particular attracted Ferri's attention was the wording of Marion True's letter to Medici, in which she announced that the museum would not be acquiring the plates. The exact wording of the end of this letter was:

I am terribly sorry about the plates myself, and I do hope that you will understand that the decision was certainly not mine. This is the first time that John [Walsh, director of the Getty] has actually refused something that I have proposed. I should have mentioned the Berlin Painter fragments in my [earlier] letter; naturally, we will return them with the plates as they were part of the Agreement. . . .

What, Ferri asked himself, was the "Agreement," and why did it merit a capital letter? There had been only so much ground they could cover in Los Angeles, and this matter was sufficiently opaque to be put on the back burner. So they never had the opportunity to ask Marion True what the exact wording meant. Searching through the Medici documents, and those supplied by the Getty, it is fair to say that no clear, coherent picture emerged. However, that is not the same as saying that the scenario was entirely blank. On the contrary, the picture that Pellegrini and Ferri teased out from the documentation was tantalizingly suggestive, and it was picked up on by the judge when Medici came to trial.

Several of the vases—eight, at least—acquired by the Getty arrived at the museum in fragments, bit by bit and piece by piece over a number of years. However, from the documentation supplied by the Getty (which had volunteered some paperwork*), the histories of only two vases were given more or less in their entirety. These were the Attic red-figure phiale by Douris, and the Attic red-figure calyx krater by the Berlin Painter. Both of these are very important vases indeed. The former was acquired in a series of sixty-three fragments between 1981 and 1990, and the latter in a series of fifty-eight fragments between 1984 and 1989. These acquisitions, combined with the fact that the Getty's behavior was so at variance with the rest of the trade in fragments, allow us to test several scenarios that had occurred to Pellegrini and Ferri.

From a detailed examination of the Getty's acquisition of the two vases, it became clear, first, that the average purchase price of a vase fragment was somewhere between $2,500 and $3,600. Obviously, this depended on size and importance, on whether the fragment related to the central theme of a vase or was incidental, for example, part of the rim. On this reckoning, however, the value of von Bothmer's donations to the Getty amount, over the years, to somewhere between 119 x $2,500 = $297,000 and 119 x $3,500 = $416,500. One might ask where von Bothmer found the means to fund these donations. Is this, perhaps, the way he liked to be remembered? According to what we have been told by other archaeologists, by attributing these fragments to known painters (if that is what he was doing), Dietrich von Bothmer would have increased the value of these fragments from 119 x $400 = $47,600 to 119 x $2,500 = $297,000, an increase of $249,900. Was he able to take a tax break on these gifts?

Now we turn to the overall price of the two vases acquired in fragments. This was, in the case of the Douris phiale, $141,300 and, in the case of the Berlin Painter calyx krater, $101,900. These prices would appear to be neither very expensive nor very inexpensive, when compared with other vases acquired by the Getty during that time, prices that ranged from $42,000 to $750,000. But $100,000-plus for a vase is still a lot of money.

On the other hand, in both cases, some of the fragments were donated to the museum. Therefore, we can say that each vase was acquired by the Getty *for less than what it was actually worth*. (We are excluding here the cost of reassembly.)

---

*See p. 204 for the circumstances.

There are two more things to consider. First, in each case the fragments were acquired from a variety of sources, though with both vases the great majority came from one dealer. For example, in the case of the Douris phiale, the bulk of the fragments came from the Nefer Gallery—from either Frida Tchacos or her husband, Werner Nussberger, or both. A few came from Bürki, and one from Symes. In the case of the Berlin Painter krater, the bulk came from Symes, quite a few came from Dietrich von Bothmer, a few came from the Nefer Gallery, and one from Fred Schultz, a dealer in New York.

What, we may ask, does this pattern mean? Does it mean anything? In both cases, more than half the fragments came from one source, though not all at the same time (the Douris phiale arrived at the Getty on thirteen separate occasions, and the Berlin Painter krater on nine separate occasions). So there was always one primary source. The existence of several subsidiary sources—if we can call them that—perhaps allowed the fiction, for the benefit of naive trustees of a museum, that these fragments were excavated separately, turned up at different moments in time, and came on to the market by different routes.

But there was one other pattern evident from the acquisition of these two vases. They arrived in spurts. In each case, several years might pass without any fragments appearing, then several would come along almost at once. In the case of the Berlin Painter krater, for instance, there was a spurt in December 1984, when fragments were acquired on the third, seventeenth, and twentieth of the month, each time from Dietrich von Bothmer. Nothing arrived in 1985 or 1986, but there was a second spurt in February 1987. Sixteen fragments arrived from von Bothmer on the eleventh of the month, and another sixteen on the seventeenth, this time from Robin Symes. In the case of the Douris phiale, the first acquisitions were made in 1981 and 1982, nothing happened in 1983 and 1984, and then there was a spurt in early 1985 when twelve fragments arrived, all from Nefer. Nothing happened in 1986 or 1987, but then in April 1988, there was another spurt, with twelve fragments arriving on two separate occasions eight days apart, again from Nefer. Nothing happened for another two years, then there was a third spurt in November 1990, when three more fragments arrived, eleven days apart, this time from Robin Symes and from the Bürkis.

Together—the sharp edges of some of the fragments, the possibility of excavation tool marks on some of them, the "outrageous" price asked by Hecht, the small number of mostly familiar names of those who supplied the fragments, Medici's withdrawal of his fragments when the deal over the plates fell through, the admission by True of an "Agreement" involving fragments, the fact that so many fragments arrived from different sources, and the fact that they arrived in spurts—all this does suggest a pattern.

Is it really likely that up to ten years after some original fragments have been discovered, and discovered to be important enough to be worthy of a museum, that tomb robbers will go back to an illicit "dig"—assuming they can remember where it was in the first place—and sift the ground for further fragments, fragments that fetch in the order of $2,500–$3,500 apiece only if they can be attributed to a recognized painter? Is it really likely that, in the case of the Douris phiale, the tomb robbers found fragments while "digging" the same site on *thirteen* separate occasions? It sounds highly improbable. It is much more likely that the fragments left the ground together. There *have* been cases where fragments that fit known vases turn up several years later, but such instances are relatively rare.

If the Douris or Berlin Painter fragments *did* leave the ground together, and fairly recently, as the evidence seems to suggest, why did they reach the Getty by different routes and at different times? How, why, and where did they become separated? We suggest that the answer lies in the fact that they arrived at the Getty in spurts. The fragments are spread around the cordata as another aspect of triangulation. It is a way for dealers in the cordata to do each other—and museums like the Getty—favors, in particular to sugar other, more important deals. This is what Medici was doing when he offered the Getty thirty-five fragments of the Berlin Painter vase *if* it bought the Attic plates. When the museum refused to buy the plates, he withdrew the fragments—the favor, the lure, was taken away. This is what the "Agreement" was about and why True knew she had to return the fragments when the deal over the plates fell through.

What this suggested to Ferri, Rizzo, and Pellegrini, therefore, although they concede that this doesn't amount to firm proof, is that a cozy arrangement is revealed, one that fulfills several functions. The acquisition of vases in fragments—"the sale of the orphans" as Pellegrini put it—enables a museum to acquire a valuable vase, not for nothing exactly, but more cheaply than if the vase were to be acquired whole or intact. The fact that, as True said, the fragments fit snugly together and were not worn may well mean that vases are broken *deliberately*, at the start of the process, to set up the subterfuge we are identifying. Second, by donating several fragments, dealers can ingratiate themselves with the museum, they can maintain good relations. Third, by publishing its acquisition of fragments, rather than a complete vase, the museum can test the water, to see if the authorities in the country where the fragments were looted from lodge complaints. (This is unlikely, because fragments hardly stir the imagination the way complete vases do. And, if a country—like Italy—has not complained in the ten years or more it can take to acquire a vase in this way, will their complaints be taken seriously at the end of that time, when the vase can be assembled? If the country hasn't complained in the interim, isn't it in a sense at least partly responsible for allowing the situation to deteriorate? And again, with all the delay involved, at some stage the statutes of limitations will kick in.) Finally, fragments can be used to sugar other deals; they are a form of hidden bonus, which the curators and those in the trade are aware of but which perhaps escapes the trustees and the rest of us. Fragments arrive in spurts, when other—bigger—deals are going through.

This scenario could only be proved if the Getty had made available *all* the documentation the Italians had requested, so that important acquisitions could be compared, alongside the arrival of fragments. But that didn't happen. As a result, the full picture regarding the sale of the orphans remains murky.

Although this picture is murky, two pieces of information have been made available since the original publication of this book which render the situation less so. In an interview in New York on November, 17, 2006, Thomas Hoving, former director of the Metropolitan Museum, confirmed that our interpretation of the market in fragments is substantially correct—that fragments are used in the way we suggest. And Dr. David Gill, classicist and archaeologist at Swansea University in Wales, whose work is discussed in the conclusion, drew our attention to another vase in the Getty, an Apulian storage jar or *pelike* attributed to the Darius Painter and showing Perseus with Andromeda (see pp. 89–90). An illustration on the Getty's own website shows a pattern of cracks in this vase, in the form of a "starburst" so regular that one is prompted to wonder whether this breakage wasn't deliberate (see the Dossier).

16

The *"Cordata"* Continues—in
Egypt, Greece, Israel, and Oxford

THE AMOUNT OF PAPERWORK generated by the prosecution of Giacomo Medici was immense. Ferri had four secretaries working for him in his fourth-floor offices in Piazzale Clodio, and it was sometimes easy to feel overwhelmed by the sheer scale of Medici's activities, the vast reams of documentation to be analyzed, the objects to be traced, the numbers of people to be questioned. Keeping track of who had handled what and when; who had covered for whom and when; who had donated what and where; who had told which lies, when, about what, and to whom—it was all daunting. Ferri's office was decorated with colorful posters of archaeological exhibitions but they were an ironical joke. No one had time to visit any museum other than the Villa Giulia, which had become an extension of the prosecutor's office.

And yet, from time to time, the load was lightened. Attitudes, and laws, have been changing across the world in regard to issues of cultural heritage. And this is true not only in the "archaeological countries" but in the market countries, too. Over the ten years since the Carabinieri's first raid on Corridor 17 in Geneva in 1995, new laws governing the trade in antiquities have been passed in Great Britain and Switzerland; and the United States, moving in its own way, has concluded bilateral agreements with several countries—among them Guatemala, Peru, Mali, Canada, and Italy—under which the importation into the United States of certain types of ancient objects is prohibited.

In recent years these new laws and agreements have begun to take effect. On top of that, countries such as Egypt, Greece, Jordan, and China have become more assertive in their attempts to prevent the illicit trade and in this regard they have adopted a common stance: It is, in the long run, more effective to stem the demand in the market countries—Western Europe, North America, Japan—than try to catch and convict the thousands of tomb robbers, who in any case make far less money than the better-heeled middlemen who are the chief culprits in the eyes of the likes of Paolo Ferri and Roberto Conforti.

This argument is substantiated by a number of other cases, parallel plots—stretching from Bombay to Cairo to Stockholm to London and Oxford to New York and Los Angeles—that have come to light in the last few years, and in each of which the names and "business practices" are only too familiar.

Ferri, Conforti, and the others were reassured by these other episodes that real change was now in the air.

In November 1995, two months after the raid on Corridor 17, a gold phiale of Sicilian origin and dating to the fourth century BC was seized in New York. The provenance of the phiale was largely unknown. It is said that sometime between 1976 and 1980, when an Italian utility company was laying cable in Sicily, workers dug up a golden platter, about the size of a pie plate. This phiale was decorated with acorns, beechnuts, and bees, and it matched one sold to the Met in 1961—by Robert Hecht. The new phiale interests us because although it was first acquired by Vincenzo Pappalardo, a private antiquities collector living in Sicily, he traded it in 1980 to Vincenzo Cammarata for artworks worth about $20,000. Cammarata, it will be remembered, was questioned by Frank di Maio, the Sicilian public prosecutor investigating the provenance of the Morgantina silver.

The case is also interesting because the phiale was eventually acquired by Robert Haber, an art dealer from New York and owner of Robert Haber & Company. Haber acquired the phiale on behalf of a client of his, Michael Steinhardt, a financier. Haber told Steinhardt that the phiale was a twin to a piece in the Metropolitan Museum of Art and charged Steinhardt $1.2 million. Steinhardt had the piece authenticated by scholars at the Metropolitan Museum of Art, and thereafter the phiale was displayed in his home from 1992 until 1995.

It was seized after an inquiry by the Italian authorities—and here it gets

murky. The U.S. government claimed that the forfeiture was proper because the phiale was stolen property and because there were false statements on the customs forms—for example, it was valued at $250,000,
when its real value was much higher. In the subsequent court case, the decision to seize the phiale was upheld, as it was on appeal, which was decided in July 1999. The gold platter was subsequently returned to Italy and
is now on display in Palermo.

But how did the authorities first come by the information that led to
this prosecution?

The episode is mentioned by Robert Hecht in his memoir: He considered the phiale a forgery, naming the Sicilian forger and some of his other
fakes. Was it he who alerted the authorities, because he was jealous of
Haber's links to a prosperous client such as Steinhardt? This is what Frida
Tchacos told Ferri at her interrogation. Hecht's trial in Rome, which began
in late 2005, may clarify this point.

In April 1997, two carved wall reliefs surfaced in London. Shlomo
Moussaieff, of Grosvenor Square, London, had applied for permission to
export one of these antiquities but was stopped by the government's official adviser, John Curtis at the British Museum. Curtis had spotted that
the relief had been looted from Iraq—it belonged in the throne-room suite
of the Sennacherib Palace in Nineveh, across the Tigris River from
Mosul.* The identification was made because of the work of Dr. John Russell, an archaeologist from Massachusetts College of Art, who excavated
at Nineveh before the first Gulf war, as part of a University of California
team, and took 900 photographs of the site.

Inquiries by Scotland Yard established that Mr. Moussif had bought
looted antiquities from Nabil el Asfar, then based in Brussels. This is the
same Asfar who had, allegedly, provided Robert Hecht with the Morgantina silver.† Mr. Moussif had been told that the reliefs had been "in
Switzerland for years."

---

*The lost palace of King Sennacherib (704–681 BC) was rediscovered in 1847 by the
British adventurer Austen Henry Layard. According to Genesis, Nineveh was among the
first cities to be built after the Flood.
†See p. 104.

At the time, Dr. Russell made it known that some ten other looted reliefs had appeared on the market. Generally, he said, he was approached by a lawyer, claiming to act on behalf of a "prospective buyer." In another case, however, involving yet another looted Iraqi relief, he had been approached by someone from the Metropolitan Museum in New York. He was able to establish that in this instance, the individual offering the relief to the museum—or who at least had provided a photograph of the proposed acquisition—was Robin Symes of London. This time the relief came from the palace of Tiglath-pileser III at Nimrud. (Tiglath-pileser III, 744–727 BC, was the real founder of the Assyrian empire.) This object was identified as loot by Richard Sobolewski, who led a Polish expedition to excavate Nimrud in 1975.

Only Mr. Moussif's objects were recovered. According to Sobolewski, the throne room in Tiglath-pileser's palace originally contained 100 stone slabs similar to those offered to the Met. Many of them are still missing.

In the late spring of 1998, Robert Guy chose not to renew his fellowship in classical archaeology at Corpus Christi College, Oxford. This brought to an end a curious set of events that was never fully explained.

In 1990, nearly a decade before, Claude Hankes-Drielsma had approached the college with a proposal that would fund, in perpetuity, a senior research fellowship in classical archaeology. Hankes-Drielsma has been a banker, a director of Robert Fleming, and chairman of the management committee of Price Waterhouse. In 1985, he masterminded the South African debt crisis; he was an adviser to the Iraqi government and did much to bring the Oil for Food scandal before the United Nations. He was one of those tasked with going through the Saddam Hussein documents after the fall of Baghdad. He is currently in charge of the appeal for the chapel at Windsor Castle (which was gutted by fire in the 1990s). An amateur antiquities collector, he is a member of the Getty Villa Council, a charity that benefits the Getty Museum's Antiquities Wing, and is himself an honorary fellow of Corpus Christi College, Oxford, where he has dining rights.

His 1990 proposal to Corpus Christi College had just two conditions: The fellowship was to be called the Beazley-Ashmole Fellowship, and the first incumbent had to be Robert Guy.

This was highly unusual. The normal practice is for fellowships to be advertised; then scholars apply, and ideally, the best candidate is appointed. When, in discussions about the fellowship, it further emerged that it was to be funded, at least in part, by the antiquities trade and that one of the dealers involved was Robin Symes, the Corpus Christi Council turned down the proposal, on the grounds that it was "inappropriate" to accept funds from such a source.

Some time afterward, Hankes-Drielsma approached the college again. This time, he said he had an alternative source of funds. The name of the donor was revealed only to the president of Corpus, but the fellows were assured that the source had a history of philanthropic giving to universities and had no links to the antiquities trade. This time, the proposal received publicity within the archaeological profession. As a result, Corpus was inundated with letters from archaeologists all over the world, protesting its proposed course of action. Almost the entire archaeological "establishment" was against the proposal—including Sir John Boardman, the distinguished author of many books on Greek vases; Donna Kurtz, the curator in charge of the Beazley Archive in Oxford; Martin Robertson, an authority on classical vase painting and professor of classical archaeology at Oxford (and an old adversary of Hecht); and Dietrich von Bothmer himself. All felt that the college should not accept funds anonymously, whatever Hankes-Drielsma said ($1.2 million was believed to be on offer), all felt the name of the fellowship was wrong and tendentious—neither Beazley nor Ashmole had anything to do with Corpus—and all felt that the fellowship should be advertised in the normal way. Those who objected to the proposal also suspected that what had originally been envisaged had been a "tame" fellowship. Funded by the trade, with the "Beazley-Ashmole" name, this fellowship would always carry the risk that the incumbent would feel obliged to satisfy dealers' commercial needs and attribute their vases to major Greek vase painters. Though commercially valuable, such a practice would be an abuse of scholarship. One of the few people who wrote in support of Guy was Marion True, at the Getty.

A college committee was set up to make a recommendation about the fellowship. The committee, however, could not agree. The members *did* agree to changing the name to the Humfrey Payne Fellowship, after a brilliant director of the British School in Athens, who had died young. Other than that, however, the divisions were fairly basic. In the end, a majority report was prepared, in favor of Guy's appointment, and a minority report was prepared by Robin Osborne, a noted classical archaeologist, who was against it. The governing body of the college then considered the issue and the whole matter was fully aired. The president of the college, Sir Keith Thomas, was in favor, and the proposal—with the name change—was eventually accepted.

Robert Guy was duly elected and served for the next seven years, as is normal, as a fellow of Corpus Christi. However, after seven years, when his renewal came up—a renewal that is usually automatic—he said he did not wish to stay, and the post was reoffered with no strings attached.

It was a curious episode, in some ways reminiscent of von Bothmer's treatment by the American Institute of Archaeology, when he failed to be elected to the board of trustees because of his actions in acquiring the Euphronios krater.* Even Robin Osborne, who was against Guy's appointment, agrees that he is a brilliant connoisseur of vases. But the original involvement of the trade in the fellowship, the anonymous nature of the money, and with the Getty in the background—all this left a nasty taste.[†]

In 1998, the Harvard Museum system put on display a 1995 purchase of 182 fifth-century BC Greek vase fragments. James Cuno, the director of Harvard's art museums, argued that the pieces had probably been removed from Italy before 1971, the date at which Harvard's acquisitions code took effect, in the wake of the UNESCO convention. The Harvard code forbids the acquisition of material of questionable provenance. The fragments were bought on the advice of museum curator David Mitten from a New York dealer who had acquired them from Robert Guy, then at the University of Oxford. *Culture Without Context*, the newsletter of the University of Cambridge Illicit Antiquities Research Centre, disagreed with Cuno.

---

* See the Prologue.
† In an interview with Peter Watson in London on February 6, 2006, Robin Symes said he had contributed $1 million to the Oxford Fellowship.

Referring to the fragments, the newsletter concluded that Guy "could only have obtained them after 1971."

In the summer of 1999, Frida Tchacos-Nussberger acquired an ancient manuscript that had been circulating in Europe and North America for some time. The so-called Gospel of Judas—thirteen codices in a Coptic translation of the ancient Greek—dates from the second century AD and is a good example of early Christian literature that was excluded as heretical from what the church had preserved in its early Greek form. The codices were allegedly found buried in the desert sand at Muh Zafat al-Minya in Egypt and had first appeared on the market in the early 1980s, via Nikolas Koutoulakis, but, proving difficult to sell, vanished again. Their resurfacing in 1999 appears to have been another attempt at a sale, for Mrs. Tchacos offered them to the Beinecke Library of Yale University for $750,000. But again there was no sale, so the manuscript was taken into a specially created Swiss foundation, which is to oversee publication, after which the codices will be returned to the Coptic Museum in Cairo.

There is a lesson here. Because no one would touch such an important—but unprovenanced—object, it is going to be properly published, and then returned to where it belongs.

In February 2000, Staffan Lunden, a Swedish journalist who was also an archaeologist, was researching a Roman funerary relief that had recently been acquired by the Museum of Mediterranean Antiquities in Stockholm. Lunden was interested in the object because, judging by stylistic criteria, it must have come from Ostia, outside Rome—but how and when?

Tracking the object back, he found that the Stockholm Museum had acquired it from Galerie Arete in Zurich in 1997. Before that, it was auctioned at Sotheby's in New York in December 1992, and before that, in 1991, it had belonged to Numismatic Fine Arts, Bruce McNall's gallery in Los Angeles. Before that, however, it was mentioned in Guntram Koch's *Roman Funerary Sculpture: Catalogue of the Collections*, published by

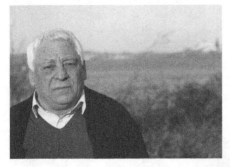

LEFT: Pietro Casasanta, the most successful tomb robber of all time, in terms of the important objects he has looted. He is shown in front of the field where he discovered the ivory head of Apollo (shown below).

RIGHT: The ivory head of Apollo, the world's rarest and most valuable looted antiquity, valued at $50 million. Looted by Casasanta, who sold it to Savoca, who sold it to Robin Symes, from whom it was recovered with the assistance of the authors.

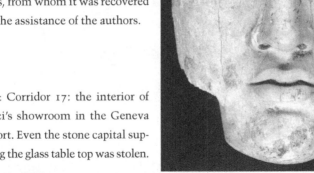

BELOW: Corridor 17: the interior of Medici's showroom in the Geneva Freeport. Even the stone capital supporting the glass table top was stolen.

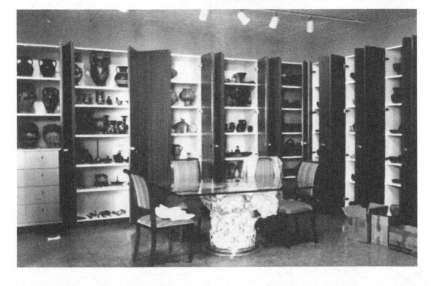

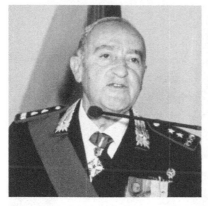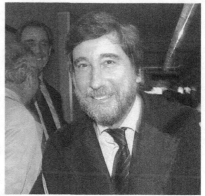

LEFT: Colonel—later General—Roberto Conforti, head of the Carabinieri art squad. RIGHT: Public Prosecutor Paolo Ferri who, with Conforti, led the Italian investigation.

RIGHT: Gianfranco Becchina, Medici's bitter enemy and leader of the rival "cordata." He operated out of Basel but retired to Sicily.

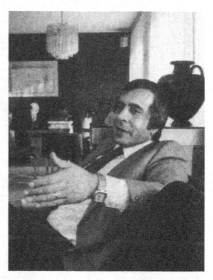

BELOW: Polaroid found in Medici's warehouse in Geneva. The central vase of the three was later in the Hunt collection, and the one on the right in the Metropolitan Museum.

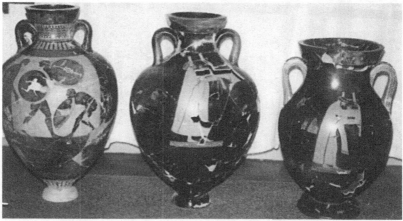

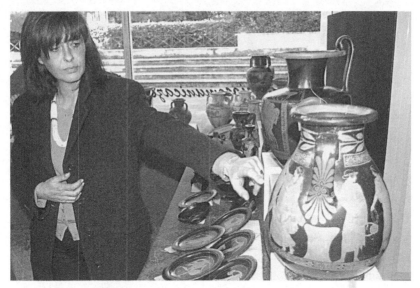

Shown alongside the restored plates is Dottoressa Daniela Rizzo, archaeologist at the Villa Giulia Museum in Rome, who helped Conforti and Ferri with technical expertise.

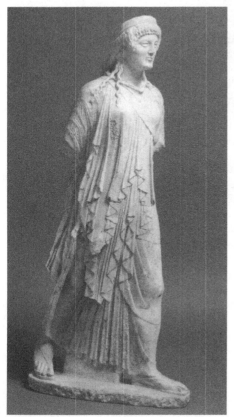

The statue of Artemis, a photograph of which was found in the glove compartment in Pasquale Camera's crashed car. This photograph was found in Robin Symes' archive. The object itself is now on display in Rome.

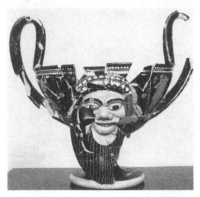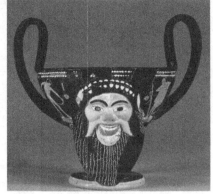

LEFT: Kantharos by Euphronios, partially restored, partially broken, in Medici's warehouse in the Geneva warehouse.

RIGHT: Kantharos by Euphronios, totally restored, on display in the J. Paul Getty Museum, Los Angeles.

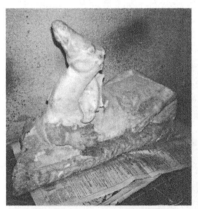

LEFT: Murky Polaroid of the Griffins, sitting on an Italian newspaper with encrusted soil, found in Medici's warehouse in Geneva.

BELOW: Medici shown alongside the restored Griffins in the J. Paul Getty Museum, Los Angeles.

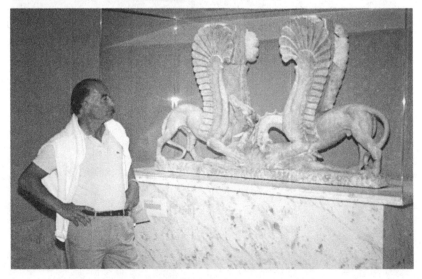

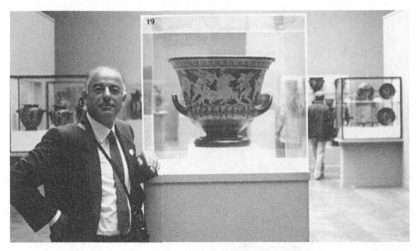

Giacomo Medici, photographed alongside the Euphronios krater in the Metropolitan Museum of Art in New York. This photograph was found during the police raid on his warehouse in Geneva Freeport. He was photographed several times with objects he had handled, after they went on display in museums around the world.

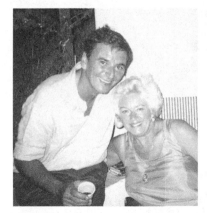

LEFT: Marion True, with Christo Michaelides, in Greece, 1998

BELOW: Robert Hecht photographed alongside the Euphronios krater in the Metropolitan Museum. This, too, was found in Medici's warehouse in Geneva.

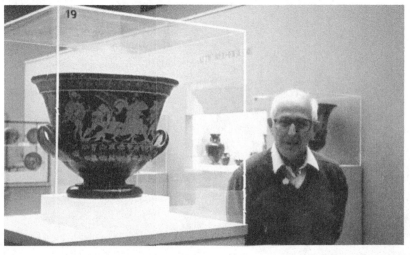

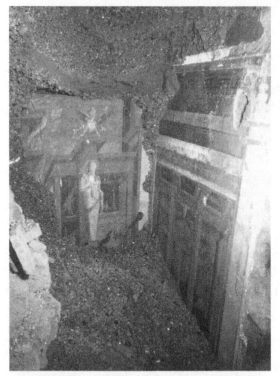

Two of the fresco walls Medici dealt in. These are shown *in situ*, as they were found, photographed by the tomb raider, and show small balls of *lapillæ*, volcanic ash, filling the room to a depth of several feet and even adhering to the ceiling.

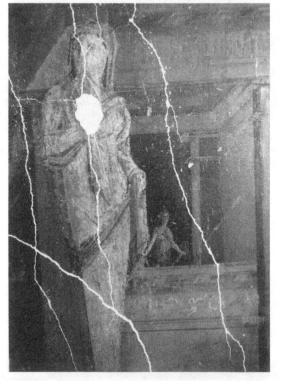

The female figure from fresco wall 1, shown partially reassembled after the looting. The joins between the pieces have been covered with plaster prior to re-painting.

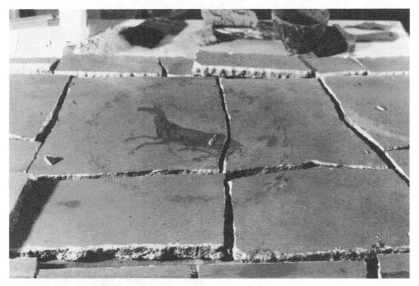

Another fresco wall, showing the pieces cut into lap-top size fragments, reassembled and laid out on the restorer's trestle table in Zurich, like a large jigsaw, prior to total restoration. The photo was found in Geneva.

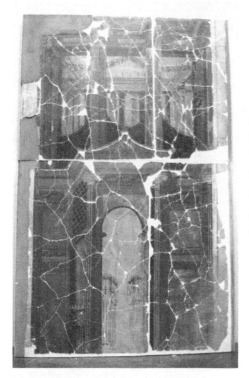

Another wall, reassembled and framed, almost ready for market. The upper panel is fresco wall 2. Beneath it is fresco wall 3. Was this entirely covered with volcanic *lapillæ* in illustration on page 6, or is it a separate wall entirely?

Christo Michaelides (left) and Robin Symes at a black-tie dinner in Monte Carlo, July 1999. The following evening, in Italy, Christo fell down some stairs, hit his head on a radiator, and died in hospital. His death triggered the fall of Robin Symes.

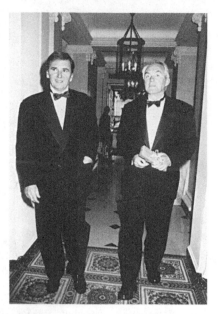

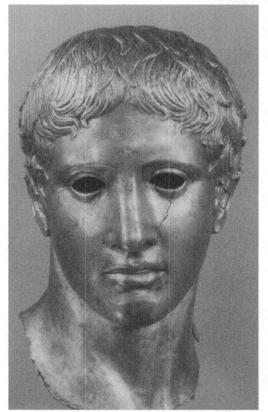

Bronze boy, showing the exceptional quality of the antiquities in the Symes' archive. Various Polaroid photographs showed this object both before and after restoration. Its present whereabouts are unknown.

the Getty. In the catalog, Koch said that the Stockholm relief had been on the "New York art market" in 1986 but didn't specify which gallery. However, also published in the catalog was a very similar one, which was in the Getty itself. Koch's text made it clear that this relief, the Getty's object, was acquired from the Summa Gallery, another of McNall's firms. Being aware of the close links between McNall and Robert Hecht, and of Hecht's reputation, Lunden wondered whether McNall-Hecht had anything to do with the Stockholm relief.

He wrote to Koch, asking which New York dealer possessed the Stockholm piece in 1986. Koch replied that he didn't know, and that the information about the object being on the New York market in that year had actually been added to the catalog manuscript by Karol Wight of the Getty, who edited the manuscript. According to Koch, the Getty had been offered the piece but had declined.

Given this information, Lunden e-mailed Karol Wight, introduced himself, and asked if she could help him with the identity of the dealer in New York who possessed the Stockholm relief in 1986.

Then something very odd happened. He got an e-mail in return later that day, but it wasn't from Karol Wight and it wasn't meant for him.

It was from Marion True, and it read:

Karol,
On second thought, I would say that we do not have this information. I am concerned about his interest in the trade and getting Bob Hecht drawn into something that could be unpleasant for us as well. Just say "New York Market." M.

A few hours later, Lunden heard from Karol Wight, who said that "they" (the Getty's Antiquities Department) were looking into his request. Five days after that, Karol Wight wrote again, to say that she had to consult Marion True, who was out of town. Then, on March 9, she wrote a third time to say that Marion True did not want to release the information, "to protect the confidentiality of the dealer and our relationship with them."

Lunden pressed her as to why the information was being withheld— was it the museum's general policy or was there something "special" about this case. She replied, "I think I'd have to put this in a 'special' category." Lunden pressed her again: "One wonders if these 'non-public' [dealers] are hiding something? Are these people not reputable dealers?"

Wight replied: "Well, I think you've hit the nail on the head (to use an old expression) regarding the nature of dealers. Some are very public and appreciate recognition, others are not, usually because they've got something to hide or an unsavory past. This dealer had a spot of trouble in the past and prefers to keep a low profile with his arrangements."

What happened here? Following Lunden's original e-mail, Wight must have contacted Marion True, who replied to her via e-mail, but somehow he received a communication never meant for his eyes.

In January 2002, Frederick H. Schultz Jr. appeared before the South District Court of New York, charged with conspiracy, and receiving and dealing in stolen antiquities. His appearance was a sensation for three reasons. In the first place, he was not just any antiquities dealer—until 2000, when he had been indicted, he was president of the National Association of Dealers in Ancient, Oriental and Primitive Art, arguably the most powerful individual in the antiquities world, a man who had advised the U.S. government on its policy toward the heritage of other nations. The NADAOPA has been active for more than twenty-five years in representing the interests of dealers, particularly in opposing U.S. ratification and implementation of the 1970 UNESCO convention.

The second reason for the sensational nature of the trial was Mr. Schultz's partner in crime, a man who had smuggled countless looted objects out of Egypt. Jonathan Tokely-Parry was an English restorer with a made-up name (he was christened Jonathan Foreman), who referred to himself in correspondence with Schultz as "006½" and called the other man "004½." Tokely-Parry's smuggling technique was to cover stone or terra-cotta antiquities in liquid plastic and paint them garish colors so that they looked like modern tourist trinkets. The Englishman's own trial in London in 1997 had itself been a sensational affair, with witnesses being threatened and with the defendant himself taking hemlock at one stage and having to be hospitalized, so that proceedings were delayed. Eventually, however, he was convicted of the dishonest handling of antiquities and given a six-year jail term.

But the most important aspect of the Schultz trial was the verdict. Having been indicted in July 2001, he filed a motion to dismiss the government's prosecution, essentially on the grounds that it did not accord with U.S. law and that the Egyptian law that had been contravened was not really an ownership law. According to an amicus curiae brief submitted to the U.S. court by Christie's, the National Association of Dealers in Ancient, Oriental and Primitive Art, and the Art Dealers Association of America, "This indictment has sent shock waves through the art world. . . . The inevitable effect of subjecting U.S. citizens to the risk of imprisonment for violating foreign patrimony laws is that dealers, collectors and museums will be forced to abandon the trade and collection of any objects that any foreign government may unilaterally claim as its 'cultural patrimony.'"

In early January 2002, however, the U.S. court issued a landmark decision, ruling that foreign governments *do* own even undiscovered antiquities, provided they have laws such as Egypt has. That ruling meant that, in this case, unprovenanced antiquities that left Egypt since 1983 are, in the eyes of U.S. law, stolen. And importing stolen goods into the United States contravenes Section 2315 of the U.S. Penal Code. Since the court's ruling, at least one major country now accepts that objects looted and smuggled from countries with strict heritage laws are, in effect, stolen property. The organization that Schultz led succeeded for years in holding up U.S. endorsement of the 1970 UNESCO protocol that outlawed dealing in unprovenanced antiquities. Where the United States leads, other countries are sure to follow.

Moreover, at the end of the case, the judge gave the jury some instructions that are of particular interest. Schultz had claimed in his defense that the government had failed to prove that he knew or believed that he was engaging in theft. The judge took care to instruct the jury that

a defendant may not purposely remain ignorant of either the facts or the law in order to escape the consequence of the law. Therefore, if you [the jury] find that the defendant, not by mere negligence or imprudence but as a matter of choice, consciously avoided learning what Egyptian law provided as to the ownership of Egyptian antiquities, you may [infer], if you wish, that he did so because he implicitly knew that there was a high probability that the law of Egypt invested ownership of these antiquities in the Egyptian government. You may treat the deliberate avoidance of positive knowledge as the equivalent of such knowledge, unless you find that the defendant actually believed that the antiquities were not the property of the Egyptian government.

In other words a sophisticated antiquities dealer cannot profess ignorance of the laws of the countries whence the objects he deals in originate.

Schultz was found guilty and in June 2002 was fined $50,000 and sentenced to thirty-three months in prison. The judge made one other comment worth recording. He said that sophisticated defendants such as Schultz were not deterred by fines and so a prison sentence formed the main part of the penalty. That verdict and penalty were upheld on appeal. Schultz left prison in December 2005.

So far as we know, Schultz was only on the edge of the Medici-Hecht cordata. It will be remembered from Chapter 15, on the matter of the orphans, that he provided one fragment of the krater by the Berlin Painter that was acquired by the Getty. The others were provided by Robin Symes, Frida Tchacos, and Dietrich von Bothmer.

In July 2002, Raffaele Monticelli, who, according to Pasquale Camera's organigram was a member of Becchina's cordata, was found guilty of conspiracy at the Foggia tribunal and sentenced to four years. In some ways, the dating of the verdict was appropriate. It came a few days before Roberto Conforti, now a general, retired, on his sixty-fifth birthday. His strategy of putting pressure on the lesser lights first was beginning to have an effect.

The Monticelli trial was notable for the many phone taps that were presented as evidence. Tomb robbers are usually extremely cagey on the phone, but the Carabinieri are patient and, just occasionally, the tomboroli let their guard slip. The following transcripts are not just vivid; they help remove any doubt about the scale of the looting and the quality of the discoveries. Among the taps presented in court was this exchange between

Orazio Di Simone* and his capo zona for the Naples region, Francesco Liberatore. At first, like a lot of transcripts of phone taps, it didn't make sense, but then it leaped into life. Apparently, the tombaroli in Campania were having problems and Liberatore was sent in to help sort it out.

> LIBERATORE: No, I don't think so. But in my opinion they need money, they're without money. Otherwise, sorry, but at this point what could they do? That thing's beautiful, I saw it again, it's beautiful but . . .
>
> DI SIMONE: We'll see . . .
>
> LIBERATORE: And then . . . anyway, be that as it may, anyway you must show it to them . . .
>
> DI SIMONE: All right.
>
> LIBERATORE: Right?
>
> DI SIMONE: Certainly.
>
> LIBERATORE: They've got an amazing job on their hands! Just amazing!
>
> DI SIMONE: But the stuff from the walls, not even as a gift, see?
>
> LIBERATORE: No, no, and what . . . OK, the stuff from the walls, if it's no good it's no good . . . It's that they can't . . . now, while they've got this job . . . There's about eighty meters [say, ninety yards] of tunnel that you can walk inside, standing up, with a wheelbarrow . . .
>
> DI SIMONE: *Merda!* Really?
>
> LIBERATORE: With lamps . . . But things . . . they're going to get something from another property, understand?
>
> DI SIMONE: Yes, yes, yes . . .
>
> LIBERATORE: They start off from the property . . . from the property on this side . . .
>
> DI SIMONE: I see, and they walk underground . . .
>
> LIBERATORE: . . . and they've got another, more or less twelve to thirteen meters [say, fifteen yards] left to go . . .
>
> DI SIMONE: OK, let's hope time will prove us right . . .

The other exchange is between Monticelli himself and Benedetto D'Aniello, of Campania.

*See p. 106.

D'Aniello: Well then, listen . . . I've got a small Etruscan gold cup, sixth to seventh century—that's why I called you, understand?

Monticelli: Eh . . .

D'Aniello: . . . of those which come out [of the ground, common tombarolo language] together with *buccheri*, that period, I don't know . . .

Monticelli: And how are those decorated?

D'Aniello: It has its little edge . . . the little edge is all incised; it's got handles—the two little handles . . . stuff of the sixth, understand?

Monticelli: It has the two . . . ?

D'Aniello: . . . the two handles, yea?

Monticelli: Hmmm . . .

D'Aniello: . . . of the sixth . . . and like those *buccheri* vases, with a little low foot which goes on the ground, an edge, and a small cup of eight to nine centimeters [3–3½ inches] in diameter; it's about five centimeters [2 inches] high. Actually it's a bit dented because it came out a bit dented, understand?

Monticelli: I understand, but it's strange, quite a number of these are coming out . . .

D'Aniello: No, these . . . there aren't . . . but because I've never seen them, never seen of . . .

Monticelli: I had two or three lately, but it's strange . . . [He suspects the cup is fake.]

D'Aniello: Huh . . . if you've had them you're lucky. I've never had them.

Monticelli: . . . very strange . . .

D'Aniello: This is the first time I've had one. Why, weren't the others good?

Monticelli: . . . the others . . . well now I'm beginning to be interested. OK, carry on . . .

D'Aniello: I don't know . . . for me, I'm certain where it comes from, understand?

Monticelli: Ah, I see . . .

D'Aniello: Eh, well, if you have . . . start to speak of these problems, then . . . I don't know what to say . . .

Monticelli: How much? How much?

D'ANIELLO: Well you don't have to ask for much; they're asking thirty million [lire = $30,000].

Finally, this:

DI SIMONE: Those things, those mural things . . . you know that at the moment there's a law which has come out in America, and it has . . . [This was a reference to the bilateral agreement between the United States and Italy, under which it was agreed that the United States would look out for Italian ancient objects being brought across its borders.]

CARRELLA [yet another tombarolo]: Yea, no . . . and OK, I know what to do . . .

DI SIMONE: Precisely, precisely.

CARRELLA: If they come out I know where . . .

DI SIMONE: Exactly, exactly . . . I know, I know . . .

CARRELLA: . . . I know where to send them.

This was the fruit of hours of phone taps. Usually, tombaroli—and even more so the capi zona—are careful what they say on the phone but, from time to time, the beauty of their discoveries gets the better of them. It was these slips, and the concurrences between them, that convicted Monticelli.

In June 2003, Vaman Ghiya was arrested in India after a six-month undercover operation by Indian police. Mr. Ghiya (see the Note on p. 386) was an Indian equivalent of Medici. He was mentioned in the documents James Hodges had leaked to the authors as someone who smuggled Indian antiquities out of the subcontinent and imported them—via companies such as Megavena and Cape Lion Logging in Switzerland—on their way to being sold at Sotheby's.

"Operation Blackhole" involved several policemen posing as beggars and rickshaw drivers stationed outside unguarded temples, on the lookout for thieves. Anand Srivastava, the superintendent in charge of the investigation, said that Ghiya had admitted to illegally smuggling more than 100 items that featured in catalogs of Sotheby's auctions that were discovered in a raid on his house. In particular, Ghiya was charged with stealing and smuggling a twelfth-century red sandstone statue from the Vilasgarth temple in September 1999, which was sold at Sotheby's in New York on September 22, 2000.

In June 2004, Ali Aboutaam was sentenced, in absentia, to fifteen years' imprisonment in Egypt for artifacts smuggling. This was part of a large initiative by the Egyptians to curb the illicit traffic, and Ali Aboutaam was one of about thirty people rounded up—including an influential politician, customs officers, police colonels, and people in charge of antiquities. The politician was given a thirty-five-year prison term, and nine foreigners—from Switzerland, France, Canada, Kenya, and Morocco—were also convicted, several in their absence.

Ali Aboutaam considered the verdicts "totally absurd." He had learned about his conviction, he told reporters, from the press. He had never received any communication from the Egyptian legal system, and although Egyptian magistrates had visited Switzerland three times in the course of their investigations, they had never contacted him. He said the only evidence against him, so far as he could see, was that one of his calling cards had been left at the home of the prominent politician who subsequently received the thirty-five-year jail sentence. Ali Aboutaam admitted to talking on the phone with the politician but added, "There are so many people who contact me to offer me ancient objects." He said he had been accused by the Egyptian press of smuggling artifacts out of Egypt, but no one had specified what, when, and where such offenses had been committed. Thus, he said, "I have nothing to do with this story."

In the very same week, Ali Aboutaam's brother, Hischam, pleaded guilty in New York to a federal charge that he had falsified a customs document about the origins of an ancient silver ceremonial drinking vessel that his gallery later sold for $950,000. He had been arrested the previous December for importing an Iranian object, described as "the most important representation of a griffin in antiquity" and for facilitating its sale to a private collector. The antiquity in question was alleged to have been part of the plundered Iranian Western Cave Treasure, said to have been looted in 1992 and dispersed around the world. The silver griffin, dated to c. 700 BC, was falsely stated as coming from Syria. According to the complaint filed in the court, the prominent collector began discussions about the object in Geneva, in 1999, discussions that included Hischam's brother, Ali. Mr. Aboutaam told the buyer at that meeting that the griffin was originally from Iran. The griffin was hand-carried into the United States by Mr. Aboutaam, and the importer of record was listed as the Bloomfield Collection. The invoice declaring Syria as the country of origin was issued by Tanis Antiquities Ltd., based in the Grenadine Islands and an affiliate of Phoenix Ancient Art. The complaint noted that Syria and Iran do not share a border. The griffin was examined by three experts to attest its authenticity, two of whom had given as their opinion that it formed part of the Western Cave Treasure.*

Coincidentally (this was a busy time for the Aboutaams), Phoenix Ancient Art was the source of a bronze statue of Apollo slaying a lizard, purchased by the Cleveland Museum of Art, which they attributed to the Greek sculptor Praxiteles. Experts were divided as to whether the statue was a Greek original or a Roman copy, but they were even more divided over the propriety of Cleveland's acquisition because of the gaps in the statue's provenance. Allegedly, the bronze was discovered lying on the ground when a retired German lawyer successfully reclaimed his family estate in the former East Germany in the 1990s. For some archaeologists this was just too convenient.

In early 2005, two Greek journalists, Andreas Apostolides and Nikolas Zirganos, broadcast the result of a four-year investigation carried out in conjunction with one of the authors of this book (Peter Watson) into the smuggling of ancient artifacts out of Greece. The investigation was wide-

*The Kalmakarra Cave, known as the Western Cave, is located about nine miles northwest of Pol-e Dokhtar in Luristan, near the Iraq border. Several hundred objects are believed to have been looted and are now dispersed in Turkey, Japan, Britain, Switzerland, and the United States. In 1993, Turkish authorities seized a number of objects believed to belong to the treasure. One of the experts who examined the griffin noted its similarities to certain objects in the Miho Museum in Japan.

ranging, but in part, it focused on familiar names—George Ortiz, Elia Borowsky, Nikolas Koutoulakis, and Christoph Leon.

Yiannis Sakellerakis, one of the best-known archaeologists in Greece, said in a TV program on antiquities that a tomb robber had admitted to him to looting two bronze Minoan statuettes, one of which had been identified as being in the Ortiz Collection. The program also revealed that as long ago as 1968, a warrant had been issued in Athens for the arrest of Elia Borowsky for his part in the smuggling of Minoan antiquities but that it had never been followed through and was allowed to lapse. The program further alleged that two Cycladic figures—one in the Met in New York, the other belonging to the Levy-Whites—had been illegally exported from Greece and had passed through Koutoulakis. The source of this information was none other than George Ortiz, who had wanted both objects but failed to get them. The program's fourth segment revealed that, in 1998, the Greek police had been alerted by the German police (in a rerun similar to the cooperation over the raid on Savoca's villa) about an almost intact classical Greek bronze figure of a youth, by the school of Polycleitus, which was on the market in Munich. The Greek police hurried to Germany, where they found that the statue was in the possession of Christoph Leon (who had handled Medici's vases, sold to Berlin) and valued at $6–$7 million. Leon was asking $1 million for his role in the deal, and when the police arrived, the statue was in a box labeled "U.S.A." They subsequently learned that Marion True, of the Getty, had been to see the statue. However, although the police brought charges against a man called Kotsaridis, who had transferred the object out of Greece (and was sentenced to fifteen years), no proceedings were brought against either Leon or True. Marion True said she had wanted to see the statue out of personal interest and had no intention of buying it.

In 2000, the collection of Attic vases built up by Borowsky was sold at Christie's in New York. This was scarcely surprising to the Greeks since the catalog text for the collection was compiled by Max Bernheimer, head of antiquities at Christie's in New York. None of these vases had any provenance, and they were of exceptional quality. Had any of them been excavated legally, they would without question have been properly published.

Finally, in 2001, the Elia Borowksy Collection went on display at the Karlsruhe Museum (its normal home was the Bible Lands Museum in

Jerusalem, where Borowsky had moved to after he left Canada). This collection, entitled Glories of Ancient Greece, consisted of a large number of superb Cretan objects, of equal quality to the Attic vases. Sakellerakis maintained that on stylistic grounds, most of the Cretan objects could only have come from a tomb in a cemetery at Poros, probably the port of Knossos, the famous site excavated by Arthur Evans. Moreover, they came from a part of the complex only discovered long after 1970.

It is depressing and distressing to see Christie's being drawn into this business alongside Sotheby's. But theirs is the only important new name. Despite the proceedings against Medici, the other members of the cordata are as active as ever.

The Fall of Robin Symes

IN SOME WAYS, the oddest set of events—the parallel plot that interested Ferri the most—began in the summer of 1999, while he was
waiting for the Swiss to make up their minds about whether or not
they were going to prosecute Medici. Of course Ferri was interested
in prosecuting Medici, Hecht, and Marion True, but the other individual
he had most in his sights was the British dealer Robin Symes. Ferri was
convinced that Symes did a large amount of business with Medici and had
a major role in the triangulations that facilitated smuggling illicit material to the Getty, the Shelby-Whites, Tempelsman, Berlin, and elsewhere.
And a major break in the case was imminent: Symes was about to suffer a
series of setbacks and disasters that would see his business, his fortune—
his entire life—implode in the most devastating way.

On July 4, 1999, Robin Symes and Christo Michaelides were guests at
a dinner in Terni, near Arezzo in Italy, given by the American collectors
Leon Levy and Shelby White. Toward the end of the dinner, Christo went
in search of some cigarettes—and didn't come back. When another guest
went to look for him, she found he had slipped on some steps and had hit
his head on a portable radiator. He died in hospital in Orvieto the next day.

It is difficult to say who was more distraught, Christo's close-knit blood
relatives, or Symes, his constant companion of more than thirty years.
Even today, members of Christo's family have difficulty putting into
words what they feel was the exact relationship between their favorite son
and Symes. The dealer, for his part, says that "Christo loved me, for 32
years" but insists that despite living together since 1970, and widely accepted from Gstaad to Los Angeles as a social couple, referred to as "the
Symeses," theirs was *not* a homosexual liaison but a long-term Platonic
friendship. At sixty-four, Symes is a stolid figure, with pale skin and silver

hair swept back off his forehead, with eyes that are magnified behind wire spectacles. Thirty years ago he suffered a double brain hemorrhage and his movements are deliberate: He doesn't rush things. Christo was six years his junior.

Symes acquired a lifestyle to match his success in the antiquities business. With Christo he had homes in London, New York, Athens, and Schinnoussa, a small island in the Cyclades, across the water from Naxos. The house in London, on Seymour Walk, on the fringes of Chelsea, boasted an underground swimming pool, decorated with classical statues, and an art deco room, filled with Eileen Gray furniture, valued, according to one estimate, at $20 million. Symes, who doesn't drive, was always chauffeured either in a silver Rolls Royce or a maroon Bentley. Their house on Schinnoussa had a studio for Robin to paint in, and a pastry kitchen for Christo, who liked to cook.

According to an interview Symes gave, the two men met in the 1960s when Christo visited Symes's shop, then on the King's Road, London, and offered him some antiquities. This contradicts what Symes said to Ferri, whom he told during interrogation that he had met Christo in a warehouse in Switzerland. Christo had a girlfriend and Symes was married, with two sons. After he was divorced, however, Symes lived in Christo's flat for a while and after that they became inseparable. Symes, with his full, baritone voice, clipped way of speaking, and tailored fawn suits, cut a more formal figure than the charismatic and handsome Christo, who was thinner, taller, and altogether more casual and relaxed. A man used to wealth (he comes from a shipowning family), who spoke six languages, Christo would think nothing of spending $100,000 on a Ferrari speedboat for his nephew, or buying him a Porsche for Christmas.

Following Symes's hemorrhage, he and Christo ran the antiquities business together. The older man found the objects, and the buyers, while the younger one organized the financial side (again, he told Ferri the exact opposite). It was a successful arrangement, and by the 1980s, they were following the calendar of the very rich: Gstaad in February; Bahamas in March; La Prairie, a spa-cum-clinic in Montreux in Switzerland, where they had their annual check-up, in the spring; London in June; Greece for the summer; New York for the sales in November. It was a near-perfect lifestyle.

Christo's family, the Papadimitrious, originated in Alexandria, Egypt, and moved to mainland Greece in 1962. They say that following Christo's death they naturally assumed that since he and Symes were equal business partners, the assets would be divided at some point on a 50–50 basis. They are a close family, so much so that they all live side by side in the same street in the fashionable Psychikos suburb of Athens. In particular, Christo was close to his sister Despina ("Deppy"), who married Nicolas Papadimitriou in 1965. Christo and "Deppy," they say, spoke to each other twice a day throughout their lives. With their experience and knowledge of shipping, they were adept at setting up offshore companies, registered in Panama, which help both ships and antiquities firms avoid paying tax. At times, they say, Despina personally guaranteed Christo and Robin's business to the tune of $17 million (shipping people talk only in dollars). In other words, the family—via Despina and Christo—was intimately involved in funding the antiquities business.

Once that summer of 1999 was over, which they all—Symes included—spent on Schinnoussa, grieving, Dimitri Papadimitriou (Christo's nephew, who was now leading the family business) told Symes that even though the business should be divided equally, Symes could keep the family's share and sell it off, over three to five years, after which time they would withdraw. Symes could live in the Seymour Walk property for the rest of his life and would always be welcome on Schinnoussa.

Privately, Symes didn't see it like that. Back in London, on his own now, he nursed the feeling that *he* had founded the business, that *he* had the "eye"—the ability to distinguish a fine object from a dud one—and that it was *he* who had found the customers who had produced the income that had caused the business to thrive. (This too was contradicted by what Symes told Ferri, that it was in fact Christo who had the "eye.")

Then there were the things that go on in all businesses but are rarely talked about. The onshore business was called Robin Symes Limited, and Symes himself was the only shareholder. Officially, Christo was an employee but, says Symes, "This was a ruse, to divert the attention of the tax people." In reality, Symes felt, "Christo and I were partners, not in the business sense, but in the husband and wife sense. While we were both alive, we shared equally in the assets and profits and debts of the company, but after death they all passed to the survivor, to me." This flatly contradicted the Papadimitrious' view.

The first inkling that Dimitri Papadimitriou had that things were not going according to plan—to his plan, anyway—did not come until May 2000, when he had a meeting at the Dorchester Hotel in London with Edmond Tavernier, Symes's Swiss lawyer, to discuss the partnership. At the lunch, Tavernier said that *if* there were a partnership between Symes and Christo, it was 70–30 in his client's favor. In a melodramatic gesture, he leaned across the table and, under Papadimitriou's nose, broke off a *grissino*, an Italian bread stick, in those proportions.

Not long after, in July 2000, Symes traveled to Athens for a commemoration service, twelve months after Christo's death. After it was over, Papadimitriou took Symes to one side and, ignoring Tavernier's outburst, reminded him that no inventory of the business had yet been prepared on which a 50–50 split could be based. At the same time, Papadimitriou handed Symes a letter from Christo's mother, Irini, pleading for her son's personal belongings to be returned. She was eighty-four, she said, and wanted to redistribute his things around the family before she died. These effects, though personal, were substantial. They included several Cartier watches made before World War II and valued at between $50,000 and $80,000 each, a Rolex made by hand in the 1950s, and a pair of Cartier cufflinks, also hand-made, inlaid with sapphires and baguette diamonds.

Although he didn't show it at the time, Symes was doubly affronted by these approaches. He had arrived to pay his respects to his former companion but instead he had, as he saw it, been ambushed and made to feel an outsider. The business was his, as were Christo's personal belongings. And in any case, Irini's demands were fanciful. "Christo didn't possess a shirt that *took* cufflinks," he says with a shudder, as if the family should have known this.

But this exchange had a catalytic—and catastrophic—impact on subsequent events. In November 2000, Symes finally sent a briefcase containing Christo's personal effects from London to the Papadimitriou "compound" in Athens. When Deppy scanned the contents, she could scarcely believe her eyes. Far from containing Cartier and Rolex watches and hand-made cufflinks set with sapphires and diamonds, as she had expected, the briefcase contained: a plastic cigarette lighter, a half-burned candle, Christo's birth cross, a plastic Swatch, a box of playing cards, refills for his pens, a cushion with a teddy bear on it, a cheap camera, some photographs.

Now, was Symes being provocative at this point? Was he deliberately trying to tease or irritate the Papadimitrious because of the pressure he felt they were putting him under? Was he trying to rub in the fact that *he*, and not they, was Christo's rightful heir? Or did he genuinely believe that these were the personal effects they were expecting? Deppy was too upset to let her mother know that the briefcase had even arrived. But the "insulting" contents hardened Dimitri Papadimitriou's heart. He had already discussed the situation with a London lawyer, Ludovic de Walden, of Lane and Partners, whose offices are near the British Museum on Bloomsbury Square. De Walden is well known in the London art world. Among his clients is the Getty Museum in Britain.

Before Papadimitriou and de Walden could decide what action to take, the family received two more shocks. In early December 2000, Symes mounted an exhibition in New York in which 152 objects—mainly antiquities—were offered for sale with a collective value of $42 million. Second, when Papadimitriou visited Seymour Walk toward the end of January 2001 to pick up some chairs that were his, he found that the entire collection of Eileen Gray art deco furniture had disappeared. Thanks to the work of a private detective nimbly hired by de Walden, they soon found out that the Gray furniture had been sold the previous September, at the Paris Biennale, for—they were told—$20 million. Far from preparing an inventory, as the family was expecting, it now seemed that Symes was selling off many of the company's assets, for cash.

Symes saw it differently. As the survivor who had inherited the business, he felt he was entirely within his rights to mount whatever exhibitions he deemed necessary; and the New York show was held in Christo's honor, with a tribute printed in the catalog, written by Symes. "It was a public exhibition," he says. "There was no question of me trying to sell things in a sneaky way—how could there be?" As far as the Eileen Gray collection was concerned, here is yet another flat contradiction. The family says they bought the furniture in the first place, but Symes says he did, and he produced a 1987 article in the *New York Times* that appears to support his claim. "In any case," he says, "it didn't fetch $20 million, but $4 million, and I told Dimitri as much on the day I made the sale." Dimitri Papadimitriou has no recollection of this conversation.

The deteriorating relations between the two sides collapsed completely in February 2001 when Symes did something that no one who was "family," in the Greek sense, would dream of doing.

Late on the morning of February 23, a Friday, the doorbell rang at Deppy's house on Diamantidou Avenue. When she went to the door, she was astonished to be served with court papers from the Athens Multi Member First Instance Court. While the family had dithered about taking Symes to court, he had got in first. *He* was suing *them*.

From their point of view, Symes's claims in his lawsuit were distressing and, yes, insulting. Far from accepting that Christo and he were partners, Symes now claimed that:

- Christo had only ever been an employee and had never participated in the business with any share, "hidden or shown";

- Neither Christo nor "any member of his family" had contributed financially to Symes's business;

- Symes had no obligation to return any property to Despina or any other Papadimitriou.

But Symes didn't stop there. Arguing that in their approaches and letters to him, Irini and Despina were interfering in his legitimate business interests, he called for them to be fined or imprisoned (for up to six months), or both, if they continued to interfere. He had inherited Christo's share of the business and that was that.

This was to seriously misread Dimitri Papadimitriou. He called de Walden in London. From now on, he said, it was war.

De Walden was ready. Just four days after Deppy received her court papers in Athens, he obtained an ex parte injunction in London to raid all Symes's premises and freeze his assets. The next day, Wednesday, February 28, 2001, at 11:30 in the morning, while Symes was in Geneva, solicitors acting under de Walden's leadership simultaneously broke into five of Symes's premises, changed the locks, and seized all documentation. As part of the same injunction, Symes was now not allowed to trade without permission of the court and his bank accounts were also frozen.

As an aggressive and successful shipowner, Dimitri Papadimitriou relishes a good scrap, and in being rich, he was able to attack his opponent in ways less well-heeled litigants could only dream of. After their successful maneuver in freezing Symes's assets and bank accounts, the next move was to have Symes followed. This was wildly expensive (the legal costs in this case amounted in the end to around $16 million). But, for Papadimitriou, the money was well spent. Using an organization run from Brighton by an ex-Scotland Yard detective, Symes was followed in no fewer than six countries—Switzerland, Britain, Germany, Italy, the United States, and Japan. The effort engaged up to fifty people and at times involved highly unorthodox methods. When Symes attended a conference in Geneva, the men following him posed as police allegedly searching for illegal immigrants; on another occasion, they pretended to be firemen; in a third case, they searched his hotel room disguised as cleaning women.

But, says de Walden, it paid off. "We discovered that Symes stored his antiquities not at five sites but at *thirty-three*. The number of objects comprising the stock of the business has snowballed to 17,000, with a value, according to stock lists, of £125 million."

Symes denies any suggestion that he has been hiding his assets. "They are my assets, no one else's. The question of 'hiding' doesn't arise."

But Papadimitriou's campaign didn't stop at surveillance. Private detectives staking out Symes's premises at Ormond Yard observed his staff disposing of several garbage bags containing shredded documents. The detectives helped themselves to the bags—twenty-three in all—which were locked away at Lane and Partners.

Symes dismisses this as scaremongering: "It was routine shredding." But Dimitri Papadimitriou and de Walden went so far as to obtain an estimate from a firm in Birmingham, England, which said it would cost £350,000 ($500,000) to reconstruct that amount of shredded paperwork. Even Papadimitriou balked at this price, but in sifting through the paper strips, de Walden noticed some that had come from a bright yellow American legal pad. Aided by this color code, he was able to reconstruct a single sheet of paper. And he struck it rich. The document was an aide-mémoire handwritten by Symes, accepting that Christo's family had given much financial help to the business in "funding many purchases and in guarantees for bank loans." In the most revealing sentence, the aide-mémoire referred to Despina Papadimitriou as a silent partner.

Although the surveillance reports make gripping reading, Symes was also photographed, dining in restaurants across Switzerland. His companions were often identified from their vehicle registration numbers, or they were followed home and identified from their addresses. This surveillance showed that Symes was regularly meeting people involved in the antiquities trade, and it convinced Papadimitriou and de Walden that Symes had assets they still didn't know about and that he was continuing to trade. On one occasion Symes was followed all the way to Japan, where he visited the Miho Museum, well known to archaeologists for its acquisitions of controversial (unprovenanced) antiquities (see Chapter 20). Symes was also followed when he was driven from Geneva to Venice, where he left a box with an acquaintance.

Symes is appalled by what he sees as a gross infringement of his privacy and insists he was doing nothing wrong. He was outside the jurisdiction of the British courts and pursuing his legitimate business interests.

As each new address of Symes was discovered, however, de Walden applied to the court to force him to reveal the contents. There were nearly thirty "interlocutory" hearings, and eventually Dimitri Papadimitriou's campaign began to pay off. Partway through 2002, the judge in the case, Justice Peter Smith, so lost patience with Symes, and what he saw as his delaying tactics in revealing all his warehouses, that he changed the burden of proof in the case. Instead of the Greeks having to prove that there *was* a partnership, Symes would now have to prove there was not. Partly as a result of this, in January the following year Symes dramatically changed tack. In Greece, on the eve of the trial in his own lawsuit, he dropped his action. In London, he performed what the judge later described as a "remarkable somersault" in his defense. He obtained permission to abandon his suggestion that Christo was a mere employee. Now he reverted to the view he had really held all along, that he and Christo were partners in the husband-and-wife sense and that, at Christo's death, the entire assets of their partnership, including the house in Seymour Walk, the house on Schinnoussa, their cars and boats, passed to Symes by survivorship.

This incensed the Papadimitrious even further. Whatever fond feelings they retained for Symes (and Deppy retained some, she said), they had no intention of letting him get his hands on their yachts, still less Schinnoussa.

However, though he had allowed the "remarkable somersault" in Symes's defense, the judge was in no mood to allow him much more leeway. The trial was set for June 2003.

It never happened. At the time he had allowed Symes to amend his defense, the judge had set a deadline of March 31, 2003, for him to disclose all the documents on which he based his new arguments. Symes failed to comply. The reason, he said, was that he ran out of lawyers. He had chopped and changed solicitors quite a bit, and due to the requirement to clear all his business transactions with the court, he wasn't always as flush with funds as he might otherwise have been. The judge was not convinced by this, again lost patience with Symes, and due to this latest noncompliance, threw out his amended defense.

This meant that the Papadimitrious had won. So far as the court was concerned, there *was* a partnership and the family was entitled to half the assets of Symes's business, as they had always maintained.

In the immediate aftermath, things got quickly worse for Symes. Following the original raids and the freezing of his assets, he had applied to the court to be able to carry on his business, so that he could live and pay his legal costs. The judge allowed this, provided Symes agreed to sell only with the permission of the court, that he agreed not to remove any "relevant chattel" from his premises without the court's permission, and that he agreed to sell objects only for "full consideration."

It had come to de Walden's notice, however, that one particular antiquity, a Granodiorite Egyptian statue of Apollo, which Symes said he sold in April 2002 to an American company, Philos, with offices in Cheyenne, Wyoming, had in fact not been sold to that company at all, which had a fictitious address. Further inquiries revealed that Symes had also lied about the price. Instead of being sold to Philos, for $1.6 million, the statue had gone to a certain Sheikh Saoud Al-Thani, in the Gulf Emirates, for $4.5 million.

For the third time in the case, the judge hit the roof. If this were true, he said, it appeared to him that Symes had committed a contempt of court and he ordered a trial in which the full circumstances of the sale of the statue would be explored. But this was a very different trial from the original case. So far, the whole business had been a matter of commercial litigation, a civil matter. Now, Symes had crossed the line and had possibly committed fraud, a criminal offense. If convicted, he could face jail.

Before the matter came to court, Symes suffered a further indignity. Eversheds, one of the seven British lawyers he had used, but not paid, finally lost patience with him and, on March 27, 2003, made him bankrupt. This meant that in addition to losing his house and full control of his business, he could now no longer be a director of any company, even his own. Then, two months later, in May 2003, Leon Levy, the American collector who had been supporting him financially, died. Symes's world was closing down around him.

Symes's defense in the contempt case was that the Granodiorite statue had indeed been sold to the sheikh for $4.5 million but that he only had one-third interest in it, which he had forgotten to mention, and that the other two-thirds were held by dealers in Switzerland, Jean Domercq and Frida Tchacos-Nussberger. Although Mr. Domercq and Mrs. Tchacos-Nussberger were joint defendants in this action, neither appeared in court to defend themselves, though a Swiss lawyer representing both did appear. The court found against the defendants and concluded that Symes owned the statue in its entirety. He was adjudged to have misled the court, to have broken the conditions of the "interlocutory regime," which forbade him to trade without the knowledge or the permission of the court, and, in July 2004, he was given a one-year suspended jail sentence. What had begun as civil litigation had resulted in something far worse.

The original action continued. The Greek relatives of Christo were still not convinced that Symes had disclosed all the assets of the business that the two partners had owned. In the course of further researches, they found that Symes appeared to have lied to the court about two other sets of objects. One was the set of art deco furniture by the designer Eileen Gray, and the second was a statue of Akhenaten. The Eileen Gray furniture, Symes said, had been sold to a Parisian dealer for $4 million. Lane and Partners eventually traced this sale and found that Symes had actually sold it for $14 million, with most of the money being lodged in a bank in Gibraltar. The statue of Akhenaten, which Symes said he had sold for $3.6 million, had in fact been sold for nearer $8 million, again to Sheikh

258 : THE MEDICI CONSPIRACY

Al-Thani, with the money this time being lodged in a bank in Liechtenstein. These sums were located, and recovered.

While Lane and Partners had been pursuing these investigations, Symes had tried to forestall further court proceedings by claiming, extraordinarily, in the autumn of 2004, that he was mentally incapable of instructing solicitors, and therefore of standing trial. This action failed and Symes was ordered to appear in court again in January 2005.

Until Christmas he had been living at an inn, in a small village near Basingstoke, about fifty miles west of London. Just before Christmas, however, he moved into the Savoy Hotel in London. Though bankrupt, Symes has a number of friends who still support him financially. When he appeared in court, however, he was unrepresented. He produced a witness statement in which he now admitted that he had lied in court, in relation to both the Eileen Gray furniture and the statue of Akhenaten. The judge took a very severe view of these (now admitted) lies to the court, which involved sums totaling $14 million. In his judgment, Justice Peter Smith concluded that Mr. Symes had committed "a serious and cynical contempt of court," designed "to conceal that he had deliberately taken the proceeds [and] used them for his own purposes." He said Symes "has told numerous lies on oath" and repeated "a false story."

The judge further said that he was not impressed by Symes's attempts to suggest that he was confused and muddled by what was going on in court. "The admitted contempts show calculated, cynical and well understood acts of deception." And he concluded: "Mr. Symes must appreciate that he will not be able, if it is his belief, simply to do his time, get his passport back and leave the jurisdiction. There remains a large number of outstanding questions to be answered. Until those questions are answered and dealt with in a meaningful way the possibility of him obtaining his passport back to enable him to leave the jurisdiction is remote. . . . I perceive [that it is] a long and necessary road that Mr. Symes still has to go down before this litigation will come to an end." On January 21, 2005, at the High Court in the Strand in London, Symes was sent to prison on two counts for contempt of court—fifteen months and nine months, to run consecutively, two years in all. He was transferred that day to Pentonville Prison, in North London.

▼

In the early part of the litigation, the Papadimitriou family had had their lawyers freeze Symes's assets and seize all his documentation. The lawyers made photocopies of everything, and because they were then hoping to prove that Symes and Christo Michaelides were business partners, not just "husband and wife," the authors of this book were given a unique opportunity to inspect Symes's records, so we might see for ourselves that the two men really did manage the business together. In the course of this inspection, we couldn't help but take note of a number of other matters that, because of our cooperation with the Italian authorities, meant more to us, perhaps, than to the Papadimitrious or their lawyers. The section that follows is based on this access.[1]

In his thirty-three warehouses (and not five, as he originally admitted), Symes had 17,000 objects worth an estimated £125 million ($210 million). The average auction sale of antiquities usually numbers somewhere between 400 and 600 lots. There are eight auctions a year, at Christie's, Sotheby's, and Bonhams, in London and New York, making between 3,200 and 4,800 lots sold annually. Between them, *in stock*, Medici and Symes had some 21,000 objects, or roughly four to five years' worth of auction supply, if we take these figures at face value. Additionally, Symes's 17,000 objects were given a collective worth of £125 million, meaning that, on average, "his" antiquities were valued at £7,353. It is notoriously difficult to value antiquities (as the "markups" discussed throughout this book show) and, indeed, when the Papadimitriou lawyers had an independent expert look at some of the Symes objects, she valued them very differently (usually lower). But even if Symes's estimates on "his" objects were twice what they should have been, that would still have valued them, on average, at £3,677 (say $5,000). This compares with an average price of £600 ($1,000) for antiquities sold at auction.

Symes had said on several occasions, in his interview with Ferri, that Xoilan Trader, his company that shared an "administrative address" with Editions Services at 7 Avenue Krieg in Geneva, was not a trading company, despite its name, but a holding company for his own collection. This was belied by the marked Sotheby's catalogs Hodges had leaked to us in the very beginning, which showed Xoilan to be selling scores of objects in the sales for which we had inside records. This picture was amplified in the documents and inventory we inspected in London.[2] One part of the inventory consisted of 105 pages of lists of objects, with approximately thirty-four items per page, a total of 3,570 artifacts. Xoilan Trader, which accounted for approximately 300 objects, made up nine pages of this list, but elsewhere there were pages and pages of objects dealt in by Xoilan through Sotheby's. There were also many dealings with Galerie Nefer (Frida Tchacos), and thirty-four numbered transactions with Giacomo Medici. Between 1979 and 1986, Robin Symes Limited, Symes's other company, conducted at least twenty-nine deals with Medici. The names Getty, Leon Levy, Kimball Museum in Texas, Naji Asfar, Koutoulakis, Savoca, Tempelsman, R. Guy, Orazio Di Simone, Sotheby's, and Christie's appeared throughout the inventory, in one context or another.

Symes's claims about Xoilan were also flatly contradicted by the copies of marked Sotheby's catalogs that James Hodges made available to us and by the documents found in Medici's warehouse. The fact is: When Symes said he didn't use Xoilan to trade under, he wasn't telling the truth. For Symes, as Justice Peter Smith discovered and observed, truth is a malleable commodity. Not one of the objects in the inventory we saw was listed with a provenance.

During the time we were going through the Symes/Michaelides archive, Peter Watson was working on the Greek television investigation referred to earlier (p. 245). The Greek journalists traveled to London and Cambridge to interview, and during their visit the conversation turned to the Symes/Michaelides partnership. Watson mentioned that he had seen several references to Michaelides' Greek family in the documentation, which did seem to suggest that the Papadimitriou family had a financial interest in the antiquities business. In particular, Watson said, there were six documents that he thought relevant.

The first was a handwritten memo by Symes, which began:

While I accept the help given by the family of the late C.M. [Christo Michaelides], both in funding many purchases and in guarantees for bankers, nonetheless I must point out that the business which ran so successfully for many years is now virtually finished; [f]or the reason that international law prohibits the export of w/art [works of art] from most host countries and it is now not possible to fragrantly [flagrantly?] disregard them. Old coll[ectors']. material does not provide suff[icient]. Funds to cont[inue]. Also there have, unfortunately, been multiple problems arising [from] four pieces which have proved to be either stolen or illegally exported. These losses over the past two years have amounted to considerable sums and have been borne by RS [Robin Symes] Ltd. In many of these instances the family should share the cost and because of their involvement be prepared for further liabilities should they occur. Many pieces were consigned to RS Ltd for sale and the costs involved should therefore the [be?] applicable to the consignors. To date they amount to $7 million and Mrs. Despina Papadimitriou was involved in all of them. Also her sleeping partnership with the firm makes her liable to the J. Paul Getty Museum for the 8 m $ paid for the half share of the limestone figure of Aphrodite should a problem arise with Italian government, who have actively been seeking its return. It is therefore a possibility and a risk I am not prepared to shoulder alone.

This was interesting on a number of grounds. It dispelled—from the horse's mouth—the convenient fiction that "old collections" provide much of the material that suddenly appears on the market. It confirmed that Symes had a hand in supplying the Getty with the Aphrodite statue. But it was interesting most of all because it detailed the intimate involvement, the "sleeping partnership," of the Papadimitriou family—Christo's sister, Despina, in particular—in financing transactions.

A separate note said that both Xoilan and SESA were owned by Christo's parents, through the fiduciary Henri Jacques. The note went on to say that Xoilan was established in the mid–1970s to receive the family's collection, and to do so confidentially.

This was as a result of unfortunate publicity surrounding one particular sale which had been made through Robin Symes Limited of an item to the British Rail Pension Fund. This had led to an investigation by Interpol. The piece in question had in fact belonged to Christo Michaelides's aunt.

These notes, it transpired, had been prepared in connection with two meetings Symes held with Britain's Inland Revenue in June 1991. During the interview, the tax inspectors asked: "How is the collection built up?" The reply was: "When RS/CM see an item, CM will tell his parents who will ask RS and/or CM to attend the auction. His parents will then instruct Henri Jacques to make arrangements. RSL will arrange for shipment."

In March 2000, Nonna Investments, another of Symes' companies, negotiated a "rolling facility" with Citibank of $14 million, later increased to $17 million—the loan guaranteed by Despina Papadimitriou. There was a letter from the Getty agreeing to buy various objects but setting off these purchases against a Diadoumenos head—part of the Fleischman Collection—and a torso of Mithras, which were being returned to Italy. In October 1992, there was paperwork in connection with a Greek statue being sold to the Getty for $18 million.

How important was all this? Neither Nikolas Zirganos nor we could be certain. The Papadimitriou family were eager just then to prove that Symes and Michaelides were business partners, not in a "marriage," and Christo's ready access to serious money—via his family—certainly seemed an important aspect of the running of their companies. That supported their argument in the London trial, but if Symes were the kind of dealer Ferri thought he was, wasn't this financial involvement by the Papadimitrious also incriminating of them?

We did not discuss it in any detail just then. Too much was going on elsewhere. Over a last lunch before Zirganos left for the airport—eaten near Symes' now-closed gallery in Mason's Yard, where we had been filming—Watson mentioned that the Symes archive, in addition to a roomful of documents, consisted of seventeen green binders showing photographs of antiquities. We didn't discuss that in any detail either. Not then.

On March 19, 2003, at a press conference, the Italian Ministry for Cultural Affairs announced that what was then the world's rarest and most important looted antiquity had been recovered by the Italian Carabinieri in London. The object, a unique life-size ivory figure, thought to be of Apollo, the Greek god of the sun, and perhaps dating from the fifth century BC, was valued at close to £30 million ($50 million) on the open market.

The ivory was of such a superb quality that Italian archaeologists who examined the head on its return believed at first that it might have been carved by Phidias, one of the greatest of classical Greek sculptors, whose carvings graced the Parthenon and the Temple of Zeus at Olympia. Pliny, Pausanias, and Lucian all sang Phidias's praises, but not a single work of his has survived. This discovery was therefore astounding to the worlds of archaeology, art history, museums, and classical scholarship.

The head was seized, partly with the help of the authors, from Robin Symes. Because relations between the Carabinieri and Scotland Yard were so poor, we served as a conduit for information between Ferri and Conforti, on the one hand, and Christo's family, and their attorneys in London, on the other, to help speed the negotiations. A fragment of a fresco, stolen from a villa near Pompeii, was also recovered at the same time. Besides the ivory head, which has its eyes, straight nose, and sensual lips intact, a series of fragments was also recovered—fingers, toes, an ear, some curls of hair. In antiquity, it was the practice for exceptionally important statues to have ivory heads, hands, and feet, with bodies of stone or wood, which were covered in gold sheets.

The ivory head and other fragments were originally discovered in 1995 by Pietro Casasanta, who showed the authors of this book the field where he says he discovered the statue, a few hundred yards from a well-known archaeological landmark, the Baths of Claudius. Casasanta told us that he believes the statue came from a large, luxurious villa that belonged to the family of the first-century Roman emperor Claudius. At the time he found the head and fragments, Casasanta also discovered three Egyptian statues of goddesses, two in green and one in black granite. He also had some pieces of mosaic, not necessarily from the same site. "This was obviously the residence of a very rich, very important family," he said. Photographs of the three statues were found by the Carabinieri at Casasanta's home when he was raided. These statues are still missing, though Casasanta believes one is in London.

Casasanta told us that the minute he set eyes on the ivory head he knew it was the most important object he—or any other tombarolo—had ever found. Only one other life-size ivory head is known to have survived in Italy, found at Montecalvo (again, near Rome) and now in the Apostolic Library in the Vatican. And only one set of life-size Chryselephantine sculptures survives in Greece. Casasanta smuggled the head and fragments, and the three statues, out of Italy himself and sold them to Nino Savoca. They agreed a fee of $10 million. Savoca, he says, showed the head to the experts or curators of two American museums, one of whom attributed it to Phidias, but neither of them was willing to risk buying such an obviously looted object. Following this, Savoca stopped paying him after $700,000, and they fell out.

Savoca died in 1998, and during a (second) raid on his premises, the Carabinieri discovered documentation that helped them close in on a number of important looted antiquities. Partly because Savoca had reneged on payment, and possibly calculating that the Carabinieri had him in their sights again, Casasanta volunteered to Conforti's men that Savoca had sold the ivory head to a London dealer, who, he told us, was "a homosexual whose partner died recently." This was clearly Robin Symes. The Carabinieri already knew this, of course, from Frida Tchacos.

Professor Antonio Giuliano, of La Sapienza University, who has examined the statue, which is now at the Museo Nazionale Romano in Rome, provisionally dated the ivory to the fifth or fourth century BC. Later studies changed this: It is now dated to the first century BC—that is, 300-plus years after Phidias. Giuliano considers the main head to be of Apollo, but he thinks that the associated fragments are from a second, somewhat smaller statue, possibly Artemis or Atona (the toe, for example, is on a smaller scale than the head).

Should we need further confirmation, there can now be no doubt of the *importance* of the objects that the Medici-Tchacos-Symes cordata dealt in. The ivory head now has an entire room to itself in a major museum in Rome. Antiquities don't come more important than that.

Robin Symes left the medical wing of Pentonville Prison, North London, after securing time off for good behavior, in September 2005. The civil action with the Papadimitriou family is still not resolved. He still has a one-year suspended sentence hanging over him. That's in Britain. In Italy, Ferri is still reviewing future cases and the fall of Robin Symes may not yet be complete.

18

THE WOODCUTTER'S ARCHIVE

WHEN OPERATION GERYON BEGAN, when Pasquale Camera's organigram was discovered, there were *some* new names in the frame, but not many. The organigram confirmed the general picture, so far as Conforti and his men understood it, but it primarily resulted in their focusing on the Italians who were masterminding the export of illicit material out of Italy—Medici, Becchina, and Savoca. The Melfi theft had led them to Savoca; then Hodges's documents leaked to us confirmed the importance of Medici; and the more Conforti and Ferri looked at Medici, the more they heard about Becchina. No one had hitherto grasped Medici's great importance, or his intimate links with Sotheby's, or the very *organized* nature of the trade and the way it was designed to protect the world's rogue museums. These were the main things to come out of the investigation.

In a sense, the organigram was a symbol of the whole exercise. As Conforti had noted, criminals invariably write things down. The same was true in the antiquities underworld. Camera had left his diagram to be found and, in Munich, Savoca's meticulous record keeping had led the Carabinieri farther forward. Medici's own records were copious, and Hecht's memoir likewise had proved to be gold dust. Thanks to Conforti's idea for a pool of magistrates, thanks to some excellent and diligent detective work among the Polaroids, thanks to Ferri's ability to use the information from Geneva to persuade other members of the cordata to cooperate, Medici's trial was at long last about to begin.

But then, one morning just before Christmas in December 2003, days after the trial had opened, the phone taps suddenly turned up trumps—and yet another archive fell into Ferri's lap. Listening in on a conversation involving one of the more familiar names, the eavesdroppers suddenly encountered someone who was entirely new, a man who was to be a revelation. They heard him talking on the phone taps, they learned that his name was Giuseppe Evangelisti, and they found that he had a nickname, *"Peppino il taglialegna"*—Peppino the woodcutter. They subsequently discovered that the nickname derived from what we might call Evangelisti's "day job": He provided wood to two whole villages. But that was not his only activity, not at all. There was also his "night job."

The phone tap had taken place just before lunchtime. That afternoon, having located Evangelisti's address from the phone number at Capo di Monte, near Lake Bolsena, north of Rome, they paid him a visit. They found him to be a tall, robust, and muscular individual in his late fifties. He was a gentle man, with receding hair and tanned skin; he looked every inch a woodcutter. He was—not unnaturally—surprised to see them, but he didn't appear nervous. On the other hand, according to one of the investigators who took part in the raid, the woodcutter's wife certainly was. The investigators told the couple they had heard Evangelisti's conversation on the telephone that day, so they knew he had looted objects and they weren't leaving until he took them to where the antiquities were located. The Carabinieri had expected to be taken to some lockup a distance away, but in fact he took them to his garage, which was under the house. And there four surprises greeted them.

In his garage they located hundreds of looted antiquities—still broken, still dirty with soil, all local, fragments in sacks and fruit boxes, *all classified by type*: Attic, Buccheri, ceramics, bronzes. In addition, they found a veritable library of archaeological books, all scientific. "This man wanted to understand the *value* of objects abroad—what foreign museums and collections were made up of," said one Carabinieri.

So far the find had been interesting but not especially sensational, the biggest surprise being that his name was new to them. That was about to change.

In the garage there was a table for restoring, with a palette, brushes, and other technical equipment. Above the table, however, was a shelf on which were a number of other books. When the Carabinieri examined these books, they got the surprise of their lives, for these books contained two precious records. In the first place, the woodcutter was a photography buff and had photographed *every* object he had ever looted—hundreds and hundreds of vases, statues, stone columns, and terra-cotta tiles. Here, in other words, was a visual record to put alongside Medici's, a visual record of what had been dug up and smuggled abroad. This record was obviously important in itself, because it means that those who traffic in illicit antiquities can no longer be sure that there is no photographic record of what they deal in, which proves that "their" objects come from Italy.

The other batch of books on the shelf in Evangelisti's garage included agendas and diaries for the years 1997 to 2002. (There were nine books of agendas in total, and seven albums of photographs.) Most exciting of all, it transpired that the woodcutter was obsessive and the agendas supplemented the photographs: *He had recorded what he had found, when, and where.* He had noted the locations he had dug at, the kind of tomb he had uncovered, even at what depth objects had been uncovered. In Daniela Rizzo's twenty-six years experience, she told us, the woodcutter was the only person—apart from Medici—to record such specific information. This was a breakthrough, not on the size of Medici's perhaps (or Symes's), but it was of the first importance all the same. Not only did Evangelisti give dates and places, but he also drew little maps of where the tombs were in which fields, with drawings showing how many paces they were from this or that tree. His descriptions of the objects were also far more scientific than other tombaroli. For example, he would write "Amphoretta with three big birds and heads of horses." It was enough for Daniela Rizzo to recognize the piece as an important Etruscan ceramic figure. "This man has a collection of figures, of Etruscan objects that the Villa Giulia dreams about—we don't have such a thing."

The woodcutter's archive named the owners of the land he dug on. The owners played an important part, because he made it clear, as Casasanta had, that the owners were paid for letting people dig on their land, and took a share of anything that was found. Occasionally, Evangelisti's agenda even gave the percentage that the owners had received. The notations for each tomb included the fate of the pieces he found and the prices they fetched. Then, even more amazingly, at the end of the year he balanced the books. Here for instance, is the woodcutter's record for:

Anno 1998

Scavate | 47 tombe | [excavated 47 tombs]
| 39 tombe a cassone | [large chest tomb in stone slabs]
| 1 fossa a terra | [trench grave]
| 4 tombe a uovo | [egg-shaped stone cave tomb]
| 1 tomba a pozzetto | [small shaft tomb]
| 2 tombe a ziro | [clay case tomb]
| Trovati 377 Pezzi | [found 377 pieces]
| Venduto 81.750.000 lire | [sold 81,750,000 lire = $68,000]

The year 2000 was a better year—sixty-eight tombs excavated, 737 pieces found, sold for 164 million lire ($135,000). In all, Pellegrini calculated that over the four years for which the records were most complete, Evangelisti had excavated 204 tombs, discovered 1,764 objects, and earned 185,000 euros ($154,000). Evangelisti himself estimated that a third of his income went in expenses so that his net gain over these four years was 130,000 euros ($108,000), or 32,500 euros per year ($27,000). This amounts to a tomb a week, each tomb yielding an average of roughly nine objects. These figures also show that, again on average, Evangelisti sold his antiquities for 105 euros (approximately $88). This compares with the average price of antiquities at auction, which is 1,000 euros (roughly $830) and the average price of Robin Symes's 17,000 antiquities (£3,750/$5,000).

Finally, Evangelisti recorded who, and on what dates, he had sold what to: Names included Medici, Cilli (whom he regarded as a "factotum" of Medici), the Aboutaams, who, he said, came to see him at home, and a prominent gallery in London's Mayfair district.

The Evangelisti discovery was almost scientific in its specificity. It removed any lingering doubt about the scale of the looting, its importance, or the role of the familiar litany of names involved.

19

THE TRIAL OF GIACOMO MEDICI

THE PALACE OF JUSTICE in the *quartiere* Clodio of Rome is by no means a beautiful building. On the contrary, it is made of gray concrete, a brutal modernist monstrosity of six stories, disfigured by rain and as dreary inside as out. It resembles nothing so much as a beached, out-of-commission aircraft carrier left to molder in dry dock. Piazzale Clodio is a large, long square of bus terminals, plane trees, and gas stations. Off it, governing the approaches to the courts, is a small, nondescript dead end with a bank, a motorcycle repair shop, and a sad café, where attorneys, police, and defendants grab a last cigarette and cappuccino before submitting themselves to a security check. This is not the Eternal City at her best.

The trial of Giacomo Medici began on December 4, 2003. Medici is of course one of the most famous names in all Italy, if not the world. Historians judge that the Florentine Medicis—"the godfathers of the Renaissance," to quote one recent study—included no fewer than fifty-four individuals worth writing about. Besides Lorenzo the Magnificent and Cosimo, there were Garcia, Gian Gastone, Giancarlo, seven Giovannis, two Giulianos, a Giulio, and a Guccio. But there has never been, until now, a Giacomo Medici. There is no danger that anyone can confuse the godfather of the Freeport with any other Medici.

The trial opened eight long years after the first arrests, since the discovery of Pasquale Camera's organigram, since the first raids in Geneva and the sealing of Corridor 17 with wax, since the first revelations about Medici's dealings at Sotheby's. During that time, Sotheby's had stopped selling antiquities in London (though sales at Bonhams had mushroomed) and had closed three departments; Felicity Nicholson had retired, and its chairman, A. Alfred Taubman, had been sent to jail for a year and a day in the United States for his part in a price-fixing scandal, when Sotheby's and Christie's had conspired to charge customers the same (increased) commission. Symes had suffered his own misfortunes, as had several others who had been Medici's collaborators.

The trafficking in illicit antiquities still went on, however, despite all these events and setbacks for the traffickers. Though he must have known that he would be followed, at least from time to time, Medici had still continued to meet tombaroli. Paolo Ferri himself bumped into Medici in Geneva on one of his visits there. Robert Hecht, on his visits to Rome, was also followed and he, too, met with fellow traffickers in looted objects.

And so, for Ferri, for Conforti (even though he had retired by then), for Rizzo, Pellegrini, and the more senior officers in the Carabinieri Art Squad, the trial could not start quickly enough. They had a mountain of evidence—and nothing in the interrogations and raids had contradicted the picture they had built up via the documentation. On the contrary, it had added to and deepened their understanding of the way the traffic works, and its far-reaching extent. So far as they were concerned, this case was triply important because Medici was by far the biggest trafficker they had ever proceeded against, because they had more documentary and other evidence against him than they had ever had against anyone else, and because his links to the international trading circuit were more established, more sophisticated—and better documented—than ever before with anyone else.

Or so they felt. Would a judge agree?

Until 1989, Italy's criminal law was based on the Napoleonic Code and had three different judicial figures—investigating magistrates, public prosecutors, and judges. Then the system was changed from the Napoleonic to the *Accusatorio*, what in English is called an adversarial system. Under this system the role of investigating magistrate has been taken over by the public prosecutor. Each case can go through three court "degrees"—first level, appeals court, and supreme court, and nearly all cases do. This is because in Italy, until March 2006, not only the defense could appeal, but the public prosecutor could as well. Under Silvio Berlusconi's government this was changed, and the prosecution can no longer appeal. If they are dissatisfied with the verdict, they can only take it to the Supreme Court. In January 2007, the Constitutional Court quashed part of the new law and further changes are expected. A defendant is considered not guilty until the definitive verdict, which is why people who have been convicted and sentenced to imprisonment may remain free for several years at the end of the first-degree trial.

A major problem with the Italian judicial system is administrative. Due to a chronic insufficiency of means, a shortage of courtrooms, of judges, of personnel in general, and in an attempt to get trials started within a certain period of time (due to the statutes of limitations), proceedings will only be in court on one day a week, or one day a month. A twelve-day trial, therefore, can—and routinely does—last for a year. Many trials, with several witnesses, go on for longer.

In an attempt to improve the situation, the Italian government introduced in 1989 the *rito abbreviato*, the "abbreviated rite." This "fast track" (by Italian standards) may be requested by the defendant during the preliminary hearing and means that the case is decided by a judge alone on the basis of documents collected by the prosecution and the defense, and means that witnesses are not called or cross-examined in court unless the judge, at his or her exclusive direction, decides that he or she wishes to hear someone. This system—which Medici chose—offers the defendant the advantage that, if found guilty, the sentence is automatically cut by one-third.

The judge in the Medici case was Guglielmo Muntoni, a small, round-faced dark-haired man, who is half Sardinian. In his mid-fifties, he is a jovial figure, with a lively sense of humor, but is a stickler for the law, insisting that all procedures be closely and correctly followed. He had been the judge in the trial of the tombarolo Pietro Casasanta, so he was familiar with many of the issues raised by the Medici case.

To this point in the book we have, essentially, given the case that the prosecutors offered at Medici's trial. The trial itself, however, gave him a chance to tell a different story.

Medici is a virile, impatient man, approaching six feet tall, with a strong physical presence, an open, round face, a high forehead, and strong-looking large hands. He favors leather jackets, drives a Maserati, and at his house in Santa Marinella, north of Rome, his study has a window in it in the shape of a capital "G."

In regard to Medici's testimony, Muntoni's approach, one can see with the benefit of hindsight, was to let the defendant talk at length—which he was very willing to do—during the course of which he would incriminate himself, both by revealing more and more of his "inside" knowledge and by contradicting himself, time and again. Once during the trial proceedings, Medici spoke for up to three hours nonstop, by the end of which his shirt was drenched in sweat. He was combative, complaining with disdain about some of the witnesses on the other side, and insisting on his expertise, talent, and standing as a connoisseur and trader. The last session was heard on December 13, 2004.

In the course of his testimony, Medici's principal defenses were that he was intending to give away the objects in his warehouses to Italian museums, that those in his home were his personal property, not for resale, and were anyway owned by his wife. At the same time, he also claimed that the majority of the objects in the Freeport were not from Italy at all but belonged to non-Italic cultures—in particular Egyptian, Syrian, Phoenician, Anatolian, Cycladic, Cretan, Rhodian, Mycenaean, Sumerian, Hittite, and so on. This made it hard to understand, as the judge observed, why he proposed to donate them to Italian (and not Greek or Egyptian or Syrian) museums.

His protestations of patriotism were fulsome but he turned coy when discussing exactly how he obtained his objects, never naming his sources.

They came from a famous Swiss collection: I bought them lovingly with only one purpose Your Honor, to bring them to Italy. Attention: donate them, not to make a museum and then take the money—donate. The collection of Villanovan clay [*impasto*] vases, from the twelfth to eighth centuries [BC], a whole series, all of one kind, very beautiful. [I] never wished to sell them. What was the purpose? To bring them to Italy and donate them all to a museum. I repeat: gift. . . . And the bronze *fibulae*, all the small Apulian Gnathian vases [which elsewhere he said he didn't like], preserved in a splendid way, new, something entirely miraculous . . . all collected with jealous care. . . . Why? Because they had to come to Italy to be donated. What do I mean by all this? I'm saying that of about three thousand objects which were seized from me, two thousand nine hundred were to be donated—that is, donated to the Italian state. Of course, Your Honour, there are a little less than one hundred objects which are valuable—it's not my fault. Those are the fruit of the sweat of my brow.

However, this sweat and toil on his part did not quite square with his claims elsewhere in his testimony, as when he told Judge Muntoni that these 2,900 objects in the Geneva warehouse "are of no value, objects which can be purchased every day in Italy and kept at home." Suddenly, the antiquities in Corridor 17 were no longer splendid examples of Anatolian or Egyptian culture, but trinkets—and Italian.

At other times he said that the objects in his warehouse had been sent by clients for restoration, "for expertise." To explain how he sold so much at Sotheby's in London (when he was supposed to be donating material to the Italian state), he said that in 1982 the Hydra Gallery had opened in Geneva, for which he became an archaeological expert and consultant. The gallery had been formed to sell an inventory of objects put together in 1980, the owner being Christian Boursaud, who also acted as shipper. The minor objects—more difficult to sell—were sold through Sotheby's in London. When Hydra was closed in 1985, he had the idea of purchasing all Hydra's objects that were in the company's warehouse and at the Geneva Freeport, and for this purpose he purchased Editions Services, a bearer-share company. He thus continued to operate as Hydra did before and "furthered his relationship with Felicity Nicholson of Sotheby's" in London. The antiquities he sent to Sotheby's never came from Italy.

Sometimes his swagger carried him away and landed him in trouble. At one point he implied that Pellegrini, the document expert, was not qualified to have written the reports for the trial and must have put his name to someone else's work. "It's obvious that these reports were not drawn up by Mr. Pellegrini, I don't understand why he or they who drew them up, did not feel it their duty—and also their pride—to sign them. They let it be signed. . . ."

JUDGE MUNTONI: Medici, you are accusing Pellegrini of criminal acts
    . . .
MEDICI: No, I'm saying . . .
JUDGE MUNTONI: No, just a minute: if you have elements to confirm
    . . . otherwise you will be answerable for libel, committed today at
    this very moment.
MEDICI: Very well, but I . . .
JUDGE MUNTONI: I've already told you before: watch what you say in

this court, because you will be held to answer for it. You have just accused Pellegrini of fraud together with others . . .

Medici's lawyer intervened, to try to lower the temperature, but Muntoni
was having none of it, saying that Medici had accused Pellegrini of signing reports that he hadn't drawn up. "That's fraud. What's more, he was
the designated consultant, so that would be doubly a fraud."

But Medici was careful to address and dismiss as irrelevant two crucial
pieces of evidence: Robert Hecht's memoir and the vast Polaroid collection in his own Freeport warehouse. Of the memoir, he said anyone could
produce such a document—even him. So far as his collection of Polaroids
was concerned and the fact that they were collected in an orderly manner
into albums, with so many objects showing soil still encrusted to them,
he offered the following explanation. As in other parts of his testimony, he
called in aid some helpfully anonymous Swiss corporations, which provided camouflage:

Well then, I mean to say, a big official in an important private Swiss
bank calls me, [and] says: "Would you feel up to consulting, but only
about the commercial value?" "Yes." I went, I descended the stairs of
this big bank, I entered this large room, there were lots of safes, he
opened them for me and inside there was God's marvel. I must tell you
the truth, it really almost seemed to me that it was stuff from recent
digs; this is stuff taken from some tomb which was surprised [discov-
ered] now, because they were really in such conditions. . . . They were
all broken, they were all badly glued, they were all full of soil and encrustation, some had been very badly restored. [He agrees, therefore,
that the objects shown in the Polaroids came from recent digs.]

I photographed them all, one by one, with the so-called famous Polaroid—careful, 'cause if Polaroid gets to know about this, they'll sue
us—because the Polaroid is [typical] of the tombaroli. According to the
consultants, some special consultants, like Dr. Pellegrini, say that the
Polaroid camera is typical of traffickers. Actually today Polaroids are little used. [This contradicts Symes, who had testified that Polaroids were
used throughout the trade and with collectors.] Anyway, I photographed
the entire collection of Marquis Guglielmi, one by one at [incomprehen-

sible]. Then they open the other vault, there were bronzes, God's marvel of bronzes. And what was there, Your Honour? The famous Tripod,
the famous Guglielmi Tripod, the stolen one was in the Geneva safe.
There was an ox this big, with a hole in his gut . . . there were so many
bronzes, all God's marvel; this doesn't interest [they said], this one we'll
show him: "What do you think of it?"—"Very beautiful stuff," I said,
"this bull is worth a lot of money; the Tripod is fragile, it's very *museale*
[museum quality] but it's very rare, a very beautiful piece." We work on
this . . . I work . . . I make out all the files, for each piece the price. Why?
Because they were selling, I don't know to whom; they were selling it
and wanted to know its commercial [value]—not from the point of view
of a collector, no, no, venal, venal, how much it's worth and if it should
be put up at auction. So I evaluated each piece, I go away and they pay
me the next day.

He said that he kept the photographs so as to be able to study them.

He denied the existence of the cordata, again in fulsome terms. "Medici
goes to the international auctions; he buys objects, also very important objects, he is in competition with all those that the prosecution today de-
fines as 'associates,' and instead they are bitter competitors Your Honour,
they really are. . . . They are people who perhaps don't speak to you for two
or three months because you nabbed the object they wanted from under
their noses." He agreed that it appeared to the outside world that he and
Hecht were associated "[but] there's a jealousy that eats our hearts, we
look daggers at each other."

At one point, he became so carried away that his self-confidence got the
better of him, his testimony verging on a rant (this was the time when his
shirt became drenched in sweat).

Somebody [a rival at an auction] will say: "Medici, remember I want
that, don't make the winning bid" and I say to them, "OK, up to what
figure do you mean to go?"—"Up to twenty thousand dollars."—"OK,
then . . . I'm a friend; when you stop, if somebody still continues, I have
the right to participate." And often that's the way it happens. Why? Because unfortunately people don't know how to do this business well,
Your Honour, believe me, and this has provoked much envy against me.

When an object is beautiful, beauty pays . . . Medici Giacomo has understood these things. So an object—I'll give you an example—is evaluated by everybody at five hundred million [lire = £250,000/$400,000+]. Medici says: "It's not so." Why? Because if it's worth five hundred million, it can be worth a billion, it can be worth a billion and a half, it can be worth two billion, and if I go mad, it's worth five billion. . . . Believe me, this is a marvellous secret which life's experience has taught me. When I used to go to auction sales, people would look at me flabbergasted and would say: "But this man's mad! Who's behind this man? Who will this man sell to? How come this man can spend all this money?" . . . they would just sit there looking at me, wondering how come I raised and raised. They said: "But the Getty Museum is on the phone! . . . is he crazy? What's he doing? Waging war on the Getty Museum?"—"But there's the Metropolitan Museum! . . . there's Fleischman, how is it possible?" . . . It was possible in this way: I knew that these gentlemen wanted to spend a certain sum, and [I] would buy for these gentlemen [i.e., with them in mind], because as countryfolk say: I waited for them at the bridge [an idiomatic Italian saying, meaning that's there's only one bridge and, if you wait there long enough, everyone comes by, to cross the river—in other words, patience and positioning pays off]. I would never seek them out, I waited [so] that it would be *they* who'd look for *me*. Then . . . there'd be a phone call, or an emissary would arrive and say: "Medici, we know you bought that object. How much do you want for it? . . . five hundred thousand dollars? We'll give you six hundred." I used to say: "I bought that object for myself, I love it. I would sell it for a million and a half dollars, otherwise don't bother me." That was my strength . . . I'm not here lying to you. . . . When I used to purchase at the auctions . . . even if I put a pencil in my mouth, to let the auctioneer understand that as long as I had the pencil in my mouth I wanted the object, somebody understood and so they knew I had bought. . . . For years I bought in Italy and nothing happened. Then, suddenly, those objects which I regularly bought became illicit.

In another self-confident—even audacious—move, but one that characterized himself as an honest man, Medici challenged Ferri to prove that even one object in the Freeport came from a tombarolo. "I challenge,

meaning it in a good sense, I challenge the prosecution to prove that one
. . . not three thousand, one object which, in inverted commas, comes
from a tombarolo. . . . Because if I, I repeat, did wrong, if I . . . if it were to
be proved from the documents of the trial that I did wrong, I must pay. Because it is right, because there are laws. . . ."

His response to the charge that he had been laundering objects through
Sotheby's was equally forthright. "If Dr. Ferri finds one single object of
those seized put there [i.e., sold at Sotheby's and bought back] by Medici
Giacomo or Editions Services, you, Your Honour, must condemn me
without attenuating circumstances, you must condemn me severely. . . .
No, no, it's I who ask."

In essence, Medici characterized himself as an innocent consultant, albeit one with an unusually large photo collection. The real villains, he
said, were elsewhere. Though his testimony was vivid, strong on rheto-
ric and expressed in a forthright manner, it was not overly rich on detail.
At the end of it all, Medici ringingly declared: "I don't consider myself
guilty of anything."

Judge Muntoni took five months to reveal his considered reaction to
Medici's performance. He began in a fairly uncompromising way.

As can be seen, even in the course of his long spontaneous declarations
made during the hearing, Medici never stopped lying and in fact accen-
tuated the distortion of reality, so as to depict himself as an innocent
subjected to persecution by the Italian Judiciary, by the Swiss Judiciary,
by the Police forces of the two countries, and by his own "work" milieu.
What strikes one most in this long series of lies, is that they were told in
spite of the fact that Medici knew very well that the documentation and
the photographic archive which had been seized from him were part of
the documents of the case and objectively give him the lie and cannot
be confuted. Medici even reached the point of several times invoking an
exemplary sentence against himself if even only one single archaeological object was proved to have been recycled. . . . Very well, the objects
that beyond doubt were recycled, as will be highlighted in the specific

paragraph, are dozens . . . Arts Franc bought all the objects at the above-mentioned auction following the indications given by Medici, at the price indicated by Medici and with the money furnished by Medici, and [were] delivered to Medici . . . for years numerous goods were sold through auctions by Medici so as to be repurchased by himself, so much so that they were found in his possession.

The judge found that 99 percent of the objects featuring in the case had no provenance.

Muntoni accepted that "innumerable objects" were sold by Medici to individual persons and to museums "by means of triangulations through Hecht, Symes-Michaelides, Bürki and others, as written by Medici himself at the bottom of Polaroids, which depict objects sold." The judge said Medici had no convincing explanation as to how, having been born into a poor family, he could open a "prestigious gallery" in the center of Rome, in the fashionable Via del Babuino, only to then transfer to Switzerland "where he could work more freely."

Nor does he explain why it was easier to trade in Switzerland through a gallery opened in Geneva, if he did not intend to trade in archaeological objects coming from thefts and clandestine digs carried out in Italy.

The purchase of archaeological material just excavated in Italy is documented by dozens and dozens of Polaroids and "scandalous" photographs which frequently show the actual stages of the digs . . . we point out that two chequered urns, clearly freshly excavated, were photographed in Medici's house in Santa Marinella. . . . The collection of *buccheri* and Villanovan objects destined to be donated to the state clashes with the fact that Medici has never donated these objects, neither before nor after their seizure, and that Medici sold . . . large quantities both of *buccheri* as well as Villanovan objects at auctions. Whilst the fact remains that Medici has in no way documented where he purchases these goods, his [declared] wish to collect them so as to donate them to the State is the umpteenth ["*ennesima*"] shameless lie.

Muntoni was not taken in by Medici's claim that the Polaroids concerned objects shown to him so as to ascertain their authenticity, or value, or sent to him for restoration. The judge pointed out that among the vast documentation there was not a single piece of paper or letter from a prospective client requesting such assistance, expertise, or advice.

No invoice has ever been made out by Medici for evaluation or restoration, yet one notices the meticulous way in which the documentation is kept with regard to his activity, from which one learns that Medici made out invoices only to the Aboutaams, through whom he used to sell his own archaeological objects. What's more, the Polaroids and photographs were not found, with the exception of very few cases, loose [or singly], but on the contrary, [they were found] well archived in specific albums which document the arrival of the goods, their condition, their initial collocation [arrangement], their temporary importation into Switzerland. . . . Medici evidently has forgotten that the catalogues titled *"Oggetti Passati"* [passed objects] contain Polaroids and photos of objects on which is marked the destination: V.CRI, V.SOTH, P.G.M., COLL, ["v." stands for *venduto,* or sold]—that is, sold through Christo Michaelides, always indicated as CRI or CR, through Bob Hecht, always indicated as BO, through Sotheby's, and sold to the Paul Getty Museum, or part of the Medici "collection."

In other words, Medici's main activity was selling, not collecting.

Muntoni himself examined the documentation that had been seized and concluded that Medici had made meticulous and "absolutely exact" records of the goods he had sold and the prices they had achieved.

It is therefore objectively proven beyond doubt that the photographic archive and the Polaroids in particular only depict objects bought and traded by Medici, who for this reason had archived the photographic documents in specific catalogues, divided into kinds of objects, their destinations. . . . The sensational falsity of Medici's statements on this point shows how well aware he is of the fact that there can be no licit justification to explain his having kept the photographic archive and he preferred denying even the evidence, in the hope perhaps that the documents seized had not been examined. In fact, it is precisely anger against those who have shown careful and intelligent examination of the seized

documents, like Maurizio Pellegrini of the Southern Etruria Superintendency, that must have made Medici throw accusations as false as they
are gratuitous.

To summarize the judge's 659-page verdict, Muntoni didn't accept
Medici's arguments on any level. He thought Medici had lied about his relationships with Robert Hecht, Marion True, and Christian Boursaud.
How could Medici have bought the Hydra Gallery from Boursaud when
the two men had fought a court battle in Switzerland in 1985 over ownership of the gallery?

He found Cottier-Angeli to be part of the cordata and found that only
2–3 percent of the goods seized were of non-Italian origin. (The report of
the three archaeological experts confirmed this.) He did not agree with
Medici that the goods the dealer sold at Sotheby's were minor artifacts.
And he did not accept for a moment that Medici was an expert. On the
contrary, Muntoni noted that Medici far more often turned to others for
expertise. He added: "Some doubts concerning Medici's capacity to recognize an authentic object—and not only to establish its period and the
maestri to whom it is attributable—necessarily occur, considering the
number of fakes found in his possession, some of which [were] bought at
public auction—unless one wishes to maintain that Medici was such a
dishonest dealer as to offer fakes which he had deliberately obtained."

Muntoni's judgment was withering.

He also had various comments and conclusions about the testimony of
others in the case.

On Robert Hecht: Muntoni concluded that Hecht was "one of the
founders of the conspiracy that was the subject of this trial," that he is
"the soul and director *(anima e regista)* of almost all the operations."

The extraordinary and adventurous human story of Hecht is well recounted in the memorandum which he himself wrote . . . a document
in which his ventures are never exalted, in fact we must perhaps think
that they contain some disinterested omissions so as to avoid problems
for his family after his death. We are obviously referring to the first draft

of the memorandum and not to the sweetened [*"edulcorata"*] version, also found in his house, which contains blatant [*"evidenti"*] corrections aimed at avoiding possible demands for reimbursement from Museums which had, at very expensive prices, purchased objects such as the Euphronios krater, about which Hecht in the first draft tells the true story—also reconstructible through other sources of evidence . . . we deduce that Hecht, together with Medici and Bürki and individuals to be identified, founded the criminal conspiracy [*"associazione per delinquere"*] between the end of the sixties and the very early seventies, the aim of which was to intercept all the important material clandestinely excavated in Etruria and most of that excavated in Puglia, thanks to a tight network [*"fitta rete"*] of relationships that Hecht personally had with individuals in positions of responsibility in many museums. . . .

On Danilo Zicchi: The judge found that all the addresses and names mentioned by Zicchi in relation to the organigram were confirmed by later investigation.

On Fritz Bürki: The judge concluded that Bürki had lied "shamelessly" about events concerning the Tripod, "adapting his version to that invented by Hecht and Rosen" (Jonathan Rosen, Hecht's partner in Atlantis Antiquities in New York). But the judge went on to "underline" the fact that Bürki had acknowledged that the archaeological objects submitted to him came from illicit digs carried out in Italy and that he was "absolutely aware of it." In regard to the Tripod, the judge concluded that Bürki had substituted Medici's name with that of Bruno.

On Harry Bürki: The judge noted, in particular and inter alia, that Harry Bürki admitted having seen the photographs of the frescoes taken in Pompeii by the tombaroli, that he could not explain the presence of a bag dirty with soil and which had a double [fake] bottom. He concluded:

Only when faced with the undeniable evidence of the proof, the two Bürkis, father and son, admitted [to] having acted as [a] "front" for Robert Hecht in the sale of objects to the Getty Museum in Los Angeles. Instead they continued to deny knowing Medici even when faced with the evidence. For them, too, therefore, dealings with him were not to be spoken of and were considered compromising: [a] denial which is in contrast with the presence of their respective names and addresses in the agendas [address books] of Bürki and Medici, [in contrast] with the restoration work done by Bürki on innumerable archaeological objects then sold by Medici, [in contrast] with the unmistakable contents of the photos seized from Medici which show objects photographed in Bürki's premises as was challenged, and [in contrast] with an association which continued for years. Proud of being citizens of a "neutral" country with respect to the one in which the clandestine digs had taken place, they shamelessly admitted that the objects they restored came from clandestine digs in Italy and even admitted having seen the photographs of the dig of the Pompeii frescoes.

On Pietro Casasanta: From his evidence the judge found it confirmed that there were competitive groups of cordate, trying to send the best objects out of Italy, and that these groups were led respectively by Nino Savoca, Gianfranco Becchina, and Medici; that "absolutely everybody in the milieu of the traffickers in archaeological material knew that Giacomo Medici was the real 'boss' who managed to intercept almost all the material excavated in Etruria," that it was well known that Hecht and Medici were partners since the sixties, that the cordate reported their rivals to the authorities whenever their interests were threatened, that Medici and Becchina had become billionaires (in Italian lire) "from nothing," that archaeological material was smuggled out of Italy thanks to "complacent shippers," that Mario Bruno was a rival of Medici's and that relations between them were very bad. Medici, concluded Muntoni, was with Hecht the "principal collector" in Italy of archaeological material coming from clandestine digs carried out in Southern Etruria and Puglia.

On Robin Symes: The judge found that Symes initially lied, trying to support Medici's "line of defense," but when faced with the Polaroid photographs, "Symes ended up by admitting some facts" and indicated as coming from Medici objects dealt with through Hecht and Fleischman.

On Wolf Dieter Heilmeyer: The evidence from Berlin, Muntoni concluded, confirmed the existence of the "criminal sodality," or cordata, between Hecht, Medici, and Symes, and that the Leon-Chamay-Cottier version of events was "pure fantasy," that the vases were restored "under Medici's watchful eye."

On Marion True: The judge thought that she had covered up her own responsibilities in these matters but had confirmed the cordata: Hecht-Bürki-Medici-Symes, and of several triangulations in connection with von Bothmer and Robert Guy, and in connection with the Hunt and Tempelsman Collections and with the Getty Museum.

Given all this, given all these uncompromising and definitive statements from Judge Muntoni and all his pithy comments and asides, showing that he had not been taken in for a moment, it came as no surprise that at the end of a massive 659-page judgment, delivered on May 12, 2005, he found Giacomo Medici guilty of the following charges: illegal export (smuggling), receiving stolen goods, and, most seriously, conspiracy. For these offenses, Muntoni sentenced Medici to ten years in prison (equivalent to fifteen years, had he not chosen the *rito abbreviato*), ordered the forfeiture of nearly all the antiquities in his possession, fined him 16,000 Euros, plus 10 million Euros as restitution of damages to the Ministry of Culture, towards payment of which his villa at Santa Marinella (the large one, with the G-shaped window, not the seaside one) and his Maserati were seized, plus another 16,000 Euros as reimbursement of legal expenses for the Civil Plaintiff (the Ministry). Medici's passport was impounded, together with other travel documents, and he was forbidden to leave the country. The judge also announced a list of Medici's objects that were to be confiscated and returned to Italy. These included objects that he was acquitted of smuggling but were seized to help offset the 10 million euros ($12 million) damages.

This was by far the heaviest punishment ever handed out in Italy to someone involved in the clandestine trade of illicit antiquities trading. As he was entitled, under the Italian system, Medici appealed. This appeal had not been heard as this book went to press.

20

TRADING WITH JAPAN, TRIALS IN ROME

THE YEAR 2007, like 2006, represents the high point of Conforti's and Ferri's achievement. Marion True and Robert Hecht are on trial in Rome, and all the world is watching. Medici's appeal will be heard and a definitive verdict obtained. But that is not all. In parallel with these events, Prosecutor Ferri is preparing to initiate proceedings against the central figure in the rival cordata—Gianfranco Becchina. And so, after ten long years since the theft at Melfi, since Operation Geryon, since the discovery of the organigram, the three figures at the top of that extraordinary piece of paper—Robert Hecht, Giacomo Medici, and Gianfranco Becchina—are all facing the music.

The trial of Marion True and Robert Hecht began on Wednesday, November 16, 2005, and is expected to last for at least two years—owing to the practice in Italy of limiting court appearances to one or two days a month.

As the trial date approached, stories began to leak out from the Getty Museum itself that were unlikely to have been helpful to Marion True. Most of these leaks came out via the *Los Angeles Times*, where two reporters—Jason Felch and Ralph Frammolino—had been working on the turbulence at the Getty since the spring. Felch had earlier worked on money laundering and political corruption, and Frammolino had exposed a scam at the L.A. County Morgue (involving the removal and sale of eye tissue from cadavers). The reporters began by looking at the troubled tenure of Getty CEO Barry Munitz, who was later forced to resign. In the course of their investigations, they were leaked more than a thousand

pages of internal Getty documents that provided the basis for several stories over the following weeks and months. As a Getty spokesperson
bluntly noted, these documents had been stolen. The thrust of the leaked
documents fell into three categories. In the first place, they showed that,
if anything, the situation inside the Getty was even worse than Ferri and
Conforti had feared. The documents appeared to show that the museum
was aware as early as 1985 that three of its principal suppliers—Hecht,
Medici, and Symes—were selling objects that had almost certainly been
looted, yet the Getty did nothing about it. There was one note from
Hecht, in his handwriting, beginning "Dear Marion," which read: "Yes-
terday my friend called me and said that since the carabinieri were looking for the pelike with the arms of Achilles he abandoned negotiations.
So I will not have it. Perhaps others may acquire it. Sorry." Then there
was a memo written by John Walsh, relating to a meeting held in September 1987 and attended by Harold Williams, then chief executive of the
museum, and Marion True, which was headed, "ANTIQUITIES ETHICS."
Walsh said it was a note of a meeting to consider ethical questions and
only considered the problem hypothetically. Nonetheless, his memo contained the lines:

HW: we are saying we won't look into the provenance{we know it's stolen
{Symes a fence

Whether this is as bad as it looks is hard to say, but in any case it paled
in comparison to a third document, a long, tightly spaced three-page
memo marked "Confidential" and written in October 1985 by antiquities curator Arthur Houghton and addressed to the Getty's deputy director, Deborah Gribbon. Houghton had been asked to comment on an
article Cornelius Vermeule had prepared on three objects in the museum
that had been acquired from Maurice Tempelsman—a statue of Apollo,
a ceremonial table with griffins, and a votive basin.* Houghton wasn't
too impressed with Vermeule's article, which considered whether the
three objects had been made or assembled as a cohesive group. As
Houghton saw it, this question could only be settled, not on grounds of

---

*See pp. 123–126 for a discussion of their quality and probable provenance.

connoisseurship but by going back through the chain of individuals who had possessed it. This he had done. His third paragraph read:

> At the beginning of this month I had a chance to discuss the matter with the dealer who had bought [the] three objects from the excavators. This individual, Giacomo Medici, had sold one (the lekanis [the votive bath]) to a second dealer, Robert Hecht, and the griffins and Apollo to a third, Robin Symes. Hecht later sold the lekanis to Symes, who then passed on the three sculptures as a group to Maurice Tempelsman, from whom we bought them. Medici informed me that he had acquired the lekanis and Apollo in 1976 or 1977, and that both had been found at the same location, a tomb which included a number of vases by the Darius Painter, at a site "not far from Taranto." Hecht said the site was Orta Nova, which lies to the northwest of Taranto not far from the Adriatic, and which has produced many fine late fourth century Italiota vases. Medici also said that the Apollo came from the same site, but was found in the ruins of a villa some 150 or 200 meters [490–650 feet] distant from the tomb whence the lekanis and griffins came. . . . I have passed on the substance of my findings to Cornelius without naming the individuals involved.

Ironically, less than a year later, Houghton resigned from the museum because he thought it was burying its head in the sand as far as illicit antiquities were concerned, not properly addressing the problems. It was Houghton who had been the person at the Getty who discovered that the Lebanese export licenses for the Sevso silver were forged. He seems to have suffered a change of heart around this time and was unable to stomach what was happening in the antiquities underworld. His resignation letter, which we have seen but were not allowed to copy, was strongly worded.

The documents leaked to Felch and Frammolino also showed that the Getty's questionable acquisitions may have been even more extensive than Ferri knew. An internal review of the documentation in connection with its holdings established that as many as half of the museum's antiquities masterpieces are of dubious origin. One case cited concerned a gold Greek funerary wreath. An Interpol cable had been turned up in the Getty files indicating that the wreath had been looted and another in which True expressed misgivings when it was first offered to the museum in 1992. During a trip to Switzerland that year, however, True arranged to view the wreath and meet its owner. For some reason, she determined that the man she did meet was an "impostor" and the prospective deal was canceled. "I am afraid that in our case it is something that is too dangerous for us to be involved with," True wrote in June 1992, to Christoph Leon, the Basel dealer who was acting as an intermediary.

Six months later, she appeared to change her mind. She asked to borrow the wreath from Leon for study, then won approval from the Getty board to buy it for $1.15 million in 1993. In 1998, Interpol sent a query to the FBI, asking the agency to interview True about her relationship with Leon, among other things. Leon declined to comment beyond confirming that he was the intermediary.

The paperwork revealed an internal note arguing that the documentation that had been turned up by the review, though "troublesome," did not need to be handed over to Ferri "because [the] Italian authorities had not specifically asked for them." The author of the note concluded: "We should point out that, while these letters are troublesome, none of them amounts to proof of Dr. True's knowledge that a particular item was illegally excavated or demonstrates her intent to join the conspiracy."

This of course takes us back to that moment when Richard Martin, the Getty's attorney, arrived at Ferri's office with a bundle of documents under his arm.* By volunteering documents, as noted earlier, the Getty did not need to provide all relevant papers, which would have been mandatory had the letters rogatory gone through. Ferri had been right to be wary of the American tactics.

Nevertheless, the Getty stood by Marion True and said that in her upcoming trial, they expected her to be exonerated. Not long after, she resigned her position as curator in the Antiquities Department. This was especially hard, for in January 2006, the original Getty Museum—the one in Malibu based on the replica of the Villa dei Papiri—was scheduled to reopen after several years; it had been closed for a $275-million renovation, redesigned specifically to represent its antiquities—including the Fleischman Collection—in more suitable surroundings.

*See p. 204.

Dr. True explained that her resignation was not directly related to the leaked documents but was because it was revealed that she had bought a vacation home in the Greek islands after Christo Michaelides—Robin Symes's Greek partner—had arranged a loan of nearly $400,000. This was in violation of the museum's ethical policy, though the museum had been aware of the loan for three years without taking any action. The museum set up a committee to examine True's behavior.

True bought her Greek vacation home in 1995, on the island of Paros. She had trouble financing the purchase because American banks wouldn't lend money on Greek property and Greek banks refused to give loans to foreigners. Christo Michaelides stepped in and introduced her to a lawyer who arranged a loan through an entity called Sea Star Corporation and deposited the funds in a Swiss bank. True repaid the loan a year later. Her attorney said, "To Ms. True's knowledge, neither Mr. Symes nor any member of the Michaelides family was involved in obtaining the loan for her, save Mr. Michaelides' introduction to Mr. Peppas [the lawyer]."

Three weeks later, the *Los Angeles Times* reported that Marion True had received a *second* loan, of $400,000, this time from Barbara and Lawrence Fleischman, which she had used to repay the first one. Furthermore, the loan was made on July 17, 1996, only three days after the Getty had agreed to acquire the Fleischman Collection. True was charged 8.25 percent interest by the Fleischmans, though the loan was unsecured. The special committee set up by the Getty to examine the affair discovered that neither Fleischman nor True had disclosed the loan in annual conflict-of-interest statements. At the time, Barbara Fleischman said she had no intention of leaving the board of the Getty. Speaking of her late husband's action, she said, "The reason he didn't hide the loan was because it was an honorable loan to a friend, with interest. There's nothing sneaky about this." She added that True had played no part in the financial negotiations over the Getty's acquisition of the Fleischman Collection.

During our research on the fall of Robin Symes, Dimitri Papadimitriou told us that Christo, his uncle, lent Marion True the money to buy her house on Paros. Christo had, he said, advanced her $360,000, plus $40,000 for legal fees and stamp duty and a Panamanian company had been set up for the purpose by a Mr. Peppas, who had been the family's lawyer until they fell out "in '96–'97." The Panamanian company made the loan to

Mrs. True, he said, but the money was "disguised," meaning that it came from Christo but was made to look as if it came from elsewhere. In the same way, he said, Christo had "bought" Felicity Nicholson's house on the Fulham Road in London.[1] Felicity Nicholson, it will be remembered, was the head of Sotheby's Antiquities Department.* Robin Symes told us that *he* had helped her pay for her house—which cost £20,000—by buying the studio in her garden for £18,000.[2] The whole setup between Christo Michaelides, Robin Symes, Felicity Nicholson, and Marion True was very cozy. Our attempts to reach Felicity Nicholson were rebuffed.

As the trial date got closer, the relationships among the various parties became strained and difficult. At one stage, Richard Martin, the Getty's lawyer, went so far as to argue to Daniel Goodman, the U.S. attorney, that Dr. Ferri had conducted his inquiry improperly. He was referring to "the efforts of the Italian prosecutor to force the Getty to de-accession from its collection a number of antiquities and send them back to Italy in order to avoid having the Curator of Antiquities be prosecuted. . . . As we have explained, the prosecutor has repeatedly used his criminal power to exert pressure on the Getty to accept a civil resolution." As in the United States, Martin said, "police and prosecutors in Italy are not permitted to use the threat of a criminal prosecution to pressure a party to reach a civil agreement." He thought there had been a breach of ethical standards and that in theory the only redress would be to initiate a criminal proceeding "in this case against Dr. Ferri." Practically speaking, though, he thought that would be futile.

At the same time, Paolo Ferri's disenchantment with Marion True had grown steadily since he heard Frida Tchacos's evidence in Limassol, when she said that the Fleischman Collection was more or less a "front" for the museum, by means of which it could still collect objects while at the same time saying that it would only acquire antiquities with a "provenance." The status of the Fleischman Collection will constitute the most dramatic focus of the evidence against Dr. True.

*See pp. 26–27.

▼

Back in 1994, when his Renault overturned near Cassino and Pasquale Camera was killed, a number of photographs of antiquities were found in the car's glove compartment. These included a picture of a vase by Asteas, one of the most important artists of Paestum in southern Italy in the fourth century BC.

The principal figure in a large workshop and one of only two southern Italian painters to sign his work, Asteas may have invented the freestanding half-palmette motif as a frame to an image. He liked myth and theatrical scenes, often explaining his compositions by means of inscriptions, and he had a biting sense of humor—for example, he delighted in showing the gods behaving in far from heroic ways. The lekythos shown in the photograph in the Renault's glove compartment was very important.

It took a while to locate the vase—because the discoveries in Medici's warehouse in the Geneva Freeport consumed most of the energies of Conforti and Ferri—but eventually, sometime in 1998, Pellegrini discovered that the Asteas lekythos was in the Getty Museum in Los Angeles. Ferri immediately wrote to the Getty, asking who had sold the museum the vase. This time, the supplier wasn't Medici but his arch-rival, Gianfranco Becchina, of Basel.

By then, of course, Camera's organigram had been discovered in Danilo Zicchi's apartment, showing that Medici and Becchina were the most important Italians in the whole underground network.* The fact that a photograph of the Asteas vase was found in the glove compartment of Camera's wrecked car, with the real thing in the Getty, gave Ferri sufficient reason to target Becchina's Basel premises—his gallery, Antike Kunst Palladion, and a warehouse in the city's Freeport—the way he had targeted Medici's warehouses in Geneva. A rogatory letter was sent to the Swiss authorities.

---

*By now, Pellegrini had worked out that the organigram must have been written down sometime between 1990 and 1993. The chart showed Mario Bruno, of Lugano, on a secondary level, below Medici and Becchina but above the capi zona. By then, the investigators had established from other interviews and interrogations that Bruno had been a prominent figure in the antiquities underworld in the 1980s, almost on a level with Hecht, but had lost some of his influence since then, though no one knew why. Bruno died in 1993, so it follows that the organigram was compiled between these dates.

While he was awaiting their reply, background checks on Becchina by the Carabinieri established that in the mid-1990s, he had moved back to Castelvetrano. Becchina is Sicilian. Now in his mid-sixties, he was born and grew up in Castelvetrano. Situated in the west of the island, inland from the port of Marsala, Castelvetrano is a small town but figures large in Sicily's criminal history. It was here that the body of Salvatore Giuliano—the legendary "bandit"—was left in 1950. His killing was a mystery. Officially, he was shot by the Carabinieri, attempting to escape. However, Giuliano was well informed and this may be the reason he was killed—he knew too much. And Castelvetrano is very near the wine-growing Belice Valley, scene of a massive earthquake in 1968, which became the subject of a major scandal when the local Mafia creamed off so much of the rescue money that was raised to help the victims that, twenty years afterward, thousands of people were still living in shacks. Castelvetrano is Cosa Nostra country.

The reality of life in Sicily is that the illicit excavation of potentially valuable antiquities cannot take place without at least the tacit permission of organized crime. This does not, of course, mean that Becchina was or is a member of the Mafia, only that any goods he received from Sicily would, in the nature of things, have come with Cosa Nostra's blessing.

Becchina appears to have moved back to Castelvetrano for two reasons. One was that he was also involved in the building materials business—he had two companies, one in Greece called Heracles Cement and one in Sicily called Atlas Cement. These companies provided building materials for the Athens subway, then under construction. The second reason for Becchina's move was the raid on Medici, which suggested to him that Switzerland was no longer the safe haven it had been.

But though Becchina had transferred back to Sicily, his wife hadn't. Becchina's wife is German. Her full name is Ursula Juraschek, but she is known as "Rosie." She remained in Basel, and her telephone calls with her husband were monitored by the Carabinieri. In fact, for eight months solid, says Ferri, he tapped all calls in and out of Becchina's Castelvetrano home. These showed that Rosie visited Sicily frequently but that Becchina—a prudent man—visited Basel only two or three times a year. All the same, the content of the phone taps confirmed that he still maintained close control over his antiquities business in Basle.

The phone taps also proved useful for what they revealed about the

Becchinas' business practices, in particular that they had more than one set of premises. And so, this time, when permission to raid the Freeport warehouse finally came through from the Swiss, and bearing in mind Ludovic de Walden's experience with Symes, rather than carry out the raid immediately, Conforti and Ferri decided to have Rosie Becchina followed.

Sure enough, she led them to two other warehouses, one inside Basel Freeport and one outside. She was observed coming and going freely in and out of these warehouses, but it also attracted the interest of both the Italian Carabinieri and the Swiss police that these other warehouses were registered not in the Becchinas' name, but in that of a well-known Mafioso.

In May 2002, the raids took place. Between the three warehouses, the raiding party discovered approximately 5,000 objects, many broken in pieces, many still dirty with soil on them, many restored. Becchina had fewer photographs than Medici, but he still had a great many, about 30 percent of which were Polaroids.

The documents found showed that one of Becchina's main suppliers was Raffaele Monticelli—another name from the organigram, a man who was convicted of trafficking in illicit antiquities in July of that very year, 2002, and sentenced to four years in prison.* Becchina had four entire folders devoted to his dealings with Monticelli, each containing long lists of objects and many Polaroids.

One interesting difference between Becchina and Medici lay in the quality of the items in the Basel warehouses. Later on, Ferri sent a small team of experts to examine the material in Basel, just as he had done in Geneva. This time it was two archaeologists and Maurizio Pellegrini, as document expert. They produced a two-volume report, physically matching on each page the photographs to the documentation, and linking them to specific sites in Italy, as had been done with the objects in Medici's warehouse. From this, one of their conclusions was that the overall quality of objects at Becchina's warehouses was, if anything, higher than in Geneva. "Medici was more *selective* than Becchina," says Ferri. "Becchina did not have the 'peaks,' the objects of world importance that Medici had, though he did have some things that were significant. But the *average* level of his objects was very high. Whereas Medici was selective,

*See pp. 240–242.

Becchina bought the whole *raccolto* [the whole harvest]." This may have been to encourage capi zona to sell to him rather than to others. The Monticelli trial showed that some of his tombaroli were paid regular wages, and perhaps this approach—employing tomb robbers full-time and buying all they unearthed—is how Becchina assured he would receive the high-quality material that was found on his premises in Basel.

The documents revealed that Becchina sold mostly through Sotheby's in London, though he did have one folder showing what he had sold at Christie's, also in London. These folders contained many photographs of what was auctioned and when, meaning that in due course, archaeologists will be able to follow the Becchina trail through the world's salesrooms.

Just as Medici used Editions Services as the main company through which he consigned material to the auction house, keeping his own name off the records, so Becchina sold 10–15 percent of his material through Mrs. Anna Spinello. This was the married name of his sister (in colloquial Italian, *"spinello"* means a cannabis "joint"). The documents seized in Basel show Becchina's handwriting alongside the lists of articles sold in Spinello's name, as he notes which objects have been sold, or bought-in (failed to sell), or withdrawn. But Becchina also used at least one other name, with an address in Buenos Aires, which may have had to do with the fact that Anna Spinello's husband is Italo-Argentinian.

In the late 1990s, it appeared to Pellegrini and to Ferri that Becchina was selling but no longer buying. Of course, some of his suppliers had themselves been arrested but it was as if, following the raid on Medici's warehouse, Becchina was running down his operations in Basel, confirming the earlier impression that Switzerland no longer offered the business opportunities it once did. However, Ferri kept up the phone taps and, in the wake of the raid, he heard Becchina say, in regard to the warehouses that had been targeted, "Have they found the other one?" This exchange led to the discovery of a fourth warehouse in Basel, consisting mainly of documents. Even this took time, however, and because the fourth warehouse was identified only in September 2005, those documents—about 30 percent of the total—have not yet been made available *in* Italy and so have not yet been properly assimilated. They may throw a different light on events.

Even so, it is already clear, according to Dr. Ferri, that Becchina had close relations with Dietrich von Bothmer, the Metropolitan Museum, the Boston Museum of Fine Arts, the Cleveland Museum, Jerome Eisenberg, a dealer with galleries in New York and London, and the Louvre in Paris. Arielle Kozlov, a curator at Cleveland, left the museum in 1997 and joined the Merrin Gallery in New York. Among the Becchina documents was a letter from the Merrin Gallery asking Becchina not to write his name on the back of the photographs he sent them, showing antiquities for sale. For Ferri, however, the main area of activity where Becchina differed from Medici concerned Japan.

The documents show that over the years, Becchina dealt mainly with two Japanese dealers, the colorfully named Tosca Fujita, whose company was Artemis Fujita, and Noriyoshi Horiuchi, a Tokyo-based dealer who at various times has had galleries in London and Switzerland. A great deal of correspondence was generated in the 1980s over the authenticity—or otherwise—of an alabastron that Horiuchi had bought from Becchina. The correspondence relating to this underlines the close relationships among Horiuchi, Becchina, Dietrich von Bothmer, and Robert Guy.

In the 1980s, Horiuchi was unknown outside the narrow world of antiquities dealing, but in 1991 his life changed. He met Mihoko Koyama and the idea for the Miho Museum was born.

The Miho Museum is a curious institution. Opened in November 1997, the museum is the brainchild of Koyama, heiress to a Japanese textile fortune who is also a disciple of the Japanese religious philosopher Mokichi Okada (1882–1955). In the early twentieth century, Okada invented an imitation diamond, which made him rich and allowed him the leisure to study art and develop his philosophical and spiritual beliefs, the chief of which was that a divine spiritual purification would "soon occur" through a global catastrophe, unless humanity could rid itself of sickness, poverty, and discord by means of "prayer, natural agriculture and the appreciation of beauty." It is the third aspect of Okada's belief system—the "soul-refining propensities of aesthetic experience"—that led to the creation of the Miho Museum.

After Okada's death, Mihoko Koyama founded her own religious sect, known as Shinji Shumeikai, which means "Divine Guidance Supreme

Light Organization" and has attracted thousands of adherents. She also began to collect Japanese tea ceremony objects and at first planned a museum devoted solely to Japanese antiquities. However, I. M. Pei, the architect for the museum, suggested to her during their discussions that the new museum should display antiquities from all over the world, making it unique in Japan.

The museum, which is about an hour's drive southeast of Kyoto, in the wooded mountains of Shigaraki, contains a dramatic entranceway: a steel-lined tunnel sliced through a mountain, leading to a 400-foot suspension bridge slung across a ravine. The museum may then be seen across the ravine, half hidden by trees and sometimes shrouded in mist.

It is said to have cost $250 million to design and build. When it opened, in November 1997, it had acquired more than 1,000 antiquities, 300 of them—by common consent—of outstanding significance. Over seven years, from 1991 to the opening, the responsibility for acquiring those antiquities—at the rate of around three a week—was Horiuchi's. Having first met Mihoko Koyama and her daughter in 1991, the trio soon became firm friends and Horiuchi was appointed consultant to the museum and given a huge budget—reportedly $200 million—to acquire non-Japanese antiquities.

During those years there was no shortage of controversy. Horiuchi had several acrimonious battles with I. M. Pei, who complained that he had constantly to redesign the museum to accommodate Horiuchi's acquisitions. There have been several allegations that Horiuchi, who has no formal training in archaeology or art history (he studied law), has bought fakes, that he won't admit it because of the loss of face involved, and that some of the pieces in the museum form part of the Treasure of the Western Cave, illegally excavated and smuggled out of Iran in the early 1990s.* It is certainly true that most of the antiquities on display in the Miho have no provenance.

By Horiuchi's own admission, very little of what he acquired was bought at auction—in what is perhaps the only full interview he has given, he said he bought from "top dealers" at "top prices."

Speaking of his first meeting with Mihoko Koyama in 1991, in that

*See pp. 244–245.

same interview, Horiuchi said, "Destiny brought us together," though there may be more to it than that.

Among the Becchina documents is an agreement signed after a creditors' meeting held in Geneva in 1991. This was a meeting held between four creditors—all Swiss antiquities dealers, of which Becchina was one—called because Horiuchi owed each of them substantial amounts of money and showed no prospect of paying. According to the agreement drawn up at the end of the meeting, and signed by all those present, the decision taken was for Horiuchi to become the agent for his creditors in Japan. In other words, so far as these four Swiss dealers were concerned, from then on Horiuchi was not allowed to buy directly from them, and sell on; instead he could only take a percentage of whatever price they chose to put on their objects.

The close proximity of this creditors' meeting and Horiuchi's meeting with Mihoko Koyama was therefore extremely fortuitous, to say the least, destiny bringing together not just these two individuals but placing the antiquities underworld cheek-by-jowl with one of the greatest sources of art funding the world has ever seen. In time, as the Becchina documents reveal more and more, we will no doubt find out just where so much of the Miho material originated.

After the raid on the first three warehouses, Rosie Becchina refused to cooperate with the Swiss and Italian authorities and she was held in prison. This produced the desired effect, to some extent, and she did admit, for example, that one of their main suppliers was Monticelli, invaluable confirmation of that cordata, from the horse's mouth. She also contacted a lawyer, Mario Roberty—the same attorney used by Frida Tchacos and Robin Symes—and Roberty called Becchina to tell him his wife had been arrested. (It was during this call that Becchina asked if the police had discovered his "other" warehouse.) Learning that his wife had been arrested, Becchina asked Roberty to tell Rosie that he was immediately leaving Sicily for Basel.

Neither Alitalia nor any other regular airline flies directly from Palermo to Basel, so Becchina had to change planes at Milan. At Malpensa airport, at the gate where the Palermo flight arrived, he was arrested and immediately taken to Rome. Before he could be interrogated, Becchina claimed that he was mad—*pazzo* in Italian—and clinically incapable of either being held in jail or of being interviewed. Once again, this well-known maneuver interested Ferri because such a claim is in Italy a standard tactic. Becchina was seen by a psychiatrist who concluded that although he did have some problems with his memory, he was quite sane enough to remain in jail. He was held for six months, after which, under Italian law, he was automatically released.

Ferri interrogated him for eight hours but didn't get very far. Becchina admitted knowing many of the people mentioned in this book—Frida Tchacos, Medici, Symes, Hecht, Cottier-Angeli, True ("a very nice woman"), and Dietrich von Bothmer—but he could scarcely deny it since their names were all over his documentation. But he admitted nothing incriminating, as his wife had admitted receiving material from Monticelli. "All he did was *fare salotto,*" says Ferri. In Italian, *salotto* means "sitting room" and the phrase means that the interrogation had all the significance of a fireside chat.

But in the course of the eight-hour interrogation, further differences did emerge between Becchina and Medici. Psychologically, whereas Medici is "*spaccone,*" a bit of a show-off, given to letting off steam, Becchina is a classical Sicilian—reserved, calm, a closed book. Small, slightly built, with straight lank hair and a sharply pointed nose, Becchina is physically very different from Medici, too. He makes no gesticulations and, while admitting nothing, Ferri says, "Unlike Medici, he has never tried to convince me he is innocent."

Robert Hecht, Giacomo Medici, Gianfranco Becchina, Robin Symes, and Marion True—all in court or in the prosecutor's sights, all involved (or alleged to be involved) in smuggling, receiving, conspiracy. This is a major event in the history of archaeology, in criminology, in the politics of cultural heritage, and in the foreign policy of the Mediterranean countries. It is a major indication of the way the world's attitudes and ethical beliefs are changing in this area. However, there is a sense that the legal fate of these figures is, if not an incidental matter, no longer the main event. The sheer scale of the illicit trade in looted antiquities, its organized nature, the routine deception, the superb quality of so much of the material, the close proximity of museum curators and major collectors to underworld figures—that is now there for all to see. Whatever verdicts are handed down, other, lesser figures in the underground network have already stood trial and been convicted.

Irrespective of the verdicts in the outstanding court cases, in November 2005, American museums started to return antiquities to Italy. The Getty set the ball rolling with the return of the Asteas vase, a photograph of which had been found in the glove compartment of Pasquale Camera's overturned Renault near Cassino (see pp. 11–13). At the same time, the museum returned two other objects, the bronze candelabrum from the Guglielmi Collection (pp. 84–86), and a stone stela with inscriptions from the archaeological site of Selinunte in Sicily.

But this paled alongside the announcement, in February 2006, that the Metropolitan Museum of Art in New York was returning the Euphronios krater, together with twenty other objects, to Italy. That transaction, and its implications, are considered in the Epilogue, because it was, and is, a special case. But the Met's move did presage several ripple effects that may be considered here.

The first of these occurred at the end of September 2006, when, after months of negotiations, the Museum of Fine Arts in Boston announced that it was returning thirteen archaeological treasures to Italy. "We are committed to seeing the end of illegal excavations and illicit trade in archaeological works of art," said director Malcolm Rogers at a formal ceremony in Rome. "This is a new era of legality." He added that his museum and the Italian authorities now had a "collegial relationship."

One of the artifacts to be returned, a two-handled amphora from the fourth century BC attributed to the Darius painter, was donated to the museum in 1991 by Shelby White. Another, a statue of Vibia Sabina, wife of the second-century emperor Hadrian, was acquired in 1979 from Fritz Bürki, with Hecht as intermediary. Several other pieces were acquired through Robert Hecht. Still others were acquired through Palladion Antike Kunst, Becchina's gallery in Basel.

Rogers insisted that the museum had acquired the objects in good faith but added that "the balance of evidence" presented by Italy now "favored the return of the objects," though he did not expand on what he meant.

The return of the objects is to be welcomed, as was the Getty's decision, a month later, to return twenty-six ancient antiquities to Rome. Those negotiations, however, did not go as smoothly as those with the Boston museum. (One observer described the Getty negotiations as "tempestuous.") The objects to be returned included many referred to in this book—for example, the Attic Red-Figured Mask Kantharos (p. 90), the Two Griffins Attacking a Fallen Doe (p. 124 and the photo section, where Medici is standing alongside the Griffins), the Douris Phiale Fragments (p. 226), and the Antefix in the Form of a Meanad and Silenos Dancing (p. 373 in the Dossier section)—but the Italians were less than satisfied. The reason for their dissatisfaction lay in the fact that by that stage they had identified no fewer than forty-six objects in the Los Angeles museum that they maintained had been illegally excavated from Italian soil. Following John Walsh's tenure at the Getty, he had been followed by Deborah Gribbon, but she had resigned abruptly, after disagreements with Barry Munitz, president of the Getty Trust (see below). She, in turn, had been succeeded by Michael Brand. Brand now said that the museum had made "substantial compromises" during the negotiations but that Italy's position "stood in the way of reaching a comprehensive agreement." Relations deteriorated still further in December, with a sharp exchange of letters and rebuttals, in which the main bone of contention was Italy's claim for a Greek bronze statue that the Getty insisted had been found in international waters. Italy rubbed in its attitude by agreeing to lend several antiquities to both the Met in New York and the Museum of Fine Arts in Boston, as an act of friendship and in response to those museums' willingness to return objects.

In the epilogue, we will make the point that the Metropolitan Museum in New York is not quite the whiter-than-white institution it makes itself out to be, but for now we will concentrate on the Museum of Fine Arts in Boston, for there is rather more to say about Boston's return of those thirteen objects than they have so far said themselves. Thanks to the research of two British academics—David Gill and Christopher Chippindale—who published their report in the *International Journal of Cultural Property*, Boston's collection comes into focus almost as much as those of the Getty and the Met. Gill and Chippindale point out that there is much more to Boston's return than meets the eye.

In the first place, they say, some of the material returned by Boston was originally said to have been in *old collections*—i.e., in collections formed before 1970, the Unesco cut-off date (as discussed in Chapter 2). Furthermore, one object that was returned, an Apulian bell-krater, was said to have been in the Holger Termer Collection in Hamburg. But, Gill and Chippindale say, this "collection" may be no more than the stock of the Galerie Neuendorf in Hamburg: They have reconstructed the collection from the archives and find that more than half of the objects passed through the Neuendorf Gallery. Earlier (p. 95), we referred to the Zbinden Collection in Switzerland and the S. Schweitzer Collection in Arlesheim, which appear to have been used as false attributions to deflect suspicion from a number of objects which would otherwise lack a history. Must we now add the Holger Termer Collection to this list?

Their second point is to question whether the thirteen objects returned so far can be an end to the matter. They identified a list of ninety-two more important items acquired through Hecht.[3] What will be the ultimate fate of this group of antiquities?

In September 2006, Giacomo Medici, awaiting his appeal, offered Paolo Ferri a deal. Although he would not talk to us, he told Vernon Silver, of Bloomberg News Service, that he was willing to return "a previously unknown masterpiece," known only as "Object X," in exchange for the abolition of his fine and a reduction in the jail time he was facing, should he lose his appeal. Medici told Silver the object he was referring to was by a famous artist from the ancient world, "whose work compares to that of Michelangelo or Leonardo da Vinci." It was, he said, "worth millions," and compared in value with the Euphronios krater.

There were other reports that, in exchange for "Object X," Ferri was willing to reduce Medici's sentence to six years, but the prosecutor was wary. "It could be a bluff," he said, adding that he would rather lose Medici's masterpiece than get duped.

Medici's offer, of course, sat oddly with his defense during his trial, or one of them anyway, that he was amassing antiquities in Geneva in order to return them to Italian museums. "To bring them to Italy and donate them all to a museum. I repeat: gift . . . " (see p. 272). Where had this "masterpiece" been in the interim? Why hadn't he donated it before, if he was so sure such objects belonged in Italy? As this book went to press, "Object X" was still in limbo.

Ferri and his colleagues were more concerned with others in and around the cordate. At the end of November 2006, the Italians asked Shelby White to consider returning twenty ancient artifacts that she and her late husband had collected. Maurizio Fiorilli, the lawyer for the Italian Culture Ministry, hastened to say on this occasion that Ms. White was not being accused of any crime and that his government was relying on "moral suasion." He said he thought the evidence spoke for itself and that the Italians hoped that her "sensitivity" to the situation would influence her to return the objects.

White insisted to us that neither she nor her late husband had ever met Medici, and had only ever bought from auction houses and dealers "considered reputable at the time." White's communications counselor, Fraser P. Seitel, said that White had always been very open about her and her late husband's collection, always making "their collection available to scholars and for public exhibition purposes. . . . In fact, you could argue that it is precisely *because* Shelby White and Leon Levy were so willing to share their collection with the public, that they have attracted attention." He said that White had, herself, initiated discussions with the Italians.

The timing of the Italians' move in connection with Shelby White was interesting. Only a few days before, the Metropolitan Museum had released its advanced publicity in connection with the opening, in April 2007, of its new Greek and Roman Galleries, which are named for and financed (to the tune of $20 million) by Mr. Levy and Ms. White. It was not clear, as this book went to press, whether any objects from the Levy-White collection would be displayed in the new galleries. Harold Holzer, a spokesman for the Met, declined to comment on the matters raised in this book.

At the Getty, there was good and bad news. One piece of good news was that, in January 2006, the Getty Villa, the original Getty Museum in Malibu—just north of Los Angeles on the Pacific coast—re-opened after a $339 million renovation, to display 1,200 of the museum's 44,000-piece collection of Greek, Roman, and Etruscan antiquities. The renovation, designed by architects Rodolfo Machado and Jorge Silvetti and featuring a bronze staircase and reflecting pool, was judged a success, described as "vibrantly splendid" by one critic and "an exquisite work of architecture" by another. It was a success with the public, too: by the end of January, the museum had sold all available tickets until the end of July.

Another piece of good news was that, in December 2006, the Getty Trust—the body that oversees the museum—announced its replacement for Barry Munitz, the president. Munitz had resigned the previous February, after eight years in the job that had been dogged by controversy. Among the charges leveled against him—mainly in the *Los Angeles Times*—were that he had lavishly spent Getty funds on himself and his wife, buying a $72,000 Porsche Cayenne, staying in $1,000-a-night hotels, traveling first class on airplanes, and even ordering his assistant to express-mail umbrellas to him where he was on his travels. (The Internal Revenue considers excessive pay, travel, and perks to be "self-dealing," the illegal use of tax-exempt resources for private benefit. Under the tax code, non-profit organizations must use their resources for the public good.) Munitz, without admitting any wrongdoing, paid the Getty Trust $250,000 "in order to resolve any continuing disputes with him" and gave up severance pay and benefits that would have exceeded $1.2 million. He was replaced by James N. Wood, an art historian and former president of the Art Institute of Chicago.

By then, the museum had specifically addressed the problem of its dealing in antiquities. At the beginning of October 2006, it was announced that the California attorney general had appointed an independent monitor to oversee reforms. It was the first time the California attorney general's office had imposed an overseer in an enforcement action against a charitable trust. At the end of the month, the museum announced that it had strengthened its rules for buying or accepting ancient artifacts. Under the new policy, the museum said it would not consider any object whose provenance did not reach back to at least 1970, the date of the landmark Unesco convention. Michael Brand said that the new rule was adopted "even though it will make it much more difficult for the museum to continue to buy antiquities."

And so, finally, the Getty—and with it, surely, most other American museums—had been dragged kicking and screaming into the twenty-first century, after months and months of scandal.

Just over a week later, Marion True, in a written "clarification" addressed to the Rome court, described the market for ancient art as probably "the most corrupt" of art markets. "I knew, in fact, that the antiquities market was filled with risks for those who wished to purchase objects, as it included many unscrupulous dealers, who had no qualms about selling fakes or objects that had been stolen or exported illegally from their country of origin," she said in a nineteen-page memo seen by Vernon Silver of Bloomberg News. "The museum had to accept the premise that the majority of antiquities available on the market had, in all probability, been exported from the countries of origin illegally." This was damning, but the rest of her statement sought to cast herself and the Getty as reformers in a corrupt market. (This had been John Walsh's argument in his depositions to the Italian court—see pp. 218–219). When she took the job of curator at the Getty in 1986, she said she had helped draft a memo to the Getty board exploring whether "it was possible to continue to collect antiquities in a tainted market." As this book had shown, the Getty *did* continue buying, but among the steps True took to battle the illicit trade, she said, was the ban on buying objects that hadn't been part of a known collection or been documented in a publication before 1995. This of course refers to the acquisition of the Fleischmann Collection (which is discussed on pp. 114–123, 193, 198, and 220), from where it will be seen that Dr. True's version of events is not the only possibility.

Later in the trial, Dr. True asked the court to admit as evidence a letter she had sent on December 18, 2006, addressed to Deborah Marrow, the Getty Trust's acting chief executive, Michael Brand, and Ron Hartwig, the trust's spokesman. In the letter, which was read in court, she accused the Getty Trust of having left her to "carry the burden" of the institution's collecting practices, even though her superiors at the museum and the trust had "approved all the acquisitions made during my tenure." She faulted the museum for a "lack of courage and integrity" and added that her Getty superiors "were fully aware of the risks involved in buying antiquities" and had still approved her decisions. She argued that the Getty Trust's failure to throw its weight behind her (though it was paying for her defense) had allowed prosecutors in Rome and Greece (see next chapter) to "place squarely on my shoulder the blame for all American collecting institutions and the illicit market."

Commenting afterward to reporters, Ferri said he thought that, on a first reading, the letter "worked against" Dr. True by suggesting that she had knowingly taken part in the acquisition of illicit artifacts. "She accuses the Getty of having been aware of all her decisions," he said, adding that she did not avoid dubious purchases. "She did not pop up out of nowhere," he said, but was "continuing an established practice."

At much the same time, in early January 2007, the *Los Angeles Times* returned to the attack. Frammolino and Felch reported on a four-month investigation into the so-called Morgantina Aphrodite. This had been, ostensibly, the Getty's most sensational acquisition. More than seven feet high, with a serene marble face and a swirling limestone gown, this, the Greek goddess of love, was acquired by the Getty for a reputed $18 million in 1986. The statue, larger than life-size, is a rare example of an almost-complete cult statue. Some idea of its importance may be gleaned from the wording of Marion True's report to the board when it was being considered for acquisition: "The proposed statue of Aphrodite would not only become the single greatest piece of ancient art in our collection; it would be the greatest piece of classical sculpture in this country and any country outside of Greece and Great Britain."

But there were early signs of trouble. Luis Monreal, a former director of the Getty Conservation Institute, now working in Geneva as general manager of the Aga Khan's Trust for Culture, said there was dirt in the folds of the gown when it arrived at the museum, and the torso had what appeared to be new fractures, "suggesting that the statue had been recently unearthed and broken apart for easy smuggling."

The reporters traced other experts who had raised doubts early on and re-created the statue's clandestine route out of Italy. This chain allegedly involved a certain Renzo Canavesi who, according to a receipt found by a Sicilian investigation, sold the statue to Robin Symes in March 1986, for $400,000.

The chances are the Aphrodite will go back to Italy. The Getty has announced that as their intention. However, should there remain any doubt in the matter, we can quote here from extracts in the Symes' archive, which we have seen and which confirm and amplify various aspects of the matter. The Symes archive shows, for example, that Symes did indeed pay $400,000 for the statue and that it was sold to the Getty for $18 million, with the first installment due in "summer 1992." A further note added that the sale "coincided with the appointment of a friend . . . as the curator of the museum." The note also says that the statue was "probably Aphrodite . . . probably from south Italy or Sicily," and that it was carved originally in pieces but had been damaged when it had been toppled either by an earthquake or vandals. The note added that the statue showed "encrustations" and deposits of "soil." Most interesting of all, however, is the fact that this file also contained photocopies of Polaroid photographs of the statue, showing how it had originally been pinned together.

One other development since the hardcover version of this book remains to be mentioned. On March 29, 2006, one of the authors, Peter Watson, gave evidence in the trial of Marion True. He recounted an unusual incident that had taken place at a conference on the trade in illicit antiquities, which had been held at the Cotsen Institute of Archaeology at the University of California in Los Angeles, in Spring 2001. The conference dinner had been held at the Getty Museum and during the course of a conversation on Medici and his tradings, Dr. True had referred to him as "Giacomo." At least two of the fellow diners who heard this reference were disconcerted by Dr. True's familiar tone.

But a much more notable event took place shortly afterward. The authors were standing outside the court room, after that day's proceedings were over, talking to Prosecutor Ferri when his cellphone rang. He listened intently and then looked up. "Marion True's house in Paros was raided today by Greek police."

21

OPERATION ECLIPSE

*Nikolas Zirganos**

IN SOUTHERN GREECE, spring comes early. Although it was still March 2006, on the island of Paros in the Cyclades the first daisies of the year had broken through and, in the morning sunshine, their white and yellow colors lined the narrow road that snaked from the port of Paroikia up the hill toward the brilliant white village of Glyssidia. Shortly after 11:00 A.M., three cars left the port and quickly reached the point where the tarmac stopped and the dirt road began, sending clouds of dust billowing into the air.

Just short of Glyssidia the cars reached a plateau where there was a high stone wall with a house hidden behind it, and stopped. Eight men got out. Six were policemen, in plainclothes. One was an archaeologist and the last was the local prosecutor. Nobody had a moment to savour the view, which was breathtaking—the islands of Antiparos and Despotico were closest, the latter with its remains of a Doric temple, beautiful but uninhabited. Beyond them the smaller islands of the Cyclades receded into the blue distance.

Captain George Gligoris, head of the Greek Art Squad, had his mind on other things. A witty, handsome man in his mid-forties, Gligoris looks—and dresses—more Italian than Greek. He always wears sunglasses and in fifteen years as an undercover agent hasn't ever worn a uniform. He was anxious that the morning's operation would go well. He approached the gate in the wall, rang the bell, and waited for the housekeeper. Beyond the wall were a number of olive trees and in among them was the house, a house that—he knew—belonged to Marion True, an American woman, and, until very recently, a curator at the Getty Museum in Los Angeles.

*Nikolas Zirganos is an investigative reporter based in Athens. He works for *Kyriakatiki Eleftheroptypia* newspaper and *Epsilon* magazine.

The housekeeper let them in. As it happened, there were plenty of people in the house that day because Dr. True had phoned that very morning to tell her staff that she would be arriving in a few days to spend her Easter vacation on the island. The staff were preparing the house for her. "As we entered the living room," Glirogis recalled later, "I spotted part of an Hellenistic idol placed on a stone windowsill. Surrounding the fireplace I saw that architectural fragments taken from ancient temples or monuments had been 'built in' to the walls as ornament while a Byzantine icon was resting on a table. The moment I saw them I took a deep breath of relief."

Gligoris was acting on a tip-off that Dr. True's villa contained unregistered antiquities. Greek law is very severe, but clear. Individuals can possess antiquities only if they are registered collectors, with special permission, or if they declare the antiquities to the authorities. Otherwise they are breaking the law. Paros is a hundred miles from Athens but most of that is the Aegean Sea so it wasn't easy, and it wasn't cheap, for Gligoris to fly his team over. But as soon as he saw the first undeclared objects in the living room, he knew his trip hadn't been wasted.

Then, inside the house, a most extraordinary thing happened. Everything went dark. The sky turned gray, a wind began, the temperature dropped sharply, and all the animals within earshot began making panicky noises. Sheep and goats bleated, turkeys cackled, hens clucked.

It was an eclipse of the sun.

"I took it as a good omen," said Gligoris. "As if someone was leading me on, as if the twelve gods were on our side, giving me the 'go-ahead.' As the sun came out again, and we resumed the investigation, one of my men suggested we now had a name for our raid—'Operation Eclipse.' Yes, but we have a saying in Greece: 'In addition to Athena's help, you must throw in a hand yourself.'"

They did. They searched the house for many hours. Paros is famous for its beaches, its traditional architecture, and its rich and ancient past, with many archaeological sites dating back to the fifth millennium BC. It is also famous for the snow-white semi-transparent marble that it carries in its bowels—Parian marble was one of the types of stone used in the construction of the sanctuaries at Delos, Olympia, and Delphi. The Venus de Milo, the Praxitilean Hermes, and the Victory of Samothrace are all hewn from Parian marble. No wonder that the house at Glyssidia—built in the traditional Cycladic style, single-story with interlocking stone, painted white—was Marion True's favorite retreat. She would spend most of her summers there, making frequent visits to the nearby island of Schinoussa to visit Robin Symes, Christo Michaelides, and his family.

A total of seventeen unregistered antiquities were discovered in her house that day of the eclipse, plus the Byzantine icon. There was a poster on display in the living room for the exhibition of the Fleischman Collection, which had been displayed at both the Cleveland Museum and the Getty Museum, under the title, "A Passion for Antiquities" (see pp. 115–118). As one of Gligoris's men remarked, "That's the passion that will lead all these people to their downfall."

None of the antiquities found in the Glyssidia residence was of particular archaeological significance. But as a curator of antiquities, with so many archaeologists—Greek and non-Greek—passing through her house every year, it is surprising that none of her friends and guests advised Dr. True to take the appropriate steps to make her possessions legal. As it was, the eighteen ancient objects were confiscated and the case referred to the district attorney's office.

The raid was more important than that, however. For the truth of the matter is that the Greek authorities had had Marion True in their sights "for decades," hoping for a reason to look more closely at her activities. Since the 1980s, reports had started coming into the offices of the Greek art squad suggesting that she had been buying, on behalf of the Getty Museum, whole consignments of Greek antiquities of mysterious provenance—perhaps without any provenance at all. In the years before the Paros raid the Greek law enforcement agencies had twice come close to prosecuting her, but both times their investigations had foundered.

In the early months of 1997, fisherman off the coast of Preveza, a small port on the Ionian coast of Greece, south of Corfu, netted a most unusual catch. It was a bronze statue of an adolescent boy, five feet high, weighing 150 pounds. It was badly corroded and covered with sea shells but even so, its quality was obvious. It was subsequently identified as coming from the workshop of Polycleitus, who, with Myron and Praxitiles, is one of the most admired sculptors of the fifth century BC. This wasn't just any sculpture, but the fishermen didn't know it.

They brought the statue ashore secretly and put out feelers among the antiquities underworld, looking for a buyer. Unfortunately for them, they approached the wrong people. When they met the middlemen with whom they thought they had arranged a sale, they were held up at gunpoint and forced to give up the statue—for nothing.

Subsequently, the bronze was hidden under boxes of grapes in a fruit truck and driven north to Germany. (These details were pieced together later by Christos Kotlidas, who was serving in the Greek Art Squad at the time.) The statue changed hands before its journey across Yugoslavia so that it was several weeks before it arrived at the town of Saarbrücken, in Saarland, on the border with France and Luxembourg. The Greek smugglers then contacted the Austrian archaeologist-turned-dealer Christoph Leon, who was operating out of Basel in Switzerland (see pp. 199–200 and 287–289 for Leon's other activities).

Nothing more was heard for several months, not until George Tzallas, the acting chief of the police department that investigates illicit antiquities, received a tip-off. It was May 21, 1998, and Tzallas learned from his informant that Christoph Leon was about to sell the bronze statue to Marion True. True, he was told, was offering $7 million on behalf of the Getty Museum, though there was believed to be another customer in the wings, a Japanese individual who had offered $6 million. Tzallas was told by his informant that Dr. True had viewed the statue "lying on a carpet at Leon's house."

Tzallas and Kotlidas immediately left for Germany, where they managed to persuade the Saarbrücken police to help them raid a hotel room occupied by a Greek immigrant, Michael Kotsarides. There was nothing incriminating in the room but, in the open-air parking lot of the hotel, they found his car, and, in the trunk, a wooden crate. Across the crate were stenciled the words, in English, "FOR EXPORT TO USA." Inside, when they opened it, were 115 small archaeological items of ancient Greek origin, 312 ancient coins—and the bronze boy from Preveza.

So far, so good. The follow-up to the raid, however, was—to say the least—unsatisfactory. The Greek government never at any point asked for a statement from either Christoph Leon or Marion True. But, at the request of the German police, the FBI did question Dr. True. According to this report, she confirmed that she had indeed "seen the statue, displayed on a carpet in Leon's residence, but turned down the sale when she realized he was acting on behalf of a third party. Having serious doubts concerning the legal status of Leon's dealings, she became suspicious as to the artwork's provenance. She never went so far as to make an offer, refusing to buy it."

Interpol sent the FBI report to the Germans, who passed it on to the Greeks, adding a note of their own: "Please inform us if further investigations are deemed necessary." They never got an answer from Athens.

Nonetheless, Kotsarides was extradited from Germany, tried, convicted, and sentenced to twelve years in prison. The statue of the youth was repatriated in 1998, restored at the National Archaeological Museum of Greece, and went on public display for the first time in an exhibition helping to celebrate the Olympic Games in Athens in the summer of 2004.

So the bronze boy did not get away. A very different story, also involving Marion True and Christoph Leon, had its beginning elsewhere in Germany in February 1992. On the twentieth of that month, the small "OHM" Gallery in Munich was packed with people. It was the opening night, the "*vernissage*," of an exhibition by a promising young Greek painter, Athanassios Seliachas. The son of an Orthodox priest, "Celia," as he was known in artistic circles, had finally managed to hold his first one-man show.

During the evening, and when his mind was obviously on other things, Celia was approached by three strangers—two Greeks and a Serb, people who appeared to have invited themselves to his show. Fourteen years later, he described what happened next.

They enquired about my connections in artistic circles. They told me they had something for sale and were looking for someone who might be interested. There, on the spot, they showed me photographs of what they wanted to sell. Then, on another day, again in the gallery, they brought me the object itself, concealed in one of those boxes they give you to carry away cakes at a pastry shop. The kind that are tied up with ribbon. They took the object out of the box and unraveled the paper it was wrapped in. And there was the most beautiful thing I had ever seen in my life. It was a Macedonian wreath made of solid gold. *Solid gold.* I was so impressed, so shocked I could hardly breath.

They asked if I could suggest someone who might buy the wreath.

The first name that came into my head was Christoph Leon. I had never met him, but I had heard about him and I knew he was in the antiquities business. Later, I found out that they did indeed go to see Leon in Basel but the meeting, I understand, was not a success.

Apparently, Leon was willing to buy the wreath but the amount he offered—200,000 marks, according to Tzallas—was much too low. Celia continued:

So they came back to me in Munich and asked me a second time if I knew anyone else who might be interested. I thought about it and answered that for such a beautiful and important antiquity it was probable that the Getty Museum in Los Angeles might be interested. Again, I found out later that they contacted Marion True.

Marion True was sent photos of the wreath that depicted it in the condition it was found. "I have kept copies of these photographs to this day," Seliachas said. And he showed them to me.

It appears, on this account, and in view of what happened later, that True would not buy from strangers. Did she prefer the security of trading with an established name, an intermediary who could distance her and the museum from the smugglers and/or the tomb robbers? At any rate, the two Greeks and the Serb went back to Christoph Leon who this time doubled his initial offer—to 400,000 marks.

What happened next isn't clear but we do know that Marion True traveled to Switzerland to inspect the wreath, where it was being held in the vault of an unknown bank in Zurich. She saw the wreath in the company of Leon and the Serbian member of the trio who had approached Seliachas. He showed these photographs to me.

Nothing was settled then. True returned to Malibu and wrote to Leon that she refused to buy the golden wreath. Yet the wreath was to prove overpoweringly enticing. Six months later, True changed her mind and decided to propose the wreath's acquisition.

Before she could do that, however, there were certain preliminaries to be complied with. In March 1993, the Getty formally notified the Greek and the Italian authorities of the museum's intention to acquire two objects, a golden wreath and an incomplete archaic kore. They sent photocopies of photographs of both pieces.

The Greek Ministry of Culture responded, saying that it disagreed with the museum's intention to acquire the two artifacts since, in its view, they could only have originated in an illicit excavation. But it added that it was unable to provide any specific details to expand and support its claim. For Greek archaeologists, it was obvious—as it had been obvious to Daniela Rizzo, Gilda Bartoloni, and other Italian archaeologists in regard to *their* antiquities—that such an important and beautiful object, had it been legally excavated, would have been widely published and known to everyone. It followed that the two acquisitions the Getty was planning to make must be dubious.

The Greek Ministry's logic was not enough. On June 10, 1993, the Getty formally acquired the wreath, for $1,150,000 (paid to Christoph Leon), and the Kore, for $3,300,000 (paid to Robin Symes). In the curator's report, prepared for the proposed acquisitions, under the heading referring to provenance, it was written that "the dealer will provide the standard warranties concerning title, export, and import in accordance with the antiquities acquisition policy of the J. P. Getty Museum." Leon was listed as the seller, the previous owner as a "Swiss Collector," and Switzerland was shown as the country of origin. In the warranty it was specifically stated by Leon that "the object was legally exported from its country of origin."

The Getty must have thought it was home-free—nothing happened for four years. Then, toward the end of 1997, Greek Interpol received, from the German police, a file of documents which showed that Greek looters—immigrant workers in Germany—had smuggled the gold wreath out of Greece into Germany and had contacted True and Leon through Athanassios Seliachas (the painter), a permanent Greek resident in Munich. The documents included a signed affidavit that Seliachas had made to the German authorities.

Early in the new year, 1998, the Greek Art Squad asked the Ministry of Culture for help in following up the investigation but the culture ministry vetoed the initiative, confirming in a confidential memorandum (I have a copy of it) that it was then engaged in diplomatic moves with the Getty aimed at securing the return of the wreath. So the police were stood down. The so-called diplomatic initiative, however, never went anywhere and, after a few years, ran into the sand. Diplomacy was tried anew every so often but, by 2005, the wreath and the kore were still in Los Angeles.

In October of that year, an officer of the Greek police, now retired, gave me copies of a set of documents with Seliachas' testimony and the golden wreath case file. Using these documents as a basis, I published a story on the wreath in *Epsilon* magazine.

Meanwhile, without my knowing it, there was a new special prosecutor in the headquarters of the Athens magistrates who read the article and decided to investigate the case. This man, Ioannis Diotis, was in many ways a parallel figure to Paolo Ferri in Italy. He had worked on some very tough cases. In particular, he had served many years in the antiterrorist department and was the man responsible for solving the case of the radical, leftist Greek terrorist group, "November 17," or "17N," as it was known. (The last victim of "17N" was Brigadier Stephen Saunders, defense attaché at the British Embassy in Athens, shot dead on his way to work in June 2000.)

Diotis, fifty-two years old, with a thick gray moustache and a strong voice, was an admirer of Giovanni Falcone, the Sicilian magistrate who was blown up by the mafia in 1992. Diotis began to look into the case of the golden wreath and it was he who realized that the Greek situation paralleled to an extent the situation in Italy—which was making news just then because, a few months before, in May 2005, the verdict against Medici was handed down. Diotis's office was on the second floor of a hundred-year-old neo-classical building inside the compound of the Athens law courts. He began burning the midnight oil, catching up with all the documents that the Greek art squad had amassed in their files.

His first move was to meet Ferri. He and Gligoris traveled to Rome together in January 2006. For four hours they compared notes and exchanged information—about True, Hecht, Medici, Symes, and Christo Michaelides. And they decided to move forward on a cooperative basis. Two months later Gligoris decided to raid Marion True's house at Glyssidia on Paros, in which those eighteen antiquities were found and confiscated. But that is not all they found.

The Greek police are old-fashioned. They rely very little on the surveillance technology the Italians use so much, but get most of their information from "sources" and tip-offs. And, during their raid on Paros, they were approached by a local informer who had something interesting to say about a nearby island and a family who had a vacation home there. The island was called Schinoussa and the family were the Papadimitrious. The informer said he had seen many antiquities "scattered around the yard" of the Papdimitirous' house.

✤

Back in Athens, after "Operation Eclipse," Gligoris moved swiftly. His first move was to check whether any of the Papadimitriou family was legally registered as a collector of antiquities. They were not. So it seemed to Gligoris that a visit to the island might be timely.

It is a six-hour crossing from Piraeus—the port of Athens—to Schinoussa, and the Aegean Sea can be rough. In early April 2006, when Gligoris took his squad to mount the island raid, the sea was as bad as ever, a furious wind sweeping across the deck of the boat like a demon. Most of the men were anxious, preoccupied. One officer usually responsible for naming operations remarked on the wind that was blowing. "Just as the wind is blowing now, Aeolos [the Greek god of the wind] is gonna blow on Schinoussa. If anything is hidden there, it will be blown clear into the open." Thus was born "Operation Aeolos," on April 12, 2006.

By late morning, Gligoris and his men had reached the Saint Basil area of Schinoussa, an enormous private peninsula owned by the Papadimitriou/Michaelides family. At the gate, they informed the watchman that they were there to search the premises. They had with them a local prosecutor and an archaeologist. Before the watchman would admit them through the gate, he insisted on calling Dimitri Papadimitriou, son of Despina and nephew of Christo Michaelides, who was now head of the ship-owning family. The watchman gave the phone to Gligoris, who explained what was happening.

"Captain, do your duty," said Papadimitriou.

The family compound was a narrow peninsula, with the sea visible on both sides. The road passed through an olive grove, then vineyards and storehouses, before the main house was reached. This house, facing south-east to avoid the wind, was a low-built construction, with a central courtyard embraced by the house on three sides, and containing an atrium and a swimming pool. The house had multicolored marble floors set into geometric patterns, not too dissimilar from the floors of the Getty Museum in Malibu. The passageways were set with cobblestone mosaics, winding between water fountains and earthen flasks full of flowers. The side facing the sea was dominated by a colonnade in the Roman villa style.

Scattered around the yard and the atrium, Gligoris and his men noticed dozens of antiquities. There were sphinxes, capitals of pillars, Byzantine tiles, an ancient metal anchor, columns, Roman fountains, Islamic mosaics, and marble lions from Roman times supporting a table made from a slab of Byzantine paving stone. Replicas of ancient sofas and other furniture were set alongside fountains hewn out of the natural bedrock.

Gligoris telephoned his superiors in Athens to report these early discoveries and to request back-up. Then he made another call and activated a second team he had standing by, back at headquarters. He ordered that this second team immediately proceed to search the residence of Despina Papadimitriou in the affluent Athens suburb of Psychico.

The search in Schinoussa took a week. Wherever they looked, they found antiquities—all of them unregistered. Outside the flower house stood two large Egyptian sphinxes made of pink granite. In the basement storeroom of the main house, in front of an array of metal shelves—on which were stored pillows and curtains, baskets and tools—stood a kneeling Venus, a copy of an original by Praxitiles. This Venus had known better times. She had once been exhibited at the Getty (she was featured in the Getty Museum *Journal*) but for reasons unknown had returned to the ownership of Christo and been forgotten. Next to the Venus was a marble face mask, ceiling panels from a Byzantine temple, two small lions, fountains, and architectural fragments from the Roman period. In another basement room, among huge refrigerators and deep-freezers—stacked on a shelf alongside candlesticks and Christmas decorations—were fragments of ancient pottery and a prehistoric obsidian stone blade.

Outside the front entrance to the villa, stacked on wooden pallets, fragments of a seventeenth-century French chapel were found. On the southern tip of the peninsula there was a chapel dedicated to Saint Basil and this too surprised the police and archaeologists. It had been built recently and was almost entirely made up of architectural segments originating from other Byzantine temples. There were bas-relief stone panels, columns, elaborate lintels, capitals, and Byzantine paving and stone masonry acquired from all over the Mediterranean.

Immediately behind, and close by the chapel, was a small grove where the remains of Christo were resting peacefully, next to those of his father, Alexander Votsi Michaelides.

Even the caretaker of the house was found to possess four ancient amphorae fished out of the sea, in his home in the village.

At the same time, in Athens, in Despina Papadimitriou's house in Psychico, Gligoris' second squad were discovering fourteen antiquities, all unregistered. Among them were nine very rare and perfectly restored pieces of Coptic weaving from the fourth-to-sixth centuries, from Egypt, two Mycenean amphorae, a marble head, and a ceramic idol with elephant feet, which the archaeologists rated as very rare, even unique.

In Schinoussa and Psychico, a total of approximately 300 ancient artworks had been discovered, all of which fell under Greek antiquities law. They had a combined value, according to the ministry of Culture, of 980,000 Euros ($1,120,000/£725,000).

The last day of the search on Schinoussa had arrived. Everyone was exhausted after nearly a week of non-stop searching. The police had, they thought, searched everywhere, including the chapel, the flower house, the pigeon house, and three private beaches. They were planning to leave in the afternoon for Athens when one of the crew entered an ironing room in a small storeroom, next to the entrance of the main villa and the caretaker's quarters. On both sides were shelves packed with towels, bed linen and blankets. On the last shelf, meticulously wrapped in bed sheets, four large Byzantine frescoes were found. They were restored but still bore signs of violent removal from a religious monument. Inside a cupboard, between boxes of cutlery, they next came across three cardboard cartons containing hundreds of photographs and some photo albums with imitation leather binding.

At first glance, all the photos depicted extremely valuable antiquities of rare beauty. In another cupboard they also found many scarlet-colored albums with personal photographs of Christo and Symes, making excursions in the Cyclades and showing details of their private life on Schinoussa. Then there were snapshots of excursions made to archaeological sites abroad—Petra, in Jordan, was easily identifiable.

Gligoris looked through the personal photographs, but did not confiscate them. He did, however, take the photographs depicting antiquities. Such was the quality that everybody in his team was under the impression that these photos portrayed artifacts from museums or private collections gathered by Christo and Symes in order to study them. The junior police officers, impatient to get back to Athens, intended to file the albums simply as a "stack of photographs." At that point, however, a more experienced officer, Dimitri Pitikakis, intervened. He insisted all the photographs be numbered on the spot and signed off. Thanks to him, what would have been a serious blunder was avoided.

Operation Aeolos brought havoc to the small island of Schinoussa. The three hundred residents were furious that the bad publicity, coming in spring, would have a negative effect on that summer's tourist trade. Those fears dispersed later in the year when three times the number of usual visitors turned up. But in the first days, with the investigation in full swing, tensions mounted: it was a small, closed community where nothing was kept secret or left without comment.

In the village coffee shop the islanders were divided on the matter, since the Michaelides/Papadimitriou family had bestowed many charities on the local church, the elderly, and the island's school. And they all agreed on one thing: the late Christo Michaelides was "the best lad" in the land. Gentle, polite, and refined, always helpful without making a show of it, he simply loved Schinoussa, and was loved in return by its inhabitants. Christo made a habit of spending his summers on Schinoussa, in the company of Robin Symes. Yet for Symes, there was not a good word from anyone.

The locals remember dozens of Greek celebrities who visited the island, although many foreign visitors and guests arrive anonymously in private yachts. However, the photo albums of Schinoussa portrayed the social entourage of Symes and Christos. Among others, there were dozens of photos of the marriage ceremony from Marion True's wedding in Paros town hall, with the director of the Benaki Museum, Angelos Delivorrias, acting as best man. He remained a close friend for many years and bravely stood up for her after her forced retirement from the Getty. True, with the same dress from the wedding, the bridegroom, and Symes also appeared in the villa on Schinoussa, while other photos show the local archaeologist of Paros, Yannis Kouragios, another close friend of Marion True, carrying a bird in a cage next to Symes. Another shot showed Symes with an assistant operating a large pneumatic drill at work on the base of an ancient capital, later to be found incorporated into the architectural ornament of Saint Basil's chapel.

Yet the most revealing were the photos from the dinner parties on Paros and Schinoussa with Christo, Robin, the collectors Shelby White and Leon Levy, the founder of the museum of ancient cycladic art in Athens, Dolly Goulandris, and many other guests present, mostly Greek and foreign archeologists.

It is something of an overstatement, often heard coming from some Greek officials, that Symes and Michaelides used Schinoussa as a base for trafficking looted antiquities. None of the witnesses interviewed by Gligoris on the island testified to anything like that. On the contrary, the villa on Schinoussa appears to have been used for the *preparation* and *closing* of deals, with important museum curators and private collectors in an idyllic setting. On the small and beautiful Cycladic island, in this huge, luxurious villa, antiquarians, museum directors, collectors, conservationists, scholars, and personalities of the economic and intellectual elite met with top dealers to discuss new deals, acquisitions, and purchases surrounded inevitably by the endless gossip of the world of art.

Christo, according to all existing reports, never appeared in person to market antiquities that originated directly from Greece. These were obtained usually from Italian middlemen such as Giacomo Medici, Gianfranco Becchina, and Nino Savoca. Officers of the Art Squad say they know, through experience, that illegally excavated Greek antiquities usually depart in trucks or commercial containers by road through one of two main routes. The northern route stretches through provinces that were previously parts of Yugoslavia and leads to Munich. This destination is reached often by antiquities originating from Crete, due to the large export of fruit and vegetables to local European markets. According to Greek police, the German route is used basically by smugglers from northern Greece. Every family in every village has a relative or friend that is an immigrant in Germany. Smugglers often use these connections in order to find a buyer and often undertake the task of exporting the artifacts themselves. These operations are usually small scale, confined to people from the same family.

The western route goes through Italy. Trucks cross over on ferries practically without any customs control due to the European common market. They end up in Switzerland, usually in the freeport of Geneva. The Italian route is more professional. Two or three Italian dealers with shady connections purchase looted antiquities from Greece on a big scale and undertake delivery including the illegal exportation. They have middlemen in Greece and decide the purchases through photographs. The Greek looter sends the photos, usually Polaroid, to Italy by post to the dealer. He in turn makes arrangements for delivery and places payment into a bank account drawn up in the name of the smuggler. The only time they are in danger of being exposed is while they are moving the artifacts. However, in a Europe without borders, who could possibly search millions of cargo shipments crossing over countries each year? Ancient artifacts furthermore are not like narcotics to be detected by trained dogs, or like illegal immigrants to be discovered through the use of biodetectors.

Back in Athens, late at night, as a member of the team that searched Schinoussa mentioned the story of how the photo albums were discovered, he remarked:

"They were bound in green-colored synthetic leather and the photos were of a professional standard, suitable even for publication."

"How many of them?" I asked.

"Seventeen, I think."

I felt I had been hit by electricity. In a flash, I thought back to one of my meetings with Peter Watson in London in 2001, when I was investigating the international network smuggling Greek antiquities, for the documentary "The Network." At that time Peter had mentioned a series of visits he had paid to the Papadimitriou lawyers' offices at Lane and Partners, in Bloomsbury Square in London. There, he had seen part of the archive kept by Symes, then in the hands of the Greek family. And he had mentioned seventeen green-colored leather-bound photo albums that contained antiquities handled by Robin and Christo.

The penny dropped. The photos from Schinoussa were probably exact copies of the original London file. If so, they were not photos showing objects in museums, for Symes and Christo to study, but were photos of their *own* objects, showing the most important antiquities to have passed through their business during the 1980s and 1990s, right up until the death of Christo in 1999. I also recalled that a spokesman for the Papadimitriou family, and also a couple of employees from the villa in Schinoussa, had claimed that shortly after Christo's death, Robin Symes and an assistant had arrived at Schinoussa and, in the absence of the Papadimitriou family, destroyed files and inventories which were kept there. "For three days and three nights they were burning documents," all three witnesses specifically reported.* The albums, however, were apparently forgotten in the storeroom of Schinoussa and had escaped destruction. Whether copies or originals, accidentally or with the assistance of Aeolos, the Symes' file of photos—that the Greeks and Italians, the prosecutors and archaeologists were so eagerly searching for—had landed in Gligoris's lap.

I called him and told him what he had.

In November 2006, charges were brought against Marion True, Christoph Leon, the two Greek looters, now named as Georgios Tsatalis and Georgios Kagias, and the Serb middleman, L. J. Kovasevic, for their involvement in the golden wreath case. On December 13, Marion True arrived in Athens to meet with prosecutor Apostolos Zavitsianos. She had been summoned to testify concerning the golden wreath. She asked for a postponement, which she received, and finally testified in January 2007, when she pleaded "not guilty" and submitted a fourteen-page defense. She was released on bail, for $19,500.

---

*This perhaps also explained something that had puzzled Ludovic de Walden, the London lawyer for the Papadimitriou family. It was known that Christo always made notes using the yellow legal pads favored by American law firms. No notes of any kind by Christo, on yellow paper, were ever found among the archives, save for the one sheet written on in Symes's distinctive handwriting (see pp. 254–255). Is this what Symes was burning on Schinoussa?

By then, however, the Getty had announced, in December 2006, that it had agreed to hand over the wreath and the marble kore because, as Michael Brand said, "There was a disturbing element regarding provenance . . ." Among this evidence were Polaroids of the wreath found in Gianfranco Becchina's archive. It seems that Becchina refused to buy the wreath but the Polaroids were a giveaway all the same. Even more important, though, were Seliachas'—the painter's—photographs.

Simultaneously, the Greek prosecutor began an inquiry into the illegal trafficking and sale of the kore. After Marion True, Robin Symes is now being investigated by both the Italian and the Greek authorities. In fact, both the wreath and the kore were returned to Greece in March 2007.

The Papadimitrious were also charged with receiving illegal goods. Despina and her three children, Alexis, Dimitri, and Angeliki all denied the charges, claiming that the seized antiquities belonged to the deceased Christo, and that some of the objects mentioned in the indictment had been bought at Christie's in New York the previous year, and hadn't been unwrapped.

It did not go unnoticed, either by Gligoris and Diotis, by Ferri (who had been given copies), or by Daniela Rizzo that the Symes/Michaelides photographs were professionally made—and displayed antiquities of equal and at times *higher* quality than is shown in either Medici's or Becchina's Polaroid archive. Whereas the main body of the Italians' inventory was made up of vases, supplemented by sculptures, bronzes, and marbles, the Symes archive—besides being huge—is chiefly comprised of marble sculptures, portrait busts, and bronzes of different kinds. The overall quality is breathtaking.

Some of these are shown in the photographic section. More than that, however, we can report that Christos Tsirogiannis, the young Greek archaeologist who accompanied Gligoris on the two raids, has now spent several months examining the Symes photographic record—and has made more than 200 matches between objects handled by him and antiquities in the world's museums and auction houses.

The Schinoussa photo archive contains 2,191 photos of 995 artifacts. All photos were shot by professional photographers except for just four Polaroids. On the reverse of the professional photos there are stamps of the studios, which range from Basel, Switzerland to Kingston-upon-Thames and Bond Street in Britain to Madison Avenue in New York.

Again according to Christos Tsirogiannis, out of the 995 artifacts shown in Symes' archive, 610 are Greco-Roman, 136 are Egyptian and 249 are from the Far East, Syria, Mesopotamia, and Persia.

Symes' photo archive was also examined by the distinguished Greek archaeologist, Professor Giannis Sakellarakis, who says that the photos from Schinoussa portray "meticulously restored artifacts of great artistic significance that could effectively constitute the contents of an entire museum in their own right." He adds: "These antiquities are of great artistic achievement and they cover an extensive spectrum of civilizations and chronological periods dating as far back as the third millennium BC up to early Christian times."

Tsirogiannis agrees that the person responsible for their selection must have an exceptionally keen eye since only significant artifacts were included, the creme de la creme, and no single item proved of inferior quality.

This fact is particularly noticeable where Greek pottery is concerned. In order to amass a collection of such outstanding quality, thousands of artifacts must have been inspected. This could only be the result of extensive looting of at least hundreds—if not thousands—of tombs and temples. Many artifacts appear unrestored in some photos, shown in the condition in which they were discovered, still smeared or encrusted with the remains of various sediments deposited during their prolonged stay in the ground or underwater, further clear indication that they derive from illegal excavations.

Comparing these unrestored antiquities with others that have undergone full restoration, it also becomes evident that the restorers employed by Symes must have been among the best in the field.

The photo archive from Schinoussa is important not only because it provides the best record of (part of) the most important unprovenanced antiquities handled by Symes but also because it allows us in many cases to match these artifacts with Polaroid pictures taken by the looters and also to match the same objects as they surface in the showcases of museums or important private collections. Here, too, as with Medici, the whole chain—from the ground to the great museums and collections—is gradually being exposed.

Here are some examples:

Symes Archive No. 1471, 1475–1483, 1950–1963: *A marble statue of the Goddess Artemis, Hellenistic period.*

In the American magazine *House and Garden* for June 1998, the statue is shown in the living room of a luxury villa belonging to an unnamed couple in Colorado, restored, surrounded by other antiquities—Cycladic idols, Etruscan vases, Egyptian, Greek, and Roman sculptures, and an art deco Eileen Gray lacquered chair. This same statue, of Artemis, matches one from the Medici photos, found in the Geneva Freeport. The statue has dirt on it and is not restored. Five other artifacts shown in the living room of the unnamed collector are also shown in Symes' files from Schinoussa.

This Artemis is, in fact, the same as the one whose photograph was found in the glove compartment of Pasquale Camera's overturned Renault the day he was killed near Monte Cassino. It is the same Artemis as the one Frida Tchacos eventually returned, having tried to mislead Ferri by first returning a fake version (see above, pp. 13–14 and 189–190). Apparently, Frida Tchacos sold the Artemis to an Italian middleman in Japan before the Colorado couple acquired it. Now it is exhibited in a museum in Rome.

Symes Archive No. 243: *A black-figure amphora, Attic workshop by the "Swing painter," dated to ca. 540–530 BC. Side A shows Dionysus flanked by two satyrs in dancing postures. On side B, the divine couple Athena and Hermes are conversing, watched by a mortal.*

This vase, described as "exceptional" by Tsirogiannis, is shown in the Medici archives, depicted in five Polaroids, where the vase appears partially restored, with holes and joins visible, encrusted with dirt, and is placed on a wooden box. The same vase, fully restored, appears in the Goulandris Cycladic Art Museum in Athens (col. No. 716), with no provenance.

Symes Archive No. 715: *Three stone vases.*

According to Professor Sakellarakis, two of these three antiquities are typical Minoan stone vases very similar to others that were found in Messara region of Crete. In the 1960s and 1970s, the Messara region was heavily looted by Greek tomb robbers.

Symes Archive No. 701–709: *A Roman bronze head of a young man.*

These black and white photographs comprise two of the four Polaroids in the Symes archive. On the back of the photos is written: "Photograph of head before clearing [or 'cleaning'?] via R. Symes."

Elsewhere in the archive, there are five photographs (not Polaroids) of the same object after restoration. Beside one photo there is a typed note: "The Minneapolis Institute of Arts, No. L.72.79.5. Lent by the Getty (head b.)"

Symes Archive No. 2205–6: *A marble sculpture, Youth with jumping weights.*

These are also Polaroid pictures. The statue is shown in the process of restoration. The same artifact is in Symes archives No. 1996–2000, semi-restored, and can also be found on the Cleveland Museum of Art website, re-stored, with the indication: "Italy, Rome, mid 1st century, No. 1985.79." No provenance is given. The website underlines that the item is not on display.

Symes Archive No. 1768: *A marble head.*

This object is also shown in the Medici archive, in two Polaroid photo-graphs. The same object was sold in a Sotheby's auction, in New York, sales catalogue, 12 June 2003, page 32–33, No. 30.

Symes Archive No. 1767: *Marble statue of Zeus enthroned.*

In Symes' photographs it is shown before restoration, apparently as it came out of the sea. The same object appears in the Getty museum, No. 92.AA.10. It is described as "Greek, about 100 BC., marble." No prove-nance is given but the museum's website entry reads: "This statuette may have served as a cult statue in a private shrine of a wealthy Greek or Roman home. As the marine incrustations indicate, this statuette spent a long period of time submerged in the sea. The unmarred left side of the sculpture was probably buried in the sand and was thus protected."

All this activity, from "Operation Eclipse" forward, marks a new era in Greece. Following the successes of the Italians in recovering so much ma-terial by targeting the middlemen, the collectors, and the museums—rather than the tomb robbers themselves—the Greeks are now employing a similar strategy. And, because of the proven depredations of the muse-ums in Baghdad and Kabul, following the armed conflicts, there is a new attitude among many Greeks—as among many other nations—toward their own heritage and the damage the illicit market is inflicting.

22

CONCLUSION: $500 MILLION + 100,000

LOOTED TOMBS = CHIPPINDALE'S LAW

D R. CHRISTOPHER CHIPPINDALE is a distinguished archaeologist based at the Museum of Archaeology and Anthropology in Cambridge, England. A large, ebullient man with a laugh that can be heard in Oxford, he was for ten years editor of *Antiquity*, the professional journal for archaeologists founded in 1927, and one of the top publications in its field. He is an authority on early rock art. And with his colleague, Dr. David Gill of Swansea, Wales, he is joint author of probably the most damning academic study of antiquities looting ever to appear.

Published in the *American Journal of Archaeology*, the official record of the Archaeological Institute of America, Chippindale and Gill have shown, in commanding detail, how our understanding of the past is now seriously threatened by the widespread scale of the looting and how it renders the bulk of the ancient objects in the high-profile new collections archaeologically meaningless. In short, their study shows that the whole antiquities business is a mess—a commercial cesspool of greed and vanity founded on loot and filled with deceit at every level.

The technique used by Chippindale and Gill is traditional scholarship: close attention to detail, plus stamina and tenacity in following up paper trails into obscure journals and dusty archives.

In the first place, Chippindale and Gill have calculated that over three selected "seasons," for which more or less complete records were available, the following proportion of antiquities that have turned up for sale at the major auction houses have no declared history—they just "surface":

	DECEMBER 1994 London	MAY 1997 New York	JULY 1997 London
Bonhams	98 percent	No sales	94 percent
Christie's	92 percent	89 percent	86 percent
Sotheby's	79 percent	[67 percent]	73 percent
Overall	89 percent	76 percent	86 percent

New York appears to be not quite as bad as London, and although Bonhams has the highest proportion of unprovenanced antiquities, the objects it sold at that time were much cheaper than at Christie's or Sotheby's (the picture has changed somewhat since, as discussed below).

Of course, one defense that the auction houses traditionally use is that unprovenanced antiquities have not necessarily been illegally excavated and smuggled out of their country of origin. They might have come out of those countries before modern laws were in operation, then held in old collections formed many years ago, or might have been hidden in attics for many years and are now being sold by widows and grandmothers who need to augment their income. The evidence of this book flatly contradicts such a picture.

Chippindale and Gill also argue that this is nonsense. In fact, they go further—and damn it as a "convenient fiction," in effect, a lie that suits the art trade. Looking at five modern collections (the Levy-White, the Fleischman, the George Ortiz, the Italy of the Etruscans exhibition at the Israel Museum in Jerusalem, and The Crossroads of Asia exhibition at the Fitzwilliam Museum in Cambridge, England, in December 1992), they traced each and every one of 569 objects back as far as its provenance would go—and found that only 101 items (18 percent) had ever been in a previous (but not necessarily old) collection. Since there is no doubt that collectors and auction houses would give details of a legitimate provenance if they had one (because it adds to the value of an object if it is licit), this shows that 82 percent of recent collections have no such provenance.

That figure should be put alongside the fact that in four other collections where the calculation was possible, 449 out of 546 objects—82 percent again—had first come to scholars' notice in the past thirty years. This is important because the Archaeological Institute of America has drawn up guidelines that forbid its members from having anything to do with antiquities that have no provenance and have appeared on the market after December 31, 1973.

It is therefore clear from the figures unearthed by Chippindale and Gill that the great majority of fine antiquities that have appeared in the last thirty years have no provenance whatsoever. Once more, the state of the market being what it is, if salesrooms or collectors could prove, for instance, that objects in their sales *had* been in attics before World War II, they would certainly publish that fact. That they do not do so speaks volumes.

Bluntly, the conclusions of this survey are inescapable: Very few antiquities have ever been in an old collection or anyone's attic. Instead, the vast majority of antiquities without a history have been illegally excavated and smuggled—and fairly recently at that.

No less revealing are the "convenient fictions" that auction houses and collectors routinely use to describe where objects come from. In the collections and sales that Chippindale and Gill examined, it turned out that 395 out of 590 artifacts—70 percent—were described in very vague and slippery ways. Some were "said to be" from such-and-such a place, others were "allegedly from" Island X; still others were "believed to be from" City Y, and some were simply labeled "?". As Chippindale and Gill pointedly say: "'Said to be'—by whom, with what motive, on what authority? And how often may 'said to be' stand for 'wanted to be'?"

Even when a place-name is given as a find site, it turns out that many are really euphemisms, phrases that are so vague as to be archaeologically meaningless. Instead of saying "Turkey," dealers use the terms "Anatolia," "Asia Minor," "Black Sea Region," "Ionia," and so forth. A spurious aura of provenance fills space in the catalog, making it appear that the collector's curators, or the sales room catalogers, have earned their fee. But the exercise is nothing more than a charade, an invention generated simply by commercial considerations.

Anyone who doubts that should consider Chippindale and Gill's next move—their most audacious, and also the most difficult for them to follow through. They managed to trace the history of a large number of objects through earlier sales and collections. This involved delving in dusty archives and locating little-known catalogs with a very limited circulation.

But their efforts, it has to be said, were amply repaid and most revealing. What they found was that the provenance of many objects had, in their words, "drifted." More bluntly, these provenances had changed, or been changed, sometimes in the most extraordinary way.

Take, for example, an object in one of the exhibitions they looked at, Art and Culture of the Cyclades, held in Karlsruhe, Germany, in 1976, one of the most important exhibitions ever held in regard to Cycladic antiquities. Number 41 in this exhibition, an abstract figure, was labeled "Provenance unknown." Almost twelve years later, however, in an exhibition held in Richmond, Virginia, in 1987, and entitled Early Cycladic Art in North American Collections, the same object was labeled "Reputedly found on Naxos." How on earth could such information have come to light in the intervening years? The catalog of the 1987 exhibition certainly did not make this clear. Similarly, a marble head, number 177 in the same Karlsruhe exhibition, was also labeled "Provenance unknown," but by the time of the Richmond exhibition it was labeled "Reputedly found on Keros." (And that description is a red flag for any right-thinking archaeologist: Keros is known to have been the site of a major illicit excavation.) Most revealing of all was a group of marble figures—a sitting female figure, two squatting females with children on their backs, plus an animal and a bowl—that were said in the Karlsruhe exhibition to be "from Attica, part of a grave group." By 1987, they were "reputedly from an islet near Porto Raphti." This group was displayed yet again, at an exhibition in 1990 at the Metropolitan Museum of Art in New York, and this time was given the provenance "said to be from Euboea." Finally, in a fourth case, a statuette of a woman, part of the Shelby White and Leon Levy Collection, shown in The Gods Delight: The Human Figure in Classical Bronze exhibition in Cleveland, Ohio, in 1988, had come from "Syria or Lebanon," according to the catalog. By the time the same figure was displayed at the Metropolitan Museum in 1990, it was labeled as "from Egypt."

These are just a few examples, but many more could be given and the implication is plain: The vast majority of these provenances are inventions—more convenient fictions that have been concocted to add to the value of the pieces and hide the fact that they are looted and smuggled.

Having dealt comprehensively with the falsehoods surrounding the provenance of so many of these objects, Chippindale and Gill next turned their spotlight on a number of prestigious museums and other institutions that have exhibited large collections of antiquities in recent years that they must have known had been looted. These institutions were: the Royal Academy in London, the Fitzwilliam Museum in Cambridge, England, the Hermitage in St. Petersburg, and the Metropolitan Museum of Art in New York.

Chippindale and Gill are explicit in their charges. Unlike the British Museum, for example, which is (now) fairly scrupulous in avoiding any association with illicit material of whatever kind, they say that these museums are more concerned with flattering collectors who help them stage glitzy shows and who might bequeath objects to them than they are with upholding the standards of disinterested scholarship. And in so doing, they allow collectors to legitimize their (mainly looted) collections. Scholarship, they insist, is corrupted by curatorial ambition and commercialism.

Let us take the earliest exhibition first. The Glories of the Past show, held at the Metropolitan Museum in New York in 1990, was the title given to an exhibition based on the Shelby White and Leon Levy Collection. Chippindale and Gill found that only 4 percent of this collection had any known provenance. Ninety percent had no provenance whatsoever, and the remaining 6 percent fell into the notorious "said to be" or "probably" categories.

The Crossroads of Asia exhibition at the Fitzwilliam Museum, Cambridge, in 1992, included a collection belonging to a mysterious organization, "A.I.C.," which was never explained but is thought to have been linked to Mr. Neil Kreitman of California, who certainly owned one of the more important objects in the collection in the early 1980s and who took part in the preparation of the show. In this collection, 88 percent of the objects had no history before the exhibition but were legitimized, say Chippindale and Gill, because the Fitzwilliam show also featured artifacts from the British Museum, the Ashmolean, and the Louvre in Paris.

And in the George Ortiz Collection exhibition, In Pursuit of the Absolute, shown at the Royal Academy in London in 1994, 23 percent had no provenance at all, with a further 62 percent made up of "said to be's," "possibly's," and "allegedly's." That left just 15 percent with some sort of provenance, however euphemistic.

The point here is not that there were one or two objects in each of these collections that were illicit but that the vast majority were. They had surfaced recently and had no secure provenance. And in none of these usually prestigious institutions did the scholars turn a hair.

Another aspect of the trade that Chippindale and Gill highlight is the close link between illegally excavated and smuggled goods, on the one hand, and widespread faking, on the other. According to the thermoluminescence laboratory in Oxford, some 40 percent of antiquities sent in for testing "are found to be of modern manufacture." (Fake Cycladic statues can be expertly aged, the story goes, by wrapping in cooked spaghetti.)

In the first place, few collectors appear willing to acknowledge even the possibility that some of the objects in their possession are fake. Much more important, however, is the fact that several unusual categories of Cycladic antiquities are known only from unprovenanced objects. Since it is very difficult to tell forged and real Cycladic figures apart (because the available scientific tests don't work with stone), it is entirely possible that whole areas of this field are forged.

Intellectually, this is a very serious problem. To begin with, in the early years when Cycladic figures became fashionable to collect, all of them were about the length of a forearm. After they became popular in the salesrooms, however, bigger statues began to turn up on the market—which fetched higher prices. But because only two of these have a secure provenance and both were discovered before 1900 (now in the National Museum in Athens), and because science can't tell the fake from the real thing, how can we be sure that *any* of these more recently acquired larger and more expensive statues are real? The answer is: We cannot. The same argument applies to male figures. Where Cycladic figures can be gendered, they are female—no male figure has ever been found with a secure provenance. So once again the *entire category* of male Cycladic figures may be fake.

The high proportion of unprovenanced and recently surfaced antiquities in a collection is one measure of the damage done by the commercially minded salesrooms and unthinking collectors. But Chippindale and Gill are more sophisticated than that. They have studied the unprovenanced objects that have been offered for sale, and acquired by modern collectors, and they have identified at least five ways in which the archaeological contexts of these artifacts are "lost." Taken together, these five forms of loss amount to a powerful indictment of collecting. For without an adequate grounding in knowledge, such collections have no point and may do more harm than good.

One form of loss has already been referred to—that the wide spread of unprovenanced antiquities, allied to the massive jumble of fakes, means that whole categories of object may be spurious. That apart, potentially the most damaging loss to archaeology is the large number of objects that are, or are supposed to be, found in groups. Chippindale and Gill give endless examples of this, but again, two will suffice.

For example, in the George Ortiz Collection, two Corinthian terracottas, a hare and a comast (a dancer), are "said to have been found in the same tomb," allegedly in Etruria. In secure circumstances, this might tell us something about the tomb, or the person buried there. The find spot might help explain the juxtaposition of hare and comast, which on the face of it is not at all an obvious pairing and may have an unusual meaning. But without such knowledge, the whole exercise is futile. In another case, two bronze statuettes of Heracles in the Crossroads of Asia collection shown at the Fitzwilliam Museum in Cambridge are said to have been found together in Afghanistan. They are more valuable if they have been found together, because this is rare. But who can tell if it is true, and in any case what was the significance of two Heracleses being found together? We may never know. There are many examples in auction catalogs of objects said to be found together, but who can prove this? We only have the salesroom's word to go on, and behind them dealers and looters with a commercial interest in these things being found together, so that they fetch more.

The sheer futility of all this is underlined by yet another phenomenon identified by Chippindale and Gill, which they term "wish fulfilment." They give three telling examples in this category. The first is a marble "egg" in the Ortiz Collection that, allegedly, comes from the Cyclades.

A date for this is given as 3200–2100 BC. But without any knowledge of its provenance, or the context in which it was found, this object is actually no more than an egg-shaped pebble that may have been picked up on any of the Greek islands. To call it an "egg," thereby implying intention on the part of the artist and a role for the object, perhaps, in religious practices, is entirely unwarranted, archaeologically speaking. It is no more than a collector's conceit.

Similarly, the Ortiz Collection also contains several clay three-legged chairs that are described as "thrones"—the basis for this being that the objects are Mycenaean and Mycenaeans are known to have constructed objects "that accompanied the deceased to their tombs." But without the context, who is to say they are Mycenaean in the first place and who is to say they are not something entirely different—milking stools, for example? Here again, the wishes of the collector may have taken over from disinterested scholarship.

A third common effect of wish fulfillment is to see all clay and marble figures as "idols," interesting statuettes that played a part in mysterious cults. Usually we do not know that: They may just as easily have been toys—"less interesting," and therefore less valuable. In addition, the very word "idol" is an interpretation; we have no idea whether the figure represents a deity or the deceased, or served some other function. "Idol" is really a vague descriptive term, and no more should be read into it.

In these varied ways, scholarship is devalued and the wishes of the collector—which may have no basis in fact—take precedence over the work of disinterested and better-informed scholars. Bluntly, these may be considered forms of intellectual corruption.

But far and away the best example of the way our understanding of the past has been distorted by the values of the auction houses and by the activities of rich and not-very-knowledgeable collectors (who nonetheless often like to pose as scholars) is the whole concept of Cycladic figures. Already plagued by fakes and copies, the collecting and salesroom framework of "art" is being imposed on an archaeology that may simply have no relation whatsoever to that structure.

The most ludicrous and revealing example of this is the practice, now widespread, of attributing this or that Cycladic figure to this or that "Master." Already we have, for example, sculptures alleged to be by the

"Doumas Master," the "Berlin Master," the "Fitzwilliam Master," and the "Copenhagen Master." In one of Christie's catalogs there is even a reference to a statue as being "in the style of the Schuster Master." Yet "Master" is a concept that was invented to cope with Renaissance art and in so doing contains two important ingredients that simply do not apply to Cycladic art and many other types of antiquities. First, it implies—as was true of the Renaissance—that there *were* masters, artists capable of producing masterpieces in their own distinctive style and good enough to be followed by other, lesser artists. Second, as traditionally used, the qualification of the master was confined to something distinctive about his style when his name wasn't known. As referred to earlier, it was based on the ideas of the Italian connoisseur, Giovanni Morrelli, taken up and developed by Bernard Berenson, who argued that authorship in an unsigned work could be identified by little, unconscious flourishes—the way the drapery was painted, for example, or the treatment of the ears. Thus, in painting we have the "Master of S. Bartholomew," named from a series of panels in Cologne and Munich and where the style suggests the painter was from Utrecht, or the "Master of the Aix Annunciation," named for a triptych now in three places—Aix, Amsterdam, and Rotterdam—in which the style suggests a Flemish artist.

In the case of Cycladic art, however, this academic tradition is corrupted. In the first place, the "Masters" are named not after the defining characteristic of the artist, which sets his work apart, or after an important work by him, which epitomizes his particular skills—instead, they are named after the owner of the object, the collection of which it forms a part, or the museum where the collection is held, the aim being either a commercial one (to suggest how good the sculptor was) or to flatter the owner. Once again, scholarly aims have been corrupted by commercialism. This is not to deny that study of the artistic variations between Cycladic figures is not possible or desirable, or that there are "subgroups" among them, just that the concept of "Master," given the evidence we have (or rather don't have), is intellectually meaningless.

Nor does it make sense, again on the available evidence, to speak of regional styles of Cycladic art, according to the islands (Naxos, Paros, Ios, and so on), since most of the provenances attributing objects to these islands are so flimsy as to be meaningless.

Some statues are said to have "canonical" proportions, presuming Cycladic artists had such a canon in mind, and others are described as "post-canonical," implying a development over time. Again, these ideas are based as much on unprovenanced—and therefore possibly fake—material as on objects that are "archaeologically secure." They imply an understanding of mathematics, in order to achieve these complex canonical proportions, for which there is as yet little evidence. Under the circumstances, any concept of a "canon," or implication of development, is premature, though that might change if more hard evidence about the circumstances of excavation became available.

On top of it all, some of the figures have been discovered with traces of blue or red paint on them, so that we are not even sure what color they originally were and how they were decorated. In such circumstances, how on earth can we judge who was a master and who was not? We do not even know if the current fashion for displaying Cycladic figures—in museums as well as in auction catalogs—in an upright vertical position is correct. They are decorated with elaborate toes pointing down—which suggests the toes were designed to be seen, but this means that the figures could never have stood by themselves. Probably, they should be displayed horizontally, not vertically.

In amassing and collating such detailed evidence, Chippindale and Gill have taken archaeologists' arguments about the damage done by looters much further than they have ever gone before. In particular, and without letting the salesrooms off the hook, they have brought collectors and museums under the spotlight, putting them on notice that their actions are no less to blame than are those of the looters themselves in causing so much damage to our understanding of the past. Collectors such as George Ortiz have often argued that even if their collections contain loot, then at least those objects are better looked after in collections like his and are available for study. Chippindale and Gill expose that for the nonsense it is. In theory, they say, the objects may be available to study; in practice, there is little that can be done when the most interesting aspects of the objects have been lost—in the looting.

The results of their investigation also showed that the loss to knowledge is in fact already far advanced, that far more damage to archaeology has already been done than anyone thought, and that in several areas—

Cycladic objects, Etruscan objects, and West African objects, together with the mixture of looted antiquities, fakes, and convenient fictions abounding—the mess is now completely unacceptable. According to Chippindale and Gill, Cycladic figures tend to be found "in about every tenth grave." This may mean that as many as 12,000 graves have been destroyed to provide the corpus of 1,600 objects currently known (140 figures have been recovered scientifically, at least 1,400 illicitly). This total, they say, represents around sixteen entire cemeteries and 85 percent of the funerary record. In the case of Cycladic art, there may now be nothing left to discover—legally or illegally.

Chippindale and Gill reserve special criticism for the Fitzwilliam Museum in Cambridge. They reveal that before the opening of the Fitzwilliam's exhibition Crossroads of Asia, in 1992, they wrote to its director, Simon Jervis, requesting assurances that the objects in the show were "archaeologically secure." This they felt entitled to do, because although the idea for the show had been mooted before Mr. Jervis took over, the guidelines of the Museums and Galleries Commission of England and Wales state in part: "A museum should not acquire, whether by purchase, gift, bequest or exchange, any work of art or object unless the governing body or responsible officer is satisfied that the museum can acquire a valid title to the specimen in question, and that in particular it has not been acquired in, or exported from, its country of origin (or any intermediate country in which it may have been legally owned) in violation of that country's laws."

No reply was ever received from the Fitzwilliam in answer to this query, or from the Ancient India and Iran Trust that sponsored the exhibition. Later, it emerged from the minutes of various meetings within the Fitzwilliam, when government indemnity was being sought, that the idea for the exhibition had actually been proposed by Neil Kreitman of California, who had put together the collection that was to form the core of the exhibition. This was disingenuous. Everyone in the antiquities field knew by that time that Gandharan sculpture was being looted on a widespread scale. It was unprofessional and irresponsible of the Fitzwilliam to ignore the provenance of this material.

Christopher Chippindale therefore wrote an editorial in *Antiquity* in which he pointed out that the bulk of the objects in that part of the forthcoming exhibition owned by A.I.C. were not secure archaeologically and that 88 percent of them had no provenance whatsoever before the show. The matter was then raised with the ethical committee of the Museums Association, the professional "union" to which most British curators belong, but the committee failed effectively to address the issue. Chippindale and Gill continue: "It seems to us that in allowing the [Crossroads of Asia] exhibition to proceed, the Fitzwilliam has publicly endorsed the display of antiquities which can reasonably be expected to have been looted. They seem to be taking the view that so long as the objects are beautiful it does not matter that the original archaeological context has been lost and can never be recovered. Such a view merely serves to encourage the market and private collectors to continue the destruction." This is another way of saying that collectors are the real looters.

When Chippindale and Gill began their research, they suspected that the proportion of unprovenanced (and therefore, almost certainly looted) antiquities sold at auction—at Bonhams, Christie's, and Sotheby's—was very high. As they delved deeper, however, they found much more than they had bargained for. In particular, they were distressed by the way provenances had been invented, the way museums and collectors "join together" objects, for which there is no evidence that they were ever an ensemble, and the way purpose is attributed to objects for which there is no context. These maneuvers were breathtaking in their audacity. The attribution of "Master" to objects that are in no way deserving of the accolade was another surprise. This intellectual vandalism and indifference to the truth was, to be blunt, shocking.

It was this distress that gave rise to "Chippindale's Law." To begin with, this was intended merely as a wry comment, a despairing joke about the naked cynicism of the trade and certain collectors and rogue museums. Chippindale's Law says, "However bad you feared it would be [so far as antiquities looting and smuggling are concerned], it always turns out worse." It was true about Chippindale and Gill's article in the *American Archaeological Journal,* and as is only too evident from this book, it is true about the world surrounding Giacomo Medici, about the world's rogue museums, the coterie of shameless collectors, leading auction houses, and the raft of deceitful and conspiratorial dealers. The more one discovers about their activities, over the years, the worse the picture revealed becomes. Layers and layers of outer evidence have been peeled away, to excavate a rotten core within, a core that not even its worst critics imagined. It is now time to sum up this core in all its stinking glory.

Let us be frank about the picture revealed during the detective work leading to Medici's trial. It has shown and confirmed the following facts:

- We may begin with the sheer scale of the looting. Medici had close to 4,000 objects in his warehouse in Geneva and photographs relating to another 4,000; Robin Symes had 17,000 objects in his thirty-three warehouses; and the woodcutter, Giuseppe Evangelisti, looted on average a tomb a week, with nine objects being unearthed per tomb. Pasquale Camera's organigram referred to a core of a dozen tombaroli but in the course of his investigations, Paolo Ferri came across hundreds of other names. If each of these were as active as Evangelisti (and why should we doubt it?), then thousands of antiquities were leaving the ground of Italy illegally each week. Ferri, of course, has by no means interviewed—or even become aware of—many other tombaroli. We have left out a lot of names encountered in the documentation. All this means that the scale of the illicit trade is enormous. No one can doubt it now, and the convenient fiction that unprovenanced antiquities have come from some ancient relative's attic must be laid to rest, once and for all. In the separate trial of Raffaele Monticelli, also mentioned in Pasquale Camera's organigram, held in Foggia in 2003, in which the defendant was found guilty and sentenced to four years, it was revealed that some tombaroli receive regular salaries rather than being paid only for their discoveries. For them, looting is a full-time job. According to one academic study, there are now as many Apulian pots in North America as there are in the museums of Italy—another measure of the "achievement" of Medici and those like him.

- Maurizio Pellegrini, Daniela Rizzo, and Paolo Ferri made calculations based on the report of Professors Bartoloni, Colonna, and Zevi, together with the activities of those names identified through Operation Geryon and the interviews with tombaroli such as Casasanta and Evangelisti. They concluded that somewhere in the region of 100,000 tombs have been excavated since Medici and Hecht built up their cordata.

• The tombaroli, as do many "collectors," like to pretend that they "love" antiquities, that they excavate carefully, that they preserve sites. This is false, and everyone concerned knows it. The scandal of the Pompeian frescoes shows that the likes of Medici, and those who supply him, do not care in the slightest about the damage they do. Not even Marion True, or Robin Symes, thought that these frescoes could be sold. No one thought they would be able to get away with displaying such obvious examples of loot—hacking them off the walls of the villa they had adorned had done too much damage to the structures where they had been embedded. The same applies to the capitals stolen from Ostia Antica that were deliberately damaged to "disguise" them. In our television program about Sotheby's and smuggled goods, we had filmed a nighttime "excavation" that had in fact been carried out by means of a mechanical digger—this was hardly a sensitive "dig." It was more like a rape. Pietro Casasanta, the tomb robber who found the ivory head, liked to say that he "excavated" villas and did not "plunder" tombs, yet Daniela Rizzo has had to pick up the pieces more than once after his illegal digs have been discovered. She confirms that Casasanta did enormous damage to the sites he "excavated." In fact, she says that he was too ignorant—archaeologically speaking—to realize the damage he was doing.

• The fiction that the traffic in illicit antiquities concerns unimportant objects has been exploded. The traffic is in fact kept in business by the interest—and demand—from some of the world's leading rogue museums and a number of rogue collectors who are interested only in very important items. The illicit traffic has provided objects for at least five of the so-called great modern collections: those of the Levy-Whites, George Ortiz, the Hunt brothers, Maurice Tempelsman, and Barbara and Lawrence Fleischman. It has also filled several of the world's leading museums. The traffic in illicit antiquities has involved hundreds if not thousands of museum-quality pieces.

The recent research of the Danish scholar Vinnie Nørskov supports—in a statistical way—many of our findings. In her book *Greek Vases in New Contexts* (2002), she concludes that in regard to ancient vases, an "invisible" market has developed. She quotes several instances to show what she means. She reveals, for instance, that the most important vases acquired by museums never appear on the auction market. In fact, the first $1 million price tag for an antiquity at auction wasn't reached until 1988, sixteen years after the trade of the Euphronios krater, by which time at least three antiquities had been sold privately to museums for well beyond that price. From the evidence in this book, we can now say that far more than three antiquities surpassed this figure—there were at least another five and maybe more. Nørskov also concluded that "the vase market has been much larger than the market described through sales catalogues."

She also found two other long-term trends. First, there was a rise in the number of south Italian vases sold at auction, which grew from the beginning of the 1970s and dropped off in the 1990s. This no doubt had something to do with the publication of Dale Trendall's scholarly works on the painters of south Italian vases, but of course it was also *exactly* the time when the Medici cordata was active. After Medici saw—as he put it in his trial—that "beauty pays," he began to be more active, around the time of the Euphronios krater affair, and more concerned with quality. His activities effectively ended when his Freeport warehouse was sealed at the end of 1995. His period of activity and the dominance of south Italian vases sold at auction overlap uncannily.

Nørskov's second point is that since around 1988, the number of vases *resold* on the auction market has snowballed, rocketing from virtually zero to more than 20 percent. There could be many reasons for this, of course, but it is not inconsistent with unscrupulous dealers buying back and reselling vases to launder them and bolster prices.

- It is true that many objects of lesser importance appear at auction, but the antiquities auctions—we now know—serve several specific purposes. Apart from their legitimate function, they exist to "launder" antiquities, so that dealers like Medici can claim that they have bought (what are in fact their own) objects on open sale, providing these objects, therefore, with a spurious provenance. These sales provide a benchmark for value—Medici (and how many others?) bid against themselves at auction to maintain the price of basic objects, against which other values can be calculated. And in offering only relatively run-of-the-mill items, the auctions helped establish the fiction that however lacking in provenance these objects are, the "antiquities trade" concerns only unimportant material.

- But far and away the most serious revelation of the Medici inquiry, and the one that supports the premise of Chippindale's Law more than any other, is the fact that the illicit trade in antiquities *is organized*. It is organized into groups—cordate, teams of people "roped" together—so as to achieve one all-important objective. This is to keep the likes of Medici, an Italian citizen who is responsible for smuggling thousands of ancient artifacts out of Italy, at a distance from the world's major museums, and collectors, so they can deny dealing directly with the underground trade. This is the tactic that in political spin-doctoring is called "deniability." Such deniability is achieved by means of triangulations—indirect routes that camouflage the actual origin of the objects. There is no need to repeat the detail here, except to reaffirm what Judge Muntoni concluded—that this was nothing less than a criminal conspiracy.

- An aspect of this organization is delay. There will be those who object to the trials of Giacomo Medici, Robert Hecht, and Marion True on the grounds that the events concerned all took place many years ago. There are several answers to this. One is that law enforcement agencies can only deal with the material available. Although many archaeologists—such as Chippindale and Gill—have argued for years that the circumstantial evidence all points to the conclusion that the vast majority of unprovenanced antiquities in museums around the world and in almost all the modern collections have been looted, both museums and the trade have resisted this reasoning. Hecht himself has said more than once that without documentary proof, he refuses to accept that the objects he deals in are looted. The evidence of Operation Geryon shows that it required both luck and clever investigation to lay bare the organization surrounding Medici. The documentary proof of the extent of the looting is now there for all to see.

Another answer is that following the landmark ruling in the Frederick Schultz case, in 2002,* antiquities looted from countries that have legislation stipulating that objects in the ground belong to that country are deemed to have been stolen—and under U.S. law, derived from British law, good title can *never* be obtained to stolen goods. So it doesn't matter how long cases take to come to court: Looted antiquities remain looted.

Yet another answer is that investigation on an international level is unwieldy and cumbersome, and therefore takes time. As this book has shown, it can take months, if not years, for questions to foreign nationals to be answered. In such circumstances, it is inevitable that prosecutions will take years to mature. This must now be accepted as a fact of life.

But we must also remember that delay is not exactly anathema to the underground trade. Objects that are held unseen in warehouses for months and years on end are, when they do surface, more difficult to match to clandestine excavations, which may have been discovered in the interim by law enforcement authorities. Before the 2002 decision by the U.S. courts, the illicit trade was often protected by the fact that statutes of limitations would come into force, preventing legal actions from being initiated (a defense that the Metropolitan Museum tried, unsuccessfully, in the case of the Lydian hoard).† As was mentioned in Chapter 15, the acquisition of fragments of vases strings out the process, making it more difficult for countries such as Italy to mount claims for these objects. The very fact that it is necessary to write in this way shows that delay, in and of itself, softens attitudes. Illegal actions of the 1980s, say, are seen as less vivid, less urgent, in some way less wrong than events of a more recent date. A moment's reflection will show that such reasoning cannot be correct. If the underground trade thinks that by delaying it can deflect the interest of law enforcement, then law enforcement agencies must insist on the opposite truth.

*See p. 239.
†See p. 103.

- In an effort to put this whole matter into context, Dr. Ferri calculated that the market price of all the objects mentioned in this book total somewhere in the region of $100 million. This is an impressive sum but still considerably less than the value Robin Symes put on his holdings, which, at $210 million, is more than twice that. According to Ferri, however, Gianfranco Becchina, whose trial will follow that of Marion True and Robert Hecht, may well have been as active as Medici, so that if his trading is taken into account, along with Savoca's, then Ferri calculates that these few names were controlling illicit traffic in antiquities easily worth $500 million—*half a billion dollars*. It is an enormous, underground business.

It is in this sense that Chippindale's Law comes into its own. Over the past thirty years, many archaeologists, policemen, and other law enforcement officials have known—in their bones—that trade in illicit antiquities was rife. But no one has guessed, even for a moment, that this trade is organized at the level it is, or that a number of rogue collectors, and a certain number of rogue museums, have been hand-in-glove with the network that surrounded Medici and, moreover, that these collectors and museums *actively cooperated* in the cordate. This is surely the most worrying revelation of all: that ostensibly honest, well-educated, highly qualified professional people—scholars, some of them—should involve themselves in such dishonest and deceitful practices, in secret and in long-term collaboration with known smugglers, fences, and tomb robbers. Christopher Chippindale is right: However bad you feared this state of affairs was, the truth is worse.

According to Paolo Ferri, it is very unlikely that we will ever again have the level of detail in regard to antiquities looting that we have in the Medici conspiracy. The set of circumstances that gave rise to Operation Geryon, the discovery of the organigram, of the Polaroids and their related correspondence, the leaks from inside Sotheby's by James Hodges—all these are the sort of episodes that are unlikely to occur together again. Furthermore, the publicity associated with the prosecution will surely change attitudes and practices—both above and below ground, as it were. Collecting habits must change, museum acquisitions policies must change, especially in the United States and Japan, and no doubt trade patterns and practices will change (fewer Polaroids, probably), though we shouldn't expect much publicity on that score.

Before we sum up, therefore, we must make it clear that Operation Geryon and its subsequent developments have lifted only one stone in the garden. What is true about the Italian antiquities-looting underworld is equally true in many other areas of the world. In parallel with the inquiries for this book, one of us (Peter Watson) has been involved in a not dissimilar investigation in Greece—with much the same results: widespread looting and not a little violence in the process. Given the other court cases described in Chapters 16 and 17, we can say with some confidence that the predicament facing Italy, Egypt, and Greece is shared by Turkey, Afghanistan, India, Pakistan—and several other countries. In Chapter 16, we described how the actions of the cordate extend to Egypt and Israel. Peter Watson worked undercover in Guatemala and Mexico, and we know that similar looting and smuggling of ancient artifacts is rife there, too, as it is in Peru, where there is even an underground trade in ancient human remains.

The Illicit Antiquities Research Centre, at Cambridge University in England, is the only outfit of its kind in the world. Its researchers have concentrated their activities outside the traditional countries of the Mediterranean, determined to show the worldwide nature of the problem. For example, Neil Brodie has conducted a longitudinal study of the London auction market in Iraqi antiquities, from 1980 through 2005. He has shown that large numbers of unprovenanced antiquities were sold, particularly after the first Gulf war of 1991. He writes: "These unprovenanced antiquities largely disappeared from the London market after UN trade sanctions were imposed through a strong new law in 2003." UN sanctions, so far as antiquities are concerned, were implemented in Britain as Statutory Instrument 1519, which crucially *inverts* the burden of proof that normally applies in a criminal prosecution. That is, it prohibits trade *unless* it is known that the objects left Iraq before 1990—in other words, objects are presumed "guilty" if there is nothing to indicate otherwise. Brodie also notes that large numbers of cuneiform tablets have been offered for sale over the past ten years with a certificate of authenticity and translation provided by one emeritus professor of Assyriology. "Presumably, if a tablet needs authenticating and translating in this way, it is because it has not previously come to the attention of the scholarly community. The alternative explanation that large numbers of previously unseen tablets have begun to surface from forgotten collections is possible, but hardly credible." The Assyriologist concerned, Wilfred Lambert, has admitted that when he authenticates an object, he does not necessarily know its origin "and he suspects that very often the dealers themselves don't know either." Brodie concludes that all this shows that those objects without provenance in the auction catalogs "really don't have one, despite trade protestations to the contrary." No less interesting, Brodie also told us: "It is also clear that through the 1990s Iraqi and Jordanian antiquities were being moved through Amman and London by means of a trading chain very similar to the cordate described here for Italy." The names are known to police forces in the countries concerned.

Brodie has also examined what he calls the "baleful effects" that the commercial market exerts on African heritage. The plundering of Africa's past, he says, is "intimately related" to the demand of Western museums and collectors. He notes the author's comments in a 1960 book, for example, that "African clay sculptures are very delicate, and are rarely to be found in museums." By 1984, all that had changed, probably brought about by an exhibition at the Zurich Kunsthaus in 1970, which sparked "a collecting frenzy." Bura statuettes from Niger were only discovered in 1983, in an official dig. But after a show toured France in the 1990s, wide-scale looting of Niger followed. Many were on sale at the Hamill Gallery in Boston in 2000, together with 44 Nok terra-cottas. Many of these latter came with a thermoluminescence date from the Bortolot Daybreak Corporation. Brodie said, "Bortolot's Web site makes for interesting reading. It claims that before 1993 most Nok terra-cottas appearing on the market were fake, and that genuine objects were usually poorly preserved fragments. Then, in 1993, a consortium of European dealers organized systematic looting of the Nok area, whereupon there was a flood of genuine heads and the fakes all but disappeared." The threat posed to the archaeology of West Africa became so serious that the International Council of Museums felt constrained to publish in May 2000 a "Red List" of African antiquities under imminent threat of looting or theft. Among the eight most threatened types of antiquity were Nok terra-cottas and Bura statuettes. In a mere seventeen years, the latter had gone from being first discovered to an "endangered species."

With his colleague Jenny Doole, Brodie also looked at the collecting of Asian antiquities by American museums. The pattern follows that disclosed in this book—namely, that older, nineteenth-century acquisitions have a much more detailed provenance than those acquired since, say, 1970. In examining the collections of such individuals as Norton Simon in California, Walter C. Mead in Denver, Sherman E. Lee in Cleveland, Avery Brundage in San Francisco, John D. Rockefeller III at the Asia Society in New York, and others, a familiar pattern emerged—the lack of provenance of most of the objects. But there was an additional and more cynical pattern—later collectors knew far less about Asian art than the nineteenth-century and early-twentieth-century collectors. Brundage, for instance, would often leave his objects in storage, unwrapped and apparently uncared for. Yet the researchers found that "Brundage loved being known as an important collector." They also noted, "In the late 1800s and early 1900s there was very little museum expertise available, and often it was the collectors themselves, men like [Ernest] Fenellosa and [A. K.] Coomaraswamy, who were hired to provide it. By the 1950s and 1960s this was no longer the case. 'Asian Art' was a well-established museum specialty with a mature professional structure. The art museum could provide the expertise if the collector could provide the money."

Doole and Brodie then go on to describe one of the consequences of this situation: In 1997, the Metropolitan Museum in New York returned a statue taken from Angkor Wat sometime before 1993; in 1999, the Met returned an eighth-century sculpture stolen in Bihar between 1987 and 1989; in the same year, the Asia Society returned an eleventh-century sandstone relief to a provincial museum in Madhya Pradesh; in 2000, Mrs. Marilyn Alsdorf returned a tenth-century piece that she found to have been stolen in 1967 from a temple in Uttar Pradesh; in 2002, the Honolulu Academy of Arts returned two more statues taken from Angkor Wat.

In a 1925 publication, there were only thirty-nine pieces of Khmer sculpture in U.S. museums. By 1997, what was published of the Alsdorf Collection alone contained thirty-eight archaeological pieces from

Cambodia and Thailand. Moreover, in the 1925 survey, twenty-five were stone heads and five were stone torsos. Of the Alsdorf pieces, three were stone heads and eleven were torsos. Doole and Brodie commented, "Clearly . . . it had become far easier to acquire complete statues."

But probably the most shocking example of what Brodie and Doole call the "Asian Art Affair" (a play on the Asian Art Fair, the trade's high-profile annual jamboree) is the experience of the German photographer Jürgen Schick, who in 1989 produced a book entitled *Die Götter verlassen das Land*, published in English nine years later as *The Gods Are Leaving the Country*. In his book, Schick provided a compelling photographic record of the appalling damage that is being done to the cultural heritage of Nepal as sculpture after sculpture disappears to feed the international market. Schick reports that since 1958, Nepal has lost more than half its Hindu and Buddhist sculpture. This large-scale plunder followed the 1964 Art of Nepal exhibition held at the Asia House in New York. By 1966, the Heeramaneck Collection contained a quantity of Nepalese sculpture, and more was acquired by the Rockefeller and Alsdorf Collections. The Boston, Cleveland, and Metropolitan Museums substantially increased their Nepalese art holdings from the 1970s onward.

Schick had intended to include more photographs in the English edition of the book, but in 1996 they were stolen from his publisher's office in Bangkok, together with the original slides of the German edition. A random theft? Or as Brodie and Doole ask, did the book have someone really rattled?

The theft of Jürgen Schick's photographs, no less than the action of the consortium of European dealers in 1993 in regard to Nok terra-cottas, are actions that underline the central argument of this book: The antiquities underworld is far more determined and far more organized than anyone has ever imagined.

What is the way forward? As we write, Marion True and Robert Hecht are on trial in Italy, charged as Medici was with conspiracy. Proceedings against Gianfranco Becchina are just beginning, and Ferri has it in mind to bring charges against a number of other prominent individuals and institutions. This will be the collective culmination of General Conforti's and Paolo Ferri's efforts over the past decade, and the world will be watching. Will Marion True be the first American curator to be convicted for doing what—one must concede—several other curators have done before her? And will Robert Hecht, after so many close shaves, finally be convicted?

The law will take its course. Meanwhile, the picture revealed in the investigation of Medici now allows us to reach certain conclusions and to make recommendations, given that we now know, *for the first time and with certainty and proof,* how the trade in illicit antiquities really works.

First, let us recall some of the people involved in the events described above. They include: Frederick Schultz, once presidential adviser in the United States and the head of a professional association of dealers; Lawrence Fleischman, once a presidential adviser and a contributor to many good causes; Barbara Fleischman, who was an adviser for President Bill Clinton; Leon Levy, who in many ways had a parallel career to Lawrence Fleischman; Maurice Tempelsman, the companion of Jacqueline Kennedy; Marion True and Dietrich von Bothmer, curators at the Getty and the Metropolitan, respectively; Ashton Hawkins, counsel and vice president of the Metropolitan Museum; George Ortiz, scion of a great family. These are not figures normally associated with a clandestine, underground network. Some of them, such as Shelby White and Leon Levy, have provided funds for archaeologists to publish their excavation reports. And that prompts a conclusion. It is that these individuals have done what they have because they have failed to adjust to the way the world has changed. Over the past thirty years, as was explained in Chapter 2, laws and attitudes and professional practices have evolved. People take cultural heritage issues far more seriously now than in the past, to the point where one can say, with the experience of this book in mind: *It is no longer possible to form a collection of classical antiquities by legitimate means.*

This is not as radical or as unusual as it may seem. It is now extremely difficult to form a first-rate collection of old master paintings, because most of the masterpieces are already in museums and the supply is drying up. The same is beginning to be true of first-rate impressionist paintings, more and more of which are locked away in museums. The experience of artworks looted by the Nazis also throws into relief the problem with looted antiquities. All the major auction houses now routinely screen their sales for paintings that have gaps in their provenance. Provenance is a major headache in the world of painting, and the salesrooms have dealt with it—or tried to—by extending their legal departments. They have taken the legal, administrative, and financial burden on the chin—because of the moral issues raised by the Holocaust. These are just some of the ways the art world, and the art market, are changing. Antiquities is not the only field facing difficult problems.

Therefore, change in regard to collecting antiquities is in the air. That said, we believe that the following specific measures are now necessary as a result of the great damage done to Italian heritage as disclosed in this book. By way of conclusion, we now argue that:

- The world's major auction houses—Bonhams, Christie's, and Sotheby's in particular—should cease selling unprovenanced antiquities. And let us be clear what "unprovenanced" means. These salesrooms should not sell antiquities whose whereabouts *since they were scientifically excavated by reputable archaeologists are not known and properly recorded*. It is no longer acceptable, as the salesrooms have recently begun to do in their catalogs, to say under "Provenance" that this or that antiquity "belonged to the vendor's mother" or that it "was acquired during World War II by an uncle who was an RAF pilot." This is emphatically *not* what archaeologists mean by "provenance," and the auction houses know it. Indeed, this sort of statement makes a mockery of what we now know to be the prevailing scenario—roughly speaking, 80–90 percent of antiquities on the open market are loot. The burden of proof should now be on the vendor to prove that the objects being put up for sale are legitimate, as it is with vendors selling paintings that have gaps in their provenance between 1933 and 1945. Vinnie Nørskov's research in this field shows that Christie's and Sotheby's account for 70 percent of the open market in antiquities (though Bonhams is catching up), and it is up to them to take a lead in this matter. Statutory Instrument 1519 marks a start in this area.

    In relation to auction houses, we mention one last piece of research, a paper given at a conference on the trade in illicit antiquities at Cambridge University, England, in 2001, by Elizabeth Gilgan of Boston University's Archaeology Department. She looked at sixty-six Sotheby's sales of pre-Columbian material in the years either side of 1991, when the government of Guatemala requested an emergency import ban on antiquities from the Petén region of the country into the United States. Until that point, Sotheby's had regularly sold antiquities with a "Petén" provenance, but after that date, sales dropped precipitately. This is what you might expect. However, in parallel with this change, Sotheby's sales saw another one, going in the opposite direction. Antiquities with a "Lowland" provenance ("Lowland" meaning Mayan Lowland, culturally very similar to Petén but wider and less specific, stretching into Mexico, Honduras, and El Salvador), which had been far fewer in Sotheby's sales, suddenly mushroomed, and in effect took the place of Petén objects. Was this another case of "drifting" provenance, and did Sotheby's really not know what was going on? It is time for the auction houses to turn from poacher into gamekeeper.

- The world's museums should not acquire—either permanently or on loan—or display, in any form whatsoever, antiquities whose whereabouts since they were scientifically excavated by reputable archaeologists are not known and properly recorded. At the same time, to help the museums of the New World exhibit some of the wonderful examples of Old World art, we urge the "archaeological countries," as John Walsh called them, to help with long-term loans of their most important and significant antiquities. Anna Maria Moretti, director of the Villa Giulia and today superintendent of archaeology for the Lazio region, has hinted to us that Italy, for one, is prepared to do exactly this. In a recent statement, the Italian Fine Arts Minister, Francesco Rutelli, has spoken of the possibility of long-term loans or exchanges, but only with museums that will "cooperate."

- Museums should not accept private collections at face value. We now know that just because an antiquity has been in a "named" collection, this does not make it legitimate. On the contrary, the evidence shows that without exception, modern collections of antiquities—those formed since World War II—are made up almost entirely of loot. By refusing to accept such collections, museums will be doing an invaluable service to archaeology and to the heritage of ancient civilizations. The long-standing informal policy of "Don't ask, don't tell," of turning a blind eye to the ugly reality underlying unprovenanced antiquities, must end. A clever loan policy by the archaeological countries would help soften the blow.

• Museums should publish full details of how they acquired the objects they do acquire. "Commercial secrecy," we can now see, is in this area too often a smoke screen for unacceptable practices. If dealers want to sell to museums, they should be prepared to have their involvement known. Only in this way can we be certain that acquisitions are above board.

• Although its laws have changed recently, Switzerland—rather than being treated as a place from which antiquities may be legally imported—should be treated with the greatest suspicion. Antiquities that have passed through Switzerland, especially through its Freeports, and have no other scientific provenance, should be looked upon as loot and treated accordingly.

• Italy has recently begun enforcing its laws regarding antiquities looting and smuggling, after a period when its attitude was more lax. (Conforti, remember, was appointed in 1990 to beef up the Carabinieri Art Squad.) Though welcome, the country might have less of a problem if its 1939 law were modernized and brought more into line with, say, Britain's. In the United Kingdom, if someone finds an archaeological object on his or her land, he or she must offer it first to the state, but the state—if it wants the piece—must pay a commercial price. The United Kingdom is not as archaeologically rich as Italy, but the law does seem to make looting and smuggling less attractive.

The case of Giacomo Medici proves the validity of Chippindale's Law. The antiquities underworld is far more organized, far more venal, far more deceitful, involves far more money, does far more damage, concerns many more objects, and corrupts far more people—and far more "respectable," "professional" people—than anyone ever imagined. Bluntly, the situation is much worse than has been envisaged. Yet the world's museums—many of them rogues until now—have it in their power to curtail this unfortunate trade. The fact is that, until now, and as this book has shown, the world's rogue museums have been the real looters. It is the demand for ancient objects that begins with them, that induces collectors to acquire objects they can subsequently donate to museums, either for social advancement or for tax breaks.

Copies of this book are being sent to all the trustees of the world's museums that have dealt in these items. They are perfectly placed to clean up this regrettable business and to staunch the enormous drain of beautiful and important objects out of Italy and elsewhere.

EPILOGUE ON FIFTH AVENUE

IN NOVEMBER 2005, Philippe de Montebello, the director of the Metropolitan Museum in New York, traveled to Rome and met with Giuseppe Proietti, an official of the Italian Ministry of Culture, to discuss the issue of the Euphronios krater and the other objects in his museum that, based on the Medici investigation, the Italians claimed had been looted. After several hours of talks, a prospective agreement was outlined, under which ownership of the objects would pass to the Italian government, but the objects themselves would either remain on display in the Met or be replaced by equally important pieces. The plan had to be approved by the Italian government and the trustees of the museum, and Mr. de Montebello at first said that he found the evidence provided by the Italians "inconclusive." Not long after, however, he changed his tune. On February 2, 2006, the Metropolitan dramatically announced that it would "relinquish ownership" of the vase to the Italian government. More than that, in documents delivered in Rome by the museum's lawyers, the Met pledged to return the Euphronios vase plus another nineteen disputed antiquities—including fifteen pieces of the Morgantina silver and four other ancient vases. The Met also proposed that it keep some of the material on display at least until 2008, after its new antiquities galleries open in Spring 2007.

De Montebello said that the exact timetable of return had not been agreed but that a resolution did not appear far off. He had first said that the museum would consider returning objects only if the Italians could provide "incontrovertible" evidence that the antiquities were illegally taken from the country. Later he conceded that the standard of evidence he had demanded was unrealistic. "I am not a lawyer," he was quoted as saying, "and the word 'incontrovertible' that I used . . . it has been brought to my attention that even in murder cases it is not used." He added that the evidence sent by the Italians in the weeks between the two announcements had satisfied him that there was a "substantial or highly probable" chance that objects were illegally removed. The museum's spokesman, Harold

Holzer, went further. "We have been congratulated on this virtuous act," he said, adding that the museum had decided to move ahead after being confronted with "irrefutable evidence." This evidence, we have been told, included a copy of Hecht's memoir with its two versions of how the Euphronios krater reached the Met. At more or less the same time, Barbara Fleischman resigned from her position as a trustee of the Getty Museum. No reason was given.

All of this is, of course, excellent news for Ferri, Conforti, and the rest of their team. The years of work have been vindicated—and in some style. Quite where these latest developments leave Marion True and Robert Hecht, legally and morally, is much less clear. Their trial in Rome is far from ending, and yet the Getty, the Metropolitan, and the Museum of Fine Arts in Boston—well ahead of any verdict—are returning objects, acquired via True and Hecht, irrespective of the court's decision.

In a sense, these actions—an apparent total climb-down by once-proud institutions—renders the True and Hecht verdicts almost a footnote. The Italians have already convicted the central driving force in the conspiracy—Medici—and he has been sentenced to ten years in jail, although his definitive appeal is still to be heard. Notwithstanding this, various types of archaeological material handled by Medici, Hecht, Becchina, and True have been returned to Italy from America in the past few months—all of it very important. Ferri and Conforti (and Pellegrini, Rizzo, Bartoloni, and the others) have therefore won the argument and the worlds of archaeology, cultural heritage, antiquities collecting, and antiquities trading will never be the same again. There is no going back to the bad old ways now, not so far as museums and would-be reputable collectors of classical antiquities are concerned. The auction market and the trade in New York, London, Paris, Munich, and Switzerland cannot but be affected.

But, despite this positive outcome, there are still some outstanding issues—and they all concern that institution on Fifth Avenue in Manhattan where this great chain of events began.

The first arises from the Metropolitan's claim that, in the negotiations, the Italians will accept that the museum acquired the various artifacts "in good faith." Now that so much important material is being returned to Italy, the authorities there—in a spirit of reconciliation and the desire for a quiet life—might accept this condition. But the rest of us should be in no doubt that such a contention is manifest nonsense. Harold Holzer may claim that he and his colleagues have been congratulated for a "virtuous act," but the facts are that the Metropolitan has hardly behaved well over the past three decades and is now trying to ease out of its responsibilities.

Consider, briefly, first, the following evidence surrounding the acquisition of the Euphronios krater:

- The most damning piece of evidence occurs in Hecht's memoir—the "Medici version" which, we hope we have done enough to show, is the real one. In that version Hecht writes about the day he took the restored krater into the museum. "When I showed [director] Hoving the invoice stating that the krater came from Dikran [Sarrafian], he laughed and said, 'I bet he doesn't exist.'"

- Hoving himself, in his memoirs, *Making the Mummies Dance*, in his chapter on the "Hot Pot," gives three examples of his "good faith" approach. On page 309, after the Met had been offered the vase, Hoving said "I thought I knew where it must have come from. An intact red-figured Greek vase of the early sixth century BC could only have been found in Etruscan territory in Italy, by illegal excavators." He was told by von Bothmer that that was unlikely, but that was Hoving's first reaction. Then, on page 315, when he was told that the krater had come from Beirut, "I tried not to laugh . . . Beirut was the cliché provenance for any smuggled antiquity out of Italy or Turkey . . . I assumed the vase had been illegally dug up in Italy." Finally, there was the episode, described on page 328 of Hoving's book, when he overheard Hecht speaking in Italian on the phone, asking his Rome lawyer "about the tombaroli—how many, their names," and how Hecht laughed when he learned that there were no photographs.

Does this *sound* like someone buying a "Hot Pot" in good faith? There was a lot of laughing all around. In an interview with us, Hoving denied that he had laughed when Hecht had mentioned Dikran Sarrafian's name, and that he had said "I bet he doesn't exist." He pointed out that it was a little late in the proceedings to say such a thing. He added some new information—that about six-to-seven months after the acquisition of the vase was announced, and because the *New York Times* was asking so many questions, the Met sent a private detective to Zurich to talk to dealers and find out as much as they could about the vase. The museum also sent its in-house attorney, Ashton Hawkins, to interview Sarrafian in Beirut. According to Hoving, Hawkins was shown "documentary evidence" that Sarrafian had been paid $900,000 for the vase ($1 million less 10 percent commission). "But of course," said Hoving, "the money could have gone into his account—and then straight out again, back to Bob Hecht for all I know."

This was all very laudable, but it was action *after* the krater had been bought. Hoving's own memoirs, referred to above, and published twenty-one years after the event, seem to confirm that the director, a swashbuckling showman, enjoyed the—shall we say—less straightforward side of his job. Does this aspect of Hoving's personality help explain, at least in part, his reaction to, and treatment of, Oscar Muscarella? This, too, is relevant to the Met's "good faith" in the Euphronios affair.

In early 2006, Muscarella was—like the Krater—still at the Metropolitan Museum in New York. As was mentioned earlier, since his court case with the Metropolitan Museum in the mid–1970s, when he was dismissed three times (despite having tenure) but reinstated, Muscarella has never received a promotion, never received a raise, other than a cost of living increment, and even that stopped in 2000. During that time, he has continued to excavate and has published several monographs and scientific papers.

His latest book, released in 2000, was called *The Lie Became Great: The Forgery of Ancient Near Eastern Cultures.* It is a detailed, scholarly examination of the many fake antiquities that Muscarella believes—controversially—are far more thickly spread around the world's museums than the world's museum authorities are willing to acknowledge (this is what the title of his book means—that museums are reluctant to acknowledge publicly what everyone inside the museum establishment knows to be true). Among the fakes he identified in his book were forty-three in the Metropolitan Museum itself, including two Anatolian figurines, two Sumerian stone statuettes, and a bronze Assyrian charioteer.

He also identified seventeen fakes in the Bible Lands Museum in Jerusalem, seven in the Boston Museum of Fine Arts, twelve in the Cleveland Museum of Arts, thirty-one in the Louvre, eleven in the British Museum, four in Copenhagen, thirty at Christie's, forty-five at Sotheby's, and two in the Levy-White Collection.

Not everyone agrees with Muscarella in his judgments about what is and is not counterfeit. But his scholarship, his attention to detail, his sheer resoluteness, has a certain magnificence. Scholarship is nothing if it is not rigorous.

Except in passing, this is a not a book about Oscar Muscarella. But his status at the Metropolitan Museum in New York does interest us, insofar as his past and continuing misfortunes at that institution are—at least in part—bound up with the Euphronios krater. For what is abundantly clear now, after the discovery of Hecht's memoir, after Conforti's phone taps and raids, after Ferri's interrogations, after Pellegrini's tracking of the paper trail, and after the discovery of so many objects—and fragments of objects—and their inspection by Professors Bartoloni, Colonna, and Zevi in Medici's warehouse, is that Muscarella was absolutely correct to say, in 1973, that the krater had been excavated illegally in Italy. The administration that has been so at odds with him has now come around to his view. It may well be, therefore, that in the aftermath of these revelations, he has a case for damages against the museum because of its treatment of him.

Now consider the Metropolitan Museum's behavior over the other objects they have agreed to return to Italy—the Morgantina silver.

After its acquisition of these items, in the early 1980s, and when the objects first came under scrutiny, the museum said that the silver came originally from Turkey and had been legally imported from Switzerland. But of course the museum had bought the items from Hecht, whose very identity should have been a red flag, even then, given the earlier controversy over the krater. Moreover, after the Met was forced to return the Lydian hoard to Turkey, the Turks did not immediately turn around and demand the Morgantina silver—where, therefore, did the Metropolitan's directors think the silver had originated? For years afterwards, the Met resisted efforts by the Italians to have the silver returned, even going so far, as we have shown, to send Hecht copies of their correspondence with General Conforti. And though the Met eventually allowed Professor Malcolm Bell to examine the silver, it at first refused him access, describing Bell (an internationally recognized and acclaimed archaeologist—like Muscarella) as "biased" and his arguments as "untrustworthy." When he did examine the objects, of course, he discovered what he later said was a mistranslation of one Greek inscription, a name (Eupolemos) that had already been found at Morgantina, and the Met's relevant curators must surely have known this. Once again, one is prompted to ask: does this *sound* like a museum acting in good faith?

Then there is the question of the museum's new antiquities galleries, due to open in Spring 2007. The Met has accepted $20 million from Shelby White for help with these galleries. They are to be called "The Leon Levy and Shelby White Court," according to the museum's internet website. But, as we have shown, the Italians claim that at least nine of the objects in the Levy-White collection were acquired via Medici and, moreover, that the documentation associated with some of these objects reveals that Shelby White and Leon Levy must have known that a good number of their antiquities have left the ground recently and been recently restored (see above, Chapter 9 and the Dossier section). It needs to be shown, therefore, that Leon Levy and Shelby White always acted in good faith. Is it fitting for the Metropolitan's new galleries to be named for them?

The Metropolitan's acquisition of the Euphronios krater remains crucial for one final, basic reason, and here again Hecht's memoir is the starting point. Remember that the "Medici version" of the krater affair was independently corroborated by others, who were not aware of what was in the memoir—such as the fact that a bronze eagle was sold to help provide funds for Medici, confirmed by Robin Symes, and the fact that Peter Wilson at Sotheby's was shown the krater—also confirmed by Symes. Buried in the pages of Hecht's memoir where he is discussing Medici is a phrase he used when speaking about "G.M." at the time that he had bought from him the kylix by Skythos (the one showing an owl between olive branches, and with a youth in the tondo). Hecht said that this deal had been an "eye-opener" for Medici and then added: "He saw that quality had a high premium."

It was a lesson that Medici learned well. During his testimony before Judge Muntoni he conceded: "[U]nfortunately people don't know how to do this business well, Your Honour, believe me, and this has provoked much envy against me. When an object is beautiful, beauty pays . . . Medici Giacomo has understood these things." Medici did indeed learn that quality has a high premium, and he never forgot that "beauty pays."

As Judge Muntoni emphasized, it was only after the Met's acquisition of the Euphronios krater—at what everyone agreed was a sensational price—that the Medici-Hecht cordata took off. It would be going too far to blame the Metropolitan Museum for all of Hecht's and Medici's crimes and misdemeanors, but there is a real sense that in paying so much over the odds for the krater, as many people remarked at the time, the Metropolitan Museum did help establish the climate in which people like Hecht, Medici, and Becchina could flourish, and so it did contribute—without question—toward the creation of the underground network that has been revealed in this book. We are told that the tombaroli of Italy "went crazy" when they heard the price that had been paid for the Euphronios krater and redoubled their efforts to search out whatever loot they could find—just in case. As we now know, several other Euphronios vases surfaced around then. Vinnie Nørskov's study of the postwar market in Greek and south Italian vases supports this. She quotes from an article by the German art critic Christian Herchenröder, titled "Der Antikensammler—von Kenner zum Investor" (The Antiquities Collector—from Connoisseur to Investor). He showed that investment funds specializing in antiquities were first founded in the early 1970s—and Nørskov says this was all due to the high price paid for the Euphronios vase.

One final thought. If the Metropolitan Museum really did acquire the Euphronios vase in good faith, then its current trustees have a fiduciary duty to reclaim the sum spent from the man who misled them and duped them into buying such a flamboyant piece of loot those many years ago. One million dollars, the all-too famous price of the krater, had it been invested instead on the stock market in 1972, would now be worth just under $15 million. Robert Hecht is well into his eighties and, under Italian law, even if found guilty in Rome, is too old to be sent to prison. That may be the least of his worries.

Acknowledgments and Dedication

The main protagonists in this story—Giacomo Medici, Robert Hecht, and Marion True—were each approached by the authors ahead of publication of the hardcover edition. They, and several others who feature in the narrative, either refused cooperation or failed to respond to our approach. The same individuals were contacted again, ahead of publication of this paperback edition. All the above-mentioned names refused cooperation once more, in each case through their attorneys, though other individuals—named at appropriate points in the text—did agree to be interviewed.

This paperback edition contains an additional chapter (Chapter 21: Operation Eclipse) on developments in Greece. In 2004, Nikolas Zirganos, the author, worked with Peter Watson on a Greek television documentary about classical antiquities being smuggled abroad. Watson shared some of his documentation on Symes and Michaelides with Zirganos, who then continued the investigation in Athens.

We would like to thank all those individuals involved in the investigations—in Italy, Switzerland, Greece, Britain, and the United States—who have helped in the research for this book, and without whom it could not have been written. In particular, we would like to acknowledge the help of those who preferred to remain anonymous. This includes the two guards at Melfi Castle, mentioned in Chapter 1, whose names were changed to protect the identity of their families. These are the only names that have been changed.

One individual we can thank by name is General Roberto Conforti, who retired during the course of the investigation. During his career as head of the Carabinieri Art Squad, he built its strength from sixty to 250. This book is dedicated to him.

DOSSIER

Pasquale Camera's handwritten "organigram," found by investigators in Danilo Zicchi's apartment.

Forensic Archaeology in the Freeport

This is a fuller list of the specific comments on particular objects as drawn up by Professor Bartoloni and her colleagues during their inspection of the contents of Corridor 17. Some details are repeated from the main text. Specialist archaeologists are referred to the actual fifty-eight-page report. Among the Medici objects were:

• An iron age *fibula* (ninth century BC) with a stirrup-shaped disk, the arch part covered in a twisted gold thread. The *fibula* is aptly described as the "grandmother" of the safety pin, but its use was rather more dramatic in antiquity, being employed to hold together the drapes in clothing. It became a decorative object in its own right and often identified the social and economic status of the wearer. The stirrup-shaped disk was the end part, where the two pins fitted together, one of the pins usually being curved, unlike modern safety pins. The experts pointed out that this *fibula* was very similar to one legally found in Tarquinia in the necropolis of Poggio dell'Impiccato, which dates from the second half of the ninth century. *Fibulae* like this one were only rarely made in gold.

• Five other *fibulae* were decorated with little ducks, a motif previously found only in Villanovan necropolises in Bologna, Tarquinia, Veio, Capua and Pontecagnano; a sixth *fibula*, decorated with a feline figure, was very similar to one found in the Tomb of the Warrior at Tarquinia.

• Several of the eighth-century BC ceramics in Medici's warehouse were specific to the necropolises of Campania, either from the Sarno Valley or Cuma—that is, they were made there, in antiquity, and nowhere else.

• Three small *amphorae* with knotted handles, two blended *bacellate* (vases decorated in bas-relief), and three ribbed *olle* (a different form of wine pitcher, like a *oinochoe* but with fat handles) with arched cordons (i.e., decorated with ribbing in the shape of arches). These designs were made *exclusively* in the Vulci area, in the eighth and seventh centuries BC, so can only have come from there.

• Thirty-two miniature cups and twenty miniature *olle* were "very similar" to a series of miniature vases (especially *olle*) found on an official dig at Bandinella, Canino, in 1992, after the discovery of an illegal dig.

- Five *kantharoi* with cusped handles (i.e., the handles were embossed with small cones, in a row), and three small *amphorae,* also with cusped handles, all dated to the seventh century BC, "can be easily recognized as coming from Crustumerium," where cups and *amphorae* "became famously cusped." Francesco di Gennaro, inspector of the Archaeological Superintendency for Rome, reported illegal digs in the Marcigliana or Monte del Bufalo area, where the necropolis of Crustumerium is located: "The greater part of information on funereal customs, architectural typologies, local artisan production and imported products, comes from the digs of the largest sepulchre complex known, the one south-east of Monte del Bufalo, where repeated clandestine digs have caused the loss of data which we presume covers half the overall number of burials. . . . The overall number of the plundered sepulchral monuments . . . is now evaluated at not less than one thousand; there is carpet-destruction and plundering of the burials. . . . Archaeological material of unquestionable Crustumerium provenance has recently been seized (for example, in Monte Rotondo near Rome, photographs of objects for sale were circulated in Cerveteri and Ladispoli) but are also exhibited for sale on the American antiquities market where a large quantity of Crustumerium objects is on show in antiquarians' shops in Manhattan. . . ."

- A silver goblet with scale-decoration (i.e., with a fishlike surface): These have "only ever been found" in very high-level tomb dowries in Palestrina, Caere, Veio, or Casal del Fosso.

- A tubular *askos* in laminated bronze (an *askos* is a smaller vase, maybe three inches long, used for oils or perfume and often in the shape of animals), decorated with a rich apparatus of small chains. There is a parallel in "the rich tomb of the Bronze Chariot in Vulci."

- One belt hook with stylized equine *protome*. A *protome* is an embossed face, human or animal. Several similar objects have been found in the Vulci area.

- So-called *impasto* ceramics (what is called "coarseware" in English) of the seventh and sixth centuries BC, similar to those found in southern Lazio or northern Campania at Teano. In recent years illegal digs have been reported around the Liri River, particularly at Teano where a sanctuary suffered "intense clandestine digs."

- Two magnificent painted Etruscan *amphorae*, "in fragments but reconstructable." This was attributed by Dr. Bartoloni and the other experts to the Painter of the Cranes, who was active in Caere in the second quarter of the seventh century BC. Another *amphora*, decorated with two huge fishes in netted squares, and a rare *askos* with a frieze of animals were both by the same Painter of the Cranes.

- One biconic vase, painted in the "white-on-red" technique, had a frieze of small Phoenician palms. A biconic vase is shaped roughly like this, ♦, like two cones, one on top of the other. "White-on-red" simply means that the decoration was white and the ground red. And, say the experts, "this is an excellent example of Cerveteri production," attributable to the "Bottega dell'Urna Calabresi." *Bottega* is Italian for "studio" or an "artist's workshop." In this case then, these biconic vases were in the manner of a well-known example, called the Urna Calabresi, but by different hands, varying slightly from the unknown painter who created the masterpiece in this particular style.

- One *olla*, also painted in "white-on-red" concentric circles, belongs—according to the experts—to the "Bolsena Group" from the Vulci hinterland. A "group" is more diffuse than a *bottega:* The vases are in the same style, but no specific master is known to name the group after, so the group is named for an area, in this case Lake Bolsena, near Vulci.

- Figured Etruscan-Corinthian ceramics (i.e., vases in the Corinthian style, but made in Etruria). The circulation of this class of vase, produced between 630 and 550 BC in southern Etruria, and to some extent in Etruscanized Campania, was limited to Etruria, ancient Lazio, and Campania, with rare sea export into Greek Gallia (southern France), Sardinia, and Carthage (North Africa). In the Medici Geneva seizure,

Etruscan-Corinthian ceramics are present in some numbers, produced by a variety of painters and "botteghe." The most antique is a rare *oinochoe* with a frieze depicting ibexes and is attributable to the Swallows Painter, who was an eastern Greek ceramicist active in Vulci at the beginning of the period of Etruscan-Corinthian ware. "Thus the vase, of modest quality, certainly comes from the Vulci area." Another vase, an *olpe* (a slender wine pitcher with high handles), is attributable to a pupil of the Bearded Sphinx Painter and "would seem to be by the same hand as the *olpe* in the Faina Museum of Orvieto." A third vase, an *oinochoe* with a narrow body, and painted in various colors ("polychrome"), is "probably attributable to the Feoli Painter, a 'second generation' maestro of Vulci ceramic masters, of whom only one other work with the same technique is known."

- One-hundred fifty-three Etrusco-Corinthian *aryballoi* and *alabastra:* ". . . the collection comes from the plundering of about 20–30 room-tombs of southern Etruria (one object still has the remains of an iron nail with which it was attached to a wall of the room)."

- Buccheri: Bucchero ceramics are a form of ceramic invented by the Etruscans and are black inside and out. They are made by firing in an oven with no oxygen. "As is known," say the experts, "they were the 'national' ceramic of the Etruscans," being produced throughout Etruria and Campania from the mid-seventh, through the sixth, to the beginning of the fifth century BC, with an early start in Caere around 675 BC. Their circulation was wider than that of Etrusco-Corinthian ceramics and even slightly touched southern Italy, Sicily, and the Po Valley in the north. In Geneva, Medici had 118 *intact* vases, all of which "appear to have been produced in southern Etruria. . . . With the knowledge we have today, the vast majority of the vases can be judged as coming from the 'botteghe,' active between 675 and 575 BC, of Caere or its cultural area." All were distinguished by graffiti in the form of "small fans" made up of dotted lines. Buccheri have been widely studied and the minute differences in the mineral composition of the clay have been associated with different specific sites. This latest science explains why the experts could be so sure which botteghe these Buccheri came from.

- One large *amphora*, dated to the end of the seventh century BC, with graffiti decorations on the body of two animal friezes, separated by horizontal cordons (rib decoration). This *amphora* is attributable to the same master painter who decorated a similar *amphora* found (legally) in Cerveteri.

- Etruscan imitation Ionic-and-Attic ceramics. Dating to the sixth and fifth centuries BC, the experts considered that all these came from the Vulci "botteghe."

- A number of Etruscan stone sculptures and *stelae* were made of the local volcanic stone, known as *nefro*. In this case, not just the style but the geology proves the sculptures' origin.

- An eastern Greek goblet was "very similar" to one found in the Panatenaica Tomb at Vulci and almost identical to a fragment found in the Sanctuary of Gravisca at Porto di Tarquinia.

- Bronze and iron statues, ornaments, necklaces, and rings—all found in Medici's warehouse—were in a style "particularly associated" with Ascoli Piceno in the central Adriatic region (on the border between the central regions of Marche and Abruzzo).

- Ceramics of Greek production: As the three experts make clear, the Greek colonies of southern Italy and Sicily, together with Etruscan cities, were primary commercial destinations for vases made in Greece—in Athens, Sparta, Euboea, and Corinth. *Amphorae* and perfume *flacons* in particular were traded. However, Etruria was obviously a special area for some reason, because only in Etruria "have objects of exceptional quality been found." Scholars believe that these exceptional objects were sent as examples, as "commercial propaganda," to show what various "botteghe" were capable of, to encourage international trade. This general picture is deduced from two types of evidence.

  First, that the vast majority of museum-quality pieces of these Greek vases have been found in Italy. One example is a famous *olpe*, found at Veio and today in the Villa Giulia Museum in Rome. A second example is the so-called Levy *oinochoe* (of Miletus production, from the ancient Greek colony of Miletus on the Ionian coast in modern-day Turkey), bought in Rome in the nineteenth century and today in the Louvre. Third, the so-called François *krater.* This was made in Athens but found in a tomb at Chiusi in Tuscany and is now in the Museum of Florence. It is a splendid monumental object, with several layers of scenes—wedding processions, battles, and so on.

The second type of evidence lies in the fact that it is also known that certain shapes of vase were produced in Greece but solely for export to Italy or Sicily. For example, the so-called Nolane vases have an Attic shape, but their most important excavation spots have been at Nola, northeast of Naples; Gela, a city founded in the eighth century BC on the southern coast of Sicily by ancient Greek colonists; Capua, situated north of Naples; and Vulci. In fact, statistical studies have shown that out of more than 800 objects known, *only one* has ever been found in Greece itself.

As the experts conclude, "One can without doubt say that the material of the Medici seizure includes an almost complete exemplification of the above-mentioned workshops." In addition, there was in the Medici warehouse a third kind of evidence. In the Freeport, even on vases of a type that *could* have come from Greece, some had "hallmarks." These were inscriptions scratched on the vases *after* their arrival at their destination, for some as yet unknown commercial reason. A seminal study by Alan W. Johnston, *Trademarks on Greek Vases* (1979), which looked at 3,500 vases of this type, concluded, "[U]p till now no vase found in continental Greece . . . bears hallmarks of this kind," which are "basically limited to vases travelling toward the west . . . Etruria, Campania or Sicily." Moreover, the hallmarks are scratched exclusively in the Etruscan alphabet. When you add in the fact that some of these vases were those found wrapped in Italian newspapers, the situation needs little further clarification. Yet more support for an Italian provenance comes from the fact that many of these vases were intact. This all-important detail is almost certainly due to the circumstance that in the Etruscan necropolises, there were entities known as room tombs, which didn't exist in ancient Greece. Almost all vases that have been found intact on legitimate digs have been found in room tombs. Finally, in regard to this matter of ceramics of Greek production, an exhibition held at Florence in 1985 of the dowry (contents) of Tomb 170 of Bufolareccia in Cerveteri, there were four objects on display almost identical to objects found in the Geneva Freeport. For the record, these were a Laconian *krater*, a Laconian *amphora* ("Laconian" refers to material from Laconia, the region of Greece where Sparta was located), an Ionic drinking goblet, and an Attic *amphora* by the Gorgon Painter.

• Not unnaturally, in view of the events described in the Prologue concerning the vase by Euphronios and because the Getty Museum acquired a *kylix* by the same painter, the experts devoted no little attention to objects by famous artists that were found on Medici's premises in Geneva. In particular, they concentrated on Exekias and Euphronios.

As the experts point out, J. D. Beazley, in his 1956 publication, *Attic Black-Figure Vase Painters*—still today a reference book for black-figure ceramics—identified sixteen vases by Exekias, for which the provenance was known, and another six for which the provenance was not known. According to Beazley, thirteen of the vases whose provenance was known came from Etruria—five from Vulci, five from Orvieto, one each from other places in Italy—whereas only three came from other countries (two from Athens, one from France). In the case of Euphronios, in a similar publication drawn up in 1963 by Beazley, *Attic Red-Figure Vase Painters*, there were thirteen vases for which the provenance was known and nine for which it was not known. For those vases of known provenance, nine came from Etruria (two from Cerveteri, two from Vulci, one each from other places), three from Greece, and one from Olbia on the Black Sea.

The experts then add that in the case of Euphronios, there was an exhibition held in 1990–1991, in Arezzo, Paris, and Berlin, in which eighteen vases, or fragments of vases not known to Beazley had come to light (this is not counting the Euphronios vase at the Metropolitan Museum in New York). *Not one of these new vases, or fragments, had any provenance at all.* Of these eighteen, eleven were in U.S. collections or museums, five in Switzerland, and two in Germany. As the experts dryly remark, "Paradoxically, objects which are part of old collections yield far more scientific data than objects of recent purchase."

The role of J. D. Beazley was important in another way, too. His prestige and eye were such that after he produced his books, even people with unprovenanced vases sought him out, because an attribution by Beazley was commercially valuable. At the back of subsequent editions of his book, therefore, Beazley illustrated these unprovenanced vases and gave them attributions. As the experts point out, the fact that Medici had in his possession vases that fall under the aegis of Beazley's publications, but are not *in* it, invites the conclusion that they have been excavated *subsequent* to the appearance of Beazley's books.

- One of the vases in Medici's warehouse was an example of Calcidian vases, which were produced in the Calcidian colony of Rhegion (Reggio Calabria). Its exportation beyond the region, or beyond Sicily, is unknown.

- One of the Laconian vases in Medici's warehouse was a single-handled pitcher, decorated with a red sash between two narrow white lines. This, the experts say, is "particularly comparable" to a vase that was "just like the one we are considering," which was part of the load of an ancient ship that was wrecked off the island of Giglio, off the coast of Tuscany.

This by no means completes the evidence amassed by the three experts. Their report was fifty-eight pages long, tightly spaced, in small print. There were many other cases where they could, for example, recognize the hand of a particular painter, or the style of a particular *bottega*, whose work is known only from sites in Italy, and there were plenty of other cases in which graffiti in the Etruscan alphabet had been scratched on to the vases.

Antiquities in the J. Paul Getty Museum That Are Pictured in the Polaroids Seized in Corridor 17 in Geneva

- A red-figure Attic kylix signed by Douris and a red-figure Attic *kalpis*, attributed to the Kleophrades Painter. Douris (fl c. 500–c. 460 BC) had a long career and produced at least 280 vases, according to Beazley. He had his own school and because his works appear in the works of other painters, it is clear that he was well known and well regarded among his collegues. The Kleophrades Painter flourished between roughly 505 and 475 BC but never signed his works, so he is named after the potter Kleophrades, son of Amasis, a well-known black-figure painter. Kleophrades' signature appears on an exceptionally large red-figure cup in the Bibliothèque Nationale in Paris. A *kalpis* was, like a *hydria*, a water jug but, unlike a *hydria*, tended not to have a neck and shoulders. Among the documentation seized in Geneva were negatives showing these objects on display in the Getty, though they were also shown in Medici's Polaroids, still in fragments. According to Getty records, these objects were bought through Robin Symes.

- Next, there was what was described in the public prosecutor's report as a "mutilated" marble statue of a *kouros* (a statue of a youth). This was acquired by the Getty in June 1993 but was never exhibited "in spite of its being an extremely important object." This statue was found in the photographs seized from Medici, still dirty with earth.

- A male marble head was acquired by the Getty in the late 1980s. This too appears in the negatives seized in Geneva, where the head is shown on display in the Getty Museum. But Pellegrini also discovered an image of the head among the Polaroids, where it was covered in dirt and earth. This object was offered to the Getty by Robin Symes, and from the documentation furnished by the museum, we learn that it arrived in the Getty with light encrustations of a mixture of iron clay and carbonate. These are the disfigurements a statue would acquire over the years while it was in the ground and are, usually, the first things a restorer or museum curator would remove.

- A red-figure Attic *amphora*, decorated with a scene in which the protagonists are fighting over a tripod. This, acquired by the Getty in 1979, was found among the Polaroids at Medici's warehouse in Geneva, pictured as covered with encrustations. According to Getty documentation provided to Ferri, this object was purchased by the museum from Antike Kunst Palladion in Basel, owned by Gianfranco Becchina.

  According to the same documentation, it was originally in the Rycroft Collection in England in 1890. If this object reached the Rycroft Collection in 1890, in a pristine state, it is difficult to see how it could have been photographed, with encrustations, with a Polaroid camera. Can the Getty's information on this be trusted? The acquisition of this vase dates from before the animosity between Medici and Becchina.

- A red-figure Attic *kylix* attributed to Epiktetos was acquired by the Getty in the early 1980s. Epiktetos flourished between 520 and 480 BC, and he was one of the major artists of the first generation of red-figure vase painters. Over 112 vases by him survive, most of which are *kylix* types, though he also painted plates. Valued at $60,000, this *kylix* appears to have been donated to the museum by Michael R. Milken in August 1983 and to have come from the Rycroft Collection in London. (Milken was "the junk bond king," the banker at Drexel Burnham Lambert, a firm that was one of the leaders of the mergers and acquisition mania of the 1980s. He was indicted in 1989, pleaded guilty to one charge of securities fraud, and was jailed for ten years.) Yet here, too, the *kylix* was found among the Polaroids in Medici's warehouse in Geneva, where it is shown as not only dirty but fragmented.

- A Corinthian *olpe*, shown in a photograph in Geneva, on which is written, "Photo sent to the P.G.M. on the 30/12/91."

- A red-figure Attic *phiale* (a shallow dish) signed by Douris, with an inscription by the ceramicist Smikros. This, bearing a graffito in Etruscan letters, was acquired in fragments (see Chapter 9 for more detail).

- A red-figure chalice-*krater*, signed by Syriskos. This was acquired for the Getty as part of the Fleischman Collection (see Chapter 9).

- A red-figure Attic chalice attributed to the Berlin Painter. This too was acquired in fragments over a period of six years (see Chapter 9).

- A Corinthian *olpe* and a three-lobed Corinthian *oinochoe* attributed to the Vatican Painter, purchased from Robin Symes in 1985.

- A mirror with cover, decorated in bas-relief, purchased from Robin Symes and acquired for the Getty as part of the Fleischman Collection (see Chapter 9).

- A polychrome marble *lekanis* (a votive bath), a marble sculpture depicting polychrome griffins, and a marble statue of Apollo with a griffin. Purchased by the Getty as part of the Maurice Tempelsman Collection (see Chapter 9). The Polaroids of these objects, all found in Geneva, all bear the same batch number. These objects are shown in fragments, resting on an Italian newspaper.

- A ceremonial table, with griffins.

- A marble head, a Roman era copy of Polycleitus's Diadoumenos. Polycleitus, along with Myron, Phidias, Lysippus, and Praxiteles, was one of the great classical Greek sculptors. The Diadoumenous, together with the Doryphorus (the ideal human form), was one of his two most famous compositions. This was actually stolen from Venosa, a town not far from Melfi from whose museum the eight vases were stolen, which had triggered off Operation Geryon. The Diadoumenos was returned to Italy. It was acquired by the Getty through the Fleischman Collection (see Chapter 9).

- An Etruscan antefix in the shape of a dancing Menades and Silenus. This was partially burned at some point in the past, and the burning is shown both on the object in the Getty and in the Polaroid photographs seized in Geneva. The antefix was acquired by the museum as part of the Fleischman Collection (see Chapter 9).

- A Roman fresco, a lunette with a mask of Hercules. There was a twin to this among the objects in Medici's warehouse in Geneva. It was acquired by the museum as part of the Fleischman Collection (see Chapter 9).

- A red-figure Apulian bell-*krater* attributed to the Choregos Painter. This, shown in the Medici Polaroids, was sold by Fritz Bürki to the Fleischmans, from whom the Getty acquired it (see Chapter 9).

- A marble statue of Tyche. Acquired by the Fleischmans from Robin Symes, it was then purchased by the Getty as part of their collection (see Chapter 9).

- A small statue of Dionysos with an animal. In the Fleischman Collection.

- A black-figure Attic *amphora* attributed by Dietrich von Bothmer to the Berlin Painter. On one of the seized photographs the following words are visible: "OK con Bo 14/2/91. TUTTA MIA" ("OK with Bo 14/2/91. ALL MINE"). "Bo" here stands for Bob Hecht, as is shown by the fact that the *amphora* had been published in Atlantis Antiquities' catalog, *Greek and Etruscan Art of the Archaic Period* (New York, 1988). The *amphora* was purchased by the Getty Museum with the Fleischman Collection.

- A black-figure Attic *amphora* attributed by von Bothmer to the Three Lines Group (a group whose distinguishing characteristic was a motif of three short lines). It was sold by Bürki to the Fleischmans in 1989 and was acquired by the Getty from them. A note in the Getty files, which they were forced to make available to the Italian public prosecutor, reported that "RG" (Robert Guy, of Princeton) had said that this object had been "*found together with*" another object, still in the possession of "REH" (Robert Emmanuel Hecht) and a vase—a *hydria* by the Würzburg Painter—still in the possession of Robin Symes (italics added). This is a clear sighting of the cordata at work.

- A red-figure Attic *kylix* attributed by Robert Guy to the Nikosthenes Painter. Sold to the Fleischmans by Robin Symes in 1988 and acquired by the Getty from them.

- A Pontic *amphora* by the Tityos Painter. Sold to the Fleischmans by Bürki in 1988 and acquired by the Getty from them.

- A red-figure Attic *amphora*, allegedly from the Rycroft Collection in England (1890), yet shown in the Polaroids seized in Geneva.

- A terra-cotta *askos* of the Clusium group, shaped like a duck. Donated to the Getty by Vasek Polak of Canada, this allegedly came from the S. Schweitzer Collection, dating from 1940. It too appears among the seized Polaroids in Geneva. Clusium, the modern city of Chiusi, near Arezzo in Umbria, was named after Clusius, son of Tyrrhenos, one of the mythical founders of Etruria.

- An Attic Gianiform *kantharos* attributed to the Vatican Class. This was purchased by the Getty from the Royal Athena Galleries in New York.

Antiquities in the Fleischman Collection That Are Pictured in the Polaroids Seized in Corridor 17 in Geneva

- A red-figure Apulian bell-*krater*, bought from Fritz Bürki.

- A marble statue of Tyche, acquired in this instance, according to the documentation, from Robin Symes. The heavily draped female figure is identified as Tyche by her turreted crown, which probably also identified the city she was meant to protect. Once again, this statue is depicted in the photographs seized in Geneva, where it is shown before it had been cleaned of the dirt that was encrusted on it. It was an important object, purchased by the museum from the Fleischmans for $2 million. In antiquity the Greek word *tyche*, meaning chance or fortune, with its inherent mutability, applied to both men and cities. The great centers of Antioch and Alexandria both established cults to the goddess Tyche, but smaller towns would have worshipped her, too.

- A Roman fresco, a lunette showing a mask of Hercules and valued at $95,000, was acquired by the Fleischmans from Bürki. On this occasion, however, the fresco was associated with Medici not because of any photographs, but because, in dimensions, subject matter, and condition, in Ferri's words, it "would appear to be a twin to another fresco" seized in Geneva from Medici. In the catalog of the Passion for Antiquities exhibition, in relation to catalog number 126, the text reads: "The superb illusionism of Second-Style Roman wall painting is brilliantly in evidence in this fragment from the upper zone of a Pompeian wall." It goes on: "The upper portion of the fresco matches precisely the upper portion of a fresco section in the Shelby White and Leon Levy Collection ... and is from the same room as catalogue number 125."

- Catalog number 125 was another fresco fragment, consisting of two rectangular panels and showing landscape scenes bathed in a light blue-green hue. The text says that based on the right-to-left orientation of the shadows on the columns, "this was part of the right-hand wall upon entering the room." These two items recall the frescoes from the Pompeian villa that Pellegrini first encountered when delving into Medici's documentation—they too were of the Second Style (see entry just above).

- There was even more of a paper trail in connection with a black-figure Attic *amphora* attributed by Dietrich von Bothmer to the Berlin Painter 1686 and dated to circa 540 BC. (This painter is called the "Berlin Painter 1686" because his name vase is also in the Berlin Museum and the "1686" refers to the museum acquisition number, to distinguish him from another Berlin Painter, whose name vase is in the same museum.) Depicted on both sides of the vase is one of the twelve labors of Hercules, one of which is the theft of the cattle of Geryon, the triple-bodied warrior, and the legend after which the original investigation of Conforti's Art Squad was named.

    This object appears in the Polaroid photos seized in Geneva, on one of which the following words are visible: "OK con Bo 14/2/91. TUTTA MIA" ("OK with Bo 14/2/91. ALL MINE"). "Bo" here stands for Bob Hecht, as is confirmed by the fact that this *amphora* featured in Hecht's Atlantis Antiquities catalog, entitled *Greek and Etruscan Art of the Archaic Period*, published in New York in 1988. Other documentation confirms that this piece was reassembled by Fritz Bürki in 1988. The *amphora*, valued at $275,000, was then acquired by the Getty with the Fleischman Collection.

- No less revealing was another black-figure *amphora* attributed by von Bothmer to the Three Lines Group (a group whose distinguishing characteristic was a motif of three short lines). This *amphora* can be seen in numerous regular photographs and Polaroids seized from

Medici in Geneva. It was offered to the Getty by the Fleischmans, having been sold to them by Fritz Bürki in June 1989. From other documentation, we find that "RG" (Robert Guy) said that this object had been "found together with" another object with gigantomachia (the revolt of the Giants against the Gods, and their consequent slaughter, a familiar theme in classical and Hellenistic art) that was still in the possession of "REH" (Robert Emmanuel Hecht), and a third vase, a *hydria* of the Würzburg painter, "still in the possession of" Robin Symes. How did Guy know this? Here, plainly, more triangulations are in operation, or in the process of beginning. This is a clear sighting of the cordata.

- A separate vase, a red-figure Attic *kylix*, attributed by Robert Guy to the Nikosthenes Painter, is also seen in the Polaroids seized in Geneva; it then became part of the Fleischman Collection, sold to them through Symes in 1988.

- In the *same* Polaroid as the Attic *kylix* was a Pontic *amphora* by the Tityos Painter, seen with prominent encrustations but also in another photograph after it has been restored. This amphora, dated to 530–510 BC and showing the scenes of Medusa's death, reached the Fleischmans through Bürki in 1988, valued at $400,000. It was acquired by the Getty with the *kylix*.

- A red-figure Apulian bell-*krater* was seen in the Medici Polaroids. By the time it reached the Fleischmans, it had been attributed (by A. D. [Dale] Trendall) to the Choregos Painter and dated to circa 380 B.C. This was different from the other vases in that it was a "comic" vase. Rather than depicting a scene from everyday life or from mythology, it showed a scene from a *phylax* play, a type of farcical comedy that was widely performed in southern Italy during the fourth and third centuries BC. The action takes place on a wooden stage, with the grain of the wood being indicated. At stage-left there is a door and steps lead down off the boards. There are a number of characters on the stage itself, two indicated by an inscription that describes them as "*choregos*." This meaning is not certain. It could mean "leaders of the chorus," but they could also be "backers of the play." The *krater* was important because of its rarity and because it was more or less complete. It has been published several times in important reference works on Greek vases. In fact this was the name-vase for the Choregos Painter, meaning it was the object used—by Trendall—to name this artist, whose work is known from a few other examples around the world. The Fleischmans acquired the *krater* from Fritz Bürki and when the Getty bought it, the vase was valued at $185,000, yet another example of the fact that Medici dealt not in everyday dross but in very important objects. Did the Fleischmans *never* ask themselves where Fritz Bürki and Robin Symes got these objects?

- The same pattern is also evident with a small statue of Dionysus, accompanied by an animal. It formed part of the Fleischman Collection and, again, is depicted in the photographs seized in Geneva.

Antiquities in the Levy-White Collection Shown in the Polaroids Seized in Corridor 17 in Geneva

- A small *kouros* statue in bronze, published on page 106, number 87 of the Levy-White catalog. "This appears in three Polaroid photos and in about ten [regular] photographs in which the small bronze clearly appears still dirty with earth."

- A Calcidian *amphora*, number 102 in the catalog, published on page 134, also appears among many seized photographs, where it is shown before proper restoration, with many gaps between the fragments.

- A Panathenaic *amphora*, attributed to the Louvre Painter F6,* number 104 in the Levy-White catalog, appears in a Polaroid in one of the albums Medici kept. In the Polaroids, the *amphora* is broken and dirty with earth. In two other photographs, in a second album, it is shown as restored. Pellegrini also traced this *amphora* as being put up for sale at Sotheby's in London, on July 17, 1985, Lot 313.

*See the explanation for this above, p. 373.

- A black-figure Attic *amphora* attributed to the Bucci Painter (540–530 BC) was number 106 in the Levy-White Collection. This too appears in the seized photographs, and it too was sold at Sotheby's in London, this time on December 9, 1985—the very sale that Brian Cook of the British Museum had warned Peter Watson about. This is actually the vase that the British Museum would have bid for, had it had a proper provenance.

- Another black-figure Attic *amphora*, this time attributed to the Medea Painter Group and dated to 520 BC, number 107 in the Levy-White Collection, is depicted in four seized Polaroid photographs.

- A whole series of seized photographs show dozens of fragments appertaining to a *psykter*, "an important black-figure object," published by von Bothmer in the catalog of the Levy-White Collection, page 149. The object in the seized photographs is completely fragmented and pictured on a kitchen tablecloth. In the Levy-White catalog it is of course totally restored but, as is evident from the motifs, it is undoubtedly the same object.

- A chalice-*krater* attributed to the Eucharides Painter (490–480 BC), showing Zeus, Ganymede, Hercules, and Iolaos, with an Etruscan inscription under the foot. This, number 117 in the Levy-White Collection, appears in fragments in the seized photographs.

- Pellegrini's report draws particular attention to two Caeretan *hydrie* (water storage vases from Cerveteri). It is especially interesting that these two vases were used to explain an article in the journal *Greek Vases in the J. Paul Getty Museum* (vol. 6 [2000]). The two vases in the Levy-White Collection were very distinctive—one showed a panther and a lioness attacking a mule, and the other showed Ulysses and his companions fleeing from Polyphemus's cavern (Polyphemus was the one-eyed giant in Homer's *Odyssey* who refused hospitality to Ulysses and his companions). Both these vases were shown in the seized photographs, where they are both broken and in fragments, with sizable gaps. In this case, however, the photographs also consisted of a number of enlargements, showing the fragments close up. What struck Pellegrini was that in the Getty article, discussing their construction and so forth, various drawings of the vases were used, and these show the vases with the original break lines *as revealed in the seized photographs*. In other words, Peggy Sanders, who made these drawings, must have seen the vases either in the stages of restoration, or she must have seen the photographs that were eventually seized.

Also, in connection with at least one of these vases, the seized documentation included correspondence between the Levy-Whites (in fact the curator of their collection) and a Dutch authority on Greek vases, Professor Jaap M. Hemelrijk, of Wanneperveen in Holland. Professor Hemelrijk was interested in publishing the *hydrie* and in the course of his letter asked if he might include the photos (which, from his phrasing, he had obviously seen) "taken before restoration of the vase." Alongside this, someone has written in hand: "Aboutaam?" The date on this letter is May 16, 1995, just over a year after the Phoenix Fine Art invoice to the Levy-Whites. In other words, it was obvious to everyone that these *hydrie* had only recently been put together.

Maurizio Pellegrini's List of Objects
Seized in Corridor 17 in Geneva That Had Been "Laundered"
Through Sotheby's in London

1. A terra-cotta head, sent to Sotheby's by Editions Services on March 2, 1990, number 44 on the consignment note. This was taken in by Sotheby's with the property number 1012763 and was Lot 344 in the company's antiquities sales on May 31, 1990. It was sold on that day for £550.

2. A Nolan *amphora*, originally sent to Sotheby's by Editions Services on March 2, 1990, was number 24 on the consignment note. This was taken in by Sotheby's with the property number 1012763 and was Lot 125 in its antiquities sale held on December 8, 1994, when it sold for £6,000.

3. An Apulian "mascheroni" *krater* (with two *protomi*, one of Medea) was sent to Sotheby's by Editions Services on September 3, 1991,

number 1 on the consignment note. It was taken in by Sotheby's with the property number 1037837 and was Lot 161 in its antiquities sale held on December 8, 1994, when it sold for £11,000.

4. A Gnathian-style *hydria* was sent to Sotheby's by Editions Services on September 13, 1989, number 25 on the consignment note. This was taken in by Sotheby's with the property number 1002611 and was Lot 295 in its antiquities sale of December 8, 1994, when it sold for £1,200. (This was the object that first alerted Pellegrini to the laundering process.)

5. Four Apulian terra-cotta vases were sent to Sotheby's by Editions Services on March 2, 1990, numbers 51 and 57 on the consignment note. They were taken in by Sotheby's with the property number 1012763, and were Lot 319 in its antiquities sale of December 8, 1994, when they sold for £1,100.

6. Two Apulian terra-cotta vases were sent to Sotheby's by Editions Services on March 2, 1990, numbers 10 and 36 on the consignment note. They were taken in by Sotheby's with the property number 1012673 and were Lot 317 in its antiquities sale held on December 8, 1994, when they sold for £600.

7. A marble torso was sent to Sotheby's by Editions Services on April 24, 1990, number 43 on the consignment note. It was taken in by Sotheby's with the property number 1016305 and was Lot 287 in its antiquities sale held on December 8, 1994, when it sold for £2,000.

8. An Etruscan Corinthian *alabastron* was sent to Sotheby's by Editions Services on March 2, 1990, number 43 on the consignment note. It was taken in by Sotheby's with the property number 1012763 and was Lot 350 in its sale of antiquities held on May 31, 1990, when it sold for £950.

9. An *impasto* biconic vase was sent to Sotheby's by Editions Services on April 24, 1990, number 9 on the consignment note. It was taken in

by Sotheby's with the property number 1002611 and was Lot 498 in its antiquities sale held on July 9, 1990, when it sold for £1,700.

10. A marble statue was sent to Sotheby's by Editions Services on September 13, 1989, numbers 35–37 on the consignment note. It was taken in by Sotheby's with the property number 1002611 and was Lot 480 in its antiquities sale held on July 9, 1990, when it sold for £1,400.

11. An Apulian *oinochoe* was sent to Sotheby's by Editions Services on September 5, 1990, number 56 on the consignment note. It was taken in by Sotheby's with the property number 1023190 and was Lot 300 in its antiquities sale held on December 8, 1994, when it sold for £2,200.

12. A terra-cotta head was sent to Sotheby's by Editions Services on September 13, 1989, number 50 in the consignment note. It was taken in by Sotheby's with the property number 1002611 and was Lot 100 in its antiquities sale held on December 11, 1989, when it sold for £2,200.

13. Four Teano ceramic vases were sent to Sotheby's by Editions Services on September 3, 1991, number 12 on the consignment note. They were taken in by Sotheby's with the property number 1037837 and were Lot 312 in its antiquities sale held on December 8, 1994, when they sold for £2,400.

14. Two terra-cotta heads were sent to Sotheby's by Editions Services on September 5, 1990, number 20 on the consignment note. They were taken in by Sotheby's with the property number 1023190 and were Lot 235 in its antiquities sale held on December 8, 1994, when they sold for £1,400.

15. A red-figure Attic *kylix* was sent to Sotheby's by Editions Services on March 2, 1990, number 17 on the consignment note. It was taken in by Sotheby's with the property number 1012763 and was Lot 228 in its antiquities sale held on December 8, 1994, when it sold for £1,800.

16. An Apulian ceramic *thymiaterion* (candelabrum) was sent to Sotheby's by Editions Services on September 5, 1990, number 47 on the consignment note. It was taken into Sotheby's with the property number 1023190 and was Lot 313 in its antiquities sale held on December 8, 1994, when it sold for £750.

17. A black-figure Attic *kylix* was sent to Sotheby's by Editions Services on April 24, 1990, number 17 on the consignment note. It was taken into Sotheby's with the property number 1016305 and was Lot 271 in its sale of antiquities held on December 8, 1994, when it sold for £1,100.

18. A black-figure Attic *oinochoe* was sent to Sotheby's by Editions Services on April 24, 1990, number 37 on the consignment note. It was taken into Sotheby's with the property number 1016305 and was Lot 232 in its sale of antiquities held on July 9, 1990, when it sold for £4,200.

19. Two Apulian vases and a bronze were sent to Sotheby's by Editions Services on September 3, 1991, number 16 in the consignment note. They were taken into Sotheby's with the property number 1037837 and comprised Lot 305 in its antiquities sale of December 8, 1994, when they sold for £1,500.

20. A black-figure Attic *amphora* was sent to Sotheby's by Editions Services. It was taken into Sotheby's under the account number 216521 and was Lot 283 in its antiquities sale held on December 14, 1987, when it sold for £17,000.

Notes

Prologue

1. The Met had already incurred the wrath of many archaeologists because, at more or less the same time, the museum had announced it was selling off—"de-accessioning," in the jargon—a collection of very rare ancient coins. These coins, about 11,000 of them, had been on loan to the American Numismatic Society, where for several decades they had formed a library for historians of art and architecture. For example, the coins were embossed with the only surviving portrayals of many ancient temples, rulers, and rites, and their dates offered important corroboration for historical events. However, for Thomas Hoving, the buccaneering director of the Met, and for Dietrich von Bothmer, the curator in the Greek and Roman Department, a magnificent vase was a much more desirable ("sexy") object to display in the museum. The sale of the coins would help defray the cost of buying the krater.
2. The source for this statement was Stuart Silver, head of the Design Department at the Met.

Chapter Two

1. Here is a little background. In the mid–1980s, one of us (Peter Watson) had been working as a writer on the *Observer* newspaper in London. A couple of times a year, Watson would have lunch with Brian Cook, the distinguished keeper in the Department of Greek and Roman Antiquities at the British Museum. In 1985, he met Watson in his office overlooking the main gates of the museum on Great Russell Street. That day, he had on his desk the catalog for the forthcoming sale of antiquities at Sotheby's—then about two weeks off. He pushed the catalog across his desk. "There," he said softly, "there's a story for you. Sotheby's is selling a whole batch of smuggled antiquities."

    He explained what he meant, and how he could be so sure. The sale included a dozen Apulian vases. Most people know these vases from museums: They usually have a black background with clear-cut, finely drawn, brownish-red figures on them and white filigree decoration. Apulia, modern Puglia, is a region of southern Italy (the "heel" in Italy's "boot"), the capital of which is Foggia, which was once part of greater Greece, or Magna Graecia. (The Melfi vases were Apulian vases.) Cook explained that the important point to grasp was that the world of Apulian vases is, in effect, a closed world, in the sense that every legally excavated vase—and some 6,000 are known to scholars—had been listed in a three-volume catalog compiled by Professor Dale Trendall and updated, to 1983, by Professor Alexander Cambitoglou. Between 1983 and the date of Watson's meeting with Cook, any other legally excavated vase would have been published in one of a small number of professional journals. Cook was familiar with these journals, he said, and none of the vases for sale at Sotheby's had been published there, or in Trendall-Cambitoglou. By definition, therefore, these vases had been illegally excavated and smuggled out of Italy.

"One or two might have been missed by Trendall or Cambitoglou," said Cook, "but not the large numbers we are now seeing in the salesrooms." Some of the vases in the Sotheby's sale were very important, he added, and there was one in particular, estimated at £60,000 in the catalog, that the British Museum would dearly have loved to acquire. But the museum considered the sale unethical and so would not be bidding for the vase. Instead, the trustees wanted such sales stopped and after due consideration had authorized Cook to speak to the press.

As Watson left the museum, Cook accompanied him part of the way, to where the museum's own Apulian vases were displayed. There he underlined how important these vases are. As general decoration they often show scenes from mythology, theater, the luxurious life of the elite, and some even make general political or sociological points. Besides being sometimes very beautiful, they are therefore valuable historical documents in themselves. Moreover, what they depict is very often related to where they are buried. Thus, if vases are illegally excavated and then smuggled abroad, important details are invariably lost to study. So the clandestine trade is more than a contravention of Italian law; it is a sad and significant loss to scholarship and our understanding of the classical world.

In addition to the Apulian vases, Hodges had documentation that concerned two specific antiquities. These were, first, a statue of the seventh-century BC Egyptian pharaoh Psammetichus. The documents showed that this was already in London when it was offered to Sotheby's to sell, but that it was in Britain illegally, because it had been smuggled out of Italy, from Rome. It became Hodges's job to export it to Switzerland and then reimport it—legally, as it were—from there. The reason for this roundabout subterfuge was that, should the statue have become the subject of any action by the Italian authorities, Sotheby's wanted to show that, so far as it was concerned, the paperwork was in order and showed that the statue had come from Switzerland—quite legally, because there were no restrictions on selling material imported from there. The paperwork that Hodges had, and leaked to us, showed that Sotheby's staff were well aware that the statue had been illegally exported from Rome and exchanges in the documentation outlined in detail how they set about overcoming this problem.

The second object for which Hodges provided the paperwork concerned a statue of another Egyptian deity, Sekhmet, the Lion Goddess, which Felicity Nicholson, the director of the Antiquities Department in London, had seen in Genoa and wanted to sell in London, where it would fetch a much higher price. This meant smuggling the statue out of Italy. On this occasion the documentation showed that she had persuaded a close friend and colleague, the London dealer Robin Symes, to actually carry out and oversee the smuggling, in return for a share of the profits when the Lion Goddess was sold. Symes did as she asked but, ironically, when the statue reached London, and then New York, ahead of being auctioned, where it was lit in order to be properly photographed, it was shown up as a fake. Symes's expenses therefore had to be reimbursed, which is how the matter generated so much internal Sotheby's documentation, paperwork that Hodges stole. Hodges' documents also identified a Mr. V. Ghiya, who was operating in much the same way out of India, via intermediary companies in Switzerland, who sold via Sotheby's.

Chapter Eight

1. These objects are important enough to feature in Mario Cristofani's book *Etruria e Lazio arcaico, Atti dell'incontro di studio (Archaic Etruria and Lazio: Documents of the Study Meeting)*, published in 1986 (p. 155 ff.). Mario Cristofani was a distinguished Etruscologist. In fact, it was Cristofani who excavated the temple dedicated to Hercules at Cerveteri in the early 1990s (see p. 202 and 384).

2. The first was a skyphos by the Trittolemos Painter, showing Menelaus and Helen at the conquest of Troy, which was sold to the museum in 1970 by Nikolas Koutoulakis. The second was an Attic kylix, showing a blacksmith sitting at the anvil, acquired from Robin Symes in 1980. The third acquisition was the most important and took place in 1983. This involved a group of twenty-one Apulian vases all coming from the same tomb. The photographs in Medici's warehouse didn't show all the vases, however, but just four of them in fragments, lying on the floor. In this case there were three series of Polaroids—one of fifteen photographs, another of six, and a third of two—that show the vases in various stages of restoration, the most important of which was a krater by the Darius Painter. Later investigation by Ferri and Pellegrini unveiled the manner in which the Berlin museum had been "tricked" into buying these objects. These maneuvers are described in Chap. 12.

Chapter Ten

1. There is further exploration in Chap. 12 of the cumbersome nature of international letters rogatory. This is the mechanism whereby law enforcement authorities in one country can officially pursue investigations in another. At the best of times, they are crude, ponderous instruments. On top of that, however, clever lawyers exploit the sheer slowness of the procedure. Knowing that a rogatory is in the works but may take months to worm its way through the system, the prudent lawyer *volunteers* to give information. This may seem surprising, but it has one crucial advantage. If a party—such as Sotheby's or the Getty, say—volunteers information, the other side is likely to accept. An investigating prosecutor, such as Dr. Ferri, will agree because it speeds up the procedure and prevents the investigation from running out of time, going beyond any statutes of limitation that may be looming. The advantage for parties being investigated is that by volunteering information, *they do not have to provide all relevant details, nor do they subject themselves to the pre-trial process of "discovery," under which they can be subpoenaed, compelled to produce all relevant documentation.* In other words, by submitting documentation voluntarily, a party can appear to be cooperating willingly with an investigation, while at the same time legally holding back certain sensitive material. This is always difficult to prove, of course, but readers may judge for themselves.

Chapter Twelve

1. That Hecht supplied other important museums with illicit material is also indicated: "My friends were loyal during this period and brought me such fine objects as the Attic r/f kylix [now in Munich] by the Elpinidos Painter with Theseus binding the rascal Sinis to a tree."

2. In a magazine article published in July 2001, Hoving added that he had bumped into Hecht the previous December, at the opening of the Hermitage Rooms in London's Somerset House, when he asked him "directly" if he had switched Sarrafian's documents on to the Met's vase. "He turned his face to the side after looking at me intently and said, 'Of course.'"

3. Perhaps the most interesting client of Summa and NFA was Gordon McLeudon of Dallas, Texas, whose father was the owner of some newspapers and a television station. "Gordon purchased fragments of Greek vases, Greek amber figurines and beads, Roman marble portraits and donated them to the Getty Museum with the connivance of Jiri Frel for an exaggerated appraisal for a tax write off. Some of the amber beads worth $5 to $25 were appraised $150 etc. It is no surprise that the IRA [Internal Revenue Administration] ordered a re-appraisal of Gordon McLeudon's gifts. Apparently Frel made the appraisal on the stationery of Royal Athena Gallery and forged the signature of J. E. [Jerome Eisenberg], the owner."

Chapter Thirteen

1. The Morgantina Venus is considered to be one of the most important objects in the Getty, and Italy has been trying to get it back for years. It is a life-size statue of Venus/Aphrodite, circa 420 BC, dressed in clinging drapery that both conceals and reveals the form of the body underneath. Opinion on the piece has ranged at various times from characterizing it as very beautiful to "scandalous." There is also a dispute as to whether the head belongs with the rest of the body. Three heads are known to have been excavated by a tombarolo at Aidone, part of Morgantina. Two of them reached the Getty via the Tempelsman Collection, but the third is missing—unless it is the one atop the body of the Morgantina Venus.

2. Symes admitted he had seen the Pompeian frescoes seized from Medici. In his opinion they could not be sold. He himself had sold the Griffins, the Tyche, and the Kore acquired from Koutoulakis. These objects went

to Koutoulakis, he said, because it was more plausible for Greek objects, originating in Macedonia, to come from a Greek dealer—in other words, the arrangement distanced them from Italy. He said he did not know they came from Medici (as the Polaroid photo of the Griffins proves). He had then sold the Kore to the Getty, the Griffins to Tempelsman, and the Tyche to Fleischman, who then sold them to the Getty (see p. 198).

Chapter Seventeen

1. This access was limited but unique.
2. Other details from the inventory: On December 19, 1998, Symes sold Leon Levy three objects: a Roman marble bust, third century AD, for $230,000; a Hellenistic over-life-size marble head of a woman, third century BC, for $500,000; and three gold vessels, north European, thirteenth century BC, for $750,000, making that day's takings $1,480,000. There was also mention in the files at that point of a fresco sold to Levy, valued at $1.6 million, which turned out to be fake.

   More details: an ivory left foot, Roman, first century AD, valued at £15,000; an Egyptian basalt seated male figure, valued at £100,000; an Egyptian blue figure of Shu, valued at £100,000 (these three amounts were Citibank's valuations for Symes's loan). A Roman wall fresco of a portico, valued at £25,000.

   Another note, addressed to "Monsieur Jacques," said that $1.5 million was due to be paid in to Xoilan on February 4 (the year was not specified), but out of that, certain payments had to be made—the note then detailed fourteen banks to which proceeds of between £2,877 and $166,888 were to be paid, banks in New York, Florida, Munich, Geneva, Zurich, London, and Guernsey.

   In March 2000, Nonna Investments, another of Symes's companies, negotiated a "rolling facility" with Citibank of $14 million, later increased to $17 million. The loan was guaranteed by Despina Papadimitriou, Christo's sister. A note of June 5, 1990, referred to a Cult Statue of a Goddess, acquired July 22, 1988, with an "unpaid principal balance of $9 million, maturing on July 21 1992, and accruing interest at 5 per cent per annum." Other documentation said that the draped statue, probably of Aphrodite, was by an unknown Greek, probably south Italy or Sicily, dated to 425–400 BC. It was around seven feet in height and had originally been carved in pieces. It had been damaged when it had toppled, caused either by an earthquake or by vandals. Part of it was encrusted with soil. There were also Polaroid photographs of the statue, showing how it was pinned together.

Another note, dated 1996, confirmed that Symes had eleven objects on loan to museums, valued in all at $9,095,000. These objects appeared to include three Villanovan, Etruscan, and Greek gold items. There was also a letter, dated July 25, 1991, from Malcolm Bell about Morgantina. It was not clear who this letter was addressed to, but it was in the Symes files alongside much material on the Getty.

There were two other notes, this time on Robin Symes Limited notepaper, dated March 1987 and March 1989, which listed, in all, nineteen objects that Symes had on consignment with George Ortiz.

Other material included Cycladic statues, Sardinian marble idols, Greek stone heads (one valued at $80,000), a marble kouros, Greek marble stelae, Greek bronzes (one valued at $65,000), a bronze Kore referred to as Griffins from Olympia, Greek arms and armor, early Greek pottery (one vase valued at $45,000), a life-size bronze head of a ruler valued at $850,000, an Etruscan bronze Hercules of the fifth century BC, Etruscan sculptures, terra-cottas, pottery, and jewelry. There was a letter from the Getty agreeing to buy various objects but setting off these purchases against a Diadoumenos head—part of the Fleischman collection—and a torso of Mithras, which were being returned to Italy. In October 1992, there was paperwork in connection with a Greek statue being sold to the Getty for $18 million.

Chapter Twenty

1. This interview took place on July 5, 2003, aboard Mr. Papadimitriou's boat, *Astrape*: Mr. Papadimitriou repeated the allegations the following day.
2. Interview, London, February 6, 2006.
3. Gill, D. W. J. and C. Chippindale, "From Boston to Rome: reflections on returning antiquities," *International Journal of Cultural Property*, Vol. 13, 2006, pp. 311–331.

Index

prosecutorial interrogations of others,
mentioned in, 150, 153–154
silver treasure, information
regarding, 148–149
tombaroli activities, scale of
recorded in the organigram, 337
Cammarata, Vincenzo, 150, 216–217,
231
Camorra, 4, 18
Campana, Marchese Gianpietro, 44
Campbell's Soup Museum (Camden,
New Jersey), 109
Canavesi, Renzo, 305
Capo zona (criminal head of a region), 6
Carabinieri Art Squad
the Bürkis, investigation of, 185–186
catalog of stolen objects, 75
commander of, 3–5
Corridor 17 materials, removal of
from Geneva to Italy, 144–145
Evangelisti, records of, 266–268
founding, organizational evolution,
and actions by, 31–32
headquarters of, 3
Hecht's apartment in Paris, raid on,
156–162
Medici investigation: beginning of
and the raid at Geneva Freeport,
19–23
the Morgantina silver and, 106
Operation Geryon (*see* Operation
Geryon)
Phoenix Ancient Art and Inanna Art
Services, raids at, 182–185
source of the demand for
antiquities, need to take on, 32
See also Conforti, Roberto
Casasanta, Pietro, 151–155, 263–264,
282, 338
Caswell, John, 96
Cenere, Armando, xiv–xv
Chamay, Jacques, 75, 110–111, 194,
199–200
China, 30, 230
Chippindale, Christopher, 299–300,
325–331, 334–336, 340, 342
Chippindale's Law
evidence supporting, 337–342
Medici as proof of the validity of,
350–351
scholarly argument and research
underlying, 325–336

statement of, 336–337
Choregos Painter, 373, 377–378
Christie's, 140, 239, 246–247, 260, 270,
326, 357. *See also* Auction houses
Church of San Saba (Rome),
sarcophagus stolen from, 19–20,
75, 148
Cilli, Roberto, 19–20
Cimicchi, Sandro, 17, 79, 180
Citibank, 262
Cleveland Museum of Art, 109, 245,
294, 357
Collectors
Alsdorf Collection, 345–346
conclusions regarding, 347–348
the Fleischman Collection, 114–123,
126, 289, 326, 372–374 (*see also*
Fleischman, Barbara; Fleischman,
Lawrence)
the Goulandris Collection, 113
growing interest of from the
eighteenth to twentieth
centuries, 43–45
the Holger Termer Collection, 300
the Hunts, 128–133 (*see also* Hunt,
Nelson Bunker; Hunt, William
Herbert)
intellectual attack on, 112–114
the Levy-White Collection (*see*
Levy-White Collection)
Medici, objects acquired that are
linked to, 118–134, 375–380
the Ortiz Collection, 133–134 (*see*
also Ortiz, George)
the Rockefeller Collection, 346
the Rycroft Collection, 371–372
scholarship, undermining of, 330–335
as sustainers of looting, 134, 338
the Tempelsman Collection,
123–125, 373 (*see also*
Tempelsman, Maurice)
unprovenanced antiquities,
percentage of collections
consisting of, 326
wish fulfillment by, 331–332
Colonna, Giovanni, 50, 52, 58, 66,
337–338
Commando Carabinieri Ministero
Pubblica Istruzione—Nucleo
Tutela Patrimonio Artistica
(TPA). *See* Carabinieri Art Squad
Concrete, invention of, 46–47

J. Paul Getty Museum (Los Angeles)
antiquities owned by that appear in
the photos from Medici's
warehouse, 370–375
Asteas lekythos at, 290
the Bürkis interview, discussed in,
187–188
Conforti's efforts to have objects
returned from, 104
controversies associated with,
81–83
the Euphronios-Onesimos kylix,
93–95
Ferri's investigation, request for
information supporting, 204
Fleischman, resignation as trustee of
Barbara, 354
the Fleischman Collection, 74,
115–118, 121–123
fragments, puzzle of the acquisition
of, 222–229
the Getty kouros, 82, 99
Greek golden wreath, acquisition
and return of, 311–312, 320–321
Hecht interrogation, discussed in,
180
leaked documents revealing the
situation at, 284–287
letterheads from found in Medici's
warehouse, 22
the Levy-White Euphronios krater,
examination of, 131–132
Medici, relations with, 75, 83–99
origins of, 80–81
prosecutorial interrogations,
mentioned in, 149–150, 197–198
recent developments at, 302–305
return of objects by, 298, 354
Roman funerary relief, publication
of, 237–238
stolen bronzes acquired by, 84–87
Symes, transactions with, 260–262,
371–372
Tempelsman collection, acquisition
of objects from, 123–125
See also True, Marion
Jacques, Henri Albert, 20, 28, 147–148,
261–262
Japan, 294–296
Jay, John, 100
Jervis, Simon, 335
John Paul II, 114–115

Johnston, Alan W., 60, 62, 368
Jordan, 230

Kagias, Georgios, 320
Karlsruhe Museum, 246
Keats, John, 43–44
Kennedy Galleries, 114
Kimball Museum, 260
Kleitias, 40
Klejman, J. J., 102
Kleophrades, 42
Kleophrades Painter, 41–42, 370–371
Koch, Guntram, 236–237
Kotlidas, Christos, 309
Kotsarides, Michael, 309–310
Kouragios, Yannis, 318
Kouros statue at the Getty, controversy
regarding, 82
Koutoulakis, Nikolas
Berlin, sale of objects in, 199
Gospel of Judas manuscript, 236
Greece antiquities, smuggling of,
246
Medici, association with, 73
name of in the organigram, 17–18
Ortiz, sale of objects to, 133
Symes, transactions with, 260
Symes interview, discussed in, 198
True interrogation, discussed in,
210
Kovasevic, L. J., 311, 320
Koyama, Mihoko, 294–296
Kozlov, Arielle, 294
Kreitman, Neil, 329, 335
Kurtz, Donna, 234

Lambert, Wilfred, 344
Lane and Partners, 257–258
Laundering of antiquities
discovery of, 136–141
impact of uncovering, 143–145
objects seized in Corridor 17
laundered through Sotheby's, list
of, 380–383
reasons for, 141–143
Layard, Austen Henry, 232
League of Nations, 28–29
Lee, Sherman E., 345
Leinster, Anne, 131
Leon, Christoph, 199–200, 246,
286–287, 309–312, 320
letters rogatory, 156

About The Authors:

Peter Watson has written for the *New York Times*, the *Los Angeles Times*, the *London Times* and *Sunday Times*, the *Observer*, and *Spectator*. Since June 1997, he has been a research associate at the McDonald Institute for Archaeological Research at the University of Cambridge. His books include *The Caravaggio Conspiracy*, *From Manet to Manhattan*, and *Sotheby's: The Inside Story*.

Cecilia Todeschini is a researcher and translator who has worked for the BBC, ITV, CBS, ABC, and CBC. For many years she specialized in reporting on the Mafia, covering the great trials in Palermo. Among many other subjects, she has also covered papal conclaves.

Nikolas Zirganos (Chapter 21) is an investigative reporter based in Athens. He works for *Kyriakatiki Eleftheroptypia* newspaper and *Epsilon* magazine.

PublicAffairs is a publishing house founded in 1997. It is a tribute to the standards, values, and flair of three persons who have served as mentors to countless reporters, writers, editors, and book people of all kinds, including me.

I.F. STONE, proprietor of *I. F. Stone's Weekly*, combined a commitment to the First Amendment with entrepreneurial zeal and reporting skill and became one of the great independent journalists in American history. At the age of eighty, Izzy published *The Trial of Socrates*, which was a national bestseller. He wrote the book after he taught himself ancient Greek.

BENJAMIN C. BRADLEE was for nearly thirty years the charismatic editorial leader of *The Washington Post*. It was Ben who gave the *Post* the range and courage to pursue such historic issues as Watergate. He supported his reporters with a tenacity that made them fearless and it is no accident that so many became authors of influential, best-selling books.

ROBERT L. BERNSTEIN, the chief executive of Random House for more than a quarter century, guided one of the nation's premier publishing houses. Bob was personally responsible for many books of political dissent and argument that challenged tyranny around the globe. He is also the founder and longtime chair of Human Rights Watch, one of the most respected human rights organizations in the world.

For fifty years, the banner of PublicAffairs Press was carried by its owner Morris B. Schnapper, who published Gandhi, Nasser, Toynbee, Truman, and about 1,500 other authors. In 1983, Schnapper was described by *The Washington Post* as "a redoubtable gadfly." His legacy will endure in the books to come.

Peter Osnos, *Founder and Editor-at-Large*